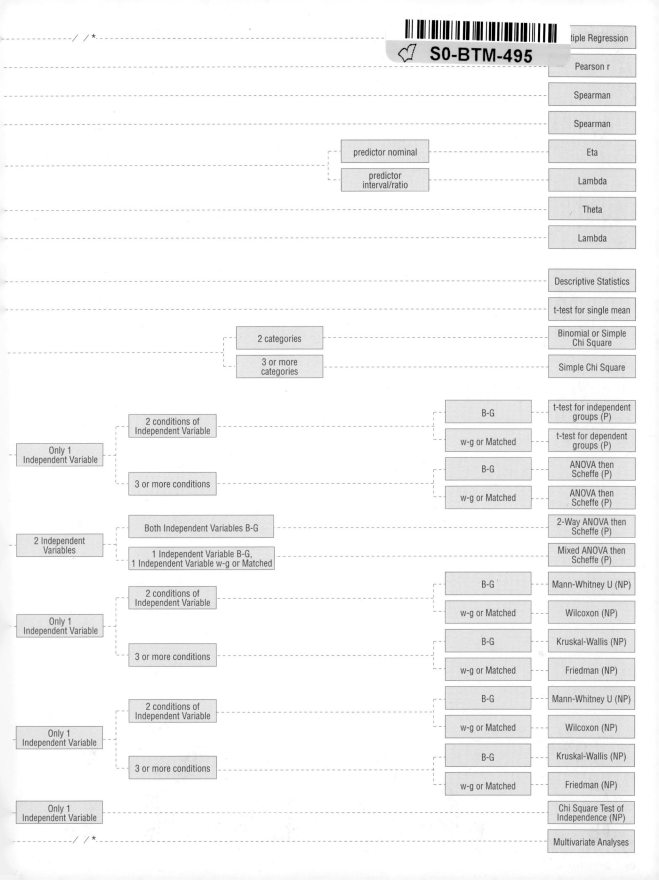

-------------------- / /* -------------------- tiple Regression

Pearson r

Spearman

Spearman

predictor nominal ---- Eta

predictor interval/ratio ---- Lambda

Theta

Lambda

Descriptive Statistics

t-test for single mean

2 categories ---- Binomial or Simple Chi Square

3 or more categories ---- Simple Chi Square

Only 1 Independent Variable

2 conditions of Independent Variable

B-G ---- t-test for independent groups (P)

w-g or Matched ---- t-test for dependent groups (P)

3 or more conditions

B-G ---- ANOVA then Scheffe (P)

w-g or Matched ---- ANOVA then Scheffe (P)

2 Independent Variables

Both Independent Variables B-G ---- 2-Way ANOVA then Scheffe (P)

1 Independent Variable B-G, 1 Independent Variable w-g or Matched ---- Mixed ANOVA then Scheffe (P)

Only 1 Independent Variable

2 conditions of Independent Variable

B-G ---- Mann-Whitney U (NP)

w-g or Matched ---- Wilcoxon (NP)

3 or more conditions

B-G ---- Kruskal-Wallis (NP)

w-g or Matched ---- Friedman (NP)

Only 1 Independent Variable

2 conditions of Independent Variable

B-G ---- Mann-Whitney U (NP)

w-g or Matched ---- Wilcoxon (NP)

3 or more conditions

B-G ---- Kruskal-Wallis (NP)

w-g or Matched ---- Friedman (NP)

Only 1 Independent Variable ---- Chi Square Test of Independence (NP)

-------------------- / /* -------------------- Multivariate Analyses

FOUNDATIONS
FOR GATHERING
AND INTERPRETING
BEHAVIORAL DATA

FOUNDATIONS FOR GATHERING AND INTERPRETING BEHAVIORAL DATA

An Introduction to Statistics

Robert Thomas Maleske

Carthage College

Brooks/Cole Publishing Company

I(T)P™ An International Thomson Publishing Company

Pacific Grove • Albany • Bonn • Boston • Cincinnati • Detroit • London • Madrid • Melbourne
Mexico City • New York • Paris • San Francisco • Singapore • Tokyo • Toronto • Washington

Sponsoring Editor: *Jim Brace-Thompson*
Marketing Representatives: *Joanne Terhaar and Jill Reinemann*
Marketing Communications: *Jean Thompson*
Editorial Associates: *Cathleen S. Collins and Patsy Vienneau*
Production Editor: *Penelope Sky*

Production Assistant: *Tessa A. McGlasson*
Manuscript Editor: *Bernard Gilbert*
Permissions Editor: *Lillian Campobasso*
Interior and Cover Design: *Lisa Berman*
Typesetting: *Doyle Graphics*
Printing and Binding: *Quebecor Printing/ Fairfield*

For more information, contact:

BROOKS/COLE PUBLISHING COMPANY
511 Forest Lodge Road
Pacific Grove, CA 93950
USA

International Thomson Publishing Europe
Berkshire House 168-173
High Holborn
London WC1V 7AA
England

Thomas Nelson Australia
102 Dodds Street
South Melbourne, 3205
Victoria, Australia

Nelson Canada
1120 Birchmount Road
Scarborough, Ontario
Canada M1K 5G4

International Thomson Editores
Campos Eliseos 385, Piso 7
Col. Polanco
11560 México D. F. México

International Thomson Publishing GmbH
Königswinterer Strasse 418
53227 Bonn
Germany

International Thomson Publishing Asia
221 Henderson Road
#05-10 Henderson Building
Singapore 0315

International Thomson Publishing Japan
Hirakawacho Kyowa Building, 3F
2-2-1 Hirakawacho
Chiyoda-ku, Tokyo 102
Japan

Printed in the United States of America

10 9 8 7 6 5 4 3 2 1

Library of Congress Cataloging-in-Publication Data

Maleske, Robert Thomas
    Foundations for gathering and interpreting behavioral data /
Robert Thomas Maleske.
      p.   cm.
    Includes index.
    ISBN 0-534-23742-8
    1. Psychology—Statistical methods.   2. Social sciences—
Statistical methods.   3. Psychology—Research—Methodology.
4. Social sciences—Research—Methodology.   I. Title.
BF39.M26   1994
150'.72—dc20   94-15947
                                     CIP

THIS BOOK IS PRINTED ON ACID-FREE RECYCLED PAPER

I dedicate this work to Marianne, my wife, whose love, support, and patience are between the lines;

to Melissa, my daughter, whose love for reading inspires me to write;

to my sister, Carol Anne Maleske Restis, and brother-in-law, Robert Restis, who supported me in high school and college after the untimely deaths of my parents;

to Marianne's parents, Frank Adamczyk and Theresa Giacchino Adamczyk, who helped us in countless ways during our graduate school years;

in loving memory of my own parents, Thomas Joseph Maleske and Dorothy Kruder Maleske, whose lives and values continue in my writing;

and to my beloved grandmother, Ruth Anderson Kruder, who, at the age of 98, continues to inspire my growth.

PREFACE

Many textbooks are available to those who are studying statistical analyses; this is not one of them. This book is for those who want or are expected to gain a fundamental understanding of the *total process* of gathering and interpreting behavioral data, and who are willing to study the basic issues and concepts involved in this process, of which statistics is only a part.

At the heart of my motivation to write this book is a firm belief that we can understand new information more easily when we can connect it with our own experience. All of us have observed the behavior of people and things; asked questions based on our observations; made our interpretations; and tested the validity of our explanations with additional observations. This universal experience is the foundation—and the only prerequisite—for using this book.

As the title indicates, my overall objective is to help readers understand the *process* of gathering and interpreting behavioral data. You will notice in the table of contents that the headings almost always contain active verbs—for example, "Recognizing the difference between data and information." This is because I emphasize actual skills rather than abstract concepts.

This book is in part my response to other texts on elementary statistics and research methods. Typically, these books focus on inferential statistical analyses *per se*, as if understanding them were an end in itself; often, the names of statistical tests—*t*-tests, for example—will be used as chapter titles. In contrast, the structure of this book emphasizes developing skills and understanding concepts that are prerequisites to knowing when and how to use statistical analyses. Specifics regarding inferential analyses are postponed until Part Four, after a larger and more coherent context is in place.

Few students find statistics intrinsically interesting. However, I have found that they are more willing to absorb the material if it emphasizes logical concepts rather than complex statistical formulas. In that case, they can recognize its relevance to everyday decision making.

Acknowledgments

I used to wonder why authors go on and on with acknowledgments; now I understand.

I'm deeply grateful to the people at Brooks/Cole, especially Jim Brace-Thompson, for his advice and support from the very beginning; Jill Reinemann and Cathleen Collins, who guided my efforts in the early stages and got my prospectus into the right hands; Patsy Vienneau, for keeping us all on schedule; Penelope Sky, for her editorial expertise and gracious efficiency; Bernard Gilbert, for his editing magic, sharp eyes, and sharp pencil; and Kelly Shoemaker, for her wonderful blend of technical expertise and artistic sensitivity.

I also appreciate the thoughtful contributions of the following reviewers: Robert Allan, Lafayette College; Linda Allred, East Carolina University; Nancy Anderson, University of Maryland at College Park; Bryan C. Auday, Gordon College; Michael Biderman, University of Tennessee at Chattanooga; Madison Dengler, Luther College; Gary François, Knox College; Richard Froman, Houghton College; David Kreiner, Central Missouri State University; Dawn Niedner, Purdue University Calumet; Kenneth D. Salzwedel, University of Wisconsin—Whitewater; and Larry Wood, Brigham Young University.

No textbook can be completed without a reality check. I appreciate the efforts of Steve Prosavac and Yi-Chun Sun of the University of Utah, who tested all the calculations, and the contributions of my students and of all readers—past, present, and future—who respect my work enough to challenge it and make thoughtful suggestions for improvement.

I could not have kept my nose to the word processor day after day without the support of my colleagues: Larry Hamilton, whose wisdom and sensitivity helped me keep everything in perspective; Ingrid Tiegel, whose professional commitment provided me with a model of persistence; George Catlin, who helped me balance the statistical with the spiritual; and Donald Michie, whose encouragement and respect added to my confidence.

To all my friends and relatives, too numerous to mention, whose encouragement and support were like fresh breezes during the doldrums every writer confronts; and to our good friend Judy Krieger, who gave Melissa a wonderful place to be when I had deadlines and Marianne had professional commitments: Thank you!

In closing, I want to recognize the wisdom of Albert Erlebacher, whose good advice during my graduate years at Northwestern has stayed with me during twenty years of teaching, and which I continue to pass on to my students: Never collect research data until you know which statistics will be appropriate!

Robert Thomas Maleske

BRIEF CONTENTS

CONTENTS

4   SELECTING AND INTERPRETING STATISTICAL ANALYSES   198

11   Selecting Statistical Analyses   201

12   Understanding Statistical Analysis Formulas   217

AN OVERVIEW

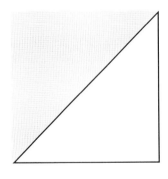

1

Understanding the Total Process of
Gathering and Interpreting Data

1

Although Part One consists of only one chapter, it is not merely a polite opening leading to the meat and potatoes of later chapters. The material in Chapter 1 lies at the core of everything that follows. Its message is that gathering data and interpreting data are not discrete processes; they are but steps in a total process. The individual chapters that follow provide the foundations for understanding that process and how the separate steps work together.

Understanding the Total Process of Gathering and Interpreting Data

After reading and studying Chapter 1 you should understand the following.

- *making observations, formulating questions, explaining observations, and making predictions are fundamental to human existence.*

- *the difference between data and information.*

- *the difference between interpreting information and making a decision based on that information.*

- *the difference between formal and informal approaches to gathering and interpreting data.*

- *gathering and interpreting data are not separate processes but elements of a total process.*

- *the difference between descriptive and inferential statistics.*

- *the difference between populations and samples.*

- *representativeness.*

- *random selection.*

- *the overall structure of this textbook.*

OBSERVING, QUESTIONING, EXPLAINING, PREDICTING

For all organisms, including humans, survival depends on responding and adapting to conditions in the environment. To respond and adapt means to (a) observe what is going on, (b) ask questions about why things happen as they do, (c) seek explanations for our questions, and (d) make predictions about what might happen. The more successful we are at responding and adapting, the more likely we are to "live long and prosper," in the words of Mr. Spock.

But there are different levels of surviving and prospering. At the most basic survival level we are concerned only with physiological needs such as food, water, and shelter. It is only when these basic needs are filled that we can focus on such higher needs as enjoyment of art and appreciation of gourmet food. However, observing, questioning, explaining, and predicting are common to all levels of the need hierarchy.

We spend most of our lives involved in this process. Even people without vision make observations in the sense that they experience their environment. It is not possible to exist normally without being curious about our observations, which in turn leads to questioning. And we cannot adapt without trying to explain what we observe and make predictions based on these explanations.

Once begun, the process is circular. It would make no sense to say that observations must precede questions or that predictions must follow observations. All elements of the process are dynamic, interdependent, and transient.

MAIN POINT SUMMARY

Survival at all levels requires a continuous process of making observations, asking questions, explaining what has happened, and predicting what will happen. But since observing, questioning, explaining, and predicting are natural activities, in everyday life they don't always occur in this sequence. Since they are activities familiar to all of us, understanding the process provides a framework for understanding what it means to gather and interpret data.

T I M E ■ O U T
Take at least ten minutes to write down questions of your own that you find particularly interesting or relevant. Try to select questions that you are genuinely interested in.

Here are some questions I generated in response to the above request.

- Why do our minds go blank when we are asked to generate questions?
- Is there a difference between a question that arises naturally and an artificial question (one that we formulate when asked to generate questions)?
- Can a 50-year-old who begins studying the piano at age 44 learn to play as well as a 12-year-old who begins at age 6?
- How many students are taking this exercise seriously?
- What does it mean to take this exercise seriously?
- How many questions will students be unwilling to share with the group due to embarrassment?
- Will any students work on this exercise more than 10 minutes?

- What is the average length of time students will spend on this exercise?

- Why are some students more motivated than others?

- What percentage of tornadoes have been predicted in the last few years, compared to 10 years ago?

- What pollutants are in my home water supply?

- Will there ever be a cure for AIDS?

- Is it possible to contract AIDS by sharing tears with someone (as in crying on each other's shoulders)?

- How many commercial passenger jets are in the air on a typical weekday afternoon?

- Is the greenhouse effect real?

In generating these questions I have tried for a free and spontaneous flow of ideas. Genuine questions seem to be free and spontaneous, without concern for what others think. I have made an effort to include questions about the behavior of both people and things, because gathering and interpreting behavioral data encompasses the behavior of all types of organisms. Although my list includes no questions about plants or nonhuman animals, their movements and changes certainly qualify as behavior.

Let's take some time to examine our questions more closely. Some of the questions on my list seek explanations.

- Why do our minds go blank when we are asked to generate questions?

- Why are some students more motivated than others?

- Is it possible to contract AIDS by sharing tears with someone (as in crying on each other's shoulders)?

- Is there a difference between a question that arises naturally and an artificial question (one that we formulate when asked to generate questions)?

- What does it mean to take this exercise seriously?

Other questions on my list are concerned with gathering information.

- How many students are taking this exercise seriously?

- What percentage of tornadoes have been predicted in the last few years, compared to 10 years ago?

- What pollutants are in my home water supply?

- How many commercial passenger jets are in the air on a typical weekday afternoon?

- Is the greenhouse effect real?

Still other questions seek to predict future behavior.

- Can a 50-year-old who begins studying the piano at age 44 learn to play as well as a 12-year-old who begins at age 6?
- How many questions will students be unwilling to share with the group due to embarrassment?
- Will any students work on this exercise more than 10 minutes?
- What is the average length of time students will spend on this exercise?
- Will there ever be a cure for AIDS?

Because all of these questions are raw and undeveloped, they are difficult to answer in their present form. Although I have not seen your questions, my past experience with students suggests that those questions that you generated most spontaneously will be among the most difficult for you to answer. Of course, if someone were to ask "What time is it?" that would be an easy question to answer. Or would it? When someone once asked Groucho Marx, "What time is it?" Groucho responded, "Do you mean now?" The question, "What time is it?" becomes obsolete the moment it is uttered, and Groucho's timely humor capitalizes on this fact.

Spontaneous questions lie at the very foundation of scientific inquiry. But students often feel that their spontaneous questioning is somehow not as important as that of scientists. Nonsense! Scientists are people like you and me who eat, sleep, go to the bathroom, get colds, have spontaneous questions, and will someday die. And their questions are driven by the same curiosity that drives ours.

One thing separating scientists from other questioners is that scientists pursue their questions with a passion. They are relentless in seeking the best possible answers. The nonscientist may remain curious but not follow this curiosity very far. Another thing separating scientist from layman is the motivation to convince other scientists that their own answers are correct. They do this with rational, logical arguments based on observable data. The inquiring layman, on the other hand, is often content to back up an answer with casual observation, personal belief, and emotional argument.

DATA VERSUS INFORMATION

A **datum** is a single piece of information, usually but not necessarily numerical. Its plural form is **data**. Consider the following data.

70°F

80°F

Without additional information these data are meaningless. But if you know that these two temperatures were reported by the National Weather Service for Chicago and Miami respectively, then you can say that the reported temperature for Chicago is lower than the reported temperature for Miami. But even this comparison is of limited value unless you know when the temperatures were measured.

If you also know that the National Weather Service reported these as current temperatures at 9:00 A.M. on May 1, 1990, then you have enough information to make a simple yet meaningful interpretation of the data. You could say that on May 1, 1990, at 9:00 A.M. it was cooler in Chicago than in Miami.

MAIN POINT SUMMARY

Data alone, without information about how and when the data are gathered, are of limited value.

The more information we have about the conditions under which data are gathered, the more useful the data will be. Also, the conditions present when data are measured will influence the conclusions we can draw from the data. For example, consider the following data and statement.

Data

Date	Location	Temperature
July 1, 1990	Miami	95°F
January 1, 1990	Chicago	10°F

Statement
The climate in Miami is more favorable than the climate in Chicago.

T I M E ■ O U T
What is your reaction to this statement?

This statement provides food for thought. What time of day were the temperatures recorded? Since the time of year was different for the two observations, the comparison is not a fair one. What does "favorable" mean? To some people 95°F is just as uncomfortable as 10°F is to other people. Is a single temperature measurement on a single day sufficient evidence for such a general statement? What about other climatic factors such as rainfall, humidity, wind, and sunshine?

My point here is that data alone do not provide information. **Information** requires that we also have a certain amount of knowledge about the context in which the data were measured.

MAIN POINT SUMMARY

The process of interpreting data should not be separated from an understanding of the context in which the data were gathered.

INTERPRETATION VERSUS DECISION MAKING

Consider the following information and interpretation

Information

Location	Average Yearly Income	Average Cost of a House
Beeg City	$50,000	$150,000
Smallville	$25,000	$75,000

Interpretation
The cost of living is the same in Smallville and Beeg City.

Given the above information the interpretation seems reasonable. If you wanted to either support or challenge this interpretation, you might wish to gather more facts. You might, for example, arm yourself with information about population of the two locations or the range of yearly incomes. However, if you were offered a job in Smallville, your decision to accept or reject the offer would involve more than an interpretation of data. Your decision would involve interpretations and judgments based on your personal values.

Let's add more information to the situation. The job you have been offered pays $40,000 a year.

T I M E ■ O U T
How might this additional information affect your decision to accept or reject the job offer?

Individuals will react differently to the job offer situation depending on experiences, values, and present circumstances. Some factors influencing such a decision are: age, current income, marital status, number of children, preference for urban or rural setting, and available housing. One individual might enjoy being among the highest paid people in Smallville, while another individual might find this uncomfortable. There are also tradeoffs to consider. Some individuals might find an above-average salary less appealing if housing options and availability are bleak in Smallville.

MAIN POINT SUMMARY

Interpreting data is a process that is distinct from the process of making decisions based on that data. While interpretations should be objective and logical, decisions are often influenced by subjective experiences and values.

FORMAL VERSUS INFORMAL PROCESSES

Imagine that you live in Chicago, it's October, and you are deciding whether to take a one-week January vacation in the Virgin Islands. Since you live in a cold climate you are likely to be curious about January weather patterns in the islands. An informal approach to satisfying this curiosity might involve talking to people who have visited the Virgin Islands in January. A formal approach might involve going to the library and researching the topic.

TIME ■ OUT
Which approach are you most likely to take? When are you most likely to take a formal rather than an informal approach to gathering and interpreting information?

Here are some of the factors that I feel influence the formality versus informality of your efforts to gather data, interpret data, and make decisions.

- The risk/payoff in making an incorrect/correct decision
- The personal relevance of the situation, i.e., is the decision about your life or someone else's life?

MAIN POINT SUMMARY

The process of gathering and interpreting data can be relatively formal or relatively informal.

THE TOTAL PROCESS OF GATHERING AND INTERPRETING DATA

In previous pages we have emphasized the following ideas about the process of gathering and interpreting data:

- Survival at all levels requires a continuous process of making observations, asking questions, explaining what has happened, and predicting what will happen. The elements of this process do not occur in any specific sequence.

- In trying to make sense of data, it is essential to know about the conditions under which the data were gathered.

- Interpreting data is a process that is distinct from the process of making decisions based on the interpretation.

- Circumstances will affect the degree of formality involved in data gathering, data interpretation, and decision making.

These ideas are meant to provide an overall perspective for the remainder of this book. As you progress into the more technical aspects of this book it will be helpful to maintain this perspective so that you won't get lost in details.

What exactly is this perspective? It is the idea that gathering data, interpreting data, and making decisions are parts of an integrated process. Specific elements of the process (for example, statistical computations) are *only* elements of the process. Intelligent decisions must take into account all aspects of the process.

DESCRIPTIVE STATISTICS VERSUS INFERENTIAL STATISTICS

One way to think about statistical techniques is to separate them into two categories: descriptive statistics and inferential statistics. **Descriptive statistics** are used when the purpose is to summarize a set of data. **Inferential statistics** are used when the purpose is to use a small sample of data from a population to understand the entire population.

POPULATIONS AND SAMPLES

You are already familiar with the word *sample* from its everyday usage. We speak of getting free samples of a new product and of sampling morsels from a serving tray. Such usage almost invariably suggests a small part taken from a larger whole. *Sample* has a similar meaning when used as a statistical term. **Statistical sampling** involves selecting a few subjects or items from the whole batch. The subset is the **sample**. The larger group from which the sample is drawn is the **population**.

The purpose of statistical sampling is to use the subset (the sample) to make inferences (guesses) about the entire group (the population). A major advantage of this arrangement is its efficiency, for it permits making inferences about relatively large groups without the need to measure every member of the population. Consider the goal of a marketing professional who wants to understand the buying behavior of all people between ages 20 and 30 in the United States. It would be impractical to survey every individual in this category. A properly selected sample from the total population of interest would allow the marketing professional to gather information from the smaller group of people, and then to generalize the results to the population.

Keep in mind, however, that this particular population (all people between ages 20 and 30 in the United States) is in turn a sample of the larger population of all people in the United States. This population is in turn a sample of the total population of all people living on earth. Thus, *sample* and *population* are almost always relative terms.

Calculations based on sample data (for example, the average of a sample of scores) are referred to as **statistics**. Calculations that are based on population data (for example, the average of a population of scores) are referred to as **parameters**.

REPRESENTATIVENESS

When using a sample to make inferences about a population, the sample should represent the population. Consider the following scenario.

In order to assess marketability of a new deodorant, the manufacturer decides to sample potential customers by giving a small package of the deodorant to the first 20 people who enter a shopping mall. They are asked to use the product for one week. At the end of the week the 20 people are contacted and questioned about the product.

T I M E ■ O U T
Would you consider this sample to represent the larger population to which the manufacturer would like to generalize?

The first 20 people to enter a mall on any given morning are not likely to represent all shoppers. For one thing, these early birds may enjoy shopping more than most people. In order to achieve a **representative sample** of the larger population, we need some way to select individuals so that no one type is more likely to be picked.

RANDOM SELECTION

ASIDE ■ See Table B.14, "Table of Random Numbers" in Appendix B for an example of a random numbers table. Also see Procedure C.30, "Using a Random Numbers Table" in Appendix C for a step-by-step example of using a random numbers table.

Random selection is one technique for selecting representative samples. A familiar example of random selection is drawing slips of paper from a hat. This simple approach provides random selection because each slip of paper is considered to have an equal chance of being drawn—assuming all slips are the same size and type of paper.

A slightly more sophisticated approach to random selection can be seen on televised lottery drawings, in which a machine forces small floating lightweight balls into a tube.

Another way to achieve random selection is to use a table of random numbers.

OVERVIEW OF THIS BOOK

This book is divided into four parts. Part One, "An Overview," consists of only one chapter, which you are completing as you read this. This chapter provides an overall philosophy and structure for the text. Part Two, "Understanding Descriptive Statistics," consists of five chapters and provides an understanding of those statistical techniques that are used to summarize and describe data. Part Three, "Understanding Inferential Statistics," consists of four chapters and provides an understanding of those statistical techniques that are used to examine data for evidence relating to the topic of inquiry. Part Four, "Selecting, Understanding, and Interpreting Statistical Analyses," consists of three chapters and provides an understanding of how to select and use the appropriate inferential statistical technique, and how to interpret results of the completed analysis.

SUMMARY

Throughout this chapter I have emphasized that gathering and interpreting data are inseparable elements of a total process. I have raised several issues related to this total process: data versus information, interpretation versus decision, formality versus informality, description versus inference, and population versus sample. The issues of representativeness and random selection were also presented.

Now is a good time to reexamine the objectives at the beginning of this chapter. For each objective, ask yourself if you now possess the understanding that was targeted there. If not, reread the relevant parts of the chapter before continuing on to Chapter 2.

KEY TERMS AND CONCEPTS

Data	Parameters
Datum	Population
Descriptive statistics	Random selection
Formal versus informal	Representative sample
Inferential statistics	Sample
Information	Statistical sampling
Information versus data	Statistics
Interpretation versus decision	

EXERCISES

1.1 Describe a formal decision-making process in which you've been involved.

1.2 Describe an informal decision-making process in which you've been involved.

1.3 After referring to Table B.14, "Table of Random Numbers" (in Appendix B) and Procedure C.30, "Using a Random Numbers Table" (in Appendix C), create a sample of 10 values randomly selected from Database A.1 in Appendix A.

1.4 Compare your random sample to those following Database A.1. Are all samples equally representative of the population? Explain.

1.5 Describe how to select a random sample of 30 students to represent your school.

1.6 Which of the following is technically more correct: "The data are ..." or "The data is ..."? Explain

1.7 The average height of a given population is 5 ft 8 in. The average height of 20 people randomly selected from this population is 5 ft 9 in. Which of these values is a parameter? Which one is a statistic?

1.8 A survey is conducted to assess public opinion of a new tax law in a city having a population of 80,000. A sample of 500 names is randomly selected from the telephone book. Is this sample representative of the population? Explain.

1.9 What is the primary purpose of inferential statistics?

1.10 What is the primary purpose of descriptive statistics?

UNDERSTANDING DESCRIPTIVE STATISTICS

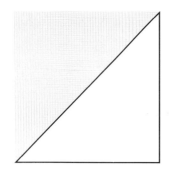

Part Two is concerned with descriptive statistics. You will recall from Chapter 1 that this category includes those statistical techniques used to summarize and describe data. Chapter 2 begins by emphasizing that our motivation to measure comes from a universal impulse to describe and make sense of our observations and experiences, and that our desire to share experience leads to standardization and objectivity. The remainder of the chapter discusses concepts related to standardizing measurements and making them more objective. Chapter 3 discusses elementary procedures for organizing measurements and applies them to the process of creating frequency distributions. Chapter 4 distinguishes data summary from data organization and introduces the procedures for calculating statistics that summarize the central tendency and variability of data sets. Chapter 5 discusses the use of tables and graphs as devices for summarizing data, including how to choose among various types of tables and graphs. Chapter 6 makes an important transition from the concept of description, which is represented by the techniques introduced in previous chapters, to the concept of inference, which begins with standardizing scores. The relationship between standard scores and the normal curve is discussed as well as the use of the normal curve in making inferences about populations

Understanding
Measurement

OBJECTIVES

After reading and studying Chapter 2 you should understand the following.

■ *observing and experiencing are essential to human existence and are the basis for gathering and interpreting data.*

■ *the terms* behavior *and* variable *as they will be used in this book.*

■ *what it means to measure a behavior or variable.*

■ *operational definitions—what they are and how to create them.*

■ *measurement validity.*

■ *the four levels of measurement and how to identify the level of a given measurement.*

■ *why it is necessary to distinguish between the four levels of measurement.*

■ *measurement precision.*

OBSERVING AND EXPERIENCING

As I've said, existence is synonymous with experiencing and observing—we continuously take in information about our environment.

TIME ■ OUT
Take at least five minutes to write down your observations since waking up this morning.

Here are some of my own observations since waking today.

1. It's 6:00 A.M.

2. The sun is shining. The temperature reading on my outdoor ther-mometer is 60°F. The leaves on the tree outside my bedroom window are rustling in the breeze.

3. Marianne, my wife, is not yet awake.

4. There are no v-neck t-shirts in my drawer.

5. Melissa, my daughter, has her head under the covers.

6. I'm traveling 45 MPH in my car. The car behind me is only 10 feet away.

7. I'm in the mailroom at Carthage College. Larry says he has 20 minutes of photocopying.

I have intentionally limited this list to objective statements lacking in opinion or judgment. Compare them to the following statements.

1. I didn't oversleep. That's good—I'll have time for a second cup of coffee.

2. It's a bright, cool, dry, and pleasant morning.

3. Marianne is still sleeping. She must be tired from the late party last night.

4. Darn it! I'm out of v-neck t-shirts again. I better buy some on my way home.

5. I think I'll look in on Melissa. She's buried under her covers with no sign of waking up. She had a long weekend—I'll bet she sleeps late today. It's her first day of summer vacation and she doesn't have to be anywhere, so that's OK.

6. What's this character behind me trying to do—kill us both? He's too close—I'll just pull over and let him pass.

7. I want to copy these student papers, but Larry is using the copying machine. I know he's in a hurry because his first summer session class begins in 30 minutes. If I help him, I'll be able to use the machine sooner.

Hopefully these two lists of my morning's observations illustrated two important points: (*a*) Beginning with the moment we awaken, our day is filled with experiences and observations; (*b*) Description of our experiences and observations can vary in amount of detail and degree of personal interpretation.

MAIN POINT SUMMARY

Observation and experience are the basis for gathering data and information about our world. As such, they are essential components of the total process described in Chapter 1. Any book that attempts to facilitate the reader's understanding of data collection (usually referred to as research methods) and data analysis (usually referred to as statistics) should never lose sight of this total process.

WHAT IS BEHAVIOR?

In colleges and universities, psychology and sociology are often categorized as behavioral sciences, which implies that these disciplines are concerned with the scientific study of human behavior. However, behavior is not limited to human activity. Similarly, this textbook, *Foundations for Gathering and Interpreting Behavioral Data*, is not limited to the behavioral sciences or to human behavior.

This book defines **behavior** as any observable change. Because change can be observed in nearly everything, this definition broadens the book's scope to include gathering and interpreting almost any data.

Here are some examples of observable change: human aggression, ocean current, human learning, prime interest rate, human depression, economic depression, human intelligence, and weather pattern. Even buildings can "behave":

> A student of architecture has gathered data to support her argument that the height of buildings decreases as the distance from the main business district of any city increases. The student is studying the behavior of buildings.

Granted, it is sometimes a bit awkward to use the word *behavior* in this way, as the term is customarily reserved for observable actions of living things. But in this book we expand the concept of behavior to include nonliving things and systems as in the assertion, "The behavior of tornadoes is affected by terrain."

Because of this awkwardness in using the word *behavior* the word *variable* is often used instead. For example, the student of architecture is studying the variable called building height. We realize that once a building is completed its height does not vary, but sentences such as the following do make sense: "Height is a variable that may change from one building to another." The concept of variable can be distinguished from the concept of behavior by defining variable as follows. A **variable** is an event that can be measured and which has the potential to change from one observation to the next.

A variable has the potential to change, whereas a behavior is a change that is actually observed. This subtle distinction is illustrated in the following scenario.

> In an effort to understand students' attentiveness in the classroom, a researcher sets up an experiment in a classroom setting. He systematically varies room temperature to ascertain if the temperature variable affects the attentiveness variable.
>
> Obviously, other elements are present in the experimental classroom situation. Some of these elements are time of day, day of week, length of lecture, topic of lecture, and instructor's voice volume. Because these other elements can take on different values

(i.e., they can vary), they too are variables and they too have the potential to influence attentiveness.

It is therefore important that the researcher set up his experiment so that temperature is the only variable that changes. This means that during the experiment he must schedule all sessions at the same time of day, use the same instructor, and so on.

It is only when the researcher actually observes change in the attentiveness variable that he can refer to attentiveness behavior of the students.

In an experiment, the variable that the researcher deliberately changes to determine its effect on another variable is referred to as the **independent variable**. The variable that may be affected by the independent variable is referred to as the **dependent variable**. In the example above, the independent variable is room temperature and the dependent variable is student attentiveness.

In a well-planned experiment, the only changes are (*a*) the manipulated variation in the independent variable that is under the researcher's control, and (*b*) any resulting change in the dependent variable. Everything else in the experimental environment is kept uniform, or as we usually say, "held constant." Only then can any change observed in the dependent variable be attributed to influence of the independent variable.

There is an apparent contradiction in this description—the idea that a variable can be held constant. Recall, however, that a variable has the potential to change; it need not actually change within a given context.

MAIN POINT SUMMARY

Variables are characteristics of people, places, or things that have the potential to change. Behavior represents an actually observable change. However, in order to observe a behavior we must observe an actual change in some variable.

MEASURING WHAT WE OBSERVE

We cannot survive without observing changes in our environment. In other words, we cannot exist without identifying variables and observing behavior. Individual survival depends on these observations; species survival depends on the ability of individuals to share these observations with one another. This need to share observations is the basis for measurement.

I suggest we use the following as a working definition of measurement in this book. **Measurement** is the process of assigning labels to variables and observed behaviors.

Consider these measurements. In each instance a label has been assigned to an observed behavior or variable.

I hold a ruler against the longest side of a book and measure the book's length to be *9 inches.*

I place a baby on a scale and measure the baby's weight to be *10 pounds.*

I give a quiz to a student and measure her understanding of the quiz material to be *88% correct.*

I listen to two students talking and measure their conversation to be *friendly.*

I look at the thermometer in my office and measure the office temperature to be *76°F.*

I look at rainfall data for July, 1989, and measure that month's rainfall to be the *third lowest for July since 1889.*

A student listens to a class lecture and measures the instructor to be *confusing.*

MAIN POINT SUMMARY

The process of assigning labels to observed behaviors and variables is called *measurement.*

In some of the examples above, assignment of a label is facilitated by using an instrument such as a ruler or thermometer. But in other cases the label assigned seems arbitrary. In order to reduce this frequent arbitrariness of measurement, we make use of operational definitions.

OPERATIONAL DEFINITIONS

You will notice in the measurement examples given in the previous section that some labels are more ambiguous than others. It would be much easier to find agreement that a baby weighs 10 pounds than it would be to find agreement that a particular conversation is friendly. To minimize such ambiguity, variables are often defined operationally. An **operational definition** describes a measurable behavior or variable such that anyone carrying out the measurement procedure will arrive at the same measurement.

Ideally, an operational definition is so clear, straightforward, and mechanical that it leaves no room for disagreement about measuring the behavior or variable. But in reality, many operational definitions still require some interpretation and this can differ from person to person. For example, we might operationally define the variable home run as *any movement of the baseball such that it lands beyond the farthest outfield boundary without going foul.* This definition may appear free of ambiguity, yet the history of baseball is filled with arguments over such questions as "did the ball go foul?" and "was it touched by a spectator before landing in the seats?"

Here are other examples of operational definitions:

Winning team: team scoring the most points.

Wealthy: person with financial assets exceeding one million dollars.

Depression: score at or above the 80th percentile on a paper and pencil inventory of depression.

Honor student: student who compiles a grade point average at or above 3.5 on a 4-point system.

The purpose of operational definitions is to standardize measurements so that information can be communicated without confusion or subjective interpretation. Here are more examples of operational definitions:

A letter grade of B is assigned whenever a student correctly answers 80% to 90% of the items on a multiple-choice test.

Temperature in a classroom is said to be uncomfortable whenever it is above 76°F or below 68°F.

A child is said to be unmotivated if absent from more than 30% of her piano lessons, not including absences due to illness.

T I M E ■ O U T
Take some time to create your own operational definitions for the following behaviors and variables: intelligence, academic success, life satisfaction, financial success, job satisfaction, birthrate, death rate, cost of living, depression, physical fitness, motivation to study, city.

In using operational definitions to simplify measurement of behaviors and variables, the realness of the behavior or variable sometimes gets lost. Consider the problem of assigning letter grades as measurements of student understanding. Although an A grade traditionally denotes excellent understanding, there are times when an A may be assigned to a student whose actual understanding does not meet this criterion. There are also times when a C may be assigned to a student with excellent understanding. And then there is the dilemma created when using final score as a measure of the better of two teams. Sports fans don't always agree that the team with more points is the better team.

This issue of truth in measurement is represented by the concept of measurement validity.

MEASUREMENT VALIDITY

One way to define **measurement validity** is to say that a measurement is valid when it represents the truth. The catch is that it is not always easy to judge if a measurement reflects reality. We could, for example, say that a person is intelligent if he has more than $100 in his possession at the time of measurement. This is an operational definition of intelligence—anyone carrying out this operational definition would arrive at the same measurement, which would also be considered to have **reliability**. Most, however, would agree that amount of money in one's pocket or purse is not a valid measure of intelligence.

Now consider this definition of physical fitness: A person between the ages of 16 and 20 is physically fit if able to run one mile in less than 10 minutes. This definition is operational—anyone carrying out the measurement procedure would arrive at the same result. And though it may not be particularly precise, most people would agree that it is a reasonably valid gauge of physical fitness for young people.

The concept of validity can be further differentiated. **Face validity** addresses whether a measurement appears to measure something that is true. **Construct validity** asks if a particular hypothetical construct (e.g., creativity) actually exists and can therefore be measured. This distinction between face validity and construct validity is an important one. In some cases, it is not sufficient to claim validity simply because a measurement appears to reflect reality. However, establishing construct validity requires using several techniques that are beyond the scope of this text. These techniques are usually studied in a course devoted to tests and measurements.

LEVELS OF MEASUREMENT

We previously stated that measurement is the process of assigning labels to observations. Look again at these two measurements.

I listen to two students talking and measure their conversation to be *friendly*.

I place a baby on a scale and measure the baby's weight to be *10 pounds*.

These measurements differ in two respects: their level of operationality and their level of quantitativeness. In the first example, the friendliness variable is not defined operationally. On the basis of the information provided, it is impossible to know how the label of friendly was assigned to the conversation. However, weighing a baby is so common that everyone understands the procedure. Of course we could get picky and ask if the baby wore clothing and what kind of scale was used.

Operationality and quantitativeness are related but separate issues. For example, the label of friendly could be operationalized as a two-person conversation in which each person smiles at least once. This definition of a friendly conversation is more operational than the original example but it is still not quantitative. Applying this definition, a conversation can be judged either friendly or not friendly; however, we still lack the means to quantify the degree of friendliness.

One goal of operational definitions is to yield easily quantified measurements. Only then is it feasible to apply a statistical technique (e.g., average) to the resulting data. For example, in measuring friendliness of conversation one might simply count the total number of smiles observed for each person during a specified number of minutes. The average smiles per minute could then be calculated.

T I M E ■ O U T
Consider the operational definition of friendly conversation. Is it valid? Do you see any problems with it? Can you create an operational definition of friendly that is more valid and/or more operational?

MAIN POINT SUMMARY

Measurements can vary with respect to both level of operationality and level of quantitativeness. The level of operationality is typically based on the clarity and ease of repeating the measurement. However, it is possible to assess reliability of an operational definition by determining the degree to which operationally defined measurements are the same from one measurement to the next.

In addition to the operationality of a measurement, it is useful to be more specific about the level of quantitativeness. These categories are referred to as **levels of measurement**.

Why Differentiate Measurement Levels?

The choice of statistical analysis for a set of data depends in part on the level at which the data were measured. For example, if the independent variable and dependent variable are both measured at the ordinal level, a Spearman r analysis is appropriate. However, if both the independent and dependent variables are measured at either the interval level or the ratio level, then a Pearson r analysis is appropriate. At this point you need not be concerned about the difference between a Spearman r and a Pearson r. But it is important to firmly grasp the distinguishing features of the four levels of measurement. These levels are ratio measurement, interval measurement, ordinal measurement, and nominal measurement.

Ratio Measurement

Like all measurements, **ratio level measurement** involves assigning labels to observed behaviors or variables. In the case of ratio measurement, the labels are numerical quantities. At the ratio level of measurement, the numbers used as labels are related to the characteristic of the behavior or variable being measured in such a way that proportional relationships between labels represent proportional relationships between actual amounts of the characteristic being measured.

For example, the behavior defined as running speed could be measured for two people. If Person A has a running speed of 15 feet per second and Person B has a running speed of 30 feet per second, we can say that Person B runs *twice as fast* as Person A, because the ratio of 30:15 is the equivalent of 2:1. Therefore running speed is measured at the ratio level.

Here are other examples of how ratio level measurements can be useful:

Arm length in inches. An adult's arm is measured as 33 inches. A child's arm is measured as 11 inches. We can say that the child's arm is one-third as long as the adult's arm because $11/33 = 1/3$.

Age in years. Amy's age is measured as 44 years. Sam's age is measured as 55 years. We can say that 55-year-old Sam is 25% older than 44-year-old Amy. This is true because $55 - 44 = 11$ and $11/44 = .25 = 25\%$.

Time in seconds. David runs 100 yards in 15 seconds. Martin runs 100 yards in 20 seconds. We can say that David (15 seconds) ran 100 yards in 75% of the time as Martin because $15/20 = .75 = 75\%$.

Ratio measurement is the most quantitatively sophisticated of the four levels. It is the only level for which ratio (i.e., proportional) relationships among measurements represent the proportional relationships that actually exist among the characteristics being measured. For example, the measurement "40 years old" represents twice as much age as the measurement "20 years old." Likewise, the measurement "33 inches of arm length" represents three times as much arm length as the measurement "11 inches of arm length."

Here are the major features of ratio level measurement.

1. The proportional or ratio relationships between numbers used as labels are the same as the same proportional relationships among the characteristics of the behaviors or variables that are being represented by the assigned numerical labels. For example, 10 seconds is twice the duration of time as 5 seconds.

2. The measurement scale has a zero point that represents total absence of the characteristic being measured. For example, 0 seconds indicates that no time has elapsed. The zero point is the same for all measurements.

3. Ratio measurement also includes all features of the other three measurement levels discussed below.

T I M E ■ O U T
Take some time to develop three of your own examples of ratio level measurement.

Interval Measurement

Interval level measurement is less sophisticated than ratio level measurement. Like the ratio level, interval level measurement utilizes numerical labels. However, at the interval level, the number on the label is related to the characteristic of the behavior or variable being measured only in such a way that equal intervals between numbers represent equal intervals between the amounts of the characteristics of the behaviors or variables being measured.

For example, the air temperature variable could be measured on three successive days. On Day 1 it is 100°F. On Day 2 it is 75°F and on Day 3 it is 50°F. We can say that the difference (i.e., interval) between temperatures on Days 1 and 2 (25°F) is the same as the interval between Days 2 and 3 (also 25°F).

However, we cannot conclude that the temperature on Day 1 (100°F) is twice as great as the temperature on Day 3 (50°F). We are not justified in making such a statement because zero degrees Fahrenheit does not represent total absence of temperature. In this case, zero degrees Fahrenheit is an arbitrary point and does not represent either the beginning of the Fahrenheit scale or total absence of temperature.

Here are three other interval level measurements.

Altitude relative to the ground. Plane A is 4000 feet above the ground; Plane B is 8000 feet above the ground. However, unless both airplanes are over the same spot of ground, it cannot be said that Plane B is twice as high as Plane A. It may be that Plane A is 4000 feet above Denver (which is one mile above sea level) and Plane B is 8000 feet above Miami (which is at sea level). Therefore, Plane A is 9280 feet above sea level and Plane B is 8000 feet above sea level. It would not, therefore, be accurate to say that Plane B is flying at twice the altitude as Plane A.

Air temperature in degrees Fahrenheit. On Day 1 the outdoor air temperature is 80°F at 2:00 P.M. on Day 2 it is 40°F at 2:00 P.M.

Calendar days. In the year 1994, Allen is born on June 8, Bart is born on June 16, and Cindy is born on June 24. It is correct to say that the interval between the births of Allen and Bart (8 days) is the same as the interval between the births of Bart and Cindy (8 days). However, even though 16 is twice as large as 8, it is not correct to say that Bart (born on June 16) is twice as old as Allen (born on June 8). Note that in this example, interval relationships among the numerical labels are equivalent to the interval relationships in calendar days. However, the ratio relationships among the same numerical labels are not equivalent to the ratio relationships in calendar days.

Here are the major features of interval level measurement.

1. There is no absolute zero point as a consistent reference for all measurements.

2. Proportional or ratio relationships among the numbers used as labels are not equivalent to the proportional relationships among the amounts of the characteristics being measured.

3. Interval measurement also includes all features of ordinal and nominal measurement.

T I M E ■ O U T
Take some time to develop three of your own examples of interval level measurement.

Ordinal Measurement

Ordinal level measurement also utilizes numbers as labels, but in a different way than the numerical labels used in ratio and interval measurements. Ordinal level measurement assigns a label based on the relative amount of some characteristic in the behavior or variable being measured.

The following examples are typical of ordinal level measurements.

Finishing position in a race. First place, second place, etc.

Status of contest winners. First place, second place, etc.

Ranking of test results. Highest grade, second highest grade, etc.

Ranking of children's heights. Shortest, second shortest, etc.

Here are the major features of ordinal level measurement.

1. Although numbers are used as labels, these numbers have limited quantitative usefulness. For example, first, second, and third place contest winners may be labeled 1, 2, and 3, but it is not meaningful to average the three numbers and conclude that the average status of contest winners is 2.

2. Differences in the characteristic being measured are not necessarily represented by differences in the labels. For example, the person who finishes a race in second place may be only two seconds behind the person who finishes in first place, while the person finishing in third place may be three minutes behind the person finishing in second place.

3. Ordinal measurement also includes all features of nominal measurement.

T I M E ■ O U T
Take some time to develop three of your own examples of ordinal level measurement.

Nominal Measurement

Unlike the other measurements, the labels assigned in **nominal level measurement** have no quantitative features—they are simply names. These names do allow us to make nonquantitative distinctions among people, places, and things. For example, the nominal labels left-handed and right-handed denote distinct traits of individuals. Assigning the right-handed label to a person probably reflects the actual trait. However, there is no implication of quantity, rank, size, or status. Although nominal labels are themselves nonquantitative, data measured at the nominal level can still be analyzed using certain statistical techniques, as we will see later in this book. For the moment, however, it is sufficient to understand that nominal level measurement assigns a nonquantitative label to an observed behavior or variable.

Here are some examples of nominal level measurement.

Names of states: Wisconsin is separate and distinct from Illinois; each has a different nominal label.

Personality type: A person who is introverted has a personality that is distinct from a person who is extroverted; each has a different nominal label.

Weather patterns: Weather that is cloudy is distinct from weather that is sunny; each has a different nominal label.

T I M E ■ O U T
Take some time to develop three of your own examples of nominal level measurement.

Philosophical Issues

The general definitions and examples I have given for each measurement level are idealized. In actual practice it is often difficult to decide which measurement level was used in collecting a set of data. One example that comes to mind is the use of numbers on athletic uniforms for purposes of readily identifying the players.

Jersey numbers worn by my daughter's baseball team are intended for nominal purposes only. However, team members have been known to attach ordinal meaning to the numbers. One child may complain because another child has a "bigger" number than hers. Or the numbers may be used ordinally to line up the players for a team photograph.

A college dean creates a course evaluation form based on a 10-point rating scale for which 1 = low and 10 = high. One of the evaluation items reads, "Rate the instructor on class preparation." What is the measurement level of the resulting ratings?

In order for the ratings to be at the interval level, one must assume that equal differences in ratings represent equal differences in the characteristic being rated. For example, it would be necessary to assume that the difference between a rating of 6 and a rating of 8 represents the same difference in rated class preparation as the difference between ratings of 7 and 9. Is this a reasonable assumption?

In order for the ratings to be at the ratio level, one must assume that ratio or proportional relationships among the ratings represent the same ratio or proportional relationships in rated class preparation. For example, it would be necessary to assume that a rating of 8 represents class preparation that is twice as high as a rating of 4. Is this a reasonable assumption?

Do gold, silver, and bronze represent metals, colors, or levels of olympic accomplishment?

When measuring tangible physical traits like weight and height, there is an overt relationship between the trait and its measurement. However, such human traits as personality and self-esteem have no tangible physical counterpart. This provides considerable freedom—and considerable ambiguity—in determining the level of measurement.

A teacher uses a 100-point quiz to measure the level of understanding achieved by students in her class. Martha's quiz grade is 100%. John's quiz grade is 50%. At which level (ratio, interval, ordinal, or nominal) is student understanding measured?

T I M E ▪ O U T
Take some time now to consider this question before reading further.

If you said ratio level, then you are willing to assume that Martha's grade of 100% represents twice as much understanding as John's grade of 50%. Is this a reasonable assumption?

Perhaps you said ordinal level. Can you compare a student with an 85% grade to a student with an 87% grade? In order for the quiz to be ordinal measurement, it is necessary to assume that the 87% grade represents more understanding than the 85% grade. Is this a reasonable assumption?

Obviously, in actual practice many instances arise in which there are no clear-cut guidelines for making judgments about measurement level. Because it can be so difficult to gauge the relationship between numerical measurements and human traits, unless there is a clear case of nominal classification or ordinal ranking, it is common practice to assume at least interval level measurement. It is also common to group interval level and ratio level together in a classification called **interval/ratio level measurement**.

A familiar application of assumed interval/ratio level measurement is the 7-point scale found on many questionnaires. A sample questionnaire item might read "Rate your amount of weekly exercise" with 1 = low and 7 = high. Despite its wide acceptance as interval/ratio measurement, some statisticians argue that this type of measurement scale is at most an ordinal measurement.

There is no simple solution to the problem of deciding which of the four levels a given measurement is at. The decision is largely a matter of philosophy regarding the relationship between numbers used as labels and the characteristic being represented by the numbers. For a more detailed discussion of this topic see Stevens (1946).

MAIN POINT SUMMARY

Established usage in statistics differentiates four levels of measurement. The basis for each level is its quantitative sophistication. In order to select an appropriate statistical technique for analyzing a set of data, it is important to determine the level at which the data were measured.

PRECISION OF MEASUREMENT

Measurement precision refers to the size of the unit of measurement. Length is one of the commonly encountered measurements. Length is a ratio level measurement because zero length represents total absence of length. The length of a neuron, the length of a bolt, your height, the distance from Milwaukee to Chicago, and the distance from Earth to the Milky Way galaxy are all examples of length measurement. But brain neurons are less than a millimeter in length, while the distance from Earth to the Milky Way is 40,000 light years. Obviously, if you wish to quantify these various lengths you will utilize various types of measuring instruments. You will also find it convenient to utilize various units of measurement.

A 12-inch ruler is appropriate for measuring the length of a bolt (2 or 3 inches). But a brain neuron is less than 0.039 inches (39 thousandths of an inch) so a 12-inch ruler won't do the job; for this you would resort to a specialized measuring device.

When measuring the bolt, your chosen unit of measurement would probably be inches and fractional inches. When measuring the neuron you would likely use some other unit of measurement such as millimeters (1 millimeter = .0393 inch).

When measuring a person's height, one typically rounds off to the nearest whole inch. For example, if Daphne's measured height is $68\frac{1}{4}$ inches; her height would be recorded as 68 inches.

The distance from Milwaukee to Chicago practically defies measurement with a ruler or even a yardstick! Nor would you express this distance as 5,892,480 inches rather than the more sane 93 miles.

The distance from Earth to the Milky Way galaxy is so astronomically large that it is cumbersome to express it as 240,000,000,000,000 miles (240 trillion miles). Instead, the distance is said to be 40,000 light years. One light year is the distance that light travels in one year, traveling at 186,000 miles per second.

Table 2.1 provides additional examples of measurable variables. Study this table in order to develop your ability to recognize (*a*) levels of measurement, (*b*) degrees of precision, and (*c*) sources of data.

REGARDING APPENDIX A

Appendix A contains eight databases that serve as the source of data for many of the examples throughout this book. Each database consists of 1000 measurements made on an imaginary population of 1000. For example, the measurements in Database A.1 are body weights for 1000 people.

For each database, several random samples have been drawn from the population. The individual measurements which make up each sample are printed below the database. Ten samples were randomly selected from Database A.1., each consisting of the body weight measurements for 20 people.

In using many examples in this book, it will often be helpful to look at all of the data in the population. You are also encouraged to generate additional random samples by practicing the skills you learn in this book. For this you may use Table B.14, "Table of Random Numbers," in Appendix B. Populations, samples, and random selection were discussed in Chapter 1.

SUMMARY

The acts of observing and measuring are essential to existence and provide natural motivation for gathering and interpreting data and information.

The term *behavior* refers to any observable change. The term *variable* refers to any characteristic that can change from one observation to another.

Measurement is the process of assigning labels to describe observed behaviors and variables.

Operational definitions are used to simplify and clarify the measurement process so that anyone who utilizes the definition will end up with the same measurement.

A measurement is said to be valid when it represents truth. Operational definitions and measurement validity are separate but related concepts. Operationality refers to how easily and unambiguously you can carry out and report a measurement. Validity addresses whether or not you are actually measuring what you claim to be measuring. It is possible to have a measurement that is operational but not valid. Is the reverse possible?

TABLE 2.1 Examples of Measurable Variables

Measurement level	Decimal accuracy	Bodily	Psychophysical	Psychological	Personal	Meteorological	Geographical	Demographic
Ratio	Integer	Weight (whole pounds) (scale) (Ex: 150 lbs)	Hand strength (millimeters) (dynamometer) (Ex: 50 mm)	Memory (words recalled) (20-word list) (Ex: 12 words)	Income (yearly) (at age 30) (Ex: $25,000)	Days of rain (yearly) (Ex: 85 days)	Altitude (feet) (above sea level) (Ex: 980 ft)	Population (people living) (Ex: 88,546)
Ratio	Tenths	Wrist diameter (tenths of inch) (Tape measure) (Ex: 7.3 in.)	Running time (tenth of sec) (100-yard dash) (Ex: 12.7 sec)	Task completion (tenths of min) (sort 52 cards) (Ex: 1.6 min)		Rainfall (tenths of inch) (yearly) (8.6 in.)		
Ratio	Hundredths		Reaction time (hundredths of second) (standard task) (Ex: 1.54 sec)		Income (hourly) (Ex: $8.50)	Rainfall (hundredth of inch) (yearly) (10.43 in.)		
Ratio	Thousandths	Hair thickness (thousandth of inch) (micrometer) (Ex: 0.012 in.)	Noticeable difference (thousandth of inch) (standard task) (Ex:0.039 in.)					
Interval	Integer	Shoe size (women's) (standard U.S.) (Ex: $6\frac{1}{2}$)					Highest point (in county) (relative to ground) (Ex: 236 ft)	
Interval	Tenths	Body temperature (waking) (Fahrenheit) (Ex: 96.8°F)				Air temperature (Fahrenheit) (average annual) (Ex: 50.5 F)		
Interval	Thousandths					Water temperature (Centigrade) (average annual) (Ex: 64°C)	Highest point (in country) (relative to ground) (Ex: 0.045 mi)	
Ordinal	Integer	Ranked height (senior class) (Ex: 37th of 300)	Ranked completion (standard task) (Ex: 8th of 22)		Class rank (high school) (Ex: 5th of 453)			Ranked population (major U.S. cities) (Ex: 3rd of all)
Nominal	(N.A.)	Eye color (Ex: green)		Personality type (Ex: extroverted)	Parents' marital status (Ex: divorced)	climate type (Ex: tropical)	Dominant land form (Ex: plains)	Dominant ethnic group (Ex: Italian)

KEY TERMS AND CONCEPTS

Behavior

Construct validity

Dependent variable

Face validity

Independent variable

Interval level measurement

Interval ratio measurement

Levels of measurement

Measurement

Measurement precision

Measurement validity

Nominal level measurement

Operational definition

Ordinal level measurement

Ratio level measurement

Reliability

Variable

EXERCISES

2.1 Fill in the empty spaces in Table 2.1 with other measurable variables. For example, try to think of a psychological variable that would be at the ratio level of measurement and would have hundredths precision (two digits to the right of the decimal point).

2.2 Identify each of the following as either a variable or a behavior:
   a.   Karen's body temperature has been increasing steadily over a one-hour period.
   b.   Martha's IQ has been measured three times during the past year and has remained at 98.
   c.   John's heart rate is being monitored while he rides an exercise bicycle.
   d.   The amount of snowfall for six Wisconsin cities is reported on the 10 o'clock news.

2.3 Jack is planning an experiment in which he will vary the time since his dog has eaten, and then measure the time the dog requires to run 50 feet. Identify the independent and dependent variables in Jack's experiment.

2.4 Is it possible to measure hair color? Explain.

2.5 Provide an operational definition for each of the following:
   a.   Musicianship
   b.   Athletic ability
   c.   Patriotism
   d.   Gender consciousness
   e.   Political conservatism
   f.   Aggressiveness
   g.   Friendliness
   h.   Androgyny

2.6 Identify the level of measurement for each of the following:
  a. Grade point average
  b. Class rank at graduation
  c. Yearly income
  d. Happiness rated on a 7-point scale
  e. Quality of an Olympic gymnastics performance as rated by panel of judges who hold up cards numbered 1 to 6.
  f. Inches of rainfall measured monthly for a given city.
  g. Percentage of correct answers on a multiple-choice quiz.

2.7 Dan Jansen was expected to win the gold medal for the 500-meter speedskating race in the 1994 Olympic Games. After the race one announcer commented that even though Dan didn't win the gold medal, everyone knew he was the fastest 500-meter skater in the world. What does the announcer's remark suggest about operational definitions of success?

2.8 Frank received grades of A, A, A, A, A, and F for six papers. Can you calculate an average grade for the six papers? If not, why not? If yes, then what is the average grade?

2.9 An Olympic ski jumper received two gold medals, one silver medal, and two bronze medals during his career. Can you calculate an average for his Olympic performance? If not, why not? If yes, then what is the average?

2.10 One teacher, Maxine, assigns only the letter grades A, B, C, and D, without using plus and minus designations. Another teacher, Mark, assigns such grades as a B+ and C−. Which grading system is more precise? Explain.

Organizing
Your
Measurements

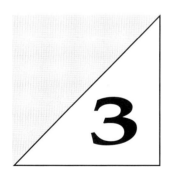

3

OBJECTIVES

After reading and studying Chapter 3 you should understand the following.

- *the act of organizing measurements is motivated by a desire to communicate information as clearly as possible.*

- *how to sort measurements.*

- *how to create categories or groups of measurements.*

- *how to create frequency counts of categorized measurements.*

- *how to create simple frequency tables.*

- *the concept of class interval; the relationship between interval size and required number of intervals.*

- *how to create grouped frequency tables of categorized measurements.*

- *the difference between apparent class intervals and real class intervals.*

- *how to create apparent class intervals and real class intervals for data sets with different degrees of precision.*

- *how to find cumulative frequencies of categorized measurements.*

SORTING MEASUREMENTS

Table 3.1 shows body weights, measured to the nearest whole pound, for each of five people randomly selected from the population of 1000 people in Database A.1.

TABLE 3.1	Body Weight Measurements for Five People (Pounds)
	(Data randomly selected from Database A.1)

128	103	102	175	145

T I M E ■ O U T
Take some time to study the data in Table 3.1. Then retrace your thinking as you pondered the data.

These were my thoughts upon encountering the data of Table 3.1: "Is 128 the largest or smallest number? Is 103 the smallest number? I guess 103 isn't the smallest number because I see that the next score is 102. I guess 128 isn't the largest number because I see that the next score is 175. The score 145 must fall somewhere in the middle of the group. Let's see now, 102 is the smallest number and 175 is the largest number. Let me list them all in order: 102, 103, 128, 145, 175."

I'm sure that your thoughts differ from mine in many ways. Yet, your thoughts and my thoughts probably both represent our efforts to make sense of the new information. This need to make sense of information is shared by all humans.

One of the most basic ways to make sense of a group of numbers (such as those in Table 3.1) is comparison and contrast. If the group is small, one can quickly compare and contrast the numbers repeatedly until ending up with a sorted list. Sorting, as we have just done, is one of the main ways to organize numerical information so that it makes more sense.

GROUPING MEASUREMENTS

Table 3.2 shows body weights, measured to the nearest whole pound, for each of seven people randomly selected from the population of 1000 people in Database A.1.

TABLE 3.2	Body Weight Measurements for Seven People (Pounds)
	(Data randomly selected from Database A.1)

144	147	174	173	144	154	173

T I M E ■ O U T
Take some time to study the data in Table 3.2. Then retrace your thinking as you studied the data.

How did your experience with the measurements in Table 3.2 differ from your experience with those in Table 3.1? One thing you may have noticed is the repetition of 144 and 173. This grouping on the basis of similarity is another basic way of organizing information so that it makes more sense. Children do this when they recognize that certain things share common traits (for example, all Barbie dolls have long legs compared with other dolls).

COUNTING MEASUREMENTS

Once we recognize that there is a repetition of certain measurements, a next logical step is to count the repetitions. Given the measurements in Table 3.2, through a combination of both sorting and counting we would arrive at the summary in Table 3.3.

TABLE 3.3	Counts of Body Weight Measurements for Seven People (Data from Table 3.2)

Body weight (lb)	Count
174	1
173	2
154	1
147	1
144	2

CREATING FREQUENCY DISTRIBUTIONS

A frequency distribution is developed by counting the number of times each measurement occurs. Table 3.3 is a simple frequency distribution.

As the number of measurements increases, so does the effort required to organize them. Not much effort was required in the examples above.

Table 3.4 shows body weights, measured to the nearest whole pound, for each of 20 people randomly selected from the population of 1000 people in Database A.1.

T I M E ■ O U T
Take some time to study the data in Table 3.4.

TABLE 3.4
Body Weight Measurements for 20 People (Pounds)
(Data randomly selected from Database A.1)

| 164 | 111 | 163 | 131 | 155 | 107 | 123 | 136 | 145 | 174 |
| 152 | 127 | 149 | 141 | 121 | 175 | 155 | 136 | 138 | 161 |

With 20 measurements to deal with, the effort required to organize and count them increases, but then so does the motivation to do so. Imagine that you have been hired by a national chain of all-you-can-eat restaurants. Your job is to estimate the amount of food that customers from a given population will eat. You have been provided with Table 3.4.

Generally, the more measurements involved, the more motivation there is to find some way to organize and summarize the data. If we use the same approach to summarizing the data in Table 3.4 as we used in developing Table 3.3 from the data in Table 3.2, we would end up with Table 3.5.

TABLE 3.5 Counts of 20 Sorted
Body Weight Measurements
(Data from Table 3.4)

Body weight (lb)	Count
175	1
174	1
164	1
163	1
161	1
155	2
152	1
149	1
145	1
141	1
138	1
136	2
131	1
127	1
123	1
121	1
111	1
107	1

Tables 3.3 and 3.5 are the crudest forms of frequency distribution. They do not display all possible score values in the range of the measurements taken. For example, Table 3.5 shows that the highest weight in the sample was 175 pounds and the lowest weight was 107 pounds. In the range from 107 to 175, there are

only 20 **actually measured scores** but 69 **possible score values**. In other words, if you counted all possible score values beginning with 107 and ending with 175, you would count 69 possible score values. Notice that only 18 of these 69 possible score values are present in this particular sample.

T I M E ■ O U T
Take some time to study the data in Table 3.5.

Table 3.6 illustrates the type of table we would end up with if we displayed the count for each of the 69 possible score values in the range from 107 to 175.

TABLE 3.6	Counts of All Possible Body Weights in the Range 107 to 175
	(Data from Table 3.4)

Body weight (lb)	Count
175	1
174	1
173	0
172	0
171	0
170	0
⋮	⋮
107	1

This type of table is called a **simple frequency distribution table**. When creating such a table the column heading *Count* is replaced with the heading *Frequency* or its abbreviation (*Freq* or *f*). Table 3.7 shows the same information as Table 3.6 but with the proper labeling.

Notice that there would be many zero frequencies if each possible body weight in the range were listed. There may be times when you would decide to create such a table. Often, however, the total range of possible score values is divided into smaller groups of score values called **class intervals** in order to provide a more concise summary. When class intervals are created, the frequency distribution is referred to as a **grouped frequency distribution**. Table 3.8 shows a grouped frequency distribution based on the same data as Tables 3.4, 3.5, 3.6, and 3.7. Notice that the size of the class interval in this table is five.

TABLE 3.7	Simple Frequency Distribution for 20 Body Weight Measurements (Data from Table 3.4)

Body weight (lb)	Freq
175	1
174	1
173	0
172	0
171	0
170	0
⋮	⋮
107	1

TABLE 3.8	Grouped Frequency Distribution for 20 Body Weight Measurements (Data from Table 3.5)

Class interval (lb)	Freq
172–176	2
167–171	0
162–166	2
157–161	1
152–156	3
147–151	1
142–146	1
137–141	2
132–136	2
127–131	2
122–126	1
117–121	1
112–116	0
107–111	2
	$n = 20$
	(Total $= 20$)

T I M E ■ O U T
Take some time to study Table 3.8.

ASIDE ■ See Procedure C.10, in Appendix C for grouped frequency distribution.

a step-by-step analysis of how to construct a

CUMULATIVE FREQUENCIES

It is often useful to determine the cumulative frequency for each class interval in a grouped frequency distribution. (We will talk more about the reasons for this later.) To accomplish this, take these steps:

Step 1. Begin with the frequency count for the lowest class interval. This is also the **cumulative frequency** count for the lowest class interval.

Step 2. Add the frequency value for the next highest class interval to the cumulative frequency that you have just determined. This gives the cumulative frequency for the next interval.

Step 3. Repeat Step 2 for all class intevals.

ASIDE ■ Cumulative frequency simply refers to the accumulated frequency count for all class intervals below and including a given interval. Since the lowest class interval has no other inter- vals below it, the cumulative frequency for the lowest interval is equivalent to the simple fre- quency for that interval.

After completing these steps for all class intervals, the results for the data in Table 3.4 would look like this:

Real class interval	Freq	Cum freq
171.5–176.5	2	20
166.5–171.5	0	18
161.5–166.5	2	18
156.5–161.5	1	16
151.5–156.5	3	15
146.5–151.5	1	12
141.5–146.5	1	11
136.5–141.5	2	10
131.5–136.5	2	8
126.5–131.5	2	6
121.5–126.5	1	4
116.5–121.5	1	3
111.5–116.5	0	2
106.5–111.5	2	2

Notice that these class intervals are different from those in Table 3.8. Those just above are **real class intervals**, while those in Table 3.8 are **apparent class intervals**. Confusing? The difference is this: Real class intervals have no gap between the intervals; apparent class intervals have a gap between them. In order to close the gap between intervals, here is what we do. For each class interval, one-half of the unit of the degree of precision is (*a*) subtracted from each lower limit and (*b*) added to each upper limit. Since the unit of precision for the data in Table 3.4 is 1.0, we subtract 0.5 from each lower limit and add 0.5 to each upper limit.

Here is the calculation for the apparent class interval 137–141:

ASIDE ■ See Procedure C.10 in Appendix C

Lower limit: $137 - 0.5 = 136.5$

for a step-by-step analysis of these calculations.

Upper limit: $141 + 0.5 = 141.5$

Therefore the real class interval is 136.5–141.5.

Table 3.9 shows a complete grouped frequency distribution (including both real and apparent class intervals) for the data in Table 3.4.

TABLE 3.9	Complete Grouped Frequency Distribution for 20 Body Weight Measurements (Data from Table 3.4)

Real class interval (lb)	Apparent class interval (lb)	Freq	Cum freq
171.5–176.5	172–176	2	20
166.5–171.5	167–171	0	18
161.5–166.5	162–166	2	18
156.5–161.5	157–161	1	16
151.5–156.5	152–156	3	15
146.5–151.5	147–151	1	12
141.5–146.5	142–146	1	11
136.5–141.5	137–141	2	10
131.5–136.5	132–136	2	8
126.5–131.5	127–131	2	6
121.5–126.5	122–126	1	4
116.5–121.5	117–121	1	3
111.5–116.5	112–116	0	2
106.5–111.5	107–111	2	2

T I M E ■ O U T

Study Table 3.9 before reading further. It may take you some time to make sense of the information there, but it is well worth the effort since it provides practice in the very useful skill of interpreting tables. As you've probably noticed, life is filled with information presented to us in the form of quantitative tables.

ASIDE ■ **TIME OUT FOR THERAPY. It's usually at about this point that most students begin to feel uncomfortable. They may look at a data display like Table 3.9 and simply go blank, as if the brain were paralyzed. If this is happening to you, I encourage you to stare at Table 3.9 until your brain begins to loosen up. This may take as long as 30 minutes. (I think the record is two hours.) Don't be intimidated by such a table. If it doesn't make sense right away this does not mean that you are stupid or that you are one of those people who doesn't understand statistics. It probably just means that you haven't had much practice interpreting tables. I promise you that whatever time you take right now to get comfortable with Table 3.9 will be well worth while. It will give you a feeling of confidence and mastery over quantitative information. This mastery is very important—not just for this course but for whatever career you choose.**

If you don't have much trouble with Table 3.9, then file away this brief therapy session for the time when your brain does freeze up. Sooner or later it happens to everyone. When it happens to you, just remember to keep staring at the material until you can make sense of it.

T I M E ■ O U T

I cannot overemphasize the importance of getting confortable with Table 3.9. Take whatever time you need.

Here are some of the things you should have noticed about Table 3.9.

1. If you add up all the frequency values you will get 20, which is the total number of body weight measurements in the sample. (This total *n*umber is often symbolized by the letter n.)
2. Table 3.9 takes up much less room than Table 3.7 would take up in its completed form.
3. There are still some zero frequency values in Table 3.9, but not nearly so many as in Table 3.7.
4. The frequency for each class interval is determined by simply adding up the number of scores falling in the range for that interval. For example, two scores fall in the apparent class interval 162–166. These scores are 163 and 164. (This information is available from either Table 3.4 or Table 3.5.)

5. The size of each apparent class interval is 5. In other words, there are five possible score values in each interval. The five possible score values in interval 137–141 are 137, 138, 139, 140, and 141.

6. Even though there are five *possible* score values in each apparent class interval, the *actual* frequency of scores need not be 5. As you can see, the frequencies for Table 3.9 range from zero to 3.

ASIDE ■ The frequency of actually measured scores in a given class interval need not be the same as the number of possible score values in the interval.

7. Each class interval is written as "lower score, hyphen, higher score." In other words, the lower score is always expressed first, followed by the higher score (for example, 117–121).

8. Class intervals are arranged so that those with the highest score values are at the top of the table and those with the lowest score values are at the bottom of the table. The class interval 172–176 is at the top of the table and contains the highest score values. The class interval 107–111 is at the bottom of the table and contains the lowest score values.

9. For any class interval, subtracting the lower score from the higher score yields a difference of 4. Thus for the class interval 152–156, $156 - 152 = 4$. (Notice that 4 is one less than the class interval size of 5.)

T I M E ■ O U T
Take some time to think about why this is true.

10. Subtracting the lower score of any class interval from the lower score of the class interval immediately above yields a difference of 5. Thus, for the class intervals 122–126 and 127–131, $127 - 122 = 5$. (Notice that this is exactly the same as the class interval size of 5.)

T I M E ■ O U T
Take some time to think about why this is true.

11. There are 14 separate class intervals.

Table 3.9 takes up less space than would a completed Table 3.7. This makes Table 3.9 a more concise summary of the data originally presented in Table 3.4. However, because Table 3.9 is more concise, we have lost some of the information in Table 3.4. For example, Table 3.9 reveals that there are two scores in the class interval 127–131 but it does not tell us what they are. Table 3.4 discloses that the two scores are 127 and 131. (In their completed form, Tables 3.5, 3.6, and .7 would also show these two scores.) This loss of detailed information in Table 3.9 when compared with Table 3.4 illustrates an important principle about organizing data for the purpose of summary: *the more concise the summary, the greater the loss of detail.*

To further illustrate this trade-off between summary and detail, let's look at two ways in which to summarize the data from Table 3.4.

1. At one extreme is the approach seen in Table 3.7. In its completed form, this table would present a frequency count for each of the 69 possible score values in the range from 107 to 175. This approach provides maximum detail and minimum summary.

2. At the opposite extreme is the approach taken in Table 3.10. Here we learn nothing about the original 20 score values, other than that they fall somewhere in the range from 107 to 175. This approach provides minimum detail and maximum summary.

TABLE 3.10 **Grouped Frequency Distribution for 20 Body Weight Measurements** (Data from Table 3.5)

Class interval (lb)	Freq
107–175	20
	$\overline{n = 20}$ (Total = 20)

Although Table 3.7 is a simple frequency distribution, we can view it as a grouped frequency distribution consisting of 69 class intervals, with each interval having a size of 1. Table 3.8 is a grouped frequency distribution of 14 class intervals, with each interval having a size of 5. Table 3.10 is a grouped frequency distribution with only one class interval, and the size of this interval is 69.

T I M E ■ O U T
Take some time to think about how Tables 3.7, 3.8, and 3.10 differ. Pay particular attention to the amount of detail as it relates to class interval size.

Table 3.11 summarizes the relationships among the characteristics of frequency distributions as seen in Tables 3.7, 3.8, and 3.10.

TABLE 3.11 **Relationships Among the Characteristics of Frequency Distributions**

	Number of class intervals	Class interval size	Degree of summary	Degree of detail	Relative amount of space required
Table 3.7	69	1	Low	High	High
Table 3.8	14	5	Medium	Medium	Medium
Table 3.10	1	69	High	Low	Low

Table 3.11 shows that if a higher degree of summary is desirable in a frequency distribution, then one should create a larger class interval size and reduce the number of intervals required to cover the range of scores measured. If more detail is desirable, then one should create a smaller interval but increase the number of intervals.

When creating grouped frequency distributions you should consider the following practical matters:

- Do you have access to computer software that creates tables?

- How much time do you have available to create the table?

- How much time does your audience have to interpret the table? If your audience doesn't have lots of time, then you'll probably want to minimize detail.

- How much space is available? Are you working with an $8\frac{1}{2}$-by-11 inch sheet of paper, a computer screen, an overhead projector, a chalkboard, or some other medium?

- How important is the detail relative to the conciseness of your summary?

APPARENT CLASS INTERVALS AND REAL CLASS INTERVALS

Now that you have a basic understanding of a grouped frequency distribution, the time has come to add some complexity. Look again at Table 3.4. Notice that all 20 scores are whole numbers. Now look at Table 3.9. Notice that the lower and upper limits for each class interval are also whole numbers. (For example, the class interval 162–166 has a lower limit of 162 and an upper limit of 166.) Notice also that the difference between the upper limit for a given interval and the lower limit for the next higher interval is 1. (For example, the difference between the upper value of 156 for the interval 152–156 and the lower value of 157 for the interval 157–161 is 1 (157 − 156 = 1). This difference of 1 represents a gap between any two adjacent class intervals. Because all the weights in Table 3.8 are whole numbers, none of them fall into one of these gaps. Every weight fits neatly into one of the class intervals. But what if one of the weight measurements had been 156.6 pounds? A score of 156.6 does not fit into any of the intervals. It's too large to fit into the interval 152–156 and too small to fit into the interval 157–161.

In order to handle such a situation, we must first determine the number of decimal places in our measurements. Then, when creating a grouped frequency distribution, class intervals must be set up so that no measurement falls into a gap between intervals. We can see that the weight measurement 156.6 falls into a gap between the class intervals set up in Table 3.8. Therefore, if any of our weight measurements are accurate to one decimal place, the intervals in Table 3.8 will not be appropriate. The column of class intervals in Table 3.8 is repeated in Table 3.9, where its heading reads "Apparent Class Interval." Table 3.9 also includes a column headed "Real Class Interval." Note that the weight measurement 156.6 does not fall into a gap between *real* class intervals, since 156.6 is within the interval 156.5–161.5. However, our problem is not yet put to rest. If the smallest unit of data precision is 0.1, we need to allow for the possibility of a weight like 156.5 and in such a case, it is not clear if we should consider 156.5 to belong in the interval 156.5–161.5 or the interval 151.5–156.5.

One solution to this quandary would be to round off all scores to whole numbers. However let's use the rainfall data in Table 3.12 to learn how to construct a grouped frequency distribution when our measures are accurate to one decimal place.

TABLE 3.12	Annual Rainfall Measurements for 20 Geographic Locations (Inches)
	(Data randomly selected from Database A.2)

8.1	10.8	6.6	8.2	10.7	7.8	9.3	9.9
9.7	9.3	10.3	12.4	7.8	4.6	5.7	7.2
9.6	8.9	5.1	9.5				

If we use the same approach to summarizing the data in Table 3.12 as we used in developing Table 3.3 from the data in Table 3.2, we would end up with Table 3.13.

TABLE 3.13	Counts of 20 Sorted Rainfall Measurements
	(Data from Table 3.12)

Rainfall (in.)	Count	Rainfall (in.)	Count
12.4	1	8.9	1
10.8	1	8.2	1
10.7	1	8.1	1
10.3	1	7.8	2
9.9	1	7.2	1
9.7	1	6.6	1
9.6	1	5.7	1
9.5	1	5.1	1
9.3	2	4.6	1

Now look at Table 3.14. It shows a grouped frequency distribution for the data in Table 3.12. Notice that two additional empty intervals have been added — one at the top (the interval 12.5–12.9) and one at the bottom (the interval 4.0–4.4). These empty intervals are added so that the frequency distribution will be anchored at the top and bottom with frequency values of zero.

TABLE 3.14 Grouped Frequency Distribution
for 20 Rainfall Measurements
(Data from Table 3.13)

Apparent class interval (in.)	Freq
12.5–12.9	0
12.0–12.4	1
11.5–11.9	0
11.0–11.4	0
10.5–10.9	2
10.0–10.4	1
9.5–9.9	4
9.0–9.4	2
8.5–8.9	1
8.0–8.4	2
7.5–7.9	2
7.0–7.4	1
6.5–6.9	1
6.0–6.4	0
5.5–5.9	1
5.0–5.4	1
4.5–4.9	1
4.0–4.4	0
	$n = 20$ (Total = 20)

T I M E ■ O U T
Take some time to compare Tables 3.14 and 3.8. Notice that class intervals for Table 3.14 have upper and lower limits with 0.1 precision. The class intervals for Table 3.8 have upper and lower limits with 1.0 precision.

As noted earlier in the chapter, it is often useful to determine cumulative frequencies for each class interval in a grouped frequency distribution. The general steps for accomplishing this were also described. If we follow these steps (for all intervals) using the data in Table 3.12, we eventually arrive at the data display seen in Table 3.15.

TABLE 3.15 Grouped Frequency Distribution for 20 Rainfall Measurements
(Data from Table 3.14)

Real class interval (in.)	Freq	Cum freq
12.45–12.95	0	20
11.95–12.45	1	20
11.45–11.95	0	19
10.95–11.45	0	19
10.45–10.95	2	19
9.95–10.45	1	17
9.45–9.95	4	16
8.95–9.45	2	12
8.45–8.95	1	10
7.95–8.45	2	9
7.45–7.95	2	7
6.95–7.45	1	5
6.45–6.95	1	4
5.95–6.45	0	3
5.45–5.95	1	3
4.95–5.45	1	2
4.45–4.95	1	1
3.95–4.45	0	0

Notice that the class intervals in Table 3.15 are different from those in Table 3.14. Intervals in Table 3.15 are real class intervals; those in Table 3.14 are apparent class intervals. Recall that real class intervals have no gaps between intervals, while apparent class intervals do have a gap. In order to close the gap between apparent class intervals, one-half of the unit of the degree of precision is (a) subtracted from each lower limit and (b) added to each upper limit. Since the unit of precision for the data in Table 3.4 is 0.1, we subtract half of this (one-half of 0.1 = 0.05) from each lower limit and add 0.05 to each upper limit.

Here is the calculation for the apparent class interval 10.0–10.4:

Lower limit: $10.0 - 0.05 = 9.95$

Upper limit: $10.4 + 0.05 = 10.45$

Therefore the real class interval is 9.95–10.45.

Table 3.16 shows a complete grouped frequency distribution for the data in Table 3.14.

| | TABLE 3.16 | Complete Grouped Frequency Distribution for 20 Rainfall Measurements (Based on information from Table 3.14) |

Real class interval (in.)	Apparent class interval (in.)	Freq	Cum freq
12.45–12.95	12.5–12.9	0	20
11.95–12.45	12.0–12.4	1	20
11.45–11.95	11.5–11.9	0	19
10.95–11.45	11.0–11.4	0	19
10.45–10.95	10.5–10.9	2	19
9.95–10.45	10.0–10.4	1	17
9.45–9.95	9.5–9.9	4	16
8.95–9.45	9.0–9.4	2	12
8.45–8.95	8.5–8.9	1	10
7.95–8.45	8.0–8.4	2	9
7.45–7.95	7.5–7.9	2	7
6.95–7.45	7.0–7.4	1	5
6.45–6.95	6.5–6.9	1	4
5.95–6.45	6.0–6.4	0	3
5.45–5.95	5.5–5.9	1	3
4.95–5.45	5.0–5.4	1	2
4.45–4.95	4.5–4.9	1	1
3.95–4.45	4.0–4.4	0	0

SUMMARY

Human beings have a natural tendency to try to make sense of new information. One of the most basic ways to make sense of a group of measurements is to organize them by sorting and grouping on the basis of similarity. Frequency distributions and frequency tables represent efforts to display such organized information in a summary form, which is easier to interpret than a simple listing of all measurements.

This chapter presented relevant issues to consider and general procedures to follow when constructing grouped frequency distributions. Procedure C.10 in Appendix C provides step-by-step instructions for creating grouped frequency distributions without the use of computer software.

KEY TERMS AND CONCEPTS

Actually measured score

Apparent class interval

Class interval

Cumulative frequency

Grouped frequency distribution

Possible score value

Real class interval

Simple frequency distribution

EXERCISES

3.1 Randomly select 25 body weights from Database A.1. Then create a complete grouped frequency distribution as seen in Table 3.16. Include columns for real class intervals, apparent class intervals, frequency, and cumulative frequency.

3.2 Use the table you've just created with sample data to make inferences about the population.

3.3 Randomly select 30 scores from Database A.3. Use this sample to create another complete grouped frequency distribution.

3.4 Use the table you've created for Exercise 3.3 to make inferences about the population that is represented by the sample.

3.5 What is the general relationship between class interval size and number of class intervals?

3.6 If the highest degree of precision is 0.1, what are the real limits of the following class intervals?

3.5–3.7

3.2–3.4

3.7 If the highest degree of precision is 0.01, what are the real limits of the following class intervals?

3.05–3.07

3.02–3.04

3.8 What is the general rule for determining real limits of class intervals?

3.9 What is one of the main differences between a frequency count and a cumulative frequency count?

3.10 What is the primary difference between an actually measured score and a possible score value?

Summarizing Your Measurements

OBJECTIVES

After reading and studying Chapter 4 you should understand the following.

- *some of the reasons for summarizing data.*

- *how to calculate the mean for a set of data.*

- *the symbols used in the formula for the mean.*

- *how to calculate the median for a set of data.*

- *how to calculate the mode for a set of data.*

- *some issues regarding the choice of the mean, the median, and the mode.*

- *the concept of* central tendency.

- *the symbols used for the mean, median, and mode of samples and populations.*

- *the concept of* variability.

- *how to calculate the range for a set of data.*

- *how to calculate the average absolute deviation for a set of data.*

- *how to calculate the variance for a set of data.*

- *the symbols used in the formula for calculating the variance.*

- *how to calculate the standard deviation for a set of data.*

- *the symbols used in the formula for calculating the standard deviation.*

- *the symbols used for the range, average absolute deviation, variance, and standard deviation of samples and populations.*

- *the difference between conceptual formulas and calculation formulas.*

INTRODUCTION

In Chapter 3, we discussed grouped frequency distributions as a means of organizing measurements. They also represent an elementary means of summarizing data: By creating class intervals and counting the number of data points present within each, we obtain a more concise statement of the information. **Summarizing data** is a process whereby we take the original data set and organize it and/or perform calculations on it so that we can obtain useful information without having to look at all the individual data points.

COMPUTING AVERAGES (MEANS)

Computing an average is one of the most common summary techniques. An **average** is simply the sum of all the data points in a given set of data divided by the total number of data points in the set. For example, if you earned the following grades on your first three tests in a class

80, 90, 100

your average would be calculated by first adding up the three scores (80 + 90 + 100 = 270) and then dividing by 3, which is the total number of data points (270 divided by 3 = 90).

In statistics, we often speak of the **mean** rather than the average; these terms are equivalent. Formally, the procedure for calculating an average is stated as follows

$$\bar{X} = \frac{\sum X}{N} \tag{4.1}$$

Let's look at the symbols in this formula one at a time, starting from the left. The first symbol

$$\bar{X}$$

can be referred to either as X-bar, which describes the symbol itself, or as the mean, which describes what the symbol represents.

The second symbol

$$=$$

is the equal-sign and requires no further explanation.

The third symbol

$$\sum$$

is a Greek letter. It can be referred to as capital sigma, which describes the symbol itself; as the summation sign, which describes its purpose in the equation; or as "the sum of . . . ," which describes the operation that it instructs us to perform. When a summation sign comes before another symbol (X in the present case), it indicates that all of the values for that symbol (all of the X values) are to be added up.

The fourth symbol

$$X$$

can be referred to either as capital X, which describes the symbol itself, or as the X value, which describes what the symbol represents. By convention, X represents a data point. For example, if there are three data points

80, 90, and 100

then we say that there are three X values. To differentiate the data points, each can be represented by X with a different subscript. For example

$$X_1 = 80, X_2 = 90, X_3 = 100$$

The fifth symbol

———

can be referred to, self-evidently, as a line or a division line, or else as "divided by," which describes the actual operation that it instructs us to perform.

The sixth symbol

$$N$$

can be referred to either as capital N, which describes the symbol itself, or as the total number of data points in the data set, which describes what the symbol represents. For example, if there are three data points in the data set, then $N = 3$.

ASIDE ■ **When we want to emphasize that our data set is a sample from a larger population then we use *n* instead of *N* to represent the number of data points.**

As we saw earlier, the mean for the three data points 80, 90, and 100 is 90. We can state this final answer symbolically as follows

$$\bar{X} = 90$$

Sometimes you will see the formula for the mean written in more detail as follows

$$\bar{X} = \frac{\sum\limits_{i=1}^{N} X_i}{N} \qquad\qquad (4.2)$$

This formula can be stated verbally as follows: The mean is equal to the sum of all the subscripted X values, starting with the X value that has the subscript 1 and ending with the last X value (that is, the X value with subscript N), divided by the total number of data points in the data set. Given the complexity of that sentence, you can perhaps appreciate the value of symbols and formulas.

Here's an example of how the formula is used

$\bar{X} = (X_1 + X_2 + X_3)$ divided by N

$\bar{X} = (80 + 90 + 100)$ divided by 3

$\bar{X} = 270$ divided by 3

$\bar{X} = 90$

Since $N = 3$, the symbols X_N and X_3 represent the same data point in this example.

While there is nothing very complicated about calculating means, it is important to feel comfortable with the symbols and the procedures involved.

T I M E ■ O U T
Take some time to practice calculating means.

By computing the mean, we are able to represent the data set with a single value. Here are two examples.

Your mean grade point (or grade point average) is a single value summarizing your grades for all the courses that you've taken. Suppose that, on a 4-point grading system, you received the following grades in the first semester of your freshman year: $A = 4, B = 3, C = 2, A = 4$. The mean is $(4 + 3 + 2 + 4)$ divided by 4, which is $13/4 = 3.25$

Your mean test grade (or test average) is a single value summarizing the grades for all the tests that you've taken in a given course. Suppose that you earned the following grades on five tests in a certain course: 80, 75, 90, 85, 92. The mean is $(80 + 75 + 90 + 85 + 92)$ divided by 5, which is $422/5 = 84.4$

COMPUTING MEDIANS

In some cases, the mean may be an inappropriate representation of the data points in a given data set. Consider Table 4.1.

TABLE 4.1		Room Temperature Measured on 20 Different Days (Degrees)							
		(Data randomly selected — with modification — from Database A.5)							
85+	85+	72	76	80	83	84	82	71	85+
85	85	85+	81	74	85+	70	85+	80	85+

Note: The measurements were taken with a thermometer with a scale that does not extend beyond 85°. Temperatures higher than 85° are denoted by 85+.

If we wanted to summarize the temperatures in Table 4.1, it would not be very accurate to calculate a mean, because there is no way to make a quantitative distinction between a value of 85 and a value of 85+. If we simply add the 85+ values as if they were 85, the mean for the data in Table 4.1 is found to be 80.9.

Now, let's imagine that someone else recorded these temperatures using a thermometer with a less limited scale, and obtained the results in Table 4.2.

TABLE 4.2		Room Temperature Measured on 20 Different Days (Degrees)							
		(Data randomly selected from Database A.5)							
90	88	72	76	80	83	84	82	71	100
85	85	105	81	74	88	70	88	80	89

Note: The measurements were taken with a thermometer with a scale that extends beyond 85°.

Notice that in Table 4.2 the data points of 85+ that we saw in Table 4.1 have been replaced with values higher than 85.

The mean for the data in Table 4.2 is 83.55. Not surprisingly, it is higher than the mean for the data in Table 4.1. Thus, the mean is not an accurate summary of the room temperatures in Table 4.1. However, these data may be more accurately represented by a measure called the median.

The **median** is that point in a data set such that the number of data points of higher value is equal to the number of data points of lower value. If the total number of data points is odd, then the median is simply equivalent in value to the middle data point. For example, if there are three data points 80, 85, and 100 in the data set, then the median is 85, the middle data point. If the total number of data points is even, then the median is the average of the two middle data points. For example, if there are four data points 80, 86, 88, and 100 in the data set, then the median is 87, the average of the two data points 86 and 88.

Getting back to the examples in Tables 4.1 and 4.2, we find that the median is the same in each case. The total number of data points is 20, an even number. Therefore, the median is equivalent to the average of the two middle scores 83 and 84, which is 83.5.

As this example makes clear, one advantage of the median is that it is less dependent than the mean upon the accuracy of the measurements. As we see for the data in Tables 4.1 and 4.2, the median is the same even though the thermometer in the first case did not allow accurate measurements above 85.

T I M E ■ O U T
Take some time to practice calculating medians.

COMPUTING MODES

In some cases, neither the mean nor the median may be appropriate to summarize the data points in a data set. For example, the owner of a t-shirt shop might wish to summarize the sizes of all the t-shirts that she sold on a given day, as listed in Table 4.3.

| TABLE 4.3 | **Sizes for 20 T-Shirts Sold on a Given Day** (Data randomly selected from Database A.6) |

L	M	S	L	M	XL	XS	XL	XS	M
L	L	M	L	L	XL	M	XL	S	S

Note: XS, extra small; M, medium; and so on.

We could calculate a mean for these data points by first converting each letter to a number (XS = 1, S = 2, M = 3, L = 4, XL = 5), as in Table 4.4. The mean for these data is 3.35. This tells us that the average size of the t-shirts sold that day is between a medium and a large. Is this a meaningful summary?

| TABLE 4.4 | **Converted Sizes for 20 T-Shirts Sold on a Given Day** (Data randomly selected from Database A.6) |

4	3	2	4	3	5	1	5	1	3
4	4	3	4	4	5	3	5	2	2

T I M E ■ O U T
Take some time to consider this question.

The mode would be a more appropriate way to summarize data like this. The **mode** is equivalent to the value of the data point that occurs most often in the data set. Table 4.5 shows the frequencies for each of the t-shirt sizes indicated in Table 4.3. (Remember the discussion of frequency distributions in Chapter 3.)

Table 4.5 indicates that there were more large t-shirts sold than any other. Therefore, the mode for this data set is "large."

TABLE 4.5	Simple Frequency Distribution for the Sizes of 20 T-Shirts Sold on a Given Day

Size	Number Sold
Extra large	4
Large	6
Medium	5
Small	3
Extra small	2
	n = 20

T I M E ■ O U T

Take some time to practice calculating modes.

CHOOSING AMONG MEANS, MEDIANS, AND MODES

Now is a good time to recall our discussion of levels of measurement in Chapter 2. The **level of measurement** for the data you are trying to summarize is one of the factors that will determine whether you choose the mean, median, or mode as your method of summary.

T I M E ■ O U T

What level of measurement is represented by t-shirt size? Take some time to consider this question.

You should examine the following issues when deciding among the mean, median, and mode.

Level of Measurement

If the measurement is at the nominal level — for example, eye color — use the mode; it would not be possible to calculate a mean or a median. If the measurement is at the ordinal level — for example, class rank — use the median; it would not make sense to calculate a mean or a mode. If the measurement is at the interval or ratio level, use the mean. Think about the level of measurement that corresponds to your data; then ask yourself which summary statistics are possible and/or meaningful to calculate.

Stability

Suppose that you randomly select several different sample data sets (10, for example) from the same population, and each data set consists of the same number of data points (20, for example). If you then calculated the mean, median, and mode for each of the sample data sets, you would probably find that the means for the 10 data sets would change the least from one sample to the other, and the modes would change the most. For this reason, the mean is said to be the most stable of the three summary statistics. **Stability** refers to the consistency of the summary statistics from one sample to another, when samples are randomly selected from the same population.

Stability should not be confused with sensitivity, which will be discussed next.

T I M E ■ O U T

Take some time to complete this exercise: Randomly select 10 samples from one of the data sets in Appendix A. Calculate the mean, median, and mode for each sample. Which of these three measures changes the least from one sample to the other?

Sensitivity

Consider a small data set consisting of four data points: 4, 5, 5, and 6. The mean for this data set is 5. The median and the mode for this data set are also 5. If the data point of 6 were to be changed to 50, the mean would increase dramatically from 5 to 16; however, the median and the mode would still be 5. In this case the mean would be the most sensitive to the change in the score. While it is often said that the mean is the most stable of the three measures, we see in this example that it may also be the most sensitive in some circumstances.

Now consider a small data set consisting of the four data points 2, 3, 3, and 40. Its mean is 12; its median is 3; and its mode is 3. If one of the 3's were changed to 40, the mean would change from 12 to 21.25; the median would change from 3 to 21.5; and the mode would change from 3 to 40. While all of these changes are relatively large, the change in the mode is the largest.

These examples illustrate that stability and sensitivity are separate issues and, also, that the relative sensitivities of the mean, median, and mode depend upon the peculiarities of a given data set.

Shape of the Distribution

If the frequency distribution is perfectly symmetrical, then the mean, median, and mode will all be virtually the same. If the distribution is negatively skewed—that is, the highest frequencies are piled up at the right end of the distribution—then the mean will be the lowest of the three measures and the mode will be the highest. If the distribution is positively skewed—that is, the highest frequencies are piled up at the left end of the distribution — then the mean will be the highest of the three measures and the mode will be the lowest. Thus, each measure represents the distribution differently, and all three measures should be reported in order to reflect the complete picture.

Purpose of the Summary

This is perhaps the most important issue to consider. In the t-shirt example, even though we could calculate a mean for the data set by converting each letter size to a number (XL = 5, and so on), the result (a mean of 3.35) is difficult to interpret. In this situation the mode would seem to be the most useful to the store owner.

Some mathematicians would argue that the mean would not be a valid summary statistic in this situation because the variable of t-shirt size is only at the ordinal level of measurement. Such mathematical issues are relevant, but the human meaning that we attach to data may be of equal importance. Consider, for example, the numerals assigned to the players on my daughter's softball team. It could be argued that these numbers are nominal-level measurements and have no quantitative meaning. However, a conversation that I overheard among some of the girls on the team led me to believe that, for these seven-year-olds, a lower numeral confers a higher social status — to the point where zero has the highest status.

To push this point even further, suppose that the men's freshmen volleyball team is trying to make a case for sex discrimination by arguing that the numerals assigned to their shirts are lower than the numerals assigned to the women's freshman volleyball team. Could they support their argument with the summary statistics in Table 4.6?

T I M E ■ O U T
Take some time to consider this question, and discuss your conclusion with other members of the class.

TABLE 4.6	Mean Jersey Numerals for Men's and Women's Freshmen Volleyball Teams
$\bar{X}_{men} = 7.3$	$\bar{X}_{women} = 8.6$

Speed of Calculation

If you are under some time pressure to provide a summary of your data set, then you might want to consider the mode, since it is often the easiest of the three summary statistics to compute. Of course, the speed of calculation will also depend on other issues. How many data points are in the data set? If there are only a few scores, then the mean is relatively easy to calculate. Are the data points already sorted? If so, then the median is relatively easy to calculate. Each situation will differ, and only you will have the information necessary to make the decision.

CENTRAL TENDENCY

Each of the three summary statistics discussed above (mean, median, and mode) is considered to be a measure of **central tendency**—in other words, a measure that represents the center of the data set. This is obviously true of the median, which is the point in the data set such that an equal number of data points are above and below it.

The mode represents the center in a different way: It indicates the most frequently occurring data point. As we will see in Chapter 5, the mode corresponds to the highest point when the frequency distribution for a given data set is graphed.

The mean represents the center in yet a different way: If the mean is subtracted from each data point in the data set and all such differences are added together, the result will always be zero.

STATISTICS AND PARAMETERS REVISITED

As we saw in Chapter 1, a calculation that summarizes data from a sample is referred to as a statistic, whereas a calculation that summarizes data from a population is referred to as a parameter. Different symbols are sometimes used to indicate whether the calculation is a statistic or a parameter. Table 4.7 illustrates the symbols used in this book for the mean of a population and the mean of a sample.

TABLE 4.7 Symbols for the Mean

	Symbol	Pronunciation	Rhymes with
Generic concept	mean	"mēn"	green
Sample statistic	$\bar{X}$	"ĕx bär"	box car
Population parameter	μ	"mü"	view

In those cases where the data are not considered to be either a population or a sample, it is appropriate to speak simply of the mean.

Tables 4.8 and 4.9 illustrate the symbols that will be used for the median and the mode.

TABLE 4.8   Symbols for the Median

	Symbol	Pronunciation
Generic concept	median	"mē'dē-ĕn"
Sample statistic	md	"mē'dē-ĕn"
Population parameter	Md	"mē'dē-ĕn"

TABLE 4.9   Symbols for the Mode

	Symbol	Pronunciation
Generic concept	mode	"mōd"
Sample statistic	mo	"mōd"
Population parameter	Mo	"mōd"

VARIABILITY

In the previous sections you learned about the concept of central tendency and the three common measures of central tendency: mean, median, and mode. Because you were already familiar with the calculation of averages, the notion of summarizing a data set by using a measure of central tendency was not totally new. Now you will be introduced to another characteristic of data sets that provides important information and, therefore, is valuable to include in any summary of the data set. This characteristic is referred to as variability. For the time being, we adopt the following *preliminary* definition: **Variability** is the degree to which the data points in a given data set are not alike. For example, consider, the small data sets in Table 4.10. In data set 1, all three data points are identical, and we say that there is no variability. On the other hand, there is some variability in data set 2, and even more variability in data set 3.

TABLE 4.10   Three Small Data Sets

Data set 1:	7,	7,	7
Data set 2:	7,	8,	9
Data set 3:	7,	56,	142

If the data points in a data set differ greatly from one another, we say that there is a high degree of variability. If the data points are very similar to one another, we say that there is a low degree of variability.

Other words that are used when referring to variability are: **heterogeneity**, **homogeneity**, and **dispersion**. These words are related as follows.

Variability	Homogeneity	Heterogeneity	Dispersion
Low	High	Low	Low
High	Low	High	High

In other words, low variability is the same as high homogeneity, low heterogeneity, and low dispersion.

Information about the variability in a data set will help us to make decisions about the relative value of certain groups of measured events. For example, two bowlers, Mary and Tom, have the same mean for a three-game series (Table 4.11); which would you rather have on your team?

TIME ■ OUT
Take some time to think about this question and prepare to discuss it with the other members of your class.

TABLE 4.11   **Bowling Scores for Mary and Tom**

Tom: 200, 220, 240	$\bar{X}_{Tom} = 220$
Mary: 210, 220, 230	$\bar{X}_{Mary} = 220$

TIME ■ OUT
Do not forget the "total process" emphasis of this text. There will be times when the discussion seems to digress, but each topic is relevant to the total process. For example, the present topic of variability is extremely important when evaluating any data that are collected in order to answer a larger question or shed light on a larger issue.

COMPUTING RANGES

The fastest way to summarize the degree of variability for a given data set is to compute the range. This concept was introduced in Chapter 3 in discussing frequency distributions.

There are three different methods for calculating the range.

Method 1

The **range** (R) is thought of as the difference between the lowest- and highest-valued data points in the data set. Using this method to calculate the ranges for the data in Table 4.10, we get the results in Table 4.12.

		Range
TABLE 4.12	**Ranges of Three Small Data Sets According to Method 1**	
Data set 1:	7, 7, 7	$7 - 7 = 0$
Data set 2:	7, 8, 9	$9 - 7 = 2$
Data set 3:	7, 56, 142	$142 - 7 = 135$

Method 2

In this case, the range is thought of as the total number of possible data values in the data set; the lowest- and highest-valued data points are included in the total. Using this method to calculate the ranges for the data in Table 4.10, we get the results in Table 4.13.

		Range
TABLE 4.13	**Ranges of Three Small Data Sets According to Method 2**	
Data set 1:	7, 7, 7	$7 - 7 + 1 = 1$
Data set 2:	7, 8, 9	$9 - 7 + 1 = 3$
Data set 3:	7, 56, 142	$142 - 7 + 1 = 136$

For data set 2, the range is 3, because there are three **possible values** between, and including, the values 7 and 9: 7, 8, and 9.

ASIDE ■ As illustrated by data set 3, there is a difference between the total number of possible values in the range (in this case, 136) and the actual number of data points (in this case, 3). This is an important distinction, which will come up again.

Method 3

In this method, the decimal precision of the data points is taken into consideration. Table 4.14 states three new data sets that are precise to one decimal place. (The data points in Table 4.10 are rounded to whole integers.)

TABLE 4.14	Three Small Data Sets

Data set 4:	7.2, 7.2, 7.2
Data set 5:	7.2, 8.2, 9.2
Data set 6:	7.2, 56.2, 142.2

As in method 2, we define the range as the total number of possible values in the set, including the lowest and highest data points. If we now assume that the values are changing in units of 0.1, we find that the ranges for data sets 4, 5, and 6 are 1, 21, and 1351 respectively. Let's look at the calculations in more detail.

For data set 4, clearly the range is 1, because there is only one possible value for the data set. For data set 5, there are 21 possible values, as follows:

7.2, 7.3, 7.4, 7.5, 7.6, 7.7, 7.8, 7.9, 8.0, 8.1, 8.2, 8.3,

8.4, 8.5, 8.6, 8.7, 8.8, 8.9, 9.0, 9.1, and 9.2

The important thing to remember here is that the number of possible values is directly related to the decimal precision of the data points. If we were to increase the precision from units of 0.1 to units of 0.01, then the range from 7.20 to 9.20 would include 201 possible values: 7.20, 7.21, 7.22, and so on.

RANGE AS AN INDEX OF VARIABILITY

Generally speaking, the more variability there is in a given data set, the larger the range will be. For example, in data set 1 there is no variability and, by method 2, the range is 1; in data set 2 there is some variability, and the range is 3; and in data set 3, which has even more variability, the range is 136. However, as an index of variability, the range can be very misleading.

Consider data sets 7 and 8 in Table 4.15. Although they both have the same range of 92 (method 2), the variability of data set 7, when calculated using a statistical formula, is actually higher. This may seem surprising since, according to our preliminary definition, variability is the degree to which the data points in a given data set are not alike. It does appear that the data points in data set 7 are more alike than those in data set 8. However, as we will see in the discussion of standard deviation below, the statistical formula for the variability takes into consideration not only the variability among the scores themselves, but also the distance of each score from the mean.

T I M E ■ O U T
Take some time to think about why the variability of the data points in data set 7 is actually higher than the variability of the points in data set 8.

TABLE 4.15	Two Small Data Sets

Data set 7:   7, 7, 7, 98
Data set 8:   7, 21, 52, 98

AVERAGE ABSOLUTE DEVIATION AS AN INDEX OF VARIABILITY

The range is very easy to calculate. However, as we see from the preceding examples, two different data sets may have the same range and yet differ in variability. It could be said that the range is a quick but unsophisticated index of variability.

How might we construct another measure of variability? We know that each data point in a data set deviates from the mean by some amount; for certain points, of course, the deviation is zero. Consider the small data set in Table 4.16.

TABLE 4.16	A Small Data Set

Data set 9:   2, 4, 6

The mean of data set 9 is 4. The deviation scores for each of the data points are stated in Table 4.17. Notice that the deviation is given a minus value when the data point is below the mean and a plus value when the data point is above the mean.

TABLE 4.17	Deviation Scores for Data Set 9

Data point	Mean	Deviation from mean
2	4	−2
4	4	0
6	4	+2

Table 4.18 shows the same information as Table 4.17, but in symbolic form: X denotes the data point; $\bar{X}$ denotes the mean; and x denotes the deviation score.

TABLE 4.18 Deviation Scores for Data Set 9

X	$\bar{X}$	x
2	4	-2
4	4	0
6	4	$+2$

The formula for the **deviation score** is as follows

$$x = X - \bar{X} \tag{4.3}$$

Table 4.19 summarizes the symbolic presentation of the deviation score. Note that the symbol used for the deviation score is a lowercase x, and it should not be confused with the uppercase X, which denotes a raw score or data point

$$x \neq X$$

The average of the deviations of data points from the mean might seem like a useful measure of variability. However, one characteristic of the deviation scores is that they sum to zero. For example, if you add up the deviation scores in Table 4.17, you will get

$$(-2) + (0) + (+2) = 0$$

Therefore, we cannot calculate an average deviation because that would require that we sum all the deviation scores, which will always result in a zero (or a value very close to zero if there are rounding errors).

TABLE 4.19 Symbol for the Deviation Score

Concept	Symbol	Pronunciation
Deviation score	x	"little ĕx"

One way around this problem would be to ignore the plus or minus sign of the deviation score and calculate an average absolute deviation. (When you ignore the plus or minus sign you then have what is referred to as an absolute value.) Even though this approach does not take into consideration whether the data point was above or below the mean, the average absolute deviation is a meaningful index of variability. The absolute deviation values for data set 9 are shown in Table 4.20.

TABLE 4.20	Absolute Deviation Scores for Data Set 9

Data point	Mean	Absolute deviation from mean
2	4	2
4	4	0
6	4	2

The **average absolute deviation** for data set 9 is obtained by first adding all of the absolute deviations

$2 + 0 + 2 = 4$

and then dividing by the number of absolute deviations

$4/3 = 1.33$

Therefore, the average absolute deviation (AAD) for data set 9 is 1.33

$AAD = 1.33$

TERMINAL STATISTICS

Although the average absolute deviation is a meaningful index of variability, it is not used to calculate any other statistics. For this reason we say that it is a **terminal statistic**.

The median and the mode are also terminal. The mean is not terminal because it is used in other calculations—for example, in the calculation of deviation scores.

Because it is terminal, the AAD is rarely calculated.

VARIANCE AS AN INDEX OF VARIABILITY

The variance is an index of varibility that is more sophisticated than the AAD, and is not terminal. It takes into consideration both the variability among the data points themselves and the extent to which they stray from the central tendency of the data set. The **variance** is the average of the squared deviations of the data points from the mean of the data set.

You already saw how to calculate deviation scores in Table 4.18, and you also know that the sum of deviation scores will be zero. We avoid this problem in calculating the variance by squaring each of the deviation scores. Table 4.21 shows the squared deviation scores for data set 9.

TABLE 4.21   Deviation Scores and Squared Deviation Scores for Data Set 9

X	$\bar{X}$	x	x^2
2	4	-2	4
4	4	0	0
6	4	$+2$	4

The variance is calculated as follows.

1. Determine the deviation score for each of the data points in the data set (as in Table 4.21).

2. Square each of the deviation scores.

3. Add up all of the squared deviation scores. This yields the *sum of the squared deviations*. For the data in Table 4.21 this would be

$$4 + 0 + 4 = 8$$

4. Get the average squared deviation score by dividing the sum of the squared deviations by the total number of data points in the data set. For the data in Table 4.21 this would be

$$8/3 = 2.67$$

The variance for data set 9 is 2.67.

The above four steps are symbolized in the following formula

$$\text{Variance} = \frac{\Sigma x^2}{N} \tag{4.4}$$

Because it is so important to understand the symbols in this formula, let's look at them one by one.

The first symbol

$$\Sigma$$

is the summation sign, which should be familiar to you from Eq. (4.1).

The second symbol

$$x^2$$

can be referred to as little x squared, which describes the symbol itself, or as deviation score squared.

The third symbol

———

is simply the division sign. It tells us to divide the sum of the squared deviation scores by N.

The fourth symbol

$$N$$

ASIDE ■ Note that n is often used to indicate

the total number of data points in a sample, while

N is often used to indicate the total number of

data points in a population.

is the total number of data points in the data set. Of course, since there is a squared deviation score for each data point in the data set, N is also the total number of squared deviation scores.

We can verbally describe this formula by saying that the variance is equal to the sum of the squared deviation scores divided by N. Note, however, that the sum of the squared deviations is not equal to the squared sum of the deviations. This can be stated symbolically as follows

$$\sum (x^2) \neq \left(\sum x\right)^2$$

This is an extremely important point, so we will examine it in detail.

Let's look at the equation for the variance again

$$\text{Variance} = \frac{\sum x^2}{N}$$

One way of stating this formula verbally would be to say that the variance is equal to the sum of the deviations squared divided by N. However, this verbal statement is flawed with a serious ambiguity. The phrase "sum of the deviations squared" can be interpreted in two very different ways.

1. Square the deviations, and then sum all the squared deviations.

2. Sum the deviations, and then square the result.

These two interpretations will result in very different calculations. Consider the results for the data in Table 4.21.

1. Square the deviations $(2^2 = 4; 0^2 = 0; 2^2 = 4)$ and then sum all the squared deviations $(4 + 0 + 4 = 8)$.

2. Sum the deviations $(-2 + 0 + 2 = 0)$ and square the result $(0^2 = 0)$.

The first of these two interpretations is correct for calculating the variance.

One way to avoid such ambiguity is by the appropriate use of parentheses. Thus, we could restate the formula for variance as follows

$$\text{Variance} = \frac{\sum (x^2)}{N}$$

The effect of these parentheses is to isolate the (x^2) operation so that each deviation will first be squared, and then the squared deviations will be summed.

This is an extremely important point, and one which is often misunderstood. Because it is so important, it is summarized again as follows:

Ambiguous form

Symbol: $\sum x^2$

Verbal interpretation: The sum of the deviations squared.

Interpretation 1

Symbol: $\sum (x^2)$

Verbal Interpretation: The sum of the squared deviations.

Example: Using deviation scores from Table 4.21, $4 + 0 + 4 = 8$

Interpretation 2

Symbol: $\left(\sum x \right)^2$

Verbal interpretation: The squared sum of the deviations.

Example: Using deviation scores from Table 4.21, $(-2 + 0 + 2) = 0$ and $0^2 = 0$.

As in the case of the mean, different symbols for the variance are used to indicate whether we are summarizing a sample of data points (in which case we have a statistic) or a population of data points (in which case we have a parameter). The symbols for the **sample variance** and **population variance** are given in Table 4.22.

| TABLE 4.22 | Symbols for the Variance | |

	Symbol
Generic concept	variance
Sample statistic	s^2
Population parameter	σ^2

STANDARD DEVIATION AS AN INDEX OF VARIABILITY

Thus far, we have seen two indices of variability that avoid the problem that deviation scores sum to zero. In the case of the average absolute deviation this problem is avoided by using the absolute value of each deviation score. In the case of variance this problem is avoided by squaring each deviation score. Of these, the average absolute deviation is much closer to the idea of an average deviation from the mean. Compare, for example, the average absolute deviation and the variance calculated for the data set in Table 4.23.

| TABLE 4.23 | Raw Data and Summary Statistics for the Arm Lengths of Five People (Inches) (Data randomly selected from Database A.7) |

Raw data: 34, 27, 31, 28, 24
Mean = 28.8
Average absolute deviation = 2.96
Variance = 11.76
Total number of data points = 5 symbolically
$\bar{X} = 28.8$
AAD = 2.96
$s^2 = 11.76$
$n = 5$

T I M E ∎ O U T
Take some time to calculate these statistics for yourself.

The value of 2.96 for the AAD of the sample seems reasonable as we look at the data points in Table 4.23: On the average, the data points seem to be about 3 units from the mean of 28.8. However, the value of 11.76 for the variance does not seem to make much sense. What happened?

Recall that, when calculating the variance, each of the deviation scores is squared. As a result, the value of the variance will often be larger than the AAD, which does not involve squaring the deviation scores.

From this point of view, it would seem that the AAD is a more practical index of variability. However, as you will see in future chapters, *the variance is much more useful because it is not terminal.*

In order to arrive at an index of variability that is not terminal, and yet has a value closer to the AAD, we take the square root of the variance and call the result the **standard deviation**.

ASIDE ■ **The complete logic behind the formula for variance is more sophisticated than this simple explanation.**

For our present purposes, you might think of it this way: We square the deviation scores to avoid summation to zero, then we average the squared deviations, and then we unsquare (that is, take the square root of) the result. This brings us back to a more interpretable index of variability.

The standard deviation of the sample in Table 4.23 is given in Table 4.24. Notice that the symbol for the standard deviation of a sample is simply a lowercase *s*. This is reasonable, in that the standard deviation is the square root of the variance. Looking at it another way, the variance is the standard deviation squared.

TABLE 4.24	Raw Data and Summary Statistics for the Arm Lengths of Five People (Inches) (Data randomly selected from Database A.7)

Raw data: 34, 27, 31, 28, 24
Mean = 28.8
Average absolute deviation = 2.96
Variance = 11.76
Standard deviation = 3.43
Total number of data points = 5

or symbolically

$\bar{X} = 28.8$
$AAD = 3$
$s^2 = 11.76$
$s = 3.43$
$n = 5$

Table 4.25 states the symbols used for the standard deviation.

TABLE 4.25	Symbols for the Standard Deviation

	Symbol
Generic concept	standard deviation
Sample statistic	s
Population parameter	σ

Take some time to get comfortable with the symbols in Table 4.25, and the relationship between the symbols in Tables 4.22 and 4.25.

The formula for the standard deviation can be stated symbolically as follows

$$\text{Standard deviation} = \sqrt{\frac{\sum (x^2)}{N}} \tag{4.5}$$

The distinction between this formula and the formula for the variance

$$\text{Variance} = \frac{\sum (x^2)}{N} \tag{4.6}$$

should be clear.

CALCULATION FORMULAS FOR STANDARD DEVIATION AND VARIANCE

Standard deviation and variance may be expressed in a form more convenient for use with a calculator. These *calculation formulas*, which are used more often than the two *conceptual* formulas stated above, are as follows

$$\text{Variance} = \frac{\sum (X^2) - \left(\frac{(\sum X)^2}{N} \right)}{N} \tag{4.7}$$

$$\text{Standard deviation} = \sqrt{\frac{\sum (X^2) - \left(\frac{(\sum X)^2}{N} \right)}{N}} \tag{4.8}$$

Note that the uppercase X in these formulas refers to score values, and should not be confused with lowercase x, which refers to deviation scores. See Procedures C.23 and 3.31 in Appendix C for step-by-step examples of calculations using these formulas.

T I M E ■ O U T
Maintaining Your Perspective Regarding Data Collection and Interpretation is a book about gathering and interpreting behavioral data and, in this chapter, we have described how to summarize measurements. However, it would be very easy to lose sight of these topics because of the many details that we have discussed. When you begin to get bogged down in minutiae, please take some time to step back and consider the major themes of the chapter and the book.

If you are a typical student, you have found the symbols, formulas, and calculations for central tendency and variability less than exciting. However, you will need to feel comfortable with this chapter if you are to master the fundamentals of gathering and interpreting behavioral data. Understanding the symbols and formulas is quite secondary to the main objective, which is to understand how we gather and interpret behavioral data. Nevertheless, just as a musician who has an understanding of fundamental musical symbols and principles is better able to master his or her art, so you can more easily master the art of information gathering and interpretation if you have an understanding of fundamental statistical symbols and principles.

SUMMARY

Chapter 4 has perhaps been the most difficult so far. Several new concepts, symbols, and formulas have been introduced. The primary concepts in this chapter have been central tendency and variability. In the middle of the chapter and again at the end the reader is reminded to keep the total process approach in mind during the side trips into more specific topics.

Both central tendency and variability characterize the distribution of measurements within a sample or population. The mean, median, and mode are three measures of central tendency. Variability is measured by the range, the standard deviation, and the variance.

Formulas for each of the measures of central tendency and variability have been presented and discussed.

KEY SYMBOLS

$N, n, \Sigma, \mu, \sigma, \sigma^2, s, s^2, X, \bar{X}, x, x^2$

KEY TERMS AND CONCEPTS

AADF	Population variance
Average	Possible values
Average absolute deviation (AAD)	Range
Central tendency	Sample variance
Deviation score	Sensitivity
Dispersion	Shape of the distribution
Heterogeneity	Stability
Homogeneity	Standard deviation

Level of measurement	Summarizing data
Mean	Terminal statistic
Median	Variability
Mode	Variance

EXERCISES

| **TABLE 4.26** | **Hand Strengths for 10 People (Kilograms)** |
| | (Data randomly selected from Database A.4) |

| 53, | 37, | 52, | 48, | 41, | 51, | 61, | 63, | 41, | 68 |

4.1 Compute the mean, median, and mode for the data in Table 4.26.

4.2 Compute the range, variance, and standard deviation for the data in Table 4.26.

4.3 Compare the results of Exercises 4.1 and 4.2 to the actual population parameters for Database A.4. Based upon this comparison, would you say that the data in Table 4.26 are a representative sample of the population? Explain.

4.4 Compute the range, AAD, s^2, and s for the data in Table 4.11.

4.5 On the basis of your calculations for Exercise 4.4 and the data in Table 4.11, which bowler would you rather have on your team? Explain.

4.6 On the basis of your calculations for Exercise 4.4, which bowler would you say has more homogeneous scores? Which bowler has more heterogeneous scores?

4.7 Describe the difference between sigma and little s.

4.8 Describe the difference between sigma and sigma squared.

4.9 Write the appropriate symbols to summarize the following data: population standard deviation = 4.6; sample standard deviation = 4.3.

4.10 In general terms, describe the difference between conceptual formulas and calculation formulas.

Showing
Your
Summaries

OBJECTIVES

After reading and studying Chapter 5 you should understand the following.

■ *some of the reasons for creating tables and graphs.*

■ *some of the fundamental guidelines for creating tables and graphs.*

■ *how to decide which type of graph is appropriate for summarizing a particular set of data.*

■ *some of the fundamental strategies for interpreting tables and graphs.*

■ *how to create tables and graphs from sets of data.*

CHOOSING BETWEEN TABLES AND GRAPHS

As we saw in Chapter 4, we compute means, medians, modes, ranges, standard deviations, and variances in an effort to organize and summarize sets of data in a way that goes beyond merely sorting and listing the data values. The purpose of tables and graphs is essentially the same.

You have already seen several tables in this book. Each table represents an attempt to organize data values so that they can be easily understood and interpreted. Graphs accomplish the same objective in a slightly different way. Consider, for example, the difference between Table 5.1 and Figure 5.1. (Note that graphs and drawings are typically referred to as figures and are captioned at the bottom. Tables are captioned at the top.) Table 5.1 and Figure 5.1 are each based upon the same information: the average (mean) grades for freshmen and seniors on quiz 1 for some imaginary class. Which do you prefer as a way of presenting the information?

T I M E ■ O U T
Take some time to consider your preference.

Some people may prefer the table, while others may prefer the figure. You could make an argument for using both, so as to reach both audiences. When deciding whether to use tables or graphs, consider the following issues.

TABLE 5.1	Average Grades for Freshmen and Seniors on Quiz 1

Freshmen: 80   Seniors: 75

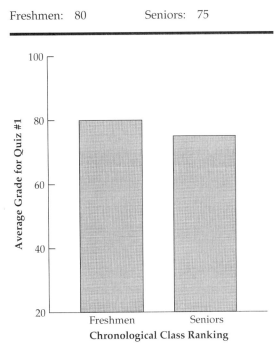

FIGURE 5.1   Average Grades for Freshmen and Seniors on Quiz 1.

- *Time and resources available.* If you're creating a table or a graph by hand, you may want to consider how much time it will take; doing a graph by hand always requires extra time. However, if you're using a computer, it may actually be easier to create a graph than a table.

- *Effectiveness of final product.* Try to imagine what the table or graph will look like when you're done. Draw a rough sketch. Think about whether the table or the graph will provide the clearest and most concise summary for your audience.

- *Your audience.* Consider such factors as the age of your audience and their level of expertise.

- *Format for presentation.* Will you be presenting your tables or graphs to your audience in printed form, as an overhead transparency, or in some other format? How much time will your audience have to see your tables or graphs?

- *Complexity of data.* The data for Table 5.1 and Figure 5.1 are so simple that the same information is available in both. However, there will be situations in which a graph may leave out information that could be presented in a table, or vice versa.

- *Level of measurement.* Although no absolute rules apply, the level of measurement will also influence the choice of table or graph. For example, if you are plotting the averages for nominal categories, as in Figure 5.1, a bar graph is more appropriate than a line graph.

- *Desired level of summary.* Some tables and graphs are intended to provide a very quick summary of the data; others are intended to provide a very high level of detail.

- *Required precision.* The precision of the data provided in tables is typically greater than that provided in figures. For example, Table 5.1 indicates the exact values of the averages, but Figure 5.1 does not.

CREATING TABLES

Consider the following issues when creating tables.

- *Avoid the temptation to include too much information in a single table.* The purpose of tables is to simplify the interpretation of the data. If too much information is present, the reader will be lost in details. It is better to create additional tables than to try to present all the available information in a single table.

- *Label your tables clearly and completely.* The reader should not have to ask for additional information when reading a table. For example, imagine how mysterious Table 5.1 would appear to the reader if there were no caption.

CREATING GRAPHS

Consider the following issues when creating graphs.

- *Avoid the tempation to include too much information in a single graph.*

- *Label your graphs clearly and completely.* For example, in Figure 5.1, if the vertical (Y) axis had not been labeled, the reader would have no clue regarding the values of the averages. Also, don't forget to provide a caption.

- *Try to have your vertical axis about two-thirds the length of your horizontal axis.* By this means, we can maintain a standard frame of reference when comparing graphs. Consider, for example, the impact of Figures 5.2 and 5.3, both of which present exactly the same data.

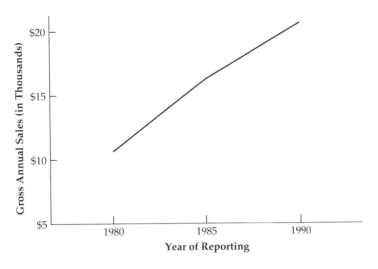

FIGURE 5.2 Gross Annual Sales Reported for Three Different Years.

ASIDE ■ It is customary for the horizontal axis to be longer, because our visual field extends further in the horizontal direction than in the vertical direction. To demonstrate this, hold your hands out to the left and right, beyond the point where you can see them, and then bring them closer together, until you can see them. Now measure the distance between your two hands. This will give you an estimate of the relative size of your horizontal field of vision. Using the same technique, estimate the relative size of your vertical field of vision. After doing this myself, I estimated the relative size of my horizontal field to be 26 inches and the relative size of my vertical field to be 15 inches. This suggests that the ratio of my vertical field to my horizontal field is 15/26 (58%). Compare this to the two-thirds (67%) ratio recommended for the vertical and horizontal axes.

TYPES OF TABLES

Since a table is essentially a summarized display of information, the possible types of tables are virtually unlimited. However, only a few major categories are used. In Chapter 3, you have already seen two very common categories of tables: *grouped frequency distribution tables* and *cumulative frequency distribution tables*. Another common category — **cross tabulation tables** — is illustrated in Table 5.2.

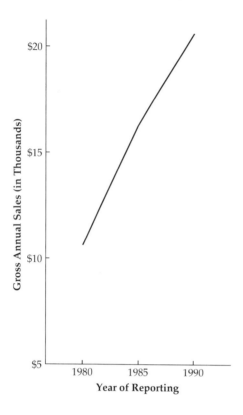

FIGURE 5.3 Gross Annual Sales Reported for Three Different Years

TABLE 5.2 Cross Tabulation of Grade Point Average by Chronological Class Rank

| | | Chronological class rank | | | | |
		Freshmen	Sophomore	Junior	Senior	Total
	A	40	50	40	35	165
	B	70	80	64	69	283
Letter grade	C	150	100	80	90	420
	D	20	15	12	4	51
	F	20	5	4	2	31
	Total	300	250	200	200	950

T I M E ■ O U T

Take some time to interpret Table 5.2.

TYPES OF GRAPHS

As with tables, types of graphs that can be constructed are virtually unlimited. However, among the most common types are line graphs, bar graphs, and pie charts.

Line Graphs

Line graphs consist of at least one variable (for example, gross annual sales in Figure 5.3) that is plotted as a function of another variable (year of report in Figure 5.3). After each point is placed appropriately, a line is drawn to connect all the plotted points.

A primary purpose in creating line graphs is to portray trends or patterns in the data. As we can see in Figure 5.3, there is an increasing trend in gross annual sales over the three years for which the data are reported. It is important to keep in mind that a line graph is only appropriate when there is a logical sequence for each of the variables being measured and plotted; in Figure 5.3 gross annual sales and year of report both vary logically and sequentially. Such a logical sequence is not present in Figure 5.4.

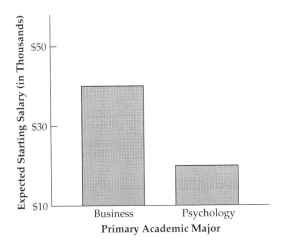

FIGURE 5.4 Bar Graph Plot of Starting Salary Expected by Seniors Majoring in Business and Psychgology (Averages of Samples Taken from Senior Class)

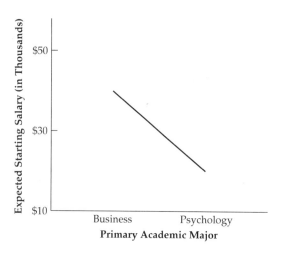

FIGURE 5.5

Inappropriate Line Graph Plot of Starting Salary Expected by Seniors Majoring in Business and Psychology (Averages of Samples Taken from Senior Class)

Generally, a bar graph is appropriate when the variable on the horizontal axis is at the nominal level. In Figure 5.4 it would not make sense to connect the plotted values for business majors and psychology majors because there is no logical sequence from business to psychology or from psychology to business. Figure 5.5 shows such an inappropriate plot.

Figure 5.5 is inappropriate because it implies that there is some possible point that falls between the labels *Business* and *Psychology*. It is appropriate to create a line graph in Figure 5.2 because there are possible points that fall between 1980 and 1985 or between 1985 and 1990.

ASIDE ■ Even though the nature of the graph may logically allow for interpolation and extrapolation, the correctness of such estimates is not guaranteed, but depends on factors such as the reliability of any trends in the data.

The process of imagining or estimating possible values between two existing values is called *interpolation*. (The prefix *inter* means *between*.) Thus, line graphs are appropriate when interpolation is at least logical for the variables measured.

Because line graphs plot variables that are logically sequenced, *extrapolation* may also be possible. (The prefix *extra* means *beyond*.) In Figure 5.5, for example, not only can we imagine (interpolate) what the gross annual sales might be in 1982, which falls *beween* the reported years of 1980 and 1985, but we can also imagine (extrapolate) what the gross annual sales might be in 1992, which falls beyond the reported year of 1990.

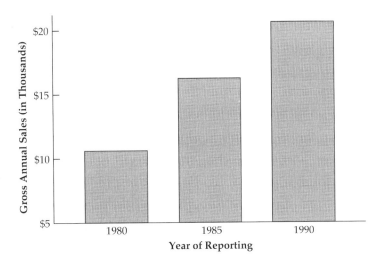

FIGURE 5.6 Bar Graph of Gross Annual Sales Reported for Three
Different Years

Bar Graphs

Bar graphs consist of at least one varible (for example, expected starting salary in
Figure 5.4) that is plotted as a function of another variable (primary academic
major in Figure 5.4). A bar is drawn separately for each plot.

As we saw in discussing Figure 5.4, a primary purpose in creating bar
graphs is to portray trends or patterns in the data when one of the variables is
nominally scaled or not logically sequenced. However, bar graphs are also often
used in circumstances where a line graph might seem more appropriate.
Consider Figure 5.6, which is the bar graph version of the information in Figure
5.2. The trend that we see in Figure 5.2 is also apparent in Figure 5.6. However, without the lines connecting the plots, interpolation is more difficult in
Figure 5.6.

Pie Charts

In **pie charts**, at least one variable is reported as a percentage or proportion of
the total number of cases. For example, in Figure 5.7, the number of declared
majors in each of the categories reported in Table 5.3 is stated as a percentage of
the total number of declared majors.

A primary purpose in creating pie charts is to portray different categories as a
proportion of the total data set. Note that the information in Figure 5.7 could also be
presented as a table, a line graph, or a bar graph. However, when the proportion of the
total is the main issue, pie charts are often preferred for their conciseness and clarity.

TABLE 5.3	Declared Majors for 25 Students in a Statistics Class	
Declared major	Frequency	Percentage of total
Business	5	20%
Geography	2	8%
Psychology	12	48%
Sociology	6	24%
Total	25	100%

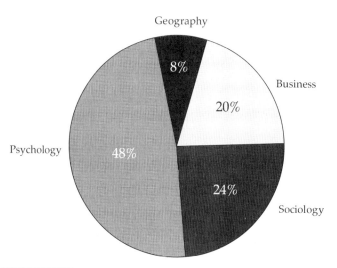

FIGURE 5.7　Percentages of Declared Majors for 25 Students in a Statistics Class

FREQUENCY DISTRIBUTIONS

In Chapter 3 you learned how to create a frequency distribution table (Table 3.8). The information contained in such a table can be graphed in several different ways.

Figure 5.8 shows a line graph of the frequency values; this is called a **frequency distribution**. Notice that the midpoints of the class intervals are used to represent each class interval along the horizontal axis, and the frequency of each class interval is plotted along the vertical axis. Notice also that the frequency values for the highest and lowest class intervals are zero. As mentioned in Chapter 3, these zero values anchor the distribution at each end.

Figure 5.9 is a bar graph version of the data in Figure 5.8. Bar graphs of frequency distributions are referred to as **histograms**.

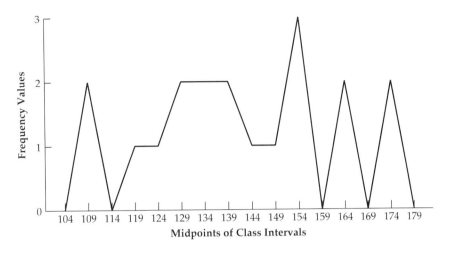

FIGURE 5.8 Line Graph of Grouped Frequency Distribution for 20 Body Weight Measurements

Both figures use identical data, but notice how the overall shape of the distribution is emphasized in Figure 5.8, which makes it easier to see the variability and central tendency of the distribution. In Figure 5.9, on the other hand, it is easier to see the actual frequencies of the individual class intervals.

Figures 5.10 and 5.11 are line graph and bar graph plots of the cumulative frequency information in Table 3.9.

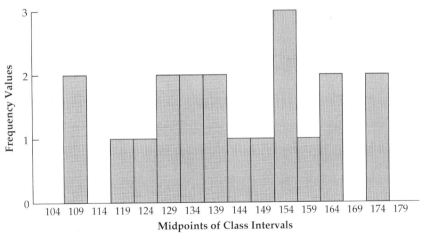

FIGURE 5.9 Histogram of Grouped Frequency Distribution for 20 Body Weight Measurements

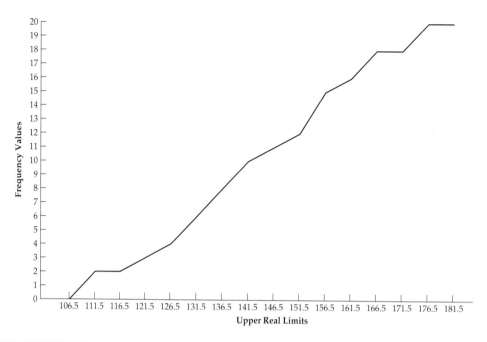

FIGURE 5.10 Line Graph of Cumulative Frequency Distribution for 20 Body Weight Measurements

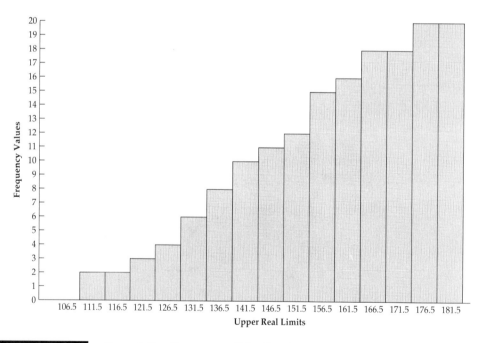

FIGURE 5.11 Cumulative Frequency Distribution Histogram for 20 Body Weight Measurements

A FINAL COMMENT ON GRAPHS

Any guidelines for deciding which type of graph to create should be viewed with caution. As we have seen from the above examples, each group of data can be approached from many different points of view. In some cases a particular type of graph may simply be illogical. Always ask yourself: "What is the primary information that I am trying to summarize? What do I want the reader to clearly see from this graph?"

SUMMARY

In this brief chapter, we have considered techniques for presenting data summaries. Whether using tables or graphs, you should always be aware of the intended audience and the purpose of your summary.

KEY TERMS AND CONCEPTS

Audience

Bar graph

Cross tabulation table

Cumulative frequency
distribution graph

Cumulative frequency
distribution table

Grouped frequency
distribution graph

Grouped frequency
distribution table

Histogram

Line graph

Pie chart

EXERCISES

5.1 Using imaginary data that is of interest to you, create one of each type of table and graph presented in this chapter.

5.2 Create a histogram based on the frequency information in the table that you created for Exercise 3.3. What does this histogram tell you about the population from which the sample was drawn? Would you say that the population is normally distributed? Explain.

5.3 Create a line graph based on the cumulative frequency information in the table that you created for Exercise 3.3. Using this graph, estimate the 75th percentile (that point in the distribution below which are 75 % of the data values).

5.4 What do you think the frequency distribution would look like for the following sample of IQ scores? Draw a sketch.

$$\bar{X}_{IQ} = 98$$

$$s_{IQ} = 15$$

$$n = 50$$

5.5 On the sketch you drew for Exercise 5.4, add a curve to express what you think the frequency distribution would look like for the following sample of IQ scores.

$$\bar{X}_{IQ} = 107$$

$$s_{IQ} = 5$$

$$n = 50$$

5.6 Discuss the differences between the samples in Exercises 5.4 and 5.5. Speculate about the different populations from which these samples might have been selected and/or about the different selection procedures that they might represent.

5.7 Discuss the differences between Figures 5.8 and 5.9. Which is easier for you to understand? Explain.

5.8 Discuss the differences between Table 5.3 and Figure 5.7. Which is easier for you to understand? Explain.

5.9. What are the important issues when deciding whether to use a table or a graph?

5.10. Find a table or figure—from a newspaper or magazine—that you find especially difficult to understand. Redraw it so that it is more comprehensible.

Standardizing Scores

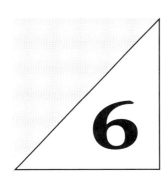

6

OBJECTIVES

After reading and studying Chapter 6 you should understand the following.

- *the difference between hypothetical and empirical distributions.*

- *the reasons for standardizing scores.*

- *the techniques used for standardizing scores.*

- *the normal curve and its relationship to standardizing scores.*

- *how the normal curve is used as a model.*

- *percentiles and their relationship to standardized scores.*

- *how to determine percentiles and percentile ranks.*

- *how to use the normal curve tables.*

- *the transition from descriptive statistics to inferential statistics.*

- *how to estimate the population mean and standard deviation from the sample mean and standard deviation.*

INTRODUCTION

Table 6.1 shows the means and standard deviations for the class grades on three imaginary quizzes. Notice that the means are the same for the second and third quizzes, while the standard deviations are the same for the first and second quizzes.

On the basis of what you learned about means and standard deviations in Chapter 4, how would you answer the following questions?

1. On which quiz was the performance of the class the highest?

2. On which quiz was the performance of the class most consistent?

TABLE 6.1	Means and Standard Deviations for Three Imaginary Quizzes	
Quiz	Mean	Standard deviation
1	75	5
2	80	5
3	80	2.5

T I M E ■ O U T

Take some time to respond to these questions.

The means for quizzes 2 and 3 are equal and higher than the mean for quiz 1. On the other hand, the standard deviations indicate that the class grades are equally consistent for quizzes 1 and 2. However, the class performance for the third quiz was the most consistent. We can see this because the standard deviation for this quiz is lower than the standard deviation of the other two (2.5 compared to 5). It is reasonable to say that the overall performance of the class was best on quiz 3, where the mean is among the highest (tied with quiz 2) and the standard deviation is the lowest.

Questions 1 and 2 are concerned with the performance of the entire class. The following questions are concerned with the performance of one person.

3. Mark earned a grade of 75 on quiz 1. How well did he do?

4. How well did Mark do on quiz 1 compared to the rest of the class?

5. Mark earned a grade of 75 on quiz 2. How well did he do?

6. How well did Mark do on quiz 2 compared to the rest of the class?

7. How well did Mark do on quiz 2 compared to quiz 1?

8. How does Mark's performance on quiz 2, relative to the class average, compare to his performance on quiz 1 relative to the class average?

T I M E ■ O U T

Take some time to answer all of these questions.

Each of these questions is different, though some may seem the same. Let's look at them one at a time.

3. Mark earned a grade of 75 on quiz 1. How well did he do? As with many such questions, it depends on the criteria. What does a grade of 75 represent? In some grading systems, it might represent a letter grade of C; in others, it might be a D. We can't provide a very specific answer to Question 3 because the question itself is not very specific. It's a poorly worded question.

4. How well did Mark do on quiz 1 compared to the rest of the class? This question is more specific and allows for a more specific response. Since the mean for the class is 75, we can say that Mark's performance was average compared to the rest of the class. He did not perform particularly well or particularly poorly; he was average.

5. Mark earned a grade of 75 on quiz 2. How well did he do? Here again, we can't provide a very specific answer because the question itself is not very specific.

6. How well did Mark do on quiz 2 compared to the rest of the class? Since the class mean for quiz 2 is 80, we can say that Mark's performance was below average compared to the rest of the class.

T I M E ■ O U T
Take some time to think about this point before continuing with Question 7. It is a concept that is fundamental to an understanding of standard scores.

7. How well did Mark do on quiz 2 compared to quiz 1? This is a very tricky question. On the one hand, it specifically asks for a comparison between Mark's quiz 1 and quiz 2 grades. As such, the answer is simple: Mark's performance was the same (75) on both quizzes. We could say that he did equally well. On the other hand, the question is ambiguous in that it doesn't specify whether we should be focusing on Mark's performance relative to himself or his performance relative to the rest of the class. The next question eliminates this ambiguity.

8. How does Mark's performance on quiz 2 relative to the class average compare to his performance on quiz 1 relative to the class average? Even though Mark's grades were the same on quizzes 1 and 2, his performance relative to the rest of the class was lower on quiz 2. On quiz 1, his grade of 75 was at the mean; it was an average grade. On quiz 2, however, his grade of 75 was below average.

The above questions illustrate that a measurement for an individual can be assessed from at least three different perspectives.

- It can be assessed in comparison to other measurements for the same individual (Mark's quiz 1 grade compared to his quiz 2 grade).

- It can be assessed in comparison to the measurement for other individuals under the same conditions (Mark's quiz 1 grade compared to the class average for quiz 1).

- It can be assessed by comparing measurements for the same individual relative to other individuals in different conditions (Mark's quiz 1 grade relative to the class average for quiz 1 compared to his quiz 2 grade relative to the class average for quiz 2).

Such assessments can become quite complex. One way to simplify these comparisons is to standardize scores.

WHAT IS A STANDARDIZED SCORE?

Mark's standardized score for quiz 1 is zero. Can you figure out why?

T I M E ■ O U T
Take some time to reflect on this question.

Mark's grade for quiz 1 is 75. We call this Mark's **raw score**. (It's raw because we haven't done anything with it yet. It's like a carrot that we just picked from the ground.) How does Mark's raw score compare to the class? If we compare his grade of 75 to the class averge of 75, we see that there is no difference. Thus, a standardized score of zero tells us that the raw score is right at the mean of the group $(75 - 75 = 0)$.

Mark's grade—and raw score—for quiz 2 is 75. When we compare this raw score of 75 to the quiz 2 class averge of 80, we see that Mark's raw score is lower by 5 $(80 - 75 = 5)$. However, this is only one step toward standardizing Mark's raw score.

Before we proceed, refer back to Table 6.1 and consider the following questions:

9. Mark earned a grade of 75 on quiz 3. How well did he do?

10. How well did Mark do on quiz 3 compared to the rest of the class?

11. How well did Mark do on quiz 3 compared to quiz 2?

Mark's performance certainly seems consistent. He earned a grade of 75 on all three quizzes. But is his performance really consistent? Our answers to Questions 9–11 will help us to decide.

9. Mark earned a grade of 75 on quiz 3. How well did he do? Once again the question is too vague to allow for much of an answer.

10. How well did Mark do on quiz 3 compared to the rest of the class? Mark's grade and raw score for quiz 3 is 75. When we compare this raw score of 75 to the quiz 3 class average of 80, we see that Mark's raw score is lower by 5.

11. How well did Mark do on quiz 3 compared to quiz 2? For both quiz 2 and quiz 3, Mark's raw score of 75 is 5 score units below the class average of 80. However, compared to the rest of the class, Mark actually did slightly better on quiz 2 than on quiz 3. Do you understand why?

T I M E ■ O U T
This is a very important question. Take some time to answer it.

The key to understanding that Mark actually did slightly better on quiz 2 than on quiz 3 is the standard deviation. Recall from Table 6.1 that the standard deviation for quiz 2 is 5, while the standard deviation for quiz 3 is 2.5. This tells us that the performance of the group was less variable on quiz 3. As such, even though Mark's grade of 75 is 5 score units below the average for both quizzes, those 5 score units represent a larger distance from the average in the case of quiz 3, where the variability of the grades in the class was lower.

The next step is to determine Mark's standard scores for both quiz 2 and quiz 3.

For quiz 2 we have already determined that Mark's raw score is 5 score units below the mean. Since the standard deviation for quiz 2 is 5, we can say that Mark's raw score of 75 is *one standard deviation below the mean*, which is essentially a verbal statement of Mark's standard score. A **standard score** is simply a statement of how many standard deviations from the mean the raw score is.

The symbolic way of expressing Mark's standard score for quiz 2 is

$$Z_{Q2} = -1.00$$

where Z is the symbol for a standard score. This expression tells us that Mark's raw score for quiz 2 is one standard deviation below the mean.

Notice that the standard deviation can change from one quiz to another. Consider Mark's standard score for quiz 3.

We have already determined that Mark's raw score for quiz 3 is 5 score units below the mean. Since the standard deviation for quiz 3 is 2.5, we can say that Mark's raw score of 75 is two standard deviations below the mean, which is a verbal statement of Mark's standard score for quiz 3.

The symbolic way of expressing Mark's standard score for quiz 3 is

$$Z_{Q3} = -2.00$$

Note that Mark's standard score for quiz 3 is further below the mean (by one standard deviation) than his standard score for quiz 2, and hence we conclude that his performance in quiz 3 is worse.

MAIN POINT SUMMARY

A standard score is simply a statement of how many standard deviations the raw score is above or below the mean.

If the raw score is below the mean, as with Mark's raw scores on quizzes 2 and 3, the standard score will have a negative value. On the other hand, if the raw score is above the mean, the standard score will have a positive value. Consider Mark's classmate, Martha.

12. Martha earned a grade of 85 on quiz 2. How well did she do on quiz 2 compared to the rest of the class?

13. Martha earned a grade of 80 on quiz 1. How well did she do on quiz 1 compared to quiz 2?

Let's examine these questions in turn.

12. Martha earned a grade of 85 on quiz 2. How well did she do on quiz 2 compared to the rest of the class? As we have seen from the above discussion, one way to answer this question is to determine Martha's standard score. What is Martha's standard score for quiz 2?

T I M E ■ O U T
Take some time to answer this question.

Martha's grade and raw score for quiz 2 is 85. When we compare this raw score of 85 to the quiz 2 class average of 80, we see that Martha's raw score is higher by 5 ($85 - 80 = 5$). Since the standard deviation for quiz 2 is 5, we state that Martha's raw score of 85 is one standard deviation above the mean for quiz 2.

The symbolic way of expressing Martha's standard score for quiz 2 is

$$Z_{Q2} = +1.00$$

T I M E ■ O U T
Take some time to examine Question 13.

13. Martha earned a grade of 80 on quiz 1. How well did she do on quiz 1 compared to quiz 2? Martha's standard score for quiz 1 is $+1$. Martha's standard score for quiz 2 is also $+1$. Therefore, in terms of her performance relative to the rest of the class, Martha did equally as well on quizzes 1 and 2.

The above statement may seem like an incorrect response to Question 13; is it?

T I M E ■ O U T
Take some time to reflect on this question.

Question 13 is not as specific as it could be. It actually implies two distinct questions:

13a. How does Martha's grade on quiz 1 compare to her grade on quiz 2?

13b. How does Martha's performance relative to the class average on quiz 1 compare to her performance relative to the class average on quiz 2?

The answers to these questions are quite clear: a) Martha's grade of 80 on quiz 1 is lower than her grade of 85 on quiz 2; b) Martha's standard score of $+1$ on quiz 1 is equivalent to her standard score of $+1$ on quiz 2.

Martha's individual grade was higher on quiz 2, but the class average was also higher and, furthermore, the variability of the grades was the same for both quizzes.

As is evident from the preceding discussion, we are able to make much more sophisticated assessments if we consider both the mean and the standard deviation for a group of scores. The use of standard scores allows us to make assessments based on a standard frame of reference: the distance of the raw score from the mean expressed in terms of the standard deviation.

As long as you know the mean and the standard deviation, you should be able to calculate the standard score for any raw score. To calculate the standard score, simply subtract the mean from the raw score and then divide the result by the standard deviation; that is

standard score = (raw score − mean)/(standard deviation)

The parentheses remind you that the difference between the raw score and the mean must first be calculated before dividing by the standard deviation.

Symbolically

$$Z = \frac{(X - \bar{X})}{s} \tag{6.1}$$

Recall from Chapter 4 that $\bar{X}$ and s represent the mean and standard deviation of the sample respectively. Thus, Eq. (6.1) represents the calculation of a standard score (a Z score) for situations in which you have the sample mean and the sample standard deviation.

Now consider the following formula

$$Z = \frac{(X - \mu)}{\sigma} \tag{6.2}$$

Recall from Chapter 4 that μ and σ represent the mean and standard deviation of the population respectively. Thus, Eq. (6.2) represents the calculation of a standard score for situations in which you have the population mean and the population standard deviation.

Finally, consider the formula

$$Z = \frac{(X - \tilde{\mu})}{\tilde{\sigma}} \tag{6.3}$$

The two new symbols $\tilde{\mu}$ (pronounced **mu tilde**) and $\tilde{\sigma}$ (**sigma tilde**) in Eq. (6.3) represent estimates of the population mean and population standard deviation obtained on the basis of sample data; more about this later. For now, suffice it to say that Eq. (6.3) represents yet another way to calculate a standard score.

UNDERSTANDING THE NORMAL CURVE

What is a curve? In statistics a curve is a line graph such as that in Figure 6.1.

One particular line graph, the **normal curve**, is very important in statistics, because it is used as a **model** (an ideal image) of the frequency distribution for

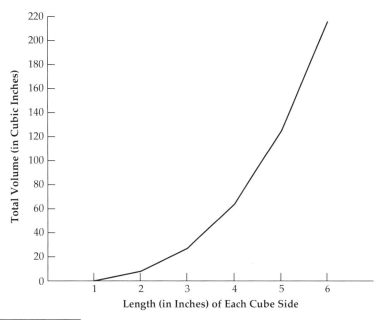

FIGURE 6.1   Total Volume (Cubic Inches) of a Cube as a Function of the Length (Inches) of Each Side

many variables. For example, what would the frequency distribution of heights (in inches) look like if everyone in the United States between the ages of 21 and 45 were measured?

T I M E ▪ O U T
Take some time to imagine what this frequency distribution would look like and then sketch the corresponding graph. Recall from Chapter 5 that a frequency distribution graph is simply a line graph that plots frequency values on the Y axis and midpoints of the class intervals on the X axis, as in Figure 5.8.

Figure 6.2 is a normal curve representing what this frequency distribution might look like. It is important to remember that this is a model, an idealized image of what we might expect the frequency distribution to look like: It is hypothetical or imaginary and is not based upon data that are actually collected. To emphasize the hypothetical nature of Figure 6.2, exact numerical frequency values are not stated. Do you agree with the general image presented here?

T I M E ▪ O U T
Take some time to answer this question.

Figure 6.2 suggests that the height measurements for all persons between the ages of 21 and 45 in the United States would be distributed normally. The general pattern portrayed by this normal curve, and by all normal curves, is that the most frequently obtained measures are at the mean. As you move away from

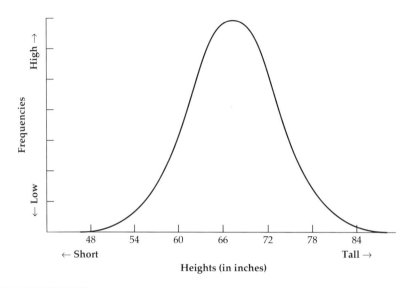

FIGURE 6.2 Idealized Normal Curve of the Frequency Distribution
of Measured Heights for All Persons between the Ages of 21
and 45 in the United States

the mean in either direction, the number of measurements obtained decreases. Wouldn't you expect, for example, that there would be more people who are 66 inches (5 feet 6 inches) tall than people who are 48 inches (4 feet) tall? Wouldn't you also expect that there would be more people who are 66 inches (5 feet 6 inches) tall than people who are 84 inches (7 feet) tall? People between the ages of 21 and 45 who are 4 feet tall are relatively infrequent. People between the ages of 21 and 45 who are 7 feet tall are also relatively infrequent. Are 4-feet-tall people just as uncommon as 7-feet-tall people?

T I M E ■ O U T
Take some time to respond to this question.

If you answered yes, then you would agree that, at least in this respect, Figure 6.2 is a reasonable model. However, if you answered no, then you are probably dissatisfied with Figure 6.2. If so, what model would you propose?

T I M E ■ O U T
If you are dissatisfied with Figure 6.2 as a model, take some time to consider this question.

HYPOTHETICAL VERSUS EMPIRICAL DISTRIBUTIONS

Database A.8 lists 1000 height measurements, for people between the ages of 21 and 45.

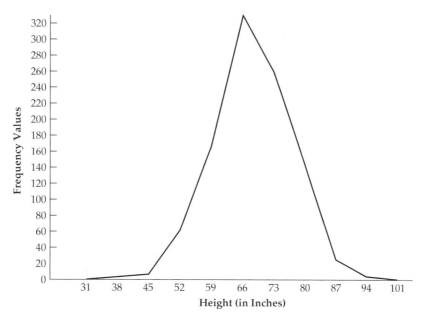

FIGURE 6.3 Line Graph of the Frequency Distribution of Heights Actually Measured for 1000 Persons between the Ages of 21 and 45 in the United States

T I M E ■ O U T
Take some time to glance at the 1000 height measurements in Database A.8 and the corresponding mean and standard deviation.

Because the data in Database A.8 represent the results of actual measurements, we say that they are **empirical data**. If you were to calculate the mean for these 1000 data points, you would find that it is 65.3 inches. If you were to calculate the standard deviation, you would find that it is 7.08 inches. Thus, the summary parameters for the data points in Database A.8 are:

$\mu = 65.3$

$\sigma = 7.08$

$N = 1000$

Now consider Figure 6.3, which plots the frequency distribution for the 1000 measured heights in Database A.8. What differences do you notice between Figures 6.2 and 6.3?

T I M E ■ O U T
Take some time to examine this question.

Recall that Figure 6.2 is hypothetical and is based on the idealized normal curve. Figure 6.3 is empirical; it is based on the actual data from Database A.8. While these distributions are similar in appearance, there are important differences:

- Figure 6.2 does not have frequency values for the Y axis.

- Figure 6.3 does have frequency values for the Y axis.

- Figure 6.2 is a smooth curve.

- Figure 6.3 is not smooth.

- Figure 6.2 has a hypothetical mean of 66 inches; that is, the average height of all persons between the ages of 21 and 45 in the United States is imagined to be 66 inches (5 ft 6 in.).

- Figure 6.3 has an empirical mean of 65.3 inches; that is, the actual calculated mean for the 1000 measured heights from Database A.8 is 65.3 inches.

- Figure 6.2 shows height values along the X axis of 48, 54, 60, 66, 72, 78, and 84. The increment between these values is 6, which is the hypothetical standard deviation of the distribution.

- Figure 6.3 shows height values along the X axis of 45, 52, 59, 66, 73, 80, and 87. The increment between these values is 7, which is the actual calculated standard deviation (7.08, to be more precise) for the 1000 measured heights from Database A.8.

To sum up, Figure 6.2 is a model: It represents what a person might expect the frequency distribution to look like if the height of every person in the United States between the ages of 21 and 45 were measured. A **hypothetical distribution** such as this might be based upon a lot of information, or it might be based upon very little information.

Figure 6.3 is an **empirical distribution** because it is based upon actual data—in this case, upon the 1000 data points in Database A.8.

TIME ■ OUT
The difference between hypothetical and empirical is extremely important for an understanding of the rest of this book. Take some time to clarify this difference in your own mind.

USING THE NORMAL CURVE AS A MODEL

As we've already established, a hypothetical normal distribution model can be based upon a lot of information or it can be based upon very little information. Regardless of how much information we have when we suggest our normal model, it will always have the following characteristics:

- The mean of the normal distribution model will always be exactly in the middle of the distribution.

- The mean, the median, and the mode of the normal model will always be equal.

- Precisely 34.13% of all the imaginary data values in the normal model will be between the mean and one standard deviation above the mean. For example, 34.13%* of the population represented by Figure 6.4 (p. 112) would be between 75 and 80.

- Precisely 34.13% of all the imaginary data values in the normal model will be between the mean and one standard deviation below the mean.

- Precisely 13.59% of all the imaginary data values in the normal model will be between one standard deviation above the mean and two standard deviations above the mean.

- Precisely 13.59% of all the imaginary data values in the normal model will be between one standard deviation below the mean and two standard deviations below the mean.

- Precisely 2.14% of all the imaginary data values in the normal model will be between two standard deviations above the mean and three standard deviations above the mean.
- Precisely 2.14% of all the imaginary data values in the normal model will be between two standard deviations below the mean and three standard deviations below the mean.

- Only 0.135% of all the imaginary data values in the normal model will be more than three standard deviations above the mean.

- Only 0.135% of all the imaginary data values in the normal model will be more than three standard deviations below the mean.

Given these characteristics of the normal model, other statements can be logically derived:

- Precisely 50% of all the imagined data values in the normal model will be above the mean.

- Precisely 50% of all the imagined data values in the normal moel will be below the mean.

- Precisely 68.26% of all the imagined data values in the normal model will be between one standard deviation below the mean and one standard deviation above the mean.

- Precisely 84.13% of all the imagined data values in the normal model will be below one standard deviation above the mean.

*Percentage values indicate the percentage of the area under the normal curve.

How are these statements derived?

T I M E ■ O U T
Take some time to respond to this question.

How do we know that these characteristics of normal curves are true? They are consequences of the mathematical structure of the curve.

The normal curve is simply a line graph of a particular mathematical equation developed by a man named Gauss in the late 1700s. Any curve can be generated by means of the appropriate mathematical formula. For example, the curve in Figure 6.1 can be generated by using the following formula:

$$Y = X^3$$

Verbally, this formula states that Y is equal to X cubed or, in other words, Y is equal to X raised to the third power. If X is 1, then

$$Y = 1 \times 1 \times 1 = 1$$

If X is 2, then

$$Y = 2 \times 2 \times 2 = 8$$

and so on. In this simple equation, there are only two variables, X and Y.

Looking again at Figure 6.1, we see that the curve represents the Y values (vertical axis) that correspond to different X values (horizontal axis). For example, for the X value of 4 we project upward to the curve and then leftward to the Y axis and find a Y value of 64 ($4 \times 4 \times 4 = 64$). To generate this curve, we simply use the equation to determine the Y values corresponding to a particular set of X values, and then draw a line graph through the resulting points.

The formula for the normal curve is much more complex

$$Y = \frac{1}{\sqrt{2\pi\sigma}} e^{-[(X - \mu)^2/2\sigma^2]} \tag{6.4}$$

In spite of the complexity of Eq. (6.4), notice that, once you know the values of the parameters for any given population (that is, the population mean and the population standard deviation), there are only two variables in the equation: Y, which is calculated by application of Eq. (6.4) itself; and X, for which we choose an appropriate range of values. All the other symbols in the formula represent either constants (π and e), which don't change for a given population, or operations such as multiplication or taking the square root.

If you applied Eq. (6.4) using specific values for the mean and the standard deviation and X values that range from three standard deviations below the mean to three standard deviations above the mean, you would obtain values for Y that, when plotted for each corresponding X, would approximate a normal curve.

MAIN POINT SUMMARY

Normal curves are simply models based upon the application of Eq. (6.4) using specific values for the mean and the standard deviation and a range of X values. Such models only approximate the true empirical frequency distribution for any given population of measurable X values.

Thus, by using the normal curve model to describe a particular population of data values, we are actually setting certain expectations about how the values are distributed in the population. This is a very useful **inferential technique**; it allows us to make inferences about populations when we actually only have information about a sample from the population. In the following example, the normal curve is used to establish letter grades for a quiz.

According to Table 6.1, the mean and standard deviation for quiz 1 are 75 and 5 respectively

$$\text{mean}_{Q1} = 75$$

$$\text{standard deviation}_{Q1} = 5$$

Assume that only 20 people took this quiz, and that the person administering the quiz is a new teacher who doesn't know what to expect from his students. Under such circumstances the teacher may wonder how to assign letter grades to the students' percentage scores. One solution to this problem would be to use the normal curve as a model of what to expect under normal circumstances.

The teacher knows that the sample mean is 75 and that the sample standard deviation is 5. If he assumes that the 20 students who took the quiz are a representative sample of some larger population of students, he could establish the normal model in Figure 6.4.

Figure 6.4 was generated by using a range of X values from 50 to 100 (representing the expected range of quiz grades for the hypothetical model) in Eq. (6.4) and adopting the hypothesis that the population mean and the population standard deviation are equal to the sample mean and the sample standard deviation—that is, 75 and 5 respectively. The model in Figure 6.4 must conform to the standard characteristics of normal curves already discussed, as follows.

- The mean of 75 is in the middle of the distribution.

- Precisely 34.13% of all the imaginary data values in Figure 6.4 are between the mean of 75 and the value of 80, which is one standard deviation above the mean.

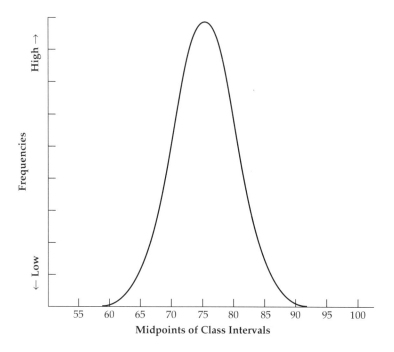

FIGURE 6.4   Normal Curve Model of Quiz Grades

- Precisely 34.13% of all the imaginary data values in Figure 6.4 are between the mean of 75 and the value of 70, which is one standard deviation below the mean.

- Precisely 13.59% of all the imaginary data values in Figure 6.4 are between 80 (one standard deviation above the mean) and 85 (two standard deviations above the mean).

- Precisely 13.59% of all the imaginary data values in Figure 6.4 are between 70 (one standard deviation below the mean) and 65 (two standard deviations below the mean).

- Precisely 2.14% of all the imaginary data values in Figure 6.4 are between 85 (two standard deviations above the mean) and 90 (three standard deviations above the mean).

- Precisely 2.14% of all the imaginary data values in Figure 6.4 are between 65 (two standard deviations below the mean) and 60 (three standard deviations below the mean).

- Only 0.135% of all the imaginary data values in Figure 6.4 will be above 90 (three standard deviations above the mean).

- Only 0.135% of all the imaginary data values in Figure 6.4 will be below 60 (three standard deviations below the mean).

Given these characteristics of the normal curve model, teachers often **grade on the curve** using the grade assignments in Table 6.2. Can you figure out where the expected percentages in Table 6.2 come from?

TABLE 6.2 Assignment of Letter Grades Based upon the Normal Curve Model for Quiz 1 Grades

Earned grade	Expected percentage below this grade	Letter grade
60	0.135%	F
65	2.275%	D
70	15.865%	C
75	50.000%	C
80	84.130%	C
85	97.720%	B
90	99.860%	A
95	99.995%	A
100	100.000%	A

T I M E ■ O U T
Take some time to think about this question.

The expected percentages in Table 6.2 are all based upon the mathematical realities of the normal curve model. For example, as we saw already, 50% of the imaginary data values are below the mean for all normal curves.

Each of the earned grades reported in Table 6.2 corresponds to a whole-number standardized score. The standardized scores are reported in Table 6.3, along with a restatement of important characteristics regarding areas of the normal curve model. How do we interpret Table 6.3?

TABLE 6.3 Standard Scores and Percentage Areas under the Normal Curve Model for Quiz 1 Grades

Earned grade	Standard score	Percentage of distribution below earned grade	Letter grade
60	−3	0.135%	F
65	−2	2.275%	D
70	−1	15.865%	C
75	0	50.000%	C
80	+1	84.130%	C
85	+2	97.720%	B
90	+3	99.860%	A
95	+4	99.995%	A
100	+5	100.000%	A

A student who earned a grade of 90 on quiz 1 would have a standard score of +3, because the standard deviation for quiz 1 is 5 and, therefore, a score of 90 is 15 score units, or three standard deviations, above the mean of 75.

Given the physical and mathematical realities of the normal curve model, we know that 99.86% of all the values in the normal distribution lie below a Z value of +3; in other words, only 0.14% (that is, fourteen-hundredths of a percent) of all the values in the distribution lie above it.

On this basis, we would have to agree that a Z value of +3 is unusually high. Logically, we would also conclude that an earned grade of 90 is unusually high, and a letter grade of A — or maybe even A+ — seems appropriate, *provided* the normal curve model is correct for our data.

Why is this proviso so important?

T I M E ■ O U T
Take some time to reflect on this question.

It is important to recognize that the normal curve model is only a guess about how some imaginary population of measurements might look. It is not an empirical distribution. If the distribution of the actual population does not conform to a normal curve, that model cannot yield correct results.

SHAPE OF THE NORMAL CURVE

As we have seen, the normal curve corresponds to a particular mathematical formula — Eq. (6.4). Figures 6.2 and 6.4 are both normal curves generated using Eq. (6.4). Notice that the values along the X axis for Figures 6.2 and 6.4 are different. This is because these normal curves were generated on the basis of different parameters. Figure 6.2 was generated on the basis of a mean of 66 and a standard deviation of 6. Figure 6.4 was generated on the basis of a mean of 75 and a standard deviation of 5. You may have also noticed that, even though Figures 6.2 and 6.4 are both normal curves, they have slightly different shapes. You should be aware that there is a whole family of normal curves with slightly different shapes. A small family is illustrated in Figure 6.5.

All three of the curves in Figure 6.5 are based upon the same mean of 75. However, each is based upon a different standard deviation. Which of these curves has the highest standard deviation and which has the lowest?

T I M E ■ O U T
Take some time to answer this question.

The curve with the highest peak has a standard deviation of 5. The curve with the lowest peak has a standard deviation of 10. The remaining curve has a standard deviation of 7. **Kurtosis** refers to the degree to which a frequency distribution curve is peaked. In Figure 6.5, the curve with the highest peak is said to be relatively **leptokurtic**; the curve with the lowest peak is said to be relatively **platykurtic**; and the middle curve is said to be relatively **mesokurtic**.

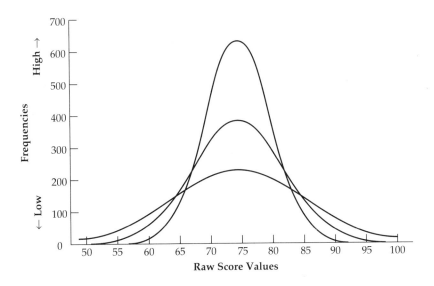

FIGURE 6.5   A Family of Three Normal Curves

Based on the above information, what would you say is the relationship between the shape of the normal curve and the standard deviation?

T I M E ■ O U T
Take some time to consider this question.

As the standard deviation increases, the peak of the normal curve becomes less pronounced. However, even though these three curves differ in shape, they are still normal curves, with all of the characteristics of normal curves. This can be illustrated by plotting each of the three curves in Figure 6.5 separately, with standard Z values along the X axis rather than raw score values (Figures 6.6, 6.7, and 6.8).

Now consider Figures 6.6, 6.7, and 6.8 as three alternative hypothetical models for the performance that might be expected on quiz 1 if 10,000 students were to take the quiz.

Model 1 (Mean: 75; Standard Deviation: 5; Figure 6.6)

This model suggests that the mean would be 75, which is consistent with the actual sample mean of quiz 1 (Table 6.1). Model 1 also suggests that we would have to go down to $Z = -4$ approximately and up to $Z = +4$ approximately in order to include all of the scores in the distribution. Since Figure 6.6 assumes a standard deviation of 5, the range from $Z = -4$ to $Z = +4$ represents a raw score range from $X = 55$ (four standard deviations below the mean) to $X = 95$ (four standard deviations above the mean).

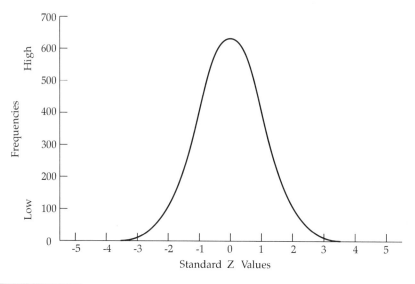

FIGURE 6.6 Normal Curve Model for a Mean of 75, a Standard Deviation of 5, and N = 10,00

Model 2 (Mean: 75; Standard Deviation: 7; Figure 6.7)

This model again suggests that the mean would be 75. Model 2 also suggests that we would have to go down to $Z = -3.5$ approximately and up to $Z = +3.5$ approximately in order to include all of the scores in the distribution. Since

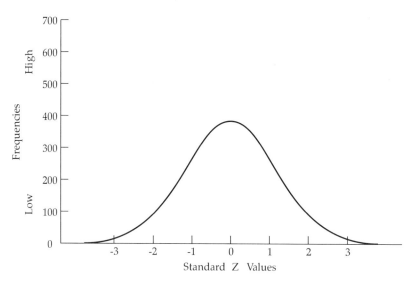

FIGURE 6.7 Normal Curve Model for a Mean of 75, a Standard Deviation of 7, and N = 10,00

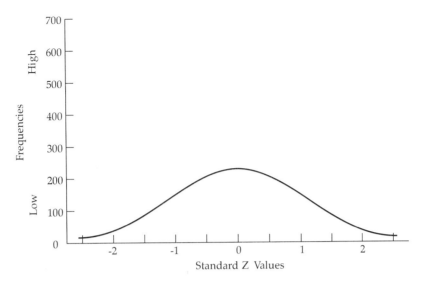

FIGURE 6.8 Normal Curve Model for a Mean of 75, a Standard Deviation of 10, and N = 10,00

Figure 6.7 assumes a standard deviation of 7, the range from $Z = -3.5$ to $Z = +3.5$ represents a raw score range from $X = 50.5$ (3.5 standard deviations below the mean) to $X = 99.5$ (3.5 standard deviations above the mean).

Model 3 (Mean: 75; Standard Deviation: 10; Figure 6.8)

Once again, this model suggests that the mean would be 75. Model 3 also suggests that we would have to go down to a $Z = -3$ approximately and up to a $Z = +3$ approximately in order to include all of the scores in the distribution. Since Figure 6.8 assumes a standard deviation of 10, the range from $Z = -3$ to $Z = +3$ represents a raw score range from $X = 45$ (three standard deviations below the mean) to $X = 105$ (three standard deviations above the mean).

The ranges covered by the distributions in Figures 6.6, 6.7, and 6.8 can also be seen in Figure 6.5. If you look closely at Figure 6.5 you will see that model 3 suggests a range of raw score values (earned grades) that go beyond the range of X values (50–100) stated along the X axis. What does this suggest about the feasibility of model 3?

T I M E ■ O U T
Take some time to respond to this question.

Since model 3 suggests X values extending beyond the range of earned grades that we would normally expect, it seems that models 1 and 2 are more appropriate. This should not surprise us: Model 1 is based upon a standard deviation of 5, which is the standard deviation of the actual earned grades for quiz 1 (Table 6.1).

USING THE NORMAL CURVE TO ESTIMATE PERCENTILES AND PERCENTILE RANKS

What is a percentile? A **percentile** represents a particular point in a distribution of measurements below which a specified percentage of scores fall. For example, the **50th percentile** is that point in a distribution below which half of all the scores fall. In the distribution illustrated in Figure 6.4, the 50th percentile is the score value of 75. Remember that a percentile is stated as a raw score value, for example, 75.

What is a percentile rank? A **percentile rank** represents the percentage of measurements in a distribution that fall below a specified raw score. For example, in the distribution illustrated in Figure 6.4, the raw score of 75 has a percentile rank of 50th: We say that the score of 75 is at the 50th percentile. We know this to be true because 50% of all the scores will fall below the mean of the distribution, *provided* we assume a normal curve. Remember that a percentile rank is a value that represents a percentage. For example, the 50th percentile represents 50%.

The ability to determine percentiles and percentile ranks is useful in many decision-making situations. Consider the following example.

You are hired as a consultant to help an employment agency find the best mechanics for vacancies in the airline industry. You are given the mean and the standard deviation for a standardized test of mechanical aptitude, as well as each candidate's raw score, but not the percentile rank. You decide to include only those candidates who scored at or above the 90th percentile on the standardized test.

Students often confuse percentiles and percentile ranks. To keep them straight, remember that, in determining a percentile, you start with a percentage value and try to establish the score value below which that percentage of scores will fall. In determining a percentile rank, start with a score value and try to establish what percentage of the scores in the distribution fall below it.

So far, we have illustrated the concepts of percentile and percentile rank for the simple example of the mean as the 50th percentile. Using similar reasoning, it is relatively easy to determine the percentile ranks of certain other scores. For example, using the data from Table 6.3, we can determine the approximate percentile ranks in Table 6.4. Do you understand how the information in Table 6.3 allows us to state the percentile ranks in Table 6.4?

TABLE 6.4 **Percentile Ranks for Quiz 1 Grades**
(Based upon Normal Model 1)

Earned grade	Standard score	Approximate percentile rank	Letter grade
60	−3	0th	F
65	−2	2nd	D
70	−1	16th	C
75	0	50th	C
80	+1	84th	C
85	+2	98th	B
90	+3	99.8th	A
95	+4	99.9th	A
100	+5	100th	A

T I M E ▪ O U T
Take some time to consider this question.

What happens when raw scores are not represented by whole-number standard scores?

Although it may seem hard to interpret Table 6.4, in fact it is relatively easy because the earned grades (raw scores) are represented by whole-number standard scores, for which the corresponding percentages in the normal curve model may be memorized without particular difficulty (Table 6.5).

Do you understand the relationship between the information in Table 6.5 and the information in Table 6.4?

TABLE 6.5 **Areas of the Normal Curve Model for Whole-Number Z Scores**

I	II	III	IV	V	VI
			Y value for X = Z, mean = 0,	Percentage area	Percentage
	Decimal area between Z	Decimal area	standard	between Z	area
Z	and mean	beyond Z	deviation = 1	and mean	beyond Z
−3	.4986	.0014	.0044	49.86%	0.14%
−2	.4772	.0228	.0540	47.72%	2.28%
−1	.3413	.1587	.2420	34.13%	15.87%
0	.0000	.5000	.3989	0.00%	50.00%
+1	.3413	.1587	.2420	34.13%	15.87%
+2	.4772	.0228	.0540	47.72%	2.28%
+3	.4986	.0014	.0044	49.86%	0.14%

Take some time to answer this question.

Table 6.5 shows just a few of the many Z scores that are possible. Table B.1 in Appendix B states information regarding areas of the normal curve model for a more extended range of Z scores.

To illustrate the use of Table B.1, consider the following question: If you earned a grade of 80 on quiz 1 (Table 6.1), what would be your percentile rank?

TIME ■ OUT
Take some time to examine this question.

There are several ways to answer this question. You might remember Table 6.4 and simply read the answer (84th percentile) from the information there. This is convenient; but what if that information was not available, and all you had was Table B.1?

Step 1. The first step is to choose the normal distribution model for use in your estimate. Thus far, we have been using a model with a mean of 75, a standard deviation of 5, and $N = 10,000$. Let's continue with that model.

Step 2. Sketch the normal distribution model that you have chosen. Recall that Figure 6.6 is a graph of the model we are using.

Step 3. Determine the standard score for the raw score in question. Remember that, by assuming a normal distribution and determining the standard score, we can estimate the percentile rank. The standard score for a raw score of 80 is $+1$. Do you understand why?

TIME ■ OUT
Take some time to reflect on this question.

Step 4. Once the standard score (Z score) is determined, we go to Table B.1 and locate that Z score.

Step 5. Once we have located the Z score in Table B.1, we locate that score on the sketch of our model. Using Figure 6.6 as our sketch, we locate the Z score of $+1$.

Step 6. Shade in the area of the sketch that we are focusing on. Using Figure 6.6 as our sketch, we would shade in the area from $Z = +1$ to the leftmost tail of the curve. This area represents the percentage of all the scores in the distribution below $Z = +1$.

Step 7. Think carefully about the relationship between the shaded area of your sketch and the information in Table B.1. This crucial step requires that you use your critical thinking skills. There are no magic instuctions; each problem is different. Also, there are several correct logical routes to any particular answer.

In the present example we might decide, as a result of Step 7, to determine the percentage of the area between $Z = +1$ and the mean (34.13%) and then add this to 50%, which is the area below the mean (50% + 34.13% = 84.13%). In this way, we would arrive at the answer provided by Table 6.4 (the 84th percentile). Do you understand why this answer is correct?

T I M E ■ O U T
This is a very important concept. Take some time to consider this question.

If you earned a grade of 85 on quiz 1 (Table 6.1), what would be your percentile rank?

T I M E ■ O U T
Take some time to answer this question.

Using the same reasoning as in the previous example, you should have concluded that a grade of 85 corresponds to the 98th percentile.
If you earned a grade of 71 on quiz 1 (Table 6.1), what would be your percentile rank?

T I M E ■ O U T
Take some time to examine this question.

By the same reasoning, a grade of 71 corresponds to the 21st percentile. Let's go through the steps with this example.

Step 1. Thus far, we have been using a model with a mean of 75, a standard deviation of 5, and $N = 10,000$. Let's continue with this model.

Step 2. We recall that Figure 6.6 is a graph of the model we are using.

Step 3. The standard score for the raw score of 71 is

$$(71 - 75)/5 = (-4)/5 = -0.8$$

Two important aspects of this standard score are that it is: 1) negative, because the raw score is below the mean; 2) not a whole number. Do you understand why the answer to step 3 is -0.8?

T I M E ■ O U T
Take some time to respond to this question.

Step 4. We locate $Z = -0.8$ in Table B.1.

Step 5. We locate $Z = 0.8$ on the sketch of our model, Figure 6.6.

Step 6. On Figure 6.6, we shade in the area that begins at $Z = -0.8$ and extends all the way to the leftmost tail of the curve. This area represents the percentage of all the scores in the distribution below $Z = -0.8$. In this case, the shaded area is below the mean.

Step 7. What relationship between the shaded area of our sketch and the information in Table B.1 would be helpful in solving this problem? One possibility is to determine the percentage of the area beyond $Z = -0.8$ (21%). In this way, we conclude that a grade of 71 corresponds to the 21st percentile.

FROM DESCRIPTIVE TO INFERENTIAL STATISTICS

In the first four chapters of Part Two, we focused on the process of measurement and the techniques used to organize and summarize measurements. In the current chapter we have begun the transition from simply describing data to making guesses (inferences) about larger groups that the data might represent. Thus, we have begun to make the transition from descriptive to inferential statistics.

Familiarity with the normal curve model is an essential foundation for your understanding of the inferential process. For example, if you had statistics for only a sample of students from your school, you would be able to make an inference about the population of all students at your school. You could also estimate percentile ranks for raw scores.

Do you recall, from Chapter 1, the difference between a sample and a population?

T I M E ■ O U T
Take some time to answer this question.

Typically, samples are relatively small groups of data that are intended to represent the population from which they are drawn. Sometimes we are not concerned about the larger population that a given sample might represent. For example, a teacher might calculate the mean and the standard deviation for a quiz and simply describe the class performance on the quiz by reporting these summary measures. Table 6.1 is an example of such a description.

Under such circumstances, would you consider the summary measures in Table 6.1 to be statistics or parameters?

T I M E ■ O U T
Take some time to reflect on this question.

Your answer to the above question will depend upon your interpretation of the situation. If you consider the group of students who took quizzes 1, 2, and 3 to be a sample that represents some larger group, then you would regard the summary measures in Table 6.1 as statistics. Strictly speaking, the summary should make use of the appropriate symbols, as in Table 6.6.

TABLE 6.6   Summary Statistics for Three Quizzes

Quiz	$\bar{X}$	s	n
1	75	5	36
2	80	5	37
3	80	2.5	35

On the other hand, if you consider the group of students who took quizzes 1, 2, and 3 to be a population in its own right, then you would regard the summary measures in Table 6.1 as parameters. Strictly speaking, the summary would then make use of the appropriate symbols indicated in Table 6.7.

TABLE 6.7   Summary Parameters for Three Quizzes

Quiz	μ	σ	N
1	75	5	36
2	80	5	37
3	80	2.5	35

Note that the same information can be regarded either as summary statistics or summary parameters, depending upon whether we consider the group of data to be a sample or a population. Note also that Table 6.1 avoids the issue by simply referring to the mean and standard deviation, without introducing symbols.

ASIDE ■ **We will discuss the issue of representativeness extensively in Chapter 8.**

It is common to avoid the issue by using these terms. Strictly speaking, the group of students who took quizzes 1, 2, and 3 is not a sample that represents a larger group. Do you agree?

T I M E ■ O U T
Take some time to examine this question.

Neither is the group of students who took quizzes 1, 2, and 3 a population, strictly speaking. Do you agree?

T I M E ■ O U T
Take some time to consider this question.

So, we might be left feeling rather vague about what to call the means and standard deviations in Table 6.1. Perhaps we should just call them summary measures.

ESTIMATING (INFERRING) PARAMETERS FROM SAMPLE STATISTICS

As you learned earlier in this chapter, the normal curve model can be used to make guesses (inferences) about larger groups of data (populations) that a smaller group of data (sample) *might* represent. However, we can't do so, unless we know the mean and standard deviation of the population. Often, we don't know what the mean and standard deviation of the population are. So we are in a Catch-22 situation: How can we use the normal curve model to make guesses about the population if we first have to know something about the population?

The answer to this apparent dilemma is that we can use the sample data to make estimates of the population mean and the population standard deviation. Making such estimates is to a large extent what inferential statistics is all about. Here's how it works.

SAMPLE MEAN AS AN ESTIMATE OF THE POPULATION MEAN

Recall the example in Chapter 4 where five data points were randomly selected from Database A.7. Table 6.8 summarizes the sample statistics again for your convenience. We will refer to these five data points as sample A.

TABLE 6.8	Raw Data and Summary Statistics for the Arm Lengths (Inches) of Five People (Data Randomly Selected from Database A.7)

Sample A:	34,	27,	31,	28,	24
$\bar{X}_A$: 28.8		s_A: 3.42		n_A: 5	

On the basis of the information in Table 6.8, what is your best guess for the mean of all 1000 measures in Database A.7?

T I M E ■ O U T
Take some time to answer this question.

Strictly on the basis of the data for sample A (Table 6.8), the best estimate we can make for the mean of all 1000 measures in Database A.7 is 28.8.

If the sample represents the population, then the sample mean is a good estimate of the population mean. Furthermore, if the sample represents the population, then the sample mean is an **unbiased estimate** of the population mean. In this context, unbiased simply means that the sample mean will not necessarily be an overestimate or an underestimate of the population mean. This is not the same as saying that the sample mean is equal to the population mean. Rather, it is saying that sometimes the sample mean may be less than the population mean and sometimes it may be greater, but it will not always be less and it will not always be greater. If it were always less, it would be a biased

ASIDE ■ It is also true that biased estimates do not overestimate or underestimate 100% of the time. Rather, biased estimates are those estimates that tend to either overestimate or underestimate most of the time.

estimate. If it were always greater, it would be a biased estimate.

What is the real population mean for Database A.7?

T I M E ■ O U T
Take some time to respond to this question.

As stated in Database A.7, the real mean for this population is 29.6. It turns out that our sample mean of 28.8 is relatively close. However, the mean of a sample randomly selected from a population may not always be so close. Look at the information for sample B in Table 6.9.

What differences do you notice between samples A and B?

T I M E ■ O U T
Take some time to reflect on this question.

ASIDE ■ Tables 6.8 and 6.9 show two separate samples taken from the population in Database A.7. Notice that the means, standard deviations, and sizes of samples A and B are denoted by subscripts A and B respectively. Always use subscripts to identify statistics and parameters when there may be some uncertainty about which sample or population is meant.

Even though each sample is the same size and was randomly selected from the same population, the sample means and the sample standard deviations are different. Notice also that, while the sample mean for sample A (28.8) is a slight underestimate of the true population mean (29.6), the sample mean for sample B (31) is a slight overestimate of the true population mean. This illustrates that the sample mean is an unbiased estimate of the population mean.

If we were to use these sample means as estimates of the population mean, the proper symbols would be as follows:

$$\tilde{\mu}_A = 28.8$$

$$\tilde{\mu}_B = 31.0$$

The tildes indicate that these are estimates of the population parameter, as opposed to the actual population parameter itself.

TABLE 6.9	Raw Data and Summary Statistics for the Arm Lengths (Inches) of Five People (Data Randomly Selected from Database A.7)

Sample B:	26, 32, 32, 31, 34		
$2\bar{X}_B$: 31.0	s_B: 2.68	n_B: 5	

SAMPLE STANDARD DEVIATION AS AN ESTIMATE
OF THE POPULATION STANDARD DEVIATION

Now that you have seen that the sample mean can be used as an estimate of the population mean without concern for bias, what would be your best estimate of the standard deviation of Database A.7?

T I M E ▪ O U T
Take some time to consider this question.

Unlike the sample mean, the sample standard deviation is a **biased estimate**. Given that it is biased, would you expect it to be an underestimate or an overestimate?

T I M E ▪ O U T
Take some time to examine this question.

The sample standard deviation will typically be an underestimate of the population standard deviation. Can you think of an explanation for this bias?

T I M E ▪ O U T
Take some time to respond to this question.

Why is the sample standard deviation typically an underestimate of the population standard deviation? There is a very logial explanation. If you have a relatively large population of measurements — for example, the 1000 arm length measurements in Database A.7 — wouldn't you expect there to be more variability among the 1000 data values in the population than there would be in a sample of five data values randomly selected from that population? Stated another way, the variability of measurements in a sample will probably be less than the variability of the measurements in the population from which the sample was randomly selected. After all, given what you know about the normal curve, isn't it likely that a randomly selected sample of data points would include more scores from around the mean of the population, where there is the greatest concentration of data points, than from the extremes of the population, where the frequency of scores decreases?

T I M E ▪ O U T
Take some time to think about this concept.

To illustrate this point, consider samples A and B in Tables 6.8 and 6.9. As noted in Database A.7, the population standard deviation is 3.5 The standard deviations of samples A and B are 3.42 and 2.68 respectively; that is, both are less than 3.5. This can be stated symbolically as follows

$s_A < \sigma$

$s_B < \sigma$

Note that the sample standard deviation will not always be less than that of the population. Consider Table 6.10, which states the score values, means, standard deviations, and sizes of 10 separate samples randomly drawn from Database A.7. Is there anything about the information in Table 6.10 that surprises you?

T I M E ■ O U T
Take some time to consider this question.

TABLE 6.10	Summary Statistics for 10 Samples

(Data Randomly Selected from Database A.7)

Sample	Measures	$\bar{X}$	s	n
C	34, 27, 31, 28, 24	28.8	3.42	5
D	26, 32, 32, 31, 34	31.0	2.68	5
E	29, 31, 31, 31, 26	29.6	1.95	5
F	31, 31, 29, 31, 25	29.4	2.33	5
G	25, 26, 28, 26, 27	26.4	1.01	5
H	25, 35, 33, 30, 25	29.6	4.07	5
I	25, 24, 30, 30, 29	27.6	2.57	5
J	29, 26, 26, 32, 31	28.8	2.48	5
K	28, 22, 27, 35, 26	27.6	4.22	5
L	32, 31, 34, 28, 29	30.8	2.13	5

It should not surprise you that the 10 sample means in Table 6.10 are not all the same, but are sometimes greater, and sometimes less, than the population mean of 29. This is consistent with the principle that the sample mean is an unbiased estimate of the population mean.

It might surprise you that two of the sample standard deviations in Table 6.10 (for samples H and K) are actually greater than the population standard deviation of 3.5. In fact, while the sample standard deviation is a biased estimate of the population standard deviation, the nature of this bias is a matter of probability. Usually the sample standard deviation will underestimate the population standard deviation, but occasionally it will not.

UNBIASED ESTIMATES OF THE POPULATION STANDARD DEVIATION

Recall the following calculation formula for the standard deviation from Chapter 4

$$\text{Standard deviation} = \sqrt{\frac{\sum(X^2) - \left(\frac{(\sum X)^2}{N}\right)}{N}}$$

If we are using this formula to calculate the standard deviation for a sample, the appropriate notation is as follows

$$s = \sqrt{\frac{\sum (X^2) - \left(\frac{(\sum X)^2}{n_{samp}}\right)}{n_{samp}}} \qquad (6.5)$$

The formula for calculating the standard deviation of a population is slightly different

$$\sigma = \sqrt{\frac{\sum (X^2) - \left(\frac{(\sum X)^2}{N_{pop}}\right)}{N_{pop}}} \qquad (6.6)$$

Do you notice the very subtle difference between these two formulas?

TIME ■ OUT
Take some time to consider this question.

Usually we do not have all the data from the population, and so Eq. (6.6) is rarely used. The use of Eq. (6.5), on the other hand, is quite common.

Using Eq. (6.5), can you arrive at the results for Samples C–L in Table 6.10?

TIME ■ OUT
Take some time to perform these calculations.

To correct the bias inherent in estimates based on the sample standard deviation, the population standard deviation may be calculated from the following formula

$$\tilde{\sigma} = \sqrt{\frac{\sum (X^2) - \left(\frac{(\sum X)^2}{n_{samp}}\right)}{n_{samp} - 1}} \qquad (6.7)$$

Do you notice the subtle difference between Eq. (6.7) and Eq. (6.5) for the sample standard deviation?

TIME ■ OUT
Take some time to respond to this question.

If you studied the formulas carefully, you probably noticed that the denominator of Eq. (6.7) is $(n_{samp} - 1)$ rather than n_{samp}, the sample size. You should also have noticed that the symbol for an unbiased estimate of the population standard deviation is $\tilde{\sigma}$. Once again, the tilde indicates that we are estimating.

If we apply this formula to sample D in Table 6.10, we arrive at the following value

$$\tilde{\sigma}_D = 3.00$$

Notice that this value, which is an unbiased estimate of the population standard deviation, is greater than the standard deviation of sample D (2.68). Thus you can see that, by attempting to correct for bias, we increase the value of the sample standard deviation. Does this make sense to you?

T I M E ■ O U T
Take some time to reflect on this question.

The correction for bias is not a perfect solution to the problem, but it does help. Some additional thought will also help you to understand that, even though the correction for bias is always the same (that is, subtracting 1 from the sample size in the denominator), its effect is greater for smaller samples. For example, if there were 10 scores in the sample, subtracting 1 would represent a 10% (1/10) reduction in the size of the denominator. If there were 100 scores in the sample, subtracting 1 would represent only a 1% (1/100) reduction in the size of the denominator. This is reasonable, in that the bias is greater for smaller samples.

STANDARDIZED SCORES REVISITED

When calculating standard scores, we are making some guesses (inferences) about the relationship of individual data points to some larger population of data points that might be represented by the smaller sample. In making such inferences, it is logical to use estimated values for the population mean and the population standard deviation. Thus, the following formula is appropriate

$$Z = \frac{(X - \tilde{\mu})}{\tilde{\sigma}} \tag{6.8}$$

This is a restatement of Eq. (6.3). Now, however, you have a better understanding of what $\tilde{\mu}$ and $\tilde{\sigma}$ are all about.

SUMMARY

In this chapter, we discussed standard scores and how they are used to make standardized comparisons within and between samples of data. We considered the normal curve and its use as a model. We then examined the concept of inferential statistics within the context of standard scores and the normal curve. Finally, we discussed the estimation of population parameters from sample data and introduced computational formulas for the population standard deviation and the unbiased estimate of the population standard deviation.

KEY SYMBOLS

$Z, \tilde{\sigma}, \tilde{\mu}$

KEY TERMS AND CONCEPTS

34.13%	Model
50th percentile	Mu tilde
Biased estimate	Normal curve
Empirical data	Normal curve model
Empirical distribution	Percentile
Formula for unbiased estimate of population standard deviation	Percentile rank
	Platykurtic
Grading on the curve	Raw score
Hypothetical distribution	Sigma tilde
Inferential technique	Standard score
Kurtosis	Unbiased estimates
Leptokurtic	Z table
Little sigma tilde	Z table
Mesokurtic	

EXERCISES

Use sample 3 from Database A.4 in the following exercises.

6.1 Calculate the mean.

6.2 Calculate the standard deviation.

6.3 Calculate the standard score that corrsponds to the raw score of 68.

6.4 Find the 50th percentile.

6.5 Find the 95th percentile.

6.6 Find the percentile rank for the score of 68.

6.7 Find the hypothetical point in the sample such that only 5% of the scores are at or below it.

6.8 Find the hypothetical point in the sample such that only 5% of the scores are at or above it.

6.9 Find limiting lower and upper points such that 5% of the scores are beyond them (that is, 2.5% below and 2.5% above).

Use the data from Table 6.11 in the following exercises.

TABLE 6.11 Hand Strength Measurements (Kilograms) for 9 People after Riding an Exercise Bike

53	68	39	50	52	60	51	61	39

6.10 Calculate the mean.

6.11 Calculate the standard deviation.

6.12 Calculate the standard score that corresponds to the raw score of 68.

6.13 Find the 50th percentile.

6.14 Find the 95th percentile.

6.15 Find the percentile rank for the sore of 68.

6.16 Find the hypothetical point in the sample such that only 5% of the scores are at or below it.

6.17 Find the hypothetical point in the sample such that only 5% of the scores are at or above it.

6.18 Find limiting lower and upper points such that 5% of the scores are beyond them (that is, 2.5% below and 2.5% above).

The following exercises require a comparison of the results of Exercises 6.1–6.9 and Exercises 6.10–6.18.

6.19 Which sample had the greatest hand strength?

6.20 Which sample had the most heterogeneous hand strengths?

6.21 How strong, relative to the rest of the population, is a hand strength of 68?

6.22 State several ways in which the two populations represented by the two samples differ.

UNDERSTANDING INFERENTIAL STATISTICS

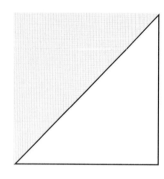

Each of the four chapters in Part Three covers a different aspect of the general category of statistics commonly referred to as *inferential statistics.* Inferential statistical techniques are typically used to test hypotheses (that is, to make predictions) about the outcomes of experiments and observations. A main objective of these techniques is the ability to generalize results from a data sample to the larger population from which the sample was taken. In Chapter 7, you will be introduced to the fundamental reasoning that underlies inferential techniques. This provides a perspective for what follows. In Chapter 8, the basic logic underlying the scientific method is outlined. This provides an important foundation for understanding how to select different inferential techniques for different types of scientific investigations. In Chapter 9, you will see the connection between the logic of scientific inquiry and the logic of inferential statistics. You will also be introduced to the rules of probability fundamental to inferential techniques. Finally, in Chapter 10, you will learn how the logic of probability can be applied to test predictions about the outcomes of observations and experiments.

Understanding the
Rationale for
Inferential Statistics

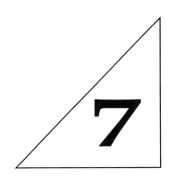

O B J E C T I V E S

After reading and studying Chapter 7 you should understand the following.

■ *that human curiosity is the basis for science.*

■ *the fundamental logic of the scientific process.*

■ *what a theory is.*

■ *what a law is.*

■ *what a hypothesis is.*

■ *the purpose of inferential statistics.*

INTRODUCTION

The rationale for inferential statistics does not require lengthy discussion; but it does deserve careful consideration as an important component of the process of gathering and interpreting behavioral data. This brief chapter is intended as an opportunity for the reader to reflect on the importance of curiosity, theories, and hypotheses. Without these fundamental driving forces, there would be no scientific process and no need for inferential statistics. An understanding of these concepts and their relationship to inferential statistics will also provide a valuable perspective for what follows.

This chapter is intended to serve an additional purpose. There are 13 chapters in this book, Chapter 7 is the median chapter, the halfway point. A short chapter will allow you time to catch your breath and to review the objectives of the previous six chapters, before heading down the home stretch.

HUMAN CURIOSITY REVISITED

Many textbooks for introductory statistics approach the topic as if the formulas for statistical analyses should be the primary focus. I believe, quite to the contrary, that the formulas are *merely* the logical results of our human curiosity, our desire to find answers. The formulas are developed from sophisticated mathematical reasoning; and, because the symbols used in the formulas are unfamiliar, they often seem intimidating to the student on first acquaintance. It is important to remember that these formulas are *merely* symbolic representations of human logic, and they are quite trivial in comparison to the human curiosity that they *serve*.

To repeat an important point from Chapter 1, it is virtually impossible for us to exist without posing an almost continuous stream of questions.

T I M E ■ O U T
Recall the process of generating questions that you went through in Chapter 1.

At this point is is important to remind you that scientific investigation begins with pure curiosity, and that one main difference between scientific questions and everyday questions is the intensity with which they are pursued.

THE SCIENTIFIC PROCESS

The **scientific process** is dynamic and circular. Strictly speaking, there are no final answers to scientific questions; those questions that have final answers are no longer a target for the scientific process. For example, if I were to ask you, "Are your biological parents still living together in the same house?" your answer would probably be a simple matter of fact: yes or no. As such, this is not the type of question that requires scientific inquiry. However, if I were to ask you, "Do the personalities of your biological mother and father differ?" your answer would not be a simple matter of fact. Even though you might respond simply by saying yes, a question of this type could easily lead to a dialogue that includes many speculations and further questions. For example, if you respond, "Yes, my father tends to be more passive than my mother," I might ask, "What do you mean by 'more passive'?" and so on.

The process of scientific inquiry is really a dialogue in which questions are proposed, observations are made, tentative answers are provided, additional questions are proposed, additional observations are made, and so on. It is important to point out that the order of these steps is not fixed: Sometimes the process begins with a question; sometimes it begins with an observation, which then leads to a question; sometimes it even begins with a tentative answer, which is then challenged by others who have questions. The main point here is that the process is dynamic and unending.

MAIN POINT SUMMARY

There are no final answers in the scientific process. If you believe you have the final answer to a question, you are no longer acting as a scientist.

WHAT IS A THEORY?

In everyday conversations we often use the word *theory* to refer to a guess or a hunch. In this book, we will be using a more specific definition: A **theory** is a tentative explanation for why or how some behavior or event has occurred. A theory is typically stated with the expectation that it will be challenged, and therefore it needs to be supported by evidence.

The tentative nature of theories cannot be emphasized enough. If an explanation is stated as final and absolute, it is no longer a theory, and no longer the subject of scientific inquiry. Although it is customary to refer to explanations that seem to be final and absolute as *laws*, there are no laws in science, strictly speaking. Even the so-called law of gravity has been challenged. Some scientists believe that they have a better explanation of the behavior that Newton attempted to describe in his theory of gravity. More practically speaking, we state explanations as **laws** when they are so well accepted in the scientific community that they are generally not challenged.

The following examples are often stated as laws:

- Boyle's law explains the relationship between the volume and pressure of a confined gas.

- Newton's law explains how physical bodies are attracted to each other.

- Muller's law of specific nerve energy explains the behavior of nerve impulses.

- Thorndike's law of effect explains how behavior is learned.

The following examples are usually stated as theories:

- James-Lange theory explains the relationship between behavior and emotions.

- Festinger's theory of cognitive dissonance explains the relationship between beliefs and behavior.

- Einstein's theory of relativity explains the relationship between time and space.

- Taylor's theory X explains human motivation to work.

- Darwin's theory of evolution explains the long-range changes of animal and plant appearance and behavior.

One way to describe the difference between theories and laws is to think of laws as highly respected theories that seem to explain behaviors very well and, therefore, are generally accepted as true. Theories, on the other hand, are more controversial.

Theories are not created only by famous people known as scientists. Each time *you* explain why something happened, you are stating a theory. Typically, you don't think of your explanations as theories because you don't consider them open to challenge, or because you don't intend to challenge them yourself. For example, consider the following scenario.

> You observe a 5-year-old child fall on a sidewalk and begin to cry. While the child is still crying, someone approaches you and asks, "Why is the child crying?" You respond, "Because the child fell and hurt himself."

Is your response a theory?

T I M E ■ O U T
Take some time to reflect on this question.

Strictly speaking, your response is a theory. You don't know with absolute certainty that the child hurt himself: It may be that the child became frightened when he fell and didn't actually hurt himself at all. Yet, you probably wouldn't think of your response as a theory because you don't consider it open to challenge.

Now consider the following scenario.

> A 5-year-old child who lives near your parents' home seems to cry frequently without any apparent reason. Next time you visit, your parents, assuming that as a college student you understand basic psychology, ask you to explain the child's behavior. You respond, "The child cries a lot because he doesn't get enough attention from his parents."

Is your response a theory?

T I M E ■ O U T
Take some time to consider this question.

Your response would seem to qualify as a theory. It is certainly much more open to challenge than your response regarding the child who fell. Also, your response attempts to explain a much broader range of behaviors than one simple incident. Generally, this is another characteristic of a theory. It attempts to explain several related behaviors, not just one incident.

Students generally have a difficult time developing theories. If we assume, for the sake of argument, that this is true, one possible explanation for why students have a difficult time—I am now about to state a theory—is that they are not motivated to explain a large body of related behaviors and are typically more content to respond specifically to individual problems and questions. You might call this Maleske's theory of why students have a difficult time developing theories.

Another theory that might explain why students do not easily develop theories is Perry's theory of cognitive development.[1] On the basis of his theory, Perry might suggest that students simply haven't lived long enough: Their cognitive skills have not yet developed to the point where they can easily formulate general explanations for large bodies of related behaviors.

These theories represent two broad categories of explanations: Maleske's theory seems to be based primarily on the motivation of students, while Perry's theory seems to be based primarily on the cognitive development of students.

Which of these theories do you think provides the better explanation?

T I M E ■ O U T
Take some time to respond to this question.

Generally speaking, anytime we provide an uncertain explanation for some event or behavior, we are stating a theory.

WHAT IS A HYPOTHESIS?

In this book, I adopt the following definition: A **hypothesis** is a prediction of what will happen in some future situation.

The terms *theory* and *hypothesis* are often used indiscriminately, as if there were no difference between the two. However, for the purposes of this book, the difference is extremely important.

Recall that a theory is a tentative explanation for why some behavior or event has already occurred. By contrast, a hypothesis is a prediction of some event that has not yet occurred.

To explore this distinction, consider again the child who cries frequently. The theory offered to explain this behavior was as follows: The child cries a lot because he doesn't get enough attention from his parents. Let's refer to this as the attention theory. On the basis of the attention theory, what prediction could you make?

T I M E ■ O U T
Take some time to answer this question.

If you were able to state a prediction based upon the attention theory, you have formulated a hypothesis.

Here's my hypothesis based upon the attention theory: If the child's parents would pay more attention to him, he wouldn't cry so much. You might not agree with this hypothesis, but you must at least accept the fact that it is a hypothesis, because it makes a prediction.

Generally speaking, anytime we make a prediction, we are stating a hypothesis.

[1] Perry, W. G. Jr. *Forms of Intellectual and Ethical Development in the College Years: A Scheme.* New York: Holt, Rinehart & Winston, 1970.

MAIN POINT SUMMARY

When you are asked to state a hypothesis, you are being asked to make a prediction about something that hasn't happened yet. When you are asked to state a theory, you are being asked to explain something that has already happened.

One reason why people often fail to distinguish between a theory and a hypothesis is that explanation and prediction are so closely related; sometimes, both occur within a single breath. For the purposes of this book, however, it is important to view explanation and prediction as separate but related processes.

Regardless of what some people may tell you, the game of science is not played in a neatly arranged sequence of steps. In reality, the scientific process evolves in a dynamic and complex manner. It includes all the ingredients of any human endeavor: hard work, fun, chance, confusion, success, and failure. Nevertheless, for purposes of instruction it is helpful to idealize and simplify the process. One way to do this for our last example is as follows:

- An observation is made: A child cries a lot.

- A person (let's call her Nancy) attempts to explain the observation. In other words, she states a theory: The child cries a lot because he doesn't get enough attention from his parents.

- In order to convince herself—and the scientific community—that her theory is correct, Nancy makes a prediction that follows logically from her theory: If the parents give the child more attention, the child will not cry as much.

This sequence of events can be summarized as follows:

- Observation
- Theory
- Hypothesis

INFERENTIAL STATISTICS

At some point in the scientific process, a hypothesis must be stated. Recall that a hypothesis is a prediction about something that hasn't happened yet. As such, it is a guess, an inference.

The role of **inferential statistics** in the scientific process is to provide a formal—and widely agreed-upon—set of procedures whereby observed data can be examined to see whether or not they support a given hypothesis. The concept is simple, although the actual procedures may be complex.

SUMMARY

This brief chapter, at the midpoint of the book, provides an important perspective for what follows. We began with the argument that human curiosity is pervasive and is basic to science. We then outlined the fundamental logic of the scientific process and defined the terms *theory* and *hypothesis*. Finally, we summarized the rationale for inferential statistics.

KEY TERMS AND CONCEPTS

Hypothesis   Scientific process

Inferential statistics   Theory

Laws

EXERCISES

7.1 Summarize the main characteristics of the scientific process as described in this chapter.

7.2 Summarize the main characteristics of a theory.

7.3 Summarize the main characteristics of a hypothesis.

7.4 Summarize the main characteristics of a law.

7.5 Make a clear distinction between a theory and a hypothesis.

7.6 Make a clear distinction between a theory and a law.

7.7 Go back to the questions that you generated in Chapter 1, or generate new questions. Then generate as many related observations, theories, and hypotheses as you can. See if you can become comfortable with the difference between a theory and a hypothesis. Always ask yourself: Am I explaining something that already happened (a theory), or am I predicting something that has not yet happened (a hypothesis)?

7.8 Look back at the hypotheses that you generated for Exercise 7.7. Indicate which of your hypotheses follow logically from your theories, and which do not.

7.9 Go to the library and find three articles published in a professional journal in your area of interest. For each article, identify the main theory and the main hypothesis.

7.10 Try to generate one or two additional hypotheses that would logically follow from each of the main theories that you've identified in Exercise 7.9.

Structuring Scientific Observations

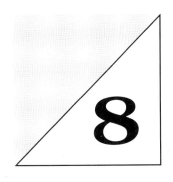

OBJECTIVES

After reading and studying Chapter 8 you should understand the following.

- *that the primary objective of scientific research is to develop the best possible explanation for why behaviors and events occur the way they do.*

- *the difference between independent and dependent variables.*

- *the difference between uncontrolled observations and controlled experiments.*

- *the difference between internal validity and external validity.*

- *the relationship between theories and hypotheses.*

- *the relationship between representativeness and random sampling.*

- *the difference between random sampling and random assignment.*

THE PRIMARY OBJECTIVE OF SCIENCE

In the previous chapter, we focused on the importance of theories and hypotheses in gathering and interpreting behavioral data. In the present chapter, we focus on strategies related specifically to the data gathering process—that is, scientific observation.

Many books provide a list of criteria for conducting scientific observations. While there is some value in considering such criteria, it seems that the primary criterion often gets left out: The primary objective in conducting scientific observations is to develop the best possible theory to explain why behaviors and events occur the way they do.

From a strictly scientific point of view, everything else is secondary. Furthermore, if this primary objective is held in focus at all times, all the other criteria will be met as a matter of course.

In all fairness to those authors who provide a more extensive list of criteria, it should be added that the phrase "best possible theory" in the above statement is somewhat vague and may be better defined by means of a list of criteria. So here's the list.

The **best possible theory**:

- is tested by hypotheses that, in turn, are supported by data gathered under the most highly controlled and repeatable conditions;

- explains the largest group of related behaviors and events in the simplest way;

- holds up against criticism by the largest group of the most critical thinkers;

- holds up under the greatest variety of circumstances;

- successfully predicts behaviors and events that occur in uncontrolled situations.

These criteria separate the scientific process from everyday speculations, which usually do not go beyond casual explanations of events after they've occurred (sometimes called **ex post facto** explanations).

Doing science represents a certain attitude about gathering and interpreting any information. The **scientific attitude** values the criteria in the preceding list. However, it is neither necessary nor appropriate for you to have a scientific attitude in every aspect of your life. Nor is it necessary to be trying to solve major or historically significant problems in order to be deemed scientific. You can be scientific in your approach to any question or problem, no matter how large or small. Scientists make a career out of pursuing problems from a scientific perspective, but anyone can be scientific in their day-to-day problem-solving activities.

UNCONTROLLED OBSERVATIONS VERSUS CONTROLLED EXPERIMENTS

According to the criteria cited in the previous section, the best possible theory is tested by hypotheses that, in turn, are supported by data gathered under the most highly controlled and repeatable conditions. What does it mean to say "highly controlled and repeatable conditions"?

T I M E ■ O U T
Take some time to consider this question.

Conditions are controlled and repeatable to the degree that all of the changeable characteristics of the situation are under the complete control of the person who is gathering the data. Consider the following scenario:

John wonders whether or not the temperature of a room might have an effect on how well a person is able to pay attention to a lecture. If John wanted to pursue an answer to this question scientifically and experimentally, he would want to measure attentiveness under conditions in which as many characteristics of the situation as possible are under his control. Such characteristics would include: the size of the room, humidity of the room, air temperature, type of lecture, person giving the lecture, time of day, number of students present, time of the year, interest value of the topic, color of the room, and so on.

In order to conduct a perfect experiment, everything about the situation would have to be controlled and kept the same while John measured attentiveness under at least two different conditions of room temperature. Attentiveness is the behavior of interest to John, and room temperature is the variable that John is predicting will affect attentiveness. Formally, the behavior of interest to the investigator is referred to as the dependent variable, and the variable that might affect the behavior of interest is the independent variable.

An **independent variable** is a variable that the researcher intends to manipulate—while holding all other factors constant—in order to determine whether or not it has an effect on the dependent variable. The **dependent variable** is the variable that, the researcher predicts, will be affected by the independent variable.

In John's experiment, what is the independent variable, and what is the dependent variable?

T I M E ■ O U T
Take some time to answer this question.

Attentiveness is the dependent variable and room temperature is the independent variable. Notice that the room temperature is the only one of these two variables that John can actually control directly.

Suppose that John is looking at two different room temperatures, 60°F and 70°F, to see if there will be a difference in the students' attentiveness. Logically, to find out if room temperature might have an effect on attentiveness, John must keep all the other experimental conditions exactly the same. It would not be a fair comparison, for example, if John measured one group in a 60° room at 7:00 A.M. and another group in a 70° room at 10:00 A.M. Why not?

T I M E ■ O U T
Take some time to respond to this question.

The problem with measuring one group in a 60° room at 7:00 A.M. and another group in a 70° room at 10:00 A.M. is that the conditions are not well controlled. Not only is the independent variable—temperature—different in the two conditions as it should be, but the time of day is also different. If John did observe that students paid better attention in the 70° room, he would not know if it was the room temperature or the time of day that made the difference.

When some variable other than the independent variable is allowed to vary systematically from one experimental condition to another, we say that the experiment is **confounded**. In the present example, we would say that time of day is the confounding variable. When an experiment is not confounded—that is, when we are certain that any possible changes in the dependent variable could only be the result of the independent variable—we say that the experiment is internally valid. **Internal validity** means that an experiment is well controlled and only the independent variable is systematically varying. A **confound** is any variable that varies systematically along with the independent variable and therefore makes it impossible to know whether any systematic changes in the dependent variable are due to the confound, the independent variable, or a combination of both.

Certainly it would be impossible to control every aspect of the situation. But the more control we have, the closer we are to having a perfect experiment. The **perfect experiment** is a hypothetical extreme case in which every conceivable variable, except for the independent variable, is held constant under all experimental conditions.

What disadvantages do you see in having a perfect experiment?

T I M E ■ O U T
Take some time to reflect on this question.

With a perfect experiment we would know for sure whether or not the independent variable was having an effect on the dependent variable. Under such conditions, we could say that the independent variable caused any observed change. Clear **causal relationships** between independent and dependent variables may only be identified if the experiment is properly controlled. However, we might wonder whether the same thing would happen in a more natural, uncontrolled setting. We face this dilemma whenever we try to answer a question by gathering information: Unless we have done a perfect experiment, we cannot be certain which variables are having an effect on the behavior of interest. On the other hand, if we have done a perfect experiment, we wonder whether or not the same behavior would be observed under more natural conditions.

Having considered the extreme case of total control, let's now consider the opposite extreme, in which there is absolutely no control over any of the variables in the situation. Consider, for example, the following scenario:

> John wonders whether or not the temperature of a room might have an effect on how well a person is able to pay attention to a lecture. If John wanted to pursue an answer to this question under natural conditions, he would want to observe the students' attentiveness under different conditions of room temperature; but he would have to avoid interfering or introducing anything artificial into the situation.

Notice how this scenario differs from the previous example. In the **experimental approach**, the goal is to control all the variables in the situation. In

natural conditions, the concern is to avoid interfering with the conditions in which the behavior normally occurs.

What disadvantages do you see in the latter approach?

T I M E ■ O U T
Take some time to examine this question.

You should be able to appreciate the advantages and disadvantages of each extreme. In reality, neither is possible, although it may seem possible to come closer to a totally **uncontrolled observation** than to a perfectly controlled experiment. However, strictly speaking, it is not possible to observe anything without somehow interfering with it.

We already know that internal validity is a measure of how perfect an experiment is. **External validity** is a measure of how certain we are that a relationship observed in a controlled experiment will also be valid outside of the conditions of that experiment. **External validity** expresses the degree to which the relationship between the independent variable and the dependent variable that is established in a particular experiment will be observed under other conditions.

There is often a misunderstanding about what external validity means. Consider the following scenario:

> John conducts a well-controlled experiment in which he finds that students pay significantly greater attention when the room is at 70°F than when the room is at 60°F. Assume, for the sake of argument, that John's experiment is internally valid. Now someone raises the question of external validity: Would we observe the same relationship between room temperature and attention in other situations?

To answer this question, John could conduct other experiments. For example, if his original experiment took place in a college classroom, he might conduct another experiment in a high school classroom. If he got the same results, we would say that the relationship between the independent variable and the dependent variable has some degree of external validity.

As with internal validity, external validity is a matter of degree. The degree of external validity increases with the number of different situations in which the same relationship between the independent variable and dependent variable is observed.

If the relationship between two variables has a high degree of external validity, we can say that the hypothesis that led to the original experiment is relatively comprehensive.

What was the hypothesis that led to John's original experiment?

T I M E ■ O U T
Take some time to respond to this question.

Actually, John's hypothesis was never stated explicitly. By implication, however, John predicted that the students' attentiveness would be different under the different temperature conditions. Such a general prediction is not the same, however, as either one of the following more specific predictions:

- The students' attentiveness will be greater in the 70° room than in the 60° room.

- The students' attentiveness will be greater in the 60° room than in the 70° room.

Notice that these two hypotheses (predictions) are exactly the opposite of each other; yet, both of them are consistent with the following more general hypothesis:

- The students' attentiveness will be different in the 70° room than in the 60° room.

Each of the two specific hypotheses is said to be **directional**; the general hypothesis is said to be **nondirectional**.

The foregoing illustrates an important point: We need not have a specific hypothesis in order to conduct an experiment. However, the more specific our hypothesis, the more impressive our prediction is if the experimental results support it. To illustrate this point, consider the following scenario:

> Mary predicts that the next card randomly drawn from a deck of cards will have a value somewhere between deuce and king. Someone draws a card, and it turns out to be a four. Mary's prediction was correct.

Are you impressed with Mary's prediction?

T I M E ■ O U T
Take some time to consider this question.

I doubt that you are impressed with Mary's prediction. Her prediction is so general that any one of 48 cards (any card other than the four aces) in the deck could have been drawn and her prediction would have been correct.

Now consider this scenario:

> Mary predicts that the next card randomly drawn from a deck of cards will be the eight of diamonds. Someone draws a card, and it turns out to be the eight of diamonds. Mary's prediction was correct.

Are you impressed with Mary's prediction?

T I M E ■ O U T
Take some time to answer this question.

You probably would be impressed with Mary's prediction. Of course, this assumes that the card was drawn randomly and there was no trickery or dishonesty on Mary's part.

MAIN POINT SUMMARY

The more specific the hypothesis that we state before gathering the data, the riskier our prediction and, therefore, the more impressive our hypothesis is if it turns out to be correct.

THE RELATIONSHIP BETWEEN THEORY AND HYPOTHESIS

Suppose, for the sake of discussion, that John's hypothesis before he gathered the data in his experiment was as follows: The students' attentiveness will be greater in the 70° room than in the 60° room. Recall that the experimental results support this hypothesis. At this level, we should be somewhat impressed with John's ability to predict. But did John have a logical basis for stating his hypothesis, or did he simply make a lucky guess?

For the moment, try putting yourself in John's shoes at the time he made his prediction. Can you imagine what reason you might have for formulating this hypothesis?

T I M E ■ O U T
Take some time to examine this question.

There are many possible reasons why you might make such a prediction. For example, you might believe that it is harder to pay attention to a lecture when you are uncomfortable than when you are comfortable. Such a belief provides a **theoretical basis** for the hypothesis. In other words, it provides some basis for an explanation of the relationship between the dependent variable and the independent variable.

Notice, however, that the hypothesis makes a statement regarding room temperature, while the theoretical basis has to do with comfort. Thus, the transition from a statement regarding comfort to a statement regarding room temperature represents a transition from a theory to a hypothesis. More specifically, we could say that the comfort theory of attention logically leads to the hypothesis regarding room temperature.

If there is a logical connection between the hypothesis and the theory that precedes it, any support for the hypothesis will also support the theory. In the present situation, for example, isn't it logical to say that the results of the experiment support the hypothesis and, therefore, support the theory?

Once the experiment is conducted, however, anyone is free to state their own explanation (theory) of the results. Can you provide an explanation other than the comfort theory to explain why the students pay more attention in the 70° room?

T I M E ■ O U T
Take some time to respond to this question.

Another possible explanation would be that the students pay more attention in a 70° room because the higher ambient temperature increases their skin temperature, which, in turn, increases neural activity. Let's call this the skin temperature theory of attention. We now have two theories, the comfort theory and the skin temperature theory, to explain the results of the room temperature experiment. Which theory is better?

T I M E ■ O U T
Take some time to consider this question.

You may have a personal preference for one of these two theories but, as far as the scientific community is concerned, the better theory is the one that meets more of the criteria for the best possible theory (p. 147).

To decide which of these two theories is better, we must examine the predictions that they make. Can we state a hypothesis that is true if the comfort theory is correct, but not true if the skin temperature theory is correct? One such hypothesis is as follows: The students' attentiveness will be greater in an 80° room than in a 70° room. Which theory is this hypothesis based upon?

T I M E ■ O U T
Take some time to reflect on this question.

The skin temperature theory seems to predict that within reasonable limits, higher skin temperature will be associated with greater neural activity, and therefore the students will be able to pay more attention. The comfort theory, however, seems to predict the opposite—that the 80° room temperature will be less comfortable, and therefore the students will pay less attention.

If the experiment were actually conducted with one room at 80°F and one room at 70°F, what would be your hypothesis?

T I M E ■ O U T
Take some time to respond to this question.

What theory would you use as the basis for your prediction?

T I M E ■ O U T
Take some time to answer this question.

From a scientific perspective, it is always beneficial to state hypotheses that will differentiate among existing theories. In this manner it is possible to eliminate theories that are not correct and gradually focus in on those that are correct.

REPRESENTATIVENESS AND RANDOM SAMPLING

For the sake of argument, suppose that the second experiment was conducted and it was found that the students in the 70° room were able to pay more attention than the students in the 80° room. Together with the assumption that the results of the first experiment also showed greater attention at the more comfortable temperature (70° versus 60°), this would seem to support the comfort theory. However, there might also be some other theory that explains the results of both experiments. Can you think of one?

The comfort theory has now been supported by two separate experiments, but many questions remain. In particular, would the results of the experiment be the same if different students were used? Can we say, for example, that the relationship between room temperature and attention in the two experiments would also be observed for all the students at the school?

T I M E ■ O U T
Take some time to consider this question.

The ability to generalize from the students who participated in the experiment to all the students in that school — or all the students in the world, for that matter — is a particular case of external validity, known as **representativeness**. You may recall that this topic was introduced in Chapter 1 when discussing samples and populations. The general question regarding representativeness is as follows: Do the subjects in the experiment represent a larger population so well that the results of the experiment would be the same if any subjects in the population were used?

One strategy for obtaining a representative sample of a population is to select subjects randomly. However, there is no guarantee that a random sample will represent the population. This important point is often misunderstood.

Consider a population that contains 80% females and 20% males. If we randomly select a sample of 15 subjects, we might find that all 15 are males, in which case the sample would not represent the gender distribution in the population.

This problem may be avoided by means of **stratified random sampling**. In this example, a stratified random sampling approach would involve randomly selecting 12 females (80% of 15) and 3 males (20% of 15) from the population. When taking a stratified random sample, you first identify certain important characteristics, and you determine what percentage of the population possesses each of these characteristics. Then you randomly select the appropriate number of subjects so that the proportions of subjects having these characteristics will be the same in the population and in the sample.

There are no magic rules for guaranteeing a sample that represents the population. Each situation is different, and depends upon which factors we are considering: age, gender, education level, and so on. The best general guide regarding representativeness is to always anticipate the kinds of criticisms that might be made after the experiment is over regarding your ability to generalize from the subjects you have used to some larger population. Do whatever you can to anticipate and avoid such criticisms when devising your sampling procedure.

What does it mean to say that representativeness is a special case of external validity?

T I M E ■ O U T
Take some time to examine this question.

RANDOM SAMPLING VERSUS RANDOM ASSIGNMENT

Random sampling and random assignment are often confused. **Random sampling** refers to the technique whereby subjects are randomly selected from some larger population. The primary purpose is to represent the population so that the results of the experiment can be generalized to the larger population; random sampling is a strategy to improve external validity. **Random assignment**, on the other hand, refers to the technique whereby subjects are randomly assigned to different experimental conditions. The primary purpose is to avoid confounds; random assignment is a strategy to improve internal validity.

Consider the following scenario:

In John's experiment regarding room temperature he randomly selected 40 students from his college to attend a lecture titled "Things You Should Know about AIDS" at 10:00 A.M. on a Saturday morning (random selection). He then randomly assigned 20 of these students to the 70° group by means of a table of random numbers. The remaining 20 were assigned to the 60° group (random assignment).

What problems are avoided by the use of random assignment?

TIME ■ OUT
Take some time to reflect on this question.

Generally speaking, the use of random assignment is designed to avoid possible confounds. For example, in John's experiment, we wouldn't want to allow students to sign up for the different groups on the basis of their own preference. It is possible that certain types of students might sign up for one group and other types might tend to sign up for the other group. Random assignment reduces the possibility that the students in one group will somehow be systematically different from the students in the other group. For example, in John's experiment you wouldn't want highly motivated students to be concentrated in one group.

SUMMARY

A primary objective of scientific research is to develop the best possible explanation for why behaviors and events occur the way they do. Such explanations are referred to as theories.

In order to test a theory, we are confronted with the dilemma of whether to control all the variables, except the independent variable, in an artificial experimental setting, or to observe the variables in a more natural setting.

Regardless of whether we choose a controlled experiment or an uncontrolled observation, we test the theory by establishing a hypothesis that follows logically from it.

Scientists seek theories that explain as much as possible. Therefore, when conducting scientific research, it is desirable to randomly select samples of people or events that represent larger populations. If a sample represents the larger population and the results of the research support the hypothesis and theory, then the hypothesis and theory can be generalized to the population of which the sample is part. Such a generalization is a special case of external validity.

Finally, it is important to distinguish between the random sampling, which is a strategy to ensure external validity, and random assignment, which is a strategy to ensure internal validity.

KEY TERMS AND CONCEPTS

Best possible theory

Causal relationship

Confound

Confounded

Dependent variable

Directional hypothesis

Experimental approach

Ex post facto

External validity

Independent variable

Internal validity

Natural conditions

Nondirectional hypothesis

Perfect experiment

Random assignment

Random sampling

Representativeness

Scientific attitude

Stratified random sampling

Theoretical basis

Uncontrolled observation

EXERCISES

8.1 State a hypothesis based upon a question of interest to you.

8.2 Describe an uncontrolled observation that you could conduct in order to test the hypothesis from Exercise 8.1.

8.3 Describe a controlled experiment that you could conduct in order to test the hypothesis from Exercise 8.1.

8.4 Evaluate the following scenarios in terms of their internal validity.

Scenario A: A researcher believes that outside temperature has an effect on a person's mood. In order to test this implied hypothesis, the researcher randomly selects 10 major cities. For each city, she records the average daily temperature on the first 20 days in January. Her research team also conducts interviews for 100 people randomly selected from each major city. After each interview, the person is given an overall mood rating, which ranges from extremely pessimistic to extremely optimistic.

Scenario B: A researcher believes that indoor relative humidity during cold weather has an effect on a person's mood. She explicitly predicts that the average mood reported by subjects when the relative humidity is kept at the level recommended by a certain humidifier manufacturer will be better than the mood reported by subjects experiencing a relative humidity 10% lower than the recommended level. The researcher randomly selects 50 subjects from all the nursing homes in a large city. From this sample, 25 subjects are randomly assigned to each of two groups. For both groups, the inside temperature is set at 70°F. On the same day, at an outside temperature of 5°F, one group is subjected to a constant relative humidity of 20% (the recommended level); for the other group, the relative humidity is maintained at 10%. Each subject is interviewed and given an overall mood rating, which ranges from extremely pessimistic to extremely optimistic.

8.5 Evaluate the above scenarios in terms of their external validity.

8.6 Identify each of the following as either a theory or a hypothesis.
   a. A researcher predicts that a person will perform better on a test if they study for the test under conditions that are the same as the conditions in which the test is given.
   b. A researcher believes that the number of murders in the United States is higher than the number of murders in Canada because there is more overcrowding in the United States.
   c. A researcher states that, when people are forced to stay in their homes during extremely cold weather, there will be more reports of child abuse.
   d. A researcher states that the increasing divorce rate is due to poor economic conditions.

8.7 Does random selection guarantee representativeness? Explain.

8.8 Describe the different purposes of random assignment and random selection.

8.9 Describe the differences between uncontrolled observations and controlled experiments. Try to use the following terms in your description: independent variable, dependent variable, internal validity, external validity.

8.10 Summarize the criteria for the best possible theory.

Making Decisions about Scientific Theories

9

After reading and studying Chapter 9 you should understand the following.

- *how null hypotheses are stated for the sake of argument.*

- *how alternative hypotheses are stated as predictions that the researcher hopes to support.*

- *how to operationally define hypotheses.*

- *how the rules of probability may be used to establish models of what to expect.*

- *when and how to use the additive rule of probability.*

- *when and how to use the multiplicative rule of probability.*

- *some general strategies for solving probability problems.*

- *the difference between replacement and nonreplacement assumptions in probability problems.*

STATING NULL HYPOTHESES

Now that you have some understanding of theories, hypotheses, and statistical inference, it's time to make the connection between statistical inference and hypothesis testing. As we do this, keep in mind that the logic of the process is far more important than the mathematical formulas that are used to serve the logic. Let's begin by considering null hypotheses.

The word "null" derives from the Latin word "nullus," which means "none." A **null hypothesis** predicts that there is no relationship between or among the variables in question. If we are conducting a controlled experiment, the null hypothesis states that the independent variable has no effect on the dependent variable. If we are conducting an uncontrolled observation, the null hypothesis states that the variables are not correlated.

When conducting research, we typically expect that there will be a relationship between or among the variables in question. However, the game of inferential statistics requires that, for the sake of argument, we assume no relationship. This assumption puts the burden of the proof on us, as researchers, to gather enough evidence to show that the null hypothesis is not correct — in other words, to show that there *is* a relationship. The logic here is extremely important, so let's go through it slowly, beginning with a more familiar reasoning process, the legal system, as an analogy. This analogy is laid out in Table 9.1.

The legal system in the United States makes use of a reasoning strategy very similar to that used in the application of statistics to scientific experimentation. The null hypothesis adopted in the legal system may be stated in general terms as follows: A person accused of breaking the law is presumed innocent until it is proven, beyond a reasonable doubt, that he or she is guilty. What is null about this hypothesis?

T I M E ■ O U T
Take some time to respond to this question.

TABLE 9.1   A Comparison of Legal Reasoning and Statistical Reasoning

Statistical Reasoning	Legal Reasoning
Assume that the null hypothesis is true until the evidence is sufficient ($p < .05$) to say that it is not true.	Assume that the person is innocent until the evidence is sufficient (beyond a reasonable doubt) to say that he or she is not innocent.
If the evidence is not sufficient, then statistically we do not say that the null hypothesis is true. Instead, we simply say that we cannot reject the null hypothesis; that is, we are unable to say that it is false.	If the evidence is not sufficient, then the jury doesn't say that the person is innocent. Instead, the jury says that the defendant is not guilty; that is, the jury is unable to say that the person is guilty.
Under these circumstances, we don't necessarily believe that the null hypothesis is true; it's just that the evidence is not convincing enough for us to say that it is false.	Under these circumstances, the jury doesn't necessarily believe that the defendant is innocent; it's just that the evidence is not convincing enough for them to say that the person is guilty.
When in doubt, assume that the null hypothesis is not false. (This is not the same as promoting the idea that the null hypothesis is true.)	When in doubt, assume that the defendant is not guilty. (This is not the same as promoting the idea that the person is innocent.)
Philosophically, the scientific and statistical system is based on the principle that it is better to let many false null hypotheses go unrejected than to reject one that isn't true.	Philosophically, our legal system is based on the principle that it is better to let many guilty people go free than to convict one innocent person.
We value truth regarding scientific predictions so much that we are unwilling to have incorrect predictions published.	We value individual freedom so much that we are unwilling to have innocent people put in jail.

By adopting the hypothesis that the person is without guilt and did not perform the illegal act, our legal system places the burden of proof on the prosecution, which must gather enough evidence to demonstrate, beyond a reasonable doubt, that the null hypothesis—the presumption of innocence—is not correct.

Some legal systems in other countries start with the assumption that the accused person is guilty. The burden is then on the defense to gather enough evidence to reject this assumption.

What is the reasoning behind the presumption of innocence?

TIME ■ OUT
Take some time to consider this question.

The legal system in the United States is founded on the belief that we would rather let 100 guilty persons go free than convict one innocent person. Of course, there is a price to pay for this reasoning; that is, we risk the high probability of letting guilty people go free.

Getting back to inferential statistics, recall John's experiment (Chapter 8), in which he measured the attentiveness of students at two different room temperatures (70° and 60°F). What would the null hypothesis be for that experiment?

TIME ■ OUT
Take some time to reflect on this question.

If we are to test the accuracy of John's hypothesis by means of statistical inference, we start by stating the following null hypothesis: Room temperature will have no effect on the attentiveness of the students. In other words, the students' attentiveness in the 70° room will be the same as the students' attentiveness in the 60° room.

Of course, this is the opposite of what John is predicting, just as the presumption of innocence is the opposite of what the prosecution is hoping to demonstrate. The burden is on John to gather data that will show, beyond a reasonable doubt, that the null hypothesis is not correct.

In a nutshell, this is the basic reasoning of many inferential statistical analyses; that is, the analyses are designed to indicate whether or not the data show, beyond a reasonable doubt, that the null hypothesis is incorrect.

The actual procedures whereby this logic is carried out will be discussed in Chapters 12 and 13. For now, it is more important to understand the logic underlying these mathematical procedures.

STATING ALTERNATIVE HYPOTHESES

The **alternative hypothesis** is the hypothesis that is true if the null hypothesis is false.

Consider the analogy with the legal system again. If enough evidence is gathered to demonstrate that the null hypothesis of innocence is not correct, the person is pronounced guilty. Guilt is the alternative hypothesis.

Can you state what the alternative hypothesis would be for John's experiment in the 60° and 70° rooms?

T I M E ■ O U T
Take some time to answer this question.

The alternative hypothesis for John's experiment could be stated as follows: Room temperature will have an effect on the students' attentiveness. This hypothesis is very general. Recall from Chapter 8 that two more specific statements would be consistent with this alternative hypothesis:

1. The students' attentiveness in the 70° room will be higher than the students' attentiveness in the 60° room.

2. The students' attentiveness in the 70° room will be lower than the students' attentiveness in the 60° room.

Even though these hypotheses are contradictory, each one is a valid alternative to the null hypothesis that room temperature will have no effect.

Which alternative is more appropriate for John's experiment?

T I M E ■ O U T
Take some time to examine this question.

The most appropriate alternative hypothesis is the one that follows logically from the theory that we wish to support. If you support the comfort theory of attention (Chapter 8), you will probably choose alternative hypothesis 1 as the most appropriate. Even if you support the skin temperature theory (Chapter 8), you will still probably choose alternative hypothesis 1.

Can you explain why the same alternative hypothesis is appropriate for both theories?

T I M E ■ O U T
Take some time to respond to this question.

Now consider John's second experiment, in which he measured the attentiveness of students at 70° and at 80°F. Which alternative hypothesis would be appropriate for the comfort theory? Which would be appropriate for the skin temperature theory?

T I M E ■ O U T
Take some time to consider these questions.

Again, there are two possible alternative hypothesis:

1. The students' attentiveness in the 80° room will be higher than the students' attentiveness in the 70° room.

2. The students' attentiveness in the 80° room will be lower than the students' attentiveness in the 70° room.

Alternative hypothesis 2 would be the more appropriate for the comfort theory. However, alternative hypothesis 1 would be the more appropriate for the skin temperature theory.

Do you understand why each theory would logically lead to a different alternative hypothesis?

T I M E ■ O U T
Take some time to answer this question.

ASIDE ■ When conducting controlled experiments, the researcher should not predict that there will be no effect due to the independent variable, because it is less convincing to accept a null hypothesis than it is to reject it. Consider, for example, a poorly conducted experiment that allows many uncontrolled factors to affect the dependent variable. Under such conditions, because of the uncontrolled variation, the researcher may fail to see a difference between the experimental conditions and, therefore, fail to reject the null hypothesis. If the researcher was predicting no effect, failure to reject the null would mean support for the researcher's hypothesis. However, we would not want to accept a research hypothesis on the basis of such poor control.

DEFINING HYPOTHESES OPERATIONALLY

Recall our discussion of operational definitions in Chapter 2. In order to carry out an experiment and determine which hypothesis—null or alternative—has more support, it is important to operationally define the variables and the experimental conditions.

In the example we have been using, John's experiment on student attentiveness, the independent variable has been defined operationally as the room temperature, in degrees Fahrenheit. However, the dependent variable, attentiveness, has not been defined operationally. Attentiveness cannot be analyzed statistically unless it is defined operationally.

One way to do so is to measure attentiveness by giving a multiple-choice test on the topics covered in the lecture. We would expect that more attentive students would score higher on the multiple-choice test.

Now that we have defined both the independent and dependent variables for John's first experiment, we can state the null hypothesis and alternative hypothesis operationally as follows:

- *Null hypothesis:* The average score on the multiple-choice test will be the same for the 70° group and the 60° group.

- *Alternative hypothesis:* The average score on the multiple-choice test will be significantly higher for the 70° group than for the 60° group.

We can also state these hypotheses using symbols that you should now be familiar with

Null hypothesis: $\mu_{70} = \mu_{60}$

Alternative hypothesis: $\mu_{70} > \mu_{60}$

Notice the following about the symbolic statements of the null and alternative hypotheses:

- The symbols represent population means, because we intend to make an inference about the populations from which the samples were drawn.

- Subscripts are used to denote the corresponding populations.

The symbolic statements of the null and alternative hypotheses are concise and unambiguous; there is very little doubt about what we are predicting. The null hypothesis, stated for the sake of argument, predicts that the average scores on the test will be the same for both groups. The alternative hypothesis, which John hopes to support by rejecting the null hypothesis, states that the average score for the 70° group will be greater than the average score for the 60° group. If the alternative hypothesis is supported, then John's prediction that the 70° group would be more attentive would also be supported. Furthermore, either the comfort theory or the skin temperature theory would be supported.

COMPARING TEST RESULTS WITH PROBABILISTIC MODELS

Recall our discussion of models in Chapter 6. From this discussion you should have learned that a model provides a guess or an estimate of what we expect a population of measurements to look like. If we use a normal curve model, we are saying that we expect the distribution of our measurements in the population to look like a normal curve and conform to all the characteristics of that curve. We also saw that we can use the normal curve as a way of making probability statements about our population—for example, to state that the probability is .50 that a measure randomly selected from the population will be greater than the average. In other words, we expect 50% of all the measurements in the population to be greater than the average.

The normal curve distribution is only one of several possible models that can be used to set expectations about populations; the binomial distribution is another. Before we get into the details of the normal and binomial models (Chapter 10), it will be helpful to understand some basics about the rules of probability.

USING THE ADDITIVE RULE OF PROBABILITY

If you toss a single unbiased coin, what is the probability that it will land either as a head or as a tail?

T I M E ■ O U T
Take some time to answer this question.

You are correct if you said that the probability is 1.00. There is a 100% chance (a probability of 1.00) that an unbiased coin will land either as a head or as a tail; one of these two outcomes is bound to occur. (In principle, the coin could land on its edge; for purposes of our discussion we will not regard this as a realistic possibility.)

In solving this problem, most people will reason to an answer using common logic and their understanding of coins. Another approach is to apply the additive rule of probability: The probability of either a head or a tail is equal to the probability of a head plus the probability of a tail. Symbolically

$$P(\text{H or T}) = P(\text{H}) + P(\text{T})$$

The solution may then be stated as follows

$$P(\text{H}) + P(\text{T}) = .5 + .5 = 1.00$$

It is useful to remember this simple example of the additive rule.

More generally, the **additive rule of probability** states that the probability that any one of two or more possible events will occur is equal to the sum of the individual probabilities of the separate events.

USING THE MULTIPLICATIVE RULE OF PROBABILITY

If you toss a single unbiased coin twice, what is the probability that it will land first as a head and then as a tail?

T I M E ■ O U T
Take some time to consider this question.

TABLE 9.2	Possible Outcomes in Two Successive Tosses of an Unbiased Coin	
	Outcome for Toss 1	Outcome for Toss 2
Series 1	head	head
Series 2	head	tail
Series 3	tail	tail
Series 4	tail	head

You are correct if you said that the probability is .25: There is a 25% chance (a probability of .25) that the coin will land as a head on the first toss and as a tail on the second toss.

This problem is not quite as easy to solve with common logic. However, people will frequently use the following strategy. If you toss a coin twice, there are four possible outcomes for the two-toss series, as in Table 9.2. There are no other possibilities. Of these four possible series, one (series 2) is represented by a head on toss 1 and a tail on toss 2. Thus, the probability of a head followed by a tail is 1 out of 4 or $1/4 = .25$.

Another approach is to apply the multiplicative rule of probability: The probability of tossing a head and then a tail is equal to the probability of tossing a head multiplied by the probability of tossing a tail. Symbolically

$$P(H, T) = P(H) \times P(T)$$

The solution is then stated as follows

$$P(H) \times P(T) = .5 \times .5 = .25$$

It is useful to remember this simple example of the multiplicative rule.

More generally, the **multiplicative rule of probability** states that the probability that each and every one of two or more independent events will occur is equal to the product of the individual probabilities.

GENERAL STRATEGIES FOR SOLVING PROBABILITY PROBLEMS

Most probability problems can be solved by applying the additive rule, the multiplicative rule, or a combination of the two. The real challenge in solving probability problems is to define the problem clearly and in such a way that it can be broken down into its additive and/or multiplicative components. Consider the following problem: If you toss a coin twice, what is the probability that it will land the same way on each toss?

T I M E ■ O U T
Take some time to answer this question.

The first step in solving this problem is to reword it so as to be more specific. For example, if you toss a coin twice, what is the probability that it will either land as a head twice in a row or that it will land as a tail twice in a row?

The next step is to convert the words into symbols

$$P[(H, H) \text{ or } (T, T)] = ?$$

Once we state the problem symbolically, we can see that both the additive rule and the multiplicative rule are involved. Breaking the problem into three components, we have the following

$$P(H, H) = P(H) \times P(H) = .5 \times .5 = .25 \text{ [multiplicative rule]}$$

$$P(T, T) = P(T) \times P(T) = .5 \times .5 = .25 \text{ [multiplicative rule]}$$

$$P[(H, H) \text{ or } (T, T)] = P(H, H) \text{ or } P(T, T) = P(H, H) + P(T, T) = .25 + .25 = .50$$
$$\text{[additive rule]}$$

This may seem like an unnecessarily long process to arrive at an answer that is obvious. But think again; the answer is not as obvious as it may seem. Although the answer of .50 seems familiar and correct because we are working with a coin tossing problem, it is actually the result of all the following operations

$$(.5 \times .5) + (.5 \times .5) = .25 + .25 = .5$$

and not the result of the simple operation $1/2 = .5$.

ASIDE ■ **Again, this logic is not the same as**

$1/2 = .5$**. Rather,** $1/4 + 1/4 = 2/4 = 1/2$**.**

Another way to demonstrate the logic involved in solving this problem is as follows. Consider again the four possible series of outcomes in Table 9.2. The problem asks for the probability that a coin will land the same way on each toss. Two of the series in Table 9.2 meet this description: (head, head) and (tail, tail). Thus, the probability of such an outcome is $2/4 = .50$.

Do you understand how the multiplicative and additive rules are being applied to this problem?

T I M E ■ O U T
Take some time to respond to this question.

Consider one more problem of this type: If you toss a pair of dice, what is the probability that the total score of the two dice will be 4?

T I M E ■ O U T
Take some time to answer this question.

The correct answer is .0833

$$eP(2, 2) \text{ or } P(3, 1) \text{ or } P(1, 3) = (\tfrac{1}{6} \times \tfrac{1}{6}) + (\tfrac{1}{6} \times \tfrac{1}{6}) + (\tfrac{1}{6} \times \tfrac{1}{6}) = (\tfrac{1}{36}) + (\tfrac{1}{36}) + (\tfrac{1}{36})$$

$$= \tfrac{3}{36} = \tfrac{1}{12} = .0833$$

Of the unlimited number of probability problems that could be generated, almost all could be solved using the following general strategy:

- Take the time to understand exactly what the problem is asking.

- Break the problem down into smaller pieces.

- State the problem symbolically so that the additive and/or multiplicative components can be identified.

- Carry out the mathematical calculations required by the additive and/or multiplicative components.

REPLACEMENT OR NONREPLACEMENT?

Consider the following problem: What is the probability of drawing two aces in a row from a well-shuffled deck of 52 cards?

T I M E ■ O U T
Take some time to reflect on this question.

There are actually two different correct answers to this question.

1. $P(A, A) = \frac{4}{52} \times \frac{4}{52} = \frac{1}{13} \times \frac{1}{13} = \frac{1}{169} = .0059$

2. $P(A, A) = \frac{4}{52} \times \frac{3}{51} = \frac{1}{13} \times \frac{1}{17} = .0045$

The first answer assumes that, if the first card is an ace, it will be replaced into the deck; the probability of drawing another ace will remain 4/52.

The second answer assumes that, if the first card is an ace, it will be kept out of the deck, so that the probability of drawing another ace will now be 3/51.

The wording of the original question is not specific enough to know which of these two answers is more correct. If you are ever faced with a problem that is not worded specifically, one good strategy is to include your interpretation of the problem in your answer. For example, you might say, "Assuming replacement, the correct answer is .0059"; or, "Assuming no replacement, the correct answer is .0045."

With respect to probability problems, **replacement** refers to the process whereby a given selected item is returned to the larger pool of items after it is selected. **Nonreplacement** refers to those situations in which the selected item is not returned to the larger pool.

As always, the most important strategy in solving problems — whether probability problems or any other type — is to think critically and carefully about the problem itself, about the various strategies for solution, and about the correctness of your solution. Challenge your own solution by asking yourself if any alternative solutions might be better.

SUMMARY

We began by describing the logic involved in using null and alternative hypotheses to test scientific theories; we chose the more familiar logic of the U.S. legal system as an analogy.

It is important to state the null and alternative hypotheses in operational terms so that everyone will know exactly what predictions are being tested. Ultimately, if you choose to play the game of statistics, the null and alternative hypotheses must be stated using the appropriate statistical symbols, for example

Null hypothesis: $\qquad \mu_{70} = \mu_{60}$

Alternative hypothesis: $\mu_{70} > \mu_{60}$

Comparing the results of hypothesis tests with probabilistic models is a powerful technique. To build a foundation for its use, we surveyed the basic rules of probability and some general strategies for solving probability problems, and we noted the distinction between replacement and nonreplacement types of probability problems.

KEY TERMS AND CONCEPTS

Additive rule of probability

Alternative hypothesis

Multiplicative rule of probability

Nonreplacement

Null hypothesis

Replacement

EXERCISES

9.1 State a hypothesis related to a question of interest to you.

9.2 Describe a controlled experiment that you could actually carry out in order to test your hypothesis from Exercise 9.1.

9.3 State the null hypothesis for the controlled experiment that you described for Exercise 9.2 in general terms.

9.4 State the null hypothesis for the controlled experiment that you described for Exercise 9.2 in operational terms.

9.5 State the null hypothesis for the controlled experiment that you described for Exercise 9.2 using appropriate symbols.

9.6 State the alternative hypothesis for the controlled experiment that you described for Exercise 9.2 in general terms.

9.7   State the alternative hypothesis for the controlled experiment that you described for Exercise 9.2 in operational terms.

9.8   State the alternative hypothesis for the controlled experiment that you described for Exercise 9.2 using appropriate symbols.

9.9   As we saw in this chapter, there is an important connection between hypothesis testing and probability theory. In your own words, desribe this connection.

9.10 What is the probability of drawing four of a kind from a well-shuffled deck of 52 cards?

9.11 In a normal distribution having a mean of 100 and a standard deviation of 20, what is the probability of randomly selecting a measurement that is either greater than 140 or less than 60?

9.12 In a normal distribution, what is the probability of randomly selecting a measurement that is either in the upper 2.5% of the distribution or in the lower 2.5% of the distribution?

9.13 In a normal distribution, what is the probability of randomly selecting a measurement that is in the lower 5% of the distribution?

9.14 In a normal distribution, what is the probability of randomly selecting a measurement that is in the upper 5% of the distribution?

9.15 What Z value marks the upper 5% of the normal distribution?

9.16 What Z value marks the lower 5% of the normal distribution?

9.17 What Z values mark the most extreme 5% of the distribution? (Careful! This is a tricky question!)

Applying the Rules of Probability to Hypothesis Testing

OBJECTIVES

After reading and studying Chapter 10 you should understand the
following.

- *how probability rules are used to test hypotheses.*

- *how to use the binomial distribution as a model for hypothesis testing.*

- *how to use the normal distribution as a model for hypothesis testing.*

- *the difference between one-tailed and two-tailed alternative hypotheses.*

- *what it means to say that the results of a hypothesis test are statistically significant.*

- *the difference between type-I and type-II errors.*

- *statistical power.*

APPLYING PROBABILITY TO HYPOTHESIS TESTING

Keeping in mind the logic of null and alternative hypotheses and the logic of probability, consider the following scenario.

> Martha claims that she can teach people how to toss a coin so that it will land the way they want. As a researcher you are wondering whether or not her claim is valid. How could you scientifically pursue this question?

TIME ■ OUT
Take some time to examine this issue.

Here is one possible approach to determining whether Martha's claim is valid:

- ■ You first ask Martha if she is willing to have her claim tested. She says yes.

- Next you ask Martha if you can randomly select one of her students to participate in a test of her coin-tossing skill. Martha says yes.

- You randomly select one of Martha's students and ask her to toss a coin once. Before she tosses the coin, you ask her to state whether she intends to have the coin land as a head or as a tail. The student says that she intends to have the coin land as a head.

- The student then tosses the coin and you record the outcome. The coin lands as a head, and you record the following in your research notebook.

Trial	Outcome
1	Correct

From a scientific point of view, would you say that Martha's claim is valid?

TIME ■ OUT
Take some time to respond to this question.

I doubt if you were impressed with the outcome of the observation. The probability that Martha's student would be correct is .50. So, perhaps you decide to make another observation, this time with two trials, and you get the following results.

Trial	Outcome
1	Correct
2	Correct

Now what do you say about Martha's coin-tossing course?

TIME ■ OUT
Take some time to consider this question.

You might be more impressed than you were after the one-trial observation, but the performance of Martha's student could still easily have occurred by chance. In fact, using your knowledge of probability, you could calculate the probability that Martha's student was just lucky. What is that probability?

TIME ■ OUT
Take some time to answer this question.

The probability of being correct by chance on two consecutive trials is $.5 \times .5 = .25$.

Still not very impressed, you decide to make a three-trial observation, and you get the following results.

Trial	Outcome
1	Correct
2	Correct
3	Correct

Are yeou impressed now? What is the probability that Martha's student could be correct by chance on three of three consecutive trials?

T I M E ■ O U T
Take some time to respond to these questions.

The probability of being correct by chance on three of three consecutive trials is $.5 \times .5 \times .5 = .125$.

At this point some readers may be impressed and others may remain unimpressed. However, from a strictly statistical point of view, you should be unimpressed. The game of statistical inference avoids the problem of subjective and individual opinion by establishing standard criteria to determine when we should be impressed.

Before we pursue these criteria, let's look back at the observations designed to test Martha's claim. What is the null hypothesis for the first one-trial observation?

T I M E ■ O U T
Take some time to consider this question.

The null hypothesis for the first observation can be stated as follows: Martha's coin-tossing course will have no effect on a person's ability to toss a coin and have it land the way they want. Another way of stating this would be that we expect any students from Martha's course to perform no better than they would if they were guessing at chance level.

Using the logic discussed earlier, we first state the null hypothesis for the sake of argument and then collect data to see if the null hypothesis can be rejected.

Looking now at the one-trial observation, what would we expect the outcome to be if the null hypothesis were true?

T I M E ■ O U T
Take some time to answer this question.

If Martha's course had no effect — in other words, if the null hypothesis were true — we'd expect the student to perform at no better than chance level. Did she?

Take some time to respond to this question.

The student was actually successful on all of the trials. However, since there was only one trial, this doesn't tell us very much. If the probability of being correct by chance is .5, we expect a person to be successful on all of the trials in a one-trial observation about 50% of the time. Another way of saying this is that, if we ran 10 people through a one-trial observation, we'd expect about five of them to be correct on that one trial.

Regardless of how it's stated, no one is likely to be impressed if Martha's student is correct on a single trial. With only one trial we really don't have enough power to challenge the null hypothesis. Martha's student did as well as she possibly could, and we're still not impressed.

So what would it take to impress you? Two correct out of two trials? Three out of three? Four out of four? More?

As we already noted, the game of statistical inference tries to avoid individual opinion. Some readers might require three out of three; others may require six out of six.

The game of statistics generally requires that, if an event is to be regarded as *not* having occurred by chance, it must occur so rarely that if it were a chance occurrence the probability of it occurring would be **.05** or less.

This is an extremely important statement. Take as long as you need to understand it fully.

The logic of this statement is applied to the coin-tossing trials as follows:

- The probability of being correct on one trial by chance is .50. This does not meet the standard statistical criterion (.50 is greater than .05). In other words, it is too likely that this just happened by chance.

- The probability of being correct on two successive trials by chance is .25. This does not meet the standard statistical criterion (.25 is greater than .05). In other words, it is too likely that this just happened by chance.

- The probability of being correct on three successive trials by chance is .125. This does not meet the standard statistical criterion (.125 is greater than .05). Once again, it is too likely that this just happened by chance.

What about four successive trials?

- The probability of being correct on four successive trials by chance is .0625. This still does not meet the standard statistical criterion (.0625 is greater than .05). It is still too likely that this just happened by chance.

What about five successive trials?

- The probability of being correct on five successive trials by chance is .03125. At last! This does meet the standard statistical criterion (.03125 is less than .05). In other words, it is unlikely that this just happened by chance. It *could* have happened by chance, but the probability is so low that we are not willing to say (on the basis of the standard criterion) that chance is the best explanation.

What if the prediction is correct on five trials out of six?

T I M E ■ O U T
Take some time to answer this question.

Perhaps you were able to follow the logic as it progressed from a probability of .5 for a single trial to .03125 for five successive trials. However, the complexity of the problem increases considerably when we consider the question of five trials out of six. In order to calculate such probabilities, we make use of the binomial model.

USING THE BINOMIAL DISTRIBUTION AS A MODEL

Like the normal curve, the binomial distribution can be used as a model of what to expect. However, we use these two models for different situations.

We adopt the **binomial model** of what to expect if the null hypothesis is true regarding behaviors (or events) that can be classified into only two possible categories, for example: pass or fail, heads or tails, win or lose, correct or incorrect, dead or alive, yes or no, and true or false.

We use the **normal model** of what to expect if the null hypothesis is true regarding behaviors (or events) that can be measured at the ratio level. (The ratio level is ideal; in practice, we settle for the interval level. (Recall our discussion of levels of measurement in Chapter 2.) Examples of behaviors measured at the interval or ratio level include: a score on the Test Anxiety Inventory, weight, the number of correct responses on a memory test, and the amount of time taken to complete an obstacle course.

Keep in mind that the logic of hypothesis testing is identical whether the normal distribution or the binomial distribution is chosen s the model.

THE BINOMIAL FORMULA

Like the normal distribution, the binomial distribution is generated from a formula. Recall that the formula for the normal distribution is

$$Y = \frac{1}{\sqrt{2\pi\sigma}} e^{-[(X-\mu)^2/2\sigma^2]}$$

(10.1)

TABLE 10.1	Values of Y as a Function of X for the Normal Curve Formula

X	Y
−3	.004
−2	.05
−1	.24
0	.40
+1	.24
+2	.05
+3	.004

Using this formula, a curve can be generated by plotting values of Y for each value of X, given certain values for μ (the mean of the population) and σ (the standard deviation of the population). Once μ and σ are known for a given population, Y varies strictly as a function of X. For example, if $\mu = 0$ and $\sigma = 1$, then $Y = .004$ when $X = 3$.

Table 10.1 shows values of Y for a series of X values in this same population ($\mu = 0$, $\sigma = 1$). If we plot these Y values as a function of X, the resulting curve (Figure 10.1) is a partial sketch of the normal distribution (partial because it is based upon only a few of the many possible values of X).

The formula for the **binomial distribution** is

$$P = {}_NC_r p^r q^{N-r} \tag{10.2}$$

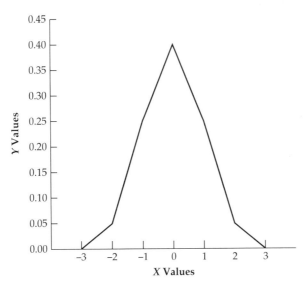

FIGURE 10.1   Partial Sketch of a Normal Distribution

where P is the probability that the combined number of outcomes of interest will occur (for example, if being correct is the outcome of interest, then P might be the probability of being correct on at least one out of two guesses); N is the number of times the binomial event will be observed and measured (for example, as in the test of Martha's coin-tossing school, a person might be allowed to guess two times and then measured as either correct or incorrect each time); C denotes the combination formula that we are using to determine the total number of different ways the outcome of interest can occur r times (for example, if we are calculating the probability of being correct on one out of two guesses, $r = 1$); p is the probability of the specific outcome of interest (for example, the probability of being correct is .5; that is, $p = .5$); q is the probability that the outcome of interest will not occur (for example, the probability of being incorrect is .5; that is, $q = .5$; note that $q = 1 - p$.

Using this formula, a histogram can be generated by plotting values of P for each value of r, given certain values for N, p, and q. Once N, p, and q are known for a given situation, P varies strictly as a function of r.

For example, if $N = 1$, $p = .5$, and $q = .5$, then $P = .5$ when $r = 0$. For these same values of N, p, and q, $P = .5$ when $r = 1$. If we plot the values of P for $r = 0$ and $r = 1$, we get the simplest case of a binomial distribution (Figure 10.2). Notice that Figure 10.2 is symmetrical, because $p = q$. When p and q are not equal, the binomial distribution will be skewed (Figure 10.3).

Note that, when we measure behavior binomially, the measure is not free to vary much at all, since there are only two possibilities that we will recognize—for example, correct and incorrect. However, if we make more than one observation of a binomial event, the combined number of outcomes of interest is more free to vary. For example, given only one opportunity to guess, a person can score 1 (if the guess is correct) or 0 (if the guess is incorrect). Given two opportunities to guess, the person may score 1, .50, or 0. Given three opportunities to guess, the person may score 1, .67, .33, or 0, and so on. In other words,

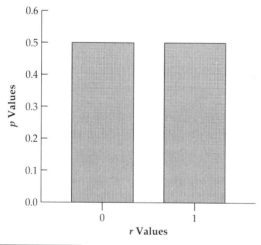

FIGURE 10.2 Binomial Distribution with $N = 1$, $p = .5$, $q = .5$

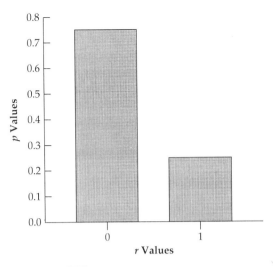

FIGURE 10.3 Binomial Distribution with $N = 1$, $p = .25$, $q = .75$

as the opportunities to guess increase, the variability in the person's score becomes greater.

T I M E ▪ O U T

I'd be very surprised if you felt comfortable with all of this information. It takes time to sort through it and master it. Are you willing to take the time? Think carefully about this question.

Let's consider the formula for the binomial distribution once again

$$P = {}_NC_r p^r q^{N-r} \tag{10.2}$$

The factor ${}_NC_r$ determines how many different ways there are for the event of interest to occur. For example, if the event of interest were one head out of two tosses, this factor would determine that there are two different ways for the event to occur. The one head could occur on the first of the two trials or on the second of the two trials.

The factor $p^r q^{N-r}$ determines the probability for each occurrence of the event of interest. For example, if the event of interest were one head out of two tosses, then this factor would determine that the probability is .25.

When these two factors are multiplied, the result will be the probability of the event of interest. For example, if the event of interest were one head out of two tosses, the result would be $2 \times .25 = .50$. This makes sense because the probability of either a head followed by a tail or a tail followed by a head is equal to the sum of the separate probabilities—that is, $.25 + .25 = .50$.

The application of this formula may seem complex at first sight. However, it is extremely valuable for you to understand how the binomial formula works, because it offers the clearest possible illustration of the relationship between probability and hypothesis testing. You should take whatever time is necessary to feel comfortable with the process by which the binomial formula creates a model of what to expect.

For the one-trial observation with Martha's student, the binomial formula would generate the following model of what to expect if the null hypothesis is true.

We will have to go through the formula twice, because there are two values for r (0 and 1). We are generating a model that will state probability values (P values) for situations in which the person is correct on none of the trials ($r = 0$) and for situations in which the person is correct on one trial ($r = 1$).

First consider the case when the person is correct on none of the trials ($r = 0$). We want to calculate $_NC_r$. It is a one-trial observation, and so $N = 1$. Using the formula

ASIDE ■ For the following calculations you should be aware that the symbol ! represents a mathematical operation known as factorialization, in which the number cited is multiplied by each successively lower integer until reaching 1. For example, $4! = 4 \times 3 \times 2 \times 1 = 24$. Note that 0! is always equal to 1. You will also need to know that any number raised to the power zero equals 1 (for example, $3^0 = 1$).

$$_NC_r = \frac{N!}{r!(N-r)!}$$

and calculating

$$N! = 1! = 1$$
$$r! = 0! = 1$$
$$(N - r)! = (1 - 0)! = 1! = 1$$

we find that

$$\frac{N!}{r!(N-r)!} = \frac{1}{1 \times 1} = \frac{1}{1} = 1$$

Next, we consider $p^r q^{N-r}$. Given that

$$p = .5, \quad r = 0, \quad q = .5, \quad \text{and} \quad N - r = 1 - 0 = 1$$

we find that

$$p^r q^{N-r} = .5^0 \times .5^1 = 1 \times .5 = .5$$

Combining the results of the two operations

$$_NC_r p^r q^{N-r} = 1 \times .5 = .5$$

Now consider the case when the person is correct on one of the trials ($r = 1$). Calculating $_NC_r$ again, we know that $N = 1$, since it was a one-trial observation. Thus

$$N! = 1! = 1$$
$$r! = 1! = 1$$
$$(N - r)! = (1 - 1)! = 0! = 1$$

Hence

$$\frac{N!}{r!(N-r)!} = \frac{1}{1 \times 1} = \frac{1}{1} = 1$$

Next, we consider $p^r q^{N-r}$. Given that

$$p = .5, \quad r = 1, \quad q = .5, \quad \text{and} \quad N - r = 1 - 1 = 0$$

we find that

$$p^r q^{N-r} = .5^1 \times .5^0 = .5 \times 1 = .5$$

Once again, combining the results of the two operations

$$_N C_r p^r q^{N-r} = 1 \times .5 = .5$$

Thus, the model predicts that, if the null hypothesis is true, the probability of being correct on none of the trials ($r = 0$) will be .5, and the probability of being correct on one of the trials ($r = 1$) will also be .5. This is the model portrayed by Figure 10.2.

ASIDE ■ If $p = .5$, we find that, as the number of opportunities to observe the specific outcome of interest increases, a given binomial distribution will come to approximate a normal distribution with a mean of Np and a standard deviation of $\sqrt{Npq}$.

Recall the question about the probability of being correct on 5 of 6 trials. The complete binomial model appropriate to this question is established by applying the formula separately for each of the 7 values of r: 0, 1, 2, 3, 4, 5, and 6. However, to determine whether 5 of 6 trials is statistically significant we need only apply the formula to the values $r = 5$ and $r = 6$, then add the resulting probability values. If the result is less than or equal to .05 then we would reject the null hypothesis; in other words, we would conclude that being correct on 5 of 6 trials is unlikely to happen by chance. The actual results of applying the model to $r = 5$ and $r = 6$ are $p = .09375$ and $p = .015625$ respectively. The sum of these two probabilities is .109375. Since this is greater than .05 we cannot reject the null hypothesis; in other words, being correct on 5 of 6 trials is likely to happen by chance. In plain English, we would conclude that Martha's School of Coin Tossing did not have a significant effect.

STATISTICAL SIGNIFICANCE AND STATISTICAL POWER

In discussing the coin-tossing experiment, we stated that the probability of a particular event (say, two correct predictions in five trials) must be .05 or less before we are prepared to reject the null hypothesis. The criterion for rejecting the null hypothesis, known as the alpha level, is usually set at .05, but other values are possible. The researcher chooses the alpha level before collecting data.

Thus, when the probability p of an event is less than or equal to the alpha level $(p \leqslant \alpha)$, the null hypothesis is rejected, and the results are said to be **statistically significant**.

In the coin-tossing observation, a correct prediction in a single trial would not surprise us. The probability of a single correct prediction is .5, which is much higher than the alpha level of .05 that we have chosen; this result is not statistically significant. In technical terms, we can say that, given the nature of the one-trial observation, there is not enough statistical power to reject the null hypothesis.

Only if we added another four trials to the experiment would it even be possible to obtain an outcome for which $p > .05$. (As we have seen, $p = .03125$ for five correct predictions out of five trials.)

Statistical power is defined as the probability of correctly rejecting a false null hypothesis. We will return to this concept later in the chapter.

USING THE NORMAL DISTRIBUTION AS A MODEL

Just as the binomial distribution can be used as a model when we are measuring a behavior at the nominal level and there are only two possible outcomes for each measurement, we can use the normal distribution as a model when we are measuring a behavior at the interval or ratio level.

Consider the following theory. Humans are able to respond to information in their environment more or less quickly depending upon the total amount of information that they are attempting to process at any given moment. Delayed responses to information occur because a person is overwhelmed with information. Rapid responses to information occur because a person is able to concentrate on the relevant information.

Consider the following research hypothesis based upon the above theory: Individuals who are allowed to clear their minds of distracting information will respond more quickly on a reaction time task.

This hypothesis may be stated more operationally as follows: If 122 people are randomly selected from a population and allowed to practice a mind clearing exercise (MCE) for 30 minutes, their average reaction time will be significantly shorter than the average reaction time of the population from which they were randomly selected.

We will go through the following **six-step process** in order to test this research hypothesis.

1. State the null hypothesis.

2. State the alternative hypothesis.

3. Establish a model of what to expect if the null hypothesis were true.

4. Establish a criterion for rejecting the null hypothesis.

5. Look at the data that were collected to see if the criterion has been met.

6. Decide which of the two hypotheses — the null or the alternate — is most reasonable in light of the model and the data.

Step 1. State the null hypothesis.

If we assume, for the sake of argument, that the mind clearing exercise will have no effect on the reaction time of those sampled from the population, then we would expect the average reaction time of the 122 people randomly selected from the population and subjected to the 30-minute MCE to be about the same as the average reaction time of the population from which they were originally selected.

Database A.3 shows the reaction time scores measured for a population of 1000 people on a standard task. Note that the mean for this population is 2.56 seconds and the standard deviation is 0.23 seconds. Given this information, the null hypothesis can be stated as follows

$$H_0: \mu_{mce} = 2.56$$

Why is the null hypothesis stated in terms of a population mean?

T I M E ■ O U T
This is an important question. Take some time to answer it.

Even though the research hypothesis makes a prediction about a sample mean, the null hypothesis is stated in terms of a population mean that the sample mean is assumed to represent. In this case, the sample of 122 subjects who participated in a mind clearing exercise is assumed to represent a hypothetical population of people who could have participated in the same exercise. For this reason, the null hypothesis could be stated as follows:

$$H_0: \bar{X}_{mce} = \mu_{mce} = 2.56$$

However, since the sample mean is assumed to represent the population mean, the sample mean is typically left out of the equation.

Step 2. State the alternative hypothesis.

Remember that the alternative hypothesis is actually the hypothesis that we hope to support; we state the null hypothesis for the sake of argument. In the present case, we hope to support the hypothesis that the average reaction time after the MCE will be less — that is, that the average reaction will be faster — than the average for the population. Hence, the alternative hypothesis is stated as follows

$$H_A: \mu_{mce} < 2.56$$

Step 3. Establish a model of what to expect if the null hypothesis were true.

In the present example, if the null hypothesis were true, we would expect the sample mean to be about the same as the population mean; that is, we would expect the mean reaction time of people who did the mind clearing exercise to be about 2.56 if the exercise had no effect.

This tells us what our model should look like with respect to central tendency. But there is another important issue to consider: What should the model look like with respect to variability?

In order to establish the variability of our model, it will be necessary to take a big step in the logic of inferential statistics and discuss the concept of sampling distributions.

ESTABLISHING SAMPLING DISTRIBUTIONS

A **sampling distribution** is a hypothetical frequency distribution of sample measurements (for example, sample means) that is based upon certain assumptions.

The binomial distribution can be used as a sampling distribution. Recall the one-trial observation regarding the prediction of a coin toss. Figure 10.2 (p. 180) is a sampling distribution of the sample measurements for the number of correct predictions in the observation. Even though sampling distributions represent distributions of frequency values, the Y axis is typically labeled with probability values. The conversion from probability values to frequency values is easy to conceptualize: For example, if Figure 10.2 represents the sampling distribution for 100 one-trial observations, a probability of .50 translates to a frequency of 50.

We can also use the normal curve as a sampling distribution, if we assume that the sample measurement is normally distributed. Let's consider how this assumption would work in the MCE example.

First, what sample measurement is of interest here?

T I M E ■ O U T
Take some time to consider this question.

Since we are testing a hypothesis regarding the mean of the population, we are interested in the sample mean. Imagine that, instead of just one sample consisting of 122 subjects, we have run all 1000 people from the original population through the MCE. Now, we take many (let's say 5000) separate samples from this population; each sample has 122 subjects in it. (Obviously, since there are only 1000 people in our total population, the reaction time score for any given person will probably be present in more than one sample.) If we were to calculate the sample mean for each of these 5000 samples and then create a frequency distribution for these 5000 sample means, this frequency distribution would be called an **empirical distribution of the sample means**, and it is an example of a sampling distribution. It would be empirical because it would be based upon data that were actually collected, in contrast to a purely hypothetical distribution. (The databases in Appendix A should be regarded as empirical databases.)

This empirical sampling distribution would be a model of what to expect regarding the means of samples of 122 subjects taken from the population and run through the mind clearing exercise.

You may be wondering why we would want such a model when we already knew the reaction time scores for all 1000 people in the population. If so, you're thinking very clearly. In reality, it is very unlikely that we would ever create a model of what to expect regarding sample means if we actually had measurements for everyone in the population. Under such conditions, we would be able to calculate the actual mean of the population, and we would not be trying to test a hypothesis about that population mean by looking at a sample mean.

T I M E ■ O U T
Take some time to think about this point.

Inferential statistics virtually always involves making inferences about a population without actually measuring all of the subjects or items in the population. Therefore, sampling distributions are virtually never empirical and virtually always hypothetical. How do we establish a **hypothetical sampling distribution?**

In the present example, we need to establish a hypothetical sampling distribution of sample means. We are trying to establish a model of what to expect regarding sample means if the null hypothesis were true. To estimate the standard deviation of the hypothetical sampling distribution, we use the following formula

$$\tilde{\sigma}_{\bar{X}} = \frac{s}{\sqrt{n_{\text{samp}} - 1}} \tag{10.3}$$

Putting this formula into words, we subtract 1 from the sample size, take the square root, and divide the result into the standard deviation of the sample.

To put all of this in perspective, we now look at some actual data values for a sample of 122 subjects randomly selected from the original population of 1000 subjects and run through the MCE exercise (Table 10.2).

If we use Eq. (10.3) and the sample statistics for the 122 measurements in Table 10.2 to estimate the standard deviation of the hypothetical sampling distribution, we get the following result

$$\tilde{\sigma}_{\bar{X}} = \frac{0.248}{\sqrt{122 - 1}} = \frac{0.248}{\sqrt{121}} = \frac{0.248}{11} = 0.0225$$

Notice that the standard deviation of the hypothetical sampling distribution of means is 0.0225, while the unbiased estimate of the standard deviation of the population is 0.249. Why would the standard deviation of the sampling distribution be so much smaller than the standard deviation of the population?

TABLE 10.2   **Reaction Time Scores for 122 Subjects after MCE**

2.45	2.59	2.18	2.69	2.75
2.79	2.52	2.40	2.74	2.95
2.49	2.39	2.67	3.03	2.37
2.00	2.64	2.83	2.38	2.75
2.86	2.46	3.09	2.68	2.43
2.19	2.96	2.72	2.75	2.88
2.50	2.20	3.06	2.86	2.30
2.30	2.97	2.74	2.94	2.96
2.43	2.52	2.83	2.52	2.81
2.93	2.54	2.55	2.69	2.39
2.52	2.40	2.47	2.28	3.09
2.74	2.63	2.30	2.60	2.49
2.39	2.35	2.65	2.39	3.01
2.68	2.69	2.36	2.66	2.92
2.63	2.23	2.88	2.52	2.59
2.52	2.73	2.66	2.27	2.34
2.38	2.51	2.62	2.88	2.27
2.57	2.33	2.37	2.62	2.75
2.74	2.39	2.28	2.60	2.97
2.70	2.62	2.32	2.96	2.25
2.09	2.50	2.54	2.29	2.78
2.65	2.32	2.95	2.42	2.51
2.57	2.48	2.20	2.97	2.44
2.45	2.68	3.15	2.64	2.22
2.19	2.31			

Note. The sample mean is 2.52, the sample standard deviation is 0.248, and the unbiased estimate of the population standard deviation is 0.249.

T I M E ■ O U T
Take some time to reflect on this question.

Wouldn't you expect that there would be more variability among the raw scores in the population than among the means of samples taken from the population? By averaging the individual scores in each sample, we eliminate some of the variability.

ASIDE ■ **The standard deviation of the hypothetical sampling distribution of the means is customarily referred to as the standard error of the mean ($\hat{\sigma}_{\bar{x}}$).**

Having obtained our estimate of the standard deviation of the hypothetical sampling distribution, we are now able to establish the complete model for what sample means to expect when the null hypothesis is true. For the MCE experiment, the model is a normal distribution of sample means in which the mean of the sample means is 2.56 (see the null hypothesis; p. 185) and the standard deviation of the sample means is 0.0225 (as estimated from the sample in Table 10.2).

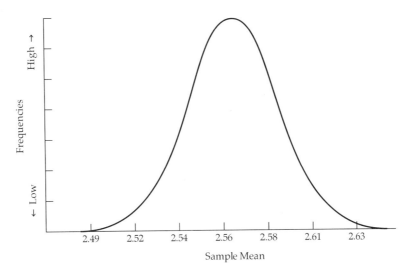

FIGURE 10.4 **Hypothetical Sampling Distribution**

Figure 10.4 illustrates our model sampling distribution. The values along the X axis are the approximate values of the sample means that we would expect to find at distances of one, two, and three standard deviations above and below the mean in this hypothetical sampling distribution.

Now that we have estimated the standard deviation of the hypothetical sampling distribution we can proceed with step 4 in testing the MCE hypothesis (p. 185).

Step 4. Establish a criterion for rejecting the null hypothesis.

Recall the null hypothesis

H_0: $\mu_{mce} = 2.56$

Recall the alternative hypothesis

H_A: $\mu_{mce} < 2.56$

If the mind clearing exercise is effective, we would expect shorter reaction times; therefore, the mean of the sample of 122 subjects should be less than the mean of the original population.

We now establish a criterion that reflects this expectation. What should this criterion be?

T I M E ■ O U T
Take some time to answer this question.

If you set a criterion of $Z = -1.645$, then your logic, based upon your understanding of Z values and the normal curve, is correct. However, because ourestimate of the standard deviation of the sampling distribution of means is based upon a sample of 122 subjects, our criterion should be based upon a t distribution rather than a Z distribution. The Z and t distributions are similar; their relationship is described by the **central limit theorem** which is stated as follows:

> When many samples of the same size (n) are randomly selected from a population, the distribution of means based upon these samples becomes increasingly similar to the normal distribution as the sample size (n) increases.

The exact steps for determining critical t values will be discussed in Chapter 12. For now, it's sufficient to understand the central limit theorem, and to know that the critical t for the present hypothesis is -1.658.

$$t_{\text{critical}} = -1.658$$

In our present example, we can reject the null hypothesis if we observe a sample mean for our experimental group that is more than 1.658 standard errors of the mean below the hypothetical population mean of 2.56.

Does this logic make sense to you?

T I M E ■ O U T
Take some time to reflect on this question.

Step 5. Look at the data that were collected to see if the criterion has been met.

Using the logic of the normal curve, we calculate a t score to determine the distance of our sample mean from the null-hypothesis mean (measured in terms of the standard error of the mean)

$$t_{\text{calc}} = \frac{\bar{X}_{\text{sample}} - \mu_{\text{null hypothesis}}}{\tilde{\sigma}_{\bar{X}}} \tag{10.4}$$

Recall that the sample mean for the 122 scores in Table 10.2 is 2.52. Using this sample mean in Eq. (10.4), what would the calculated t value be?

T I M E ■ O U T
Take some time to respond to this question.

The result obtained is as follows

$$t_{\text{calc}} = \frac{2.52 - 2.56}{0.0225} = \frac{-0.04}{0.0225} = -1.78$$

Step 6. Decide which of the two hypotheses—the null or the alternate—is most reasonable in light of the model and the data.

Since $t_{critical} = -1.658$ and $t_{calc} = -1.78$ for a sample mean of 2.52, we reject the null hypothesis.

Do you understand the logic here?

T I M E ■ O U T
Take some time to consider this question.

ASIDE ■ This logic is extremely important and reasonably complex. You should not be discouraged if you did not follow the argument the first time through. However, please keep trying until you are comfortable with the reasoning; it is an extremely important foundation for the remainder of this book—and for your career!

The logic is as follows. We know that a sample mean that is 1.658 standard errors of the mean (or further) below the null-hypothesis mean would occur less than 5% of the time. Therefore, if we obtain such a sample mean, we can conclude that the null-hypothesis mean is unlikely to be true. In this example, the sample mean of 2.52 is actually 1.78 standard errors of the mean below the null-hypothesis mean of 2.56. This is beyond $t_{critical} = -1.658$. Therefore, we reject the null-hypothesis mean and prefer the alternate hypothesis, which states that the population mean is less than 2.56.

In plain English, the MCE appears to have had an effect in reducing the average reaction time of the sample.

SAMPLING DISTRIBUTION OF DIFFERENCES

In the MCE example, the null and alternative hypotheses both refer to a single mean for the population. It is actually more common for null and alternative hypotheses to make statements about the relationship between two or more population means.

In discussing John's experiment on student attention in Chapter 8, we made a distinction between directional and nondirectional hypotheses (p. 151). The nondirectional hypothesis was that students' attentiveness would be different in a 70° room than in a 60° room. This is consistent with two contradictory directional hypotheses: that the students' attentiveness will be greater in the 70° room, and that their attentiveness will be greater in the 60° room. Each of these hypotheses makes a statement regarding the relationship between two means.

The null hypothesis could be conceptualized as follows: Imagine that the subjects in the 60° room and the 70° room represent separate populations. If there is no difference in the effects of the two temperatures, then, for all practical purposes, the two populations are identical and, therefore, the means will also be identical. Symbolically

$$H_0: \mu_{60} = \mu_{70}$$

Now imagine pairs of samples drawn randomly from each of these two populations. We wouldn't expect the means of the samples in each pair to be equal, even if the means of the populations from which they are drawn were equal. By chance, we would expect each pair of means to differ by some amount. If we randomly selected many pairs of sample means and found the difference between the means in each pair, we would expect that the average of all these differences would approach zero if the population means are equal. Symbolically

$$\mu_{\bar{X}_{60} - \bar{X}_{70}} = 0$$

The empirical frequency distribution of the differences between the means of a large number of pairs of sample is referred to as the **sampling distribution of differences**. This should be contrasted with the simpler sampling distribution of means already described.

Now notice that each of John's alternative hypotheses could be restated in terms of the sampling distribution of differences. The hypothesis that the students' attentiveness will be greater in the 70° room could be restated in the following form

$$H_A: \mu_{\bar{X}_{60} - \bar{X}_{70}} < 0$$

The hypothesis that the students' attentiveness will be greater in the 60° room could be restated in the following form

$$H_A: \mu_{\bar{X}_{60} - \bar{X}_{70}} > 0$$

Finally, the hypothesis that the students' attentiveness will be different in the 70° and 60° rooms could be restated in the following form

$$H_A: \mu_{\bar{X}_{60} - \bar{X}_{70}} \neq 0$$

John's nondirectional hypothesis simply states that the means of the two experimental conditions will be unequal. In the case of such nondirectional hypotheses, the null hypothesis could be rejected either because the empirical results fall in the extreme left tail of the sampling distribution of differences (where unusually large negative differences rarely occur), or because the empirical results fall in the extreme right tail of the sampling distribution of differences (where unusually large positive differences rarely occur). For this reason, nondirectional alternative hypotheses are often referred to as **two-tailed alternative hypotheses**. When the alternative hypothesis is two-tailed, the most unusual 5% of the sampling distribution is divided equally between the two tails, with 2.5% in each tail.

Each of John's directional hypotheses implies that the null hypothesis could be rejected only if the results fall in the extreme portion of only one of the two tails. For example, the hypothesis that the students' attentiveness will be greater in the 70° room implies that, if they are to allow rejection of the null hypothesis, the empirical results will show an extremely large negative difference (in the leftmost tail of the sampling distribution of differences). On the other hand, the hypothesis that the students' attentiveness will be greater in the 60° room implies that, if they are to allow rejection of the null hypothesis, the empirical results will show an extremely large positive difference (in the rightmost tail of the sampling distribution of differences). Thus, these are **one-tailed alternative hypotheses**.

THE LOGIC OF SAMPLING DISTRIBUTIONS

Whenever testing hypotheses using inferential statistics, the logic is essentially the same: We establish a model based upon certain assumptions. The model is a sampling distribution based partially on some existing knowledge of the variable (for example, in the MCE example, the mean and standard deviation of the sampling distribution were based upon the observed sample data) and partially on the mathematics of the chosen model (for example, the mathematical equation for the normal distribution).

We will not go through the calculations involved in establishing all the sampling distributions relevant to the inferential analyses in this book. However, it is important to recognize the fundamental logic common to all these analyses. More information regarding the different models used for inferential analyses may be found in Chapter 12.

Now that you have an understanding of sampling distributions, you are in a better position to comprehend the concept of statistical significance. In your own words, finish the following statement: "The results of an experiment are said to be statistically significant when . . . "

T I M E ■ O U T
Take some time to complete this exercise.

Adopting an alpha level of .05, we could complete this statement as follows: The results of an experiment are said to be statistically significant when the empirical data would occur only rarely (less than 5% of the time) in the null hypothesis sampling distribution.

TYPE-I VERSUS TYPE-II ERRORS

Once the researcher has chosen the alpha level (usually .05), the criterion for statistical significance is established by setting either one point (in the case of a one-tailed alternative hypothesis) or two points (in the case of a two-tailed alternative hypothesis) in the sampling distribution such that any sample values beyond that point (or those points) would occur less than 5% of the time if the null hypothesis were true. If, for example, in John's experiment there was a negative difference between the sample means of the $70°$ group and the $60°$ group so large that it would occur less than 5% of the time in the null sampling distribution of differences (which has a mean of zero), then the null hypothesis would be rejected. Of course, there is always a possibility that the null hypothesis should not have been rejected, and that the large difference observed was simply one of those relatively rare events that do in fact occur 5% of the time or less. Such an error is referred to as a type-I error. We expect that if the criterion is set at 5% then we will probably make a type-I error 5% of the time.

Does this make sense to you?

TIME ■ OUT
Stop and consider this question.

The standard 5% criterion may be stated symbolically as follows

$\alpha = .05$

Type-I error is defined as the error we make by rejecting the null hypothesis when the null hypothesis is actually true. **Type-II error** is defined as the error we make by failing to reject the null hypothesis when the null hypothesis is actually false.

In general, it is fair to say that, the greater the probability of making a type-I error, the lower the probability of making a type-II error. However, while the probability of a type-I error is set by the researcher (usually .05), the probability of a type-II error (also referred to as the **beta level** or symbolically as β) is much more difficult to determine.

STATISTICAL POWER REVISITED

It is appropriate to consider statistical power again here in the context of type-I and type-II errors. Verbally, **statistical power** can be described as the probability of correctly rejecting a false null hypothesis. Symbolically

$Power = 1 - \beta$

The following factors all influence the power of a statistical analysis:

■ the alpha level set by the researcher. (A lower alpha level corresponds to a greater likelihood of making a type-II error and hence to higher beta and lower power.)

- the number of observations made in the experiment. (Fewer observations correspond to lower power. An example of this is illustrated in the case of the binomial distribution where it can be demonstrated that, with a low probability of the event of interest—$p = .167$, say—and a small number of trials—three, say—P could never be low enough to reject the null hypothesis even if the event of interest was found to occur on every trial.)

- the real effect of the independent variable. (If the independent variable in fact has a strong effect, the researcher is more likely to see this effect and to correctly reject a false null hypothesis.)

- the degree of experimental control. (A more controlled experiment corresponds to a greater likelihood of detecting any genuine effect of the independent variable and, therefore, of correctly rejecting a false null hypothesis.)

Table 10.3 illustrates the relationship between type-I and type-II errors and power. Table 10.4 illustrates the analogy between type-I and type-II errors and the legal system.

TABLE 10.3   Type-I and Type-II Errors and Statistical Power

| | | Decision regarding the null hypothesis | |
		Reject null	Fail to reject null
Truth regarding the null hypothesis	Null is true	Type-I error (alpha)	No error
	Null is false	Correct (power)	Type-II error (beta)

TABLE 10.4   The Legal System Analogy to Type-I and Type-II Errors

| | | Jury's decision | |
		Guilty	Not guilty
Truth regarding the accused person	Innocent	Type-I error (innocent person goes to jail)	Correct verdict (defense wins)
	Guilty	Correct verdict (prosecution wins)	Type-II error (guilty person goes free)

SUMMARY

First, we considered the comparison of research data with probabilistic models—the binomial distribution and the normal distribution—as a means of testing the research hypothesis. You should recall that research hypotheses are reasonable only to the degree that the null hypothesis can be rejected because it is unreasonable.

We then worked through a step-by-step example of how the normal model is used to test a hypothesis (specifically, the hypothesis that a mind clearing exercise would significantly decrease reaction time).

We also discussed sampling distributions, statistical power, statistical significance, one-tailed and two-tailed alternative hypotheses, and type-I and type-II errors.

KEY SYMBOLS

$\tilde{\sigma}_{\bar{X}}$, α, β, $1 - \beta$

N, r, P, p, q, $_NC_r$, H_0, H_A

KEY TERMS AND CONCEPTS

.05

Alpha level

Beta level

Binomial distribution

Binomial formula

Binomial model

Central limit theorem
   of sample means

Empirical distribution

Hypothetical sampling distribution

Normal distribution

Normal model

Null hypothesis

One-tailed alternative hypothesis

Sampling distribution

Sampling distribution of differences

Six-step process of hypothesis testing

Standard error of the mean

Statistical power

Statistical significance

Two-tailed alternative hypothesis

Type-I error

Type-II error

EXERCISES

10.1 Randomly select 20 data values from Database A.3.

10.2 Randomly select 10 of the 20 data values in Exercise 10.1 and label them as the control group. Imagine that the remaining 10 data values represent the reaction time scores of an experimental group before they drink 4 ounces of alcohol. Would you expect the reaction times for these 10 people to change after drinking 4 ounces of alcohol? If so, add an amount to, or subtract an amount from, each of the 10 data values to represent the effect of drinking the alcohol.

10.3 Exercises 10.1 and 10.2 are designed to create an imaginary experiment. State the null hypothesis for this imaginary experiment in general terms.

10.4 State the null hypothesis from Exercise 10.3 in operational terms.

10.5 State the null hypothesis from Exercise 10.3 using the appropriate symbols.

10.6 State the alternative hypothesis for this imaginary experiment in general terms.

10.7 State the alternative hypothesis from Exercise 10.6 in operational terms.

10.8 State the alternative hypothesis from Exercise 10.6 using the appropriate symbols.

10.9 Is your alternative hypothesis one-tailed or two-tailed? Explain.

10.10 What type of sampling distribution would you establish as a model to test the null hypothesis?

10.11 In which of the following situations would there be more statistical power?
a. The researcher sets the alpha level at .01.
b. The researcher sets the alpha level at .05.

10.12 In which of the following situations would there be less statistical power?
a. The researcher randomly selects 60 subjects and randomly assigns 30 to each of two experimental groups.
b. The researcher randomly selects 40 subjects and randomly assigns 20 to each of two experimental groups.

SELECTING, UNDERSTANDING, AND INTERPRETING STATISTICAL ANALYSES

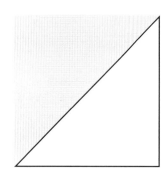

Part Four consists of three chapters that are designed to help you: decide which satistical analysis to use in a particular situation; understand the logic that underlies some of the most commonly used statistical analyses; and understand how to interpret the results of these analyses. Just as importantly, these chapters will help you understand how to design data collection procedures appropriate to your level of understanding of statistics, so that, whenever possible, you will have a particular statistical analysis in mind before you actually begin collecting your data.

4

In Part Four, our discussion focuses on the principles and procedures for some of the most commonly used inferential analyses. If you understand these principles and procedures, then you will be able to apply them to all of the analyses included in the decision tree located inside the front and back covers of this book, though not all those analyses are discussed here. On those occasions when you need a complete and detailed presentation of a particular analysis, you can refer to Appendix C, which provides comprehensive coverage of each analysis — including calculations — within the context of a particular scenario. Each scenario illustrates a total process, beginning with the researcher's motivation to collect the data and ending with a plain English statement regarding the results of the statistical analysis as they relate to the researcher's hypothesis.

In Chapter 11, we discuss the relationship between the researcher's original question and the strategies available for collecting data. Next, we consider the relationship between the strategies for data collection and the available choices for analyzing the data. These issues are then related to the use of the decision tree for determining which statistical analysis to use (located inside the front and back covers). Finally, we illustrate the use of the decision tree in various scenarios. In Chapter 12, we discuss the logic underlying some of the more commonly used statistical analyses: Pearson r, Spearman r, t-test, analysis of variance, Scheffe, and chi square. The formulas for these analyses are presented and discussed within the larger context of understanding how they may be used to test null hypotheses. Null hypotheses related to the scenarios in Chapter 11 are used as examples. In Chapter 13, taking the next logical step, we discuss the interpretation of the actual results of statistical analyses for the scenarios in Chapter 11. We also consider general issues regarding the interpretation of these analyses.

Selecting Statistical Analyses

Relationship between Hypotheses and Data Collection Strategies

Relationship between Data Collection Strategies
and the Choice of Statistical Analysis

Relationship between the Type of Data
and the Choice of Statistical Analysis

Determining Which Statistical Analysis to Use
by Means of the Decision Tree

Examples of the Decision-Making Process

Summary

Key Terms and Concepts

Exercises

OBJECTIVES

After reading and studying Chapter 11 you should understand the following.

- *the differences among between-groups, within-groups, and matched groups designs.*

- *the general relationship between the researcher's original question and strategies for collecting the data.*

- *the general relationship between the data collection strategies and the choice of statistical analysis.*

- *the general relationship between the type of data collected and the choice of statistical analysis.*

- *how to determine the appropriate type of statistical analysis by means of the decision tree provided.*

- *the assumptions underlying parametric analyses.*

RELATIONSHIP BETWEEN HYPOTHESES AND DATA COLLECTION STRATEGIES

As we noted in Chapter 8, the primary objective of scientific observation is to develop the best possible theory to explain why behaviors and events occur the way they do.

The quality of a theory is dependent in part on how well it generates testable hypotheses that turn out to be correct. In other words, a good theory makes correct predictions. From a scientific point of view, we have the most confidence if our hypothesis is demonstrated to be correct under controlled conditions that are not confounded — in other words, when we have conducted an internally valid experiment. Under such conditions, we will be able to say with confidence whether or not the independent variable is causing a change in the dependent variable.

Scientifically, then, we would like to test our theory by generating a hypothesis that can be tested in a controlled **experiment**. However, the degree of control we can exert over the variables of interest will depend both on the nature of our theory and on the nature of the behavior or event that we are trying to explain. Suppose, for example, that we are trying to explain why the number of violent crimes reported in a particular city in 1993 increased by 110% as compared to 1992. In this situation, clearly, we will not be able to conduct a highly controlled experiment in which we manipulate some variable to see if it has an effect on violent crime; too many variables are beyond our control.

T I M E ■ O U T
Take some time to name some variables that might affect the number of violent crimes.

Suppose we have a theory that attributes the increase in violent crime to an increase in the amount of violence portrayed on television. Since we cannot directly control the amount of violence portrayed on television, we cannot directly predict that an increase in the amount of violence portrayed on television will result in an increase in the amount of violent crime. We can, however, predict that, if our theory is correct, there should be a significant positive correlation between the amount of violence portrayed on television during specific periods of time for specific viewing audiences and the amount of violent crime reported during specific periods of time for the same viewing audiences. Note that a significant positive correlation between television violence and reported violent crime, although necessary to support the theory, is not sufficient. In other words, if we find that there is a significant positive correlation, our theory is still reasonable, but we cannot say with confidence that there is a causal relationship.

ASIDE ■ **The conditions under which the data are gathered and the results of the statistical analysis are both important in making decisions about causal relationships. Neither alone is sufficient; the total process must be considered.**

When variables are observed in an uncontrolled setting and found to be related in a predictable way, we can only say that they are correlated. When variables are manipulated (independent variable) and observed (dependent variable) in controlled experiments and found to be related in a predictable way, we can say that they are causally related. The conditions under which the data are collected determine whether we can claim a causal relationship if and when the results of our statistical analysis are significant.

RELATIONSHIP BETWEEN DATA COLLECTION STRATEGIES AND THE CHOICE OF STATISTICAL ANALYSIS

For purposes of clarity at the introductory level, the **decision tree** (see inside cover) forces a choice between observation and experiment. The ease with which a particular data collection procedure can be placed into either category depends on the degree of control the researcher has over the variables in question. If the researcher can manipulate quantitative or qualitative aspects of at least one particular variable, we conceptualize that variable as an independent variable in a controlled experiment. If the researcher exerts no control over any of the variables, we refer to these variables simply as variables in an uncontrolled observation. However, there are times when the researcher exerts some degree of control over a variable, but not enough for it to be considered a true independent variable. For example, without actually manipulating a variable, a researcher may select for observation a limited number of categories for a qualitative variable, such as political philosophy, or a limited number of values for a quantitative variable, such as age. The decision to conceptualize such procedures as **quasi experiments** is somewhat arbitrary, but may be guided by the following consideration.

- If there are only two variables, with one being considered as a predictor of the other, and the number of categories or values of the predictor variable is less than five, then the predictor variable can be conceptualized as a **quasi-independent variable.** The results can then be analyzed as if it were a controlled experiment. However, if the analysis indicates a systematic relationship between the variables, it can only be concluded that the predictor variable is correlated with, *not causally related to*, the other variable.

Consider, for example, a case in which the researcher is predicting that females have a higher pain tolerance than males. Ten males and 10 females are randomly selected and measured for pain tolerance. Gender could be considered a quasi-independent variable, and the two categories of male and female could be conceptualized as separate conditions of a quasi experiment. However, if it is found that the average pain tolerance for the females is significantly higher than for the males, it could be said only that gender is correlated with pain tolerance. It would not be appropriate to say that gender has an effect on pain tolerance.

The conditions under which the data are collected also determine the precise nature of the null hypothesis and, therefore, the particular type of statistical analysis that is appropriate.

Observations

If only two variables are observed under uncontrolled conditions — for example, the amount of television violence and the number of violent crimes reported — the null hypothesis would be stated as follows: There is no correlation between the amount of television violence and the number of violent crimes reported.

There are several inferential statistical analyses designed to test the probable truth of null hypotheses that pertain to correlations. Those included in this book are: Pearson r, Spearman r, eta, lambda, and theta. Notice that these analyses appear in the **observation** branch of the decision tree for determining which statistical analysis to use (located inside the front and back covers of this book).

Experiments

If we have one independent variable—for example, the temperature of a room—and one dependent variable—for example, a test score—the null hypothesis would be stated as follows: Room temperature has no effect on test scores.

There are several inferential statistical analyses designed to test the probable truth of null hypotheses that pertain to causal relationships between independent and dependent variables. Those included in this book are: t-test, analysis of variance, Scheffe, Mann-Whitney U, Wilcoxon, Kruskal-Wallis, and Friedman. Notice that these analyses appear in the experiment branch of the decision tree.

Thus, you can see that the choice of a particular type of statistical analysis will depend in part on whether the data were collected in an uncontrolled **observation** or in a controlled **experiment**. For this reason, it is important, whenever possible, to identify certain aspects of your data collection strategy—for example, observation versus experiment—before you collect your data. If you do so, you will know exactly which statistical analysis you will be using. If you don't follow this advice, you may end up with data that you cannot analyze using an inferential analysis.

RELATIONSHIP BETWEEN THE TYPE OF DATA AND THE CHOICE OF STATISTICAL ANALYSIS

As we noted in Chapter 2, the choice of which statistical analysis to use for a particular situation depends in part on the level of measurement for the data. Thus, you should also identify the level of measurement before you collect your data. This point will be illustrated in the following scenarios.

The first three scenarios are related to the general null hypothesis that there is no correlation between television violence and actual violent crime.

Scenario 11.1. Television violence is operationally defined as the total number of gunshots counted by a team of research assistants who watched all the programs on four major networks during the hours from 7:00 P.M. to 9:00 P.M. Monday through Saturday during the period February through May in each of 10 major cities. Actual violent crime is operationally defined as the total number of deaths due to bullet wounds counted by the police departments in the same cities.

Scenario 11.2. Television violence is operationally defined as follows. An independent research organization conducts a telephone survey and ranks 10 major cities with respect to the amount of television violence that viewers watch. The city with the viewers who watch the most violence is given the highest ranking, and so on. Actual violent crime is operationally defined as the ranking of the same 10 cities with respect to deaths due to bullet wounds based upon federal government statistics.

Scenario 11.3. Television violence is operationally defined as in Scenario 11.1. Actual violent crime is operationally defined by having a panel of experts categorize each of the same 10 cities as extremely violent, moderately violent, or nonviolent.

In each of these scenarios, the researchers would like to show that television violence and actual reported crime are positively correlated; that is, the greater the amount of television violence, the greater the amount of violent crime. If such a correlation could be found, it would be possible to predict the amount of violent crime in a given area by knowing the amount of television violence viewed in that same area. We could then say that television violence, the **predictor variable**, is a predictor of actual violent crime, the **predicted variable**.

ASIDE ■ Two general cases should be identified regarding uncontrolled observations in which two variables, x and y, are being measured. One case involves a research hypothesis that implies that variation in x directly causes variation in y. The other case involves a research hypothesis that does not imply a direct causal relationship, but explicitly states that variation in x can be used as a predictor of variation in y. In both cases, because it is not a controlled experiment, one can only speak of a correlation between x and y; and in both cases, it should be stated that variable x is the predictor variable, while variable y is the predicted variable.

Given this information, we can now look at the decision tree inside the front and back covers of this book to determine which particular statistical analysis would be appropriate.

For Scenario 11.1, both variables are at the ratio level of measurement; therefore, as indicated in the decision tree, the Pearson r analysis would be appropriate.

For Scenario 11.2, both variables are at the ordinal level of measurement; therefore, the Spearman r analysis would be appropriate.

T I M E ■ O U T
Take some time to determine which analysis would be appropriate for Scenario 11.3 using the decision tree.

You are correct if you decided to use a lambda analysis, because the predictor variable is at the ratio level and the other variable is at the nominal level.

The next two scenarios are related to the general null hypothesis that room temperature has no effect on test scores.

Scenario 11.4. The independent variable, room temperature, is manipulated by setting the temperature at 60°F for one group of subjects and at 70° for another group of subjects. The dependent variable, test score, is measured by counting the number of correct choices on a 100-item multiple choice test covering a lecture presented at each of the two temperatures.

Scenario 11.5. The independent variable, room temperature, is manipulated as in Scenario 11.4. The dependent variable is measured simply by indicating whether each person at each temperature passed or failed the test. (They passed if they scored 70% or more.)

Given the information in these two scenarios, we can use the decision tree to determine which statistical analysis to use.

In Scenario 11.4, we have one dependent variable measured at the ratio level and two different conditions (60° and 70°) of one independent variable (room temperature). Therefore, as indicated in the decision tree, a *t*-test would be an appropriate analysis. (The question of whether to use a *t*-test for independent groups or a *t*-test for dependent groups will be discussed in the next section.)

In Scenario 11.5, we have one dependent variable measured at the nominal level and the same independent variable as in Scenario 11.4. Therefore, we would choose a chi square test of independence.

MAIN POINT SUMMARY

Scenarios 11.1–11.5 illustrate that at the elementary level, in order to select an appropriate statistical analysis, you need to know whether the data were collected in an uncontrolled observation or in a controlled experiment, and you need to know the level of measurement corresponding to your variables.

DETERMINING WHICH STATISTICAL ANALYSIS TO USE BY MEANS OF THE DECISION TREE

If you are simply going to describe some data, without testing a null hypothesis, you can choose from the various summary techniques discussed in previous chapters. If you intend to test a null hypothesis, however, you need to answer the following questions in order to choose an appropriate statistical analysis:

- Are you conducting a relatively uncontrolled observation in which there are no true independent and dependent variables, or are you conducting a relatively controlled experiment? (See pages 203–204.)

- How many variables will you be measuring? Which, if any, are independent variables? Which, if any, are dependent variables?

- What level of measurement (nominal, ordinal, interval, or ratio) corresponds to each measured variable?

- If you are conducting an uncontrolled observation, which is your predictor variable?

- If you are conducting a controlled experiment, which is your independent variable? How many different levels or conditions of this independent variable are there?

- What level of measurement corresponds to your dependent variable?

Given a scenario that includes all the relevant information, you should be able to answer each of the above questions on the basis of what you have learned in previous chapters. If you have gone down the experiment branch of the decision tree, there are two additional questions:

- Have you met the parametric assumptions?

- Is your experiment a between-groups (B-G) experiment, a within-groups (w-g) experiment, or a matched-groups experiment?

In order to answer these questions, you need some new concepts.

Parametric Assumptions

Whenever you are conducting a true experiment, you will have a dependent variable that you are measuring. As you can see in the decision tree, if you have only one dependent variable, and this variable is at the interval or ratio level, then you must decide which path to take on the basis of whether the assumptions are met or not met. The assumptions referred to here are the **parametric assumptions**. Given your understanding of what a parameter is, can you imagine what the parametric assumptions might be?

T I M E ▪ O U T
Take some time to consider this question.

As you may have determined, the parametric assumptions have something to do with the characteristics of the population from which the experimental sample was drawn. (Recall that, in most experiments, you have randomly selected subjects or items from a larger population, to which you hope to generalize the experimental results.)

If you are willing to make the three parametric assumptions, you can conduct a *parametric inferential statistical analysis*. (Notice that the first six end-points in the experiment branch of the tree are **parametric analyses**.) The three parametric assumptions are as follows.

1. Normal distribution of the dependent variable.

2. Random selection of subjects or items from the population.

3. Homogeneity of variance.

In order to meet the first assumption, you should be reasonably sure that the dependent variable is normally distributed in the population from which you are sampling. In other words, if you measured all subjects or items in the population and then plotted a frequency distribution, the graph should resemble a normal curve.

The parametric statistical analyses require not only that the dependent variable be normally distributed in the population, but also that your sample adequately represent this normal distribution. The second assumption—random selection—meets this requirement.

In order to satisfy the third parametric assumption, you should be reasonably sure that the variances are the same in each of the imaginary populations from which you are sampling. This may seem confusing, since, in reality, you have only sampled from one population. However, once the subjects or items in your samples have been subjected to the influence of the independent variable, each of these samples represents a new imaginary population that has been subjected to the same influence of the independent variable. You must now imagine that you have calculated the variance (that is, the squared standard deviation) for each of these new imaginary populations, and that these variances are reasonably equal.

There are sophisticated techniques for testing the homogeneity of variance. For our purposes, however, it is sufficient to suggest that, if the standard deviations for each of your treatment samples are reasonably similar, you may meet this assumption.

In order to meet each of the three parametric assumptions with confidence, it would be necessary to conduct certain tests that are beyond the scope of an elementary statistics text. For this reason, students are traditionally advised to assume that they can meet each of the assumptions unless there is strong evidence to the contrary. If, after serious consideration, you find yourself wondering whether the evidence is strong, you should probably assume that it isn't.

There is an ongoing debate among statisticians regarding the relative benefits and disadvantages of meeting or failing to meet the parametric assumptions. If, given a dependent variable at the interval or ratio level, we fail to meet the parametric assumptions, we must conduct a **nonparametric analysis** (see the decision tree). However, under certain conditions, the likelihood of a type-II error is greater when using a nonparametric analysis.

Without going into detail, suffice it to say that the student of elementary statistics should be aware of the controversy among statisticians regarding how strictly we should meet the parametric assumptions. (Example: Blair et al. (1985))

Between-Groups Designs

If you were to describe the most typical example of an experiment, it would have one independent variable with two different conditions (the experimental group and the control group) and one dependent variable at the interval or ratio level. A certain number of subjects (20, for example) would be randomly selected from a population, and half would be randomly assigned to each group (10 to the experimental group and 10 to the control group). This is referred to as a **between-groups experimental design**, because of the random assignment of the subjects to the two different experimental groups, or sometimes as an **independent-groups design**, because the assignment of subjects to one of the experimental groups is totally independent of the assignment of subjects to the other group. Any effect due to the independent variable will be recognized by observing a significant difference between the experimental and the control groups with respect to the dependent variable.

> *Scenario 11.6 (Between-Groups).* The researcher randomly selects 20 people from the general population and then randomly assigns 10 of these people to a control group and the remaining 10 to an experimental group. In the control group, each of the 10 people is asked to sit in a room for 15 minutes and to try to relax as best as they can. In the experimental group, each of the 10 people is asked to sit in a room for 15 minutes and try to relax by listening to classical music. All subjects in both the experimental and control groups are tested for their reaction times after the 15-minute relaxation period.

Within-Groups Design

Perhaps the most common example of a within-groups design is the **before-after design**. In such an experiment, there is only one group of subjects. This group is measured on some dependent variable both before and after some change in the independent variable. Any effect due to the independent variable will be recognized by observing a significant difference within the single group. Because the same subjects are used in all conditions of a **within-groups design**, the observed measurements of the dependent variable in one condition are related to — that is, not independent of — the observed measurements of the dependent variable in any other condition. For this reason, a within-groups design is also referred to as a **dependent-groups design**.

> *Scenario 11.7 (Within-Groups).* The researcher randomly selects 20 people from the general population. All of these 20 people are first measured for their reaction times on a standard task. Then, each of these 20 people is asked to sit in a room for 15 minutes and to try to relax by listening to classical music. After this 15-minute relaxation period, all 20 people are measured again for their reaction times on the same standard task.

Matched-Groups Designs

It is true to say that all independent-groups designs are between-groups designs; and it is true to say that all within-groups designs are dependent-groups designs. Strictly speaking, however, it is not true to say that all dependent-groups designs are within-groups designs. Another subcategory of dependent-groups designs consists of matched-groups designs.

In a **matched-groups design**, the subjects are not independently assigned to the experimental conditions. Instead, the subjects or items are assigned to the experimental conditions in such a way that they will be matched on the basis of some characteristic that is believed to be related to the dependent variable. We already know (Chapter 8) that the purpose of random assignment is to ensure that there is no difference between the subjects or items in the different experimental conditions before the introduction of the independent variable. The purpose of matched assignment is the same, but in this case the researcher is not content to let randomness eliminate any differences among the experimental conditions. Consider the following example.

Scenario 11.8 (Matched-Groups). The researcher randomly selects 20 people from the general population. All of these 20 people are first measured for their reaction times on a standard task. On the basis of the results, they are ranked from fastest to slowest and placed into matched pairs (the first and second ranked as one pair, the third and fourth ranked as another pair, and so on). Then one member of each matched pair is randomly assigned to the control group and the other member to the experimental group. After all matched assignments are made, there are 10 subjects in the control group and 10 subjects in the experimental group. Each of the 10 subjects in the control group is asked to sit in a room for 15 minutes and to try to relax. After this 15-minute relaxation period, all 10 people are measured again for their reaction times on the same standard task. Each of the 10 subjects in the experimental group is asked to sit in a room for 15 minutes and try to relax while listening to classical music. After this 15-minute relaxation period, all 10 people are measured again for their reaction times on the same standard task.

T I M E ■ O U T
Use the decision tree to determine which statistical analysis would be appropriate for each of Scenarios 11.6–11.8.

If you used the decision tree correctly, you should have arrived at the following decisions:

- A *t*-test for independent groups is appropriate for Scenario 11.6.

- A *t*-test for dependent groups is appropriate for Scenario 11.7.

- A *t*-test for dependent groups is appropriate for Scenario 11.8.

The reasons for these decisions will be spelled out in the next section.

EXAMPLES OF THE DECISION-MAKING PROCESS

One of the goals of this book is to provide you with clear guidelines for making decisions about which statistical analysis to use for a given situation. Given your elementary level of understanding at this point, it is useful to simplify this decision-making process by grouping all data collection procedures that involve testable hypotheses into two broad categories: observation and experiment. This classification is consistent with the first decision you face when using the decision tree.

One simple way to decide whether you are dealing with an uncontrolled observation or a controlled experiment is to ask yourself if there is a true independent variable involved. If there is, you have an experiment; if not, you have an observation. Admittedly, this is a simplification of what can be a rather complex issue, but it is justified at the elementary level, in view of the limited number of statistical analyses that you have mastered. (Recall the discussion on pages 203–204.)

Having made the basic decision regarding observation or experiment, you can begin to work your way through the decision tree. The decision process for Scenarios 11.1–11.8 is summarized in Table 11.1. On the basis of Table 11.1, you can see that, knowing certain things about how the data were collected, you can use the decision tree to determine an appropriate inferential statistical analysis.

| TABLE 11.1 | Decision Processes for Scenarios 11.1–11.8 |

Scenario 11.1

Type of research:	Observation
Number of variables:	2
Levels of measurement:	Both variables at interval/ratio level
Choice of analysis:	**Pearson r**

Scenario 11.2

Type of research:	Observation
Number of variables:	2
Levels of measurement:	Both variables at ordinal level
Choice of analysis:	**Spearman r**

Scenario 11.3

Type of research:	Observation
Number of variables:	2
Levels of measurement:	Predictor: interval/ratio
	Other variable: nominal
Choice of analysis:	**Lambda**

TABLE 11.1   Decision Processes for Scenarios 11.1–11.8 (*continued*)

Scenario 11.4

Type of research	Experiment
Number of dependent variables	1
Level of measurement	Interval/ratio
Assumptions met?	Yes
Number of independent variables	1
Conditions of independent variable	2
Type of design	Between-groups (B-G)
Choice of analysis	**t-test for independent groups**

Scenario 11.5

Type of research	Experiment
Number of dependent variables	1
Level of measurement	Nominal
Number of independent variables	1
Conditions of independent variable	2
Choice of analysis	**Chi square test of independence**

Scenario 11.6

Type of research	Experiment
Number of dependent variables	1
Level of measurement	Interval/ratio
Assumptions met?	Yes
Number of independent variables	1
Conditions of independent variable	2
Type of design	Between-groups
Choice of analysis	**t-test for independent groups**

Scenario 11.7

Type of research	Experiment
Number of dependent variables	1
Level of measurement	Interval/ratio
Assumptions met?	Yes
Number of independent variables	1
Conditions of independent variable	2
Type of design	Within-groups
Choice of analysis	**t-test for dependent groups**

Scenario 11.8

Type of research	Experiment
Number of dependent variables	1
Level of measurement	Interval/ratio
Assumptions met?	Yes
Number of independent variables	1
Conditions of independent variable	2
Type of design	Matched-groups
Choice of analysis	**t-test for dependent groups**

SUMMARY

In this chapter, we discussed the ways in which the researcher's original question can determine the data collection strategy. In this context, we reviewed the differences between uncontrolled observations and controlled experiments and the related issue of correlation versus causality. We also discussed how the null hypothesis differs for uncontrolled observations and controlled experiments.

The determination of the most appropriate type of analysis in any particular situation can be complex, but is much simplified by means of the decision tree provided (inside the front and back covers of this book). In explaining that decision tree, we discussed the influence of data collection strategies and of the type of data collected on the choice of statistical analysis.

We also examined the assumptions that underlie parametric analysis, and we distinguished between three types of experimental designs: between-groups, within-groups, and matched-groups designs. Finally, as an illustration, we worked through the decision tree for eight brief scenarios.

KEY TERMS AND CONCEPTS

Before-after design

Between-groups design

Chi square test of independence

Decision tree

Dependent-groups design

Experiment

Independent-groups design

Lambda

Matched-groups design

Nonparametric analysis

Observation

Parametric analysis

Parametric assumptions

Pearson *r*

Predicted variable

Predictor variable

Quasi experiments

Quasi independent variable

Spearman *r*

t-test for dependent groups

t-test for independent groups

Within-groups design

EXERCISES

11.1 Use the decision tree to determine an appropriate statistical analysis for each of the following scenarios.

Scenario A: A researcher randomly selects 20 people from a population of people known to be depressed and then randomly assigns 10 of these people to a Freudian therapy group and the remaining 10 to a drug therapy group. All subjects are measured for their depression, after six weeks of therapy, by counting the number of times they smile during a 30-minute interview. The researcher is predicting that the drug therapy group will show lower levels of depression—that is, will smile more.

Scenario B: A researcher randomly selects 20 people from a population of people known to be depressed. At the beginning of the investigation, each person's attention span is measured: Each subject is asked to watch a complex computer-generated pattern until he or she gets bored and turns it off. The total number of seconds is recorded. At the beginning of the investigation, all subjects are also measured for their depression by counting the number of times they smile during a 30-minute interview. The researcher is predicting that in general, the people who smile more will also have the highest attention spans.

Scenario C: A researcher randomly selects 30 people from the population of all students at a particular college and then randomly assigns 10 students to each of three groups. In one group, 10 students are asked to drink 2 ounces of water. In the second group, 10 other students are asked to drink a mixture containing 1 ounce of water and 1 ounce of vodka. In the third group, the remaining 10 students are asked to drink 2 ounces of vodka. All 30 students are given a standard reaction time test 5 minutes after drinking. Reaction times are measured accurate to the nearest one-thousandth of a second. The researcher predicts that a higher alcohol consumption will correspond to longer reaction times.

Scenario D: In the same conditions as scenario C, the researcher decides that the variances of the three groups are not sufficiently homogeneous.

Scenario E: In the same conditions as scenario C, the researcher would like to look at a second independent variable: social pressure. Half of the students in each of the three experimental groups take the reaction time test while no one is watching; the other half take the reaction time test while an audience of 10 people is watching. The researcher predicts that the effect of alcohol will be reduced for those who perform in front of an audience.

11.2 Create your own scenarios that would lead to two analyses at the end of the observation branch of the decision tree which were not covered by Exercise 11.1.

11.3 Create your own scenarios that would lead to two analyses at the end of the experiment branch of the decision tree which were not covered by Exercise 11.1.

11.4 Using one of the questions that you generated in Chapter 1, generate a related hypothesis, state the related null hypothesis, create a scenario that describes how you would test the null hypothesis, and, finally, use the decision tree to determine an appropriate statistical analysis.

11.5 What is the nonparametric alternative to the *t*-test for independent groups?

11.6 What is the nonparametric alternative to the *t*-test for dependent groups?

11.7 Summarize the parametric assumptions.

11.8 Describe the difference between a between-groups design and a within-groups design.

11.9 Describe the difference between a before-after design and a matched-groups design.

11.10 What is the nonparametric alternative to the analysis of variance (ANOVA) for a between-groups design with one independent variable?

Understanding Statistical Analysis Formulas

OBJECTIVES

After reading and studying Chapter 12 you should understand the following.

■ *the logic of null-hypothesis testing as it applies to the calculation formulas for Pearson* r, *Spearman* r, *t-test, F-test (analysis of variance), Scheffe, and chi square analyses.*

■ *the inflated alpha problem.*

■ *what it means to say that two independent variables interact.*

■ *the relationship between research design and appropriate formulas for inferential analysis.*

■ *factors that lead to complex research designs.*

■ *when nonparametric analyses are used.*

REVIEW OF HYPOTHESIS TESTING LOGIC

As we saw in Chapter 9, although we typically expect that there will be a relationship among the variables in our research, inferential statistics requires that, for the sake of argument, we assume no relationship. The burden of proof is on us, as researchers, to show that the null hypothesis is not correct. All of the inferential statistical analyses in the decision tree have the same general purpose: to make an educated guess about the truth of the null hypothesis. The researcher hopes that the results of statistical analysis will show that the null hypothesis is probably not true.

You have learned that there are two major categories of null hypotheses: In the case of uncontrolled observations, the null hypothesis states that there will be no correlation between the variables; in the case of controlled experiments, the null hypothesis states that the independent variable will have no effect on the dependent variable. Because of these differences in the null hypothesis, and because of other differences corresponding to the choice points in the decision tree, each inferential statistical analysis uses a different mathematical approach to test the truth of the null hypothesis.

In the present chapter, we look at some common inferential analysis formulas, in order to understand how these different approaches address the same general objective.

GENERAL LOGIC OF INFERENTIAL STATISTICAL ANALYSIS

In Chapter 10, we formulated the following six-step process for hypothesis testing:

1. State the null hypothesis.

2. State the alternative hypothesis.

3. Establish a model of what to expect if the null hypothesis were true.

4. Establish a criterion for rejecting the null hypothesis.

5. Look at the data that were collected to see if the criterion has been met.

6. Decide which of the two hypotheses—the null or the alternative—is most reasonable in light of the model and the data.

Steps 3–6 represent the essence of most inferential statistical analyses. In the binomial analysis, for example, the binomial formula establishes a model of what to expect if the null hypothesis were true. Specifically, we obtain information on what to expect by constructing a hypothetical sampling distribution.

As we saw in Chapter 10, a sampling distribution is a hypothetical frequency distribution of sample measurements. This distribution is derived from the assumptions of the model we have chosen—for example, the binomial model. In some cases—for example, for the normal model—the sampling distribution is also based upon information obtained from the observation or experiment itself.

T I M E ■ O U T
If this all seems confusing, take some time to review the relevant sections of Chapter 10.

To understand the significance of the hypothetical sampling distribution, let's review the MCE example from Chapter 10. The researcher predicts that a mind clearing exercise will decrease reaction time. The null hypothesis states that the MCE will have no effect on reaction time and, therefore, that the average reaction time after the exercise will be the same as the average reaction time for the population from which the sample was originally drawn—specifically, 2.56 seconds. After the mind clearing exercise, the mean of the sample is measured to be 2.52 seconds, and the standard deviation of the sample is 0.248 seconds.

On the basis of the null hypothesis, the hypothetical sampling distribution of sample means is assumed to have a mean of 2.56. To calculate the standard deviation of the sampling distribution of sample means, we substitute the standard deviation of the sample (0.248) into Eq. (10.3), which gives a result of 0.0225.

The essence of the subsequent analysis is Eq. (10.4), which calculates the t value for the mean of the experimental group

$$t_{calc} = \frac{\bar{X}_{sample} - \mu_{null\ hypothesis}}{\tilde{\sigma}_{\bar{X}}} \qquad (10.4)$$

The logic of the **t-test** in Eq. (10.4) is very important because essentially the same logic is used whenever we test a null hypothesis by means of inferential analysis.

ASIDE ■ **It is helpful to think about the sampling distribution as a model of what to expect if the null hypothesis is true. Strictly speaking, however, it is not necessary to construct the sampling distribution. We need only compare the calculated statistic to a critical value found in standard tables compiled for the particular sampling distribution that corresponds to a given model. In the present example, we use the t distribution as a model and, therefore, need only compare $t_{calc} = -1.78$ to $t_{critical} = -1.658$. If t_{calc} is further from the mean than $t_{critical}$, we reject the null hypothesis. The same logic will apply to all of the inferential analyses discussed in this chapter.**

Notice that the numerator in Eq. (10.4) calculates the difference between the actual results of the experiment (the sample mean) and what we expect if the null hypothesis were true (the null-hypothesis mean). In the MCE example, the researcher predicted that the sample mean would be less than the null-hypothesis mean. As it turns out, this prediction is true because 2.52 is less than 2.56. The difference is 0.04. However, the size of this difference alone does not give us enough information to decide whether or not we can reject the null hypothesis. This difference must be looked at relative to how much the sample means will normally vary, which is given by the denominator in Eq. (10.4). In the case of the t analysis, the denominator is the standard deviation of the sample means (also known as the standard error of the mean).

In the MCE example, using Eq. (10.3), we obtained an estimate of 0.0225 for the standard deviation of the sample means. Dividing 0.04 by 0.0225, we find that the sample mean is 1.78 standard deviations below the null-hypothesis mean. But we know that, in a normal distribution, the probability of a point at a distance of 1.658 standard deviations from the mean is only 5%, and hence such an event is extremely unusual. Consequently, we can reject the null hypothesis. In plain English, the researcher was correct in predicting that the mind clearing exercise would reduce the reaction time.

The t formula, like other formulas for inferential statistical analysis, determines how far an actual observation varies from what we would expect if the null hypothesis were true, and then compares this variance to an estimate of **normally occurring variance**.

PEARSON r ANALYSIS

As with the *t*-test, there are two components to the **Pearson r analysis**. First, the statistic itself is calculated. In the *t* analysis, this statistic is the sample mean. In Pearson *r* analysis, this statistic is the correlation coefficient *r*. Whereas the sample mean is a summary statistic that gives us an idea of the central tendency of a given sample, the Pearson *r* is a summary statistic that gives us an idea of the relative variation of two variables in a sample. A **positive Pearson** *r* value indicates a positive **correlation**. This means that the measurements vary systematically, in such a way that high values of one variable tend to occur together with high values of the other variable; likewise, low values of one variable tend to occur together with low values of the other variable. The relationship between the amount of snowfall and the number of children having snowball fights is an example of a positive correlation.

A **negative Pearson** *r* value indicates a negative correlation. This means that high values of one variable tend to occur with low values of the other variable. The relationship between the amount of snowfall and the number of people on time for work is an example of a negative correlation.

Note the following Pearson *r* formula

ASIDE ■ **This formula is presented here to illustrate the logic of the Pearson *r* analysis. The calculation formula in Calculation C.17 (Appendix C) is much easier to use, but does not illustrate the logic of the analysis.**

$$r = \frac{\Sigma(Z_x Z_y)}{N} \qquad (12.1)$$

When calculating a Pearson *r*, we are trying to find the degree of correlation between two measured variables. We refer to one of these variables as *x* and the other as *y*.

In order to use Eq. (12.1), we start with pairs of measurements of **variables x and y**. For example, we might sample 20 locations and measure the number of inches of snowfall (*x*) and the number of children having snowball fights (*y*) for each location. We would then calculate Z_x, the Z score for each *x* measurement, and Z_y, the Z score for each *y* measurement. Next we would multiply each pair of Z scores and add up the results of all these multiplications. Finally, we would divide the results by *N*, the total number of pairs (*N* = 20 in this example).

Each Z value represents the distance of a particular measurement from the mean of all the other measurements in the same sample or population. Therefore, as the correlation between the two variables *x* and *y* improves, their Z values become more similar. If the correlation is perfect, the Z values in each pair will be identical, and the sum of $Z_x Z_y$ will be equivalent to the sum of Z^2, which is equivalent to *N*. In other words, if the correlation is perfect, $\Sigma Z_x Z_y = N$, and Eq. (12.1) will result in *r* = 1.00. With perfect positive correlations, the Z values would be such that *r* = +1.00; with perfect negative correlations, the Z values would be such that *r* = −1.00. It is important to remember that the magnitude of the correlation and the direction of the correlation are separate issues; for example, +1.00 and −1.00 both indicate perfect correlations.

If there is no correlation between the variables, then $r = 0$. Values of $r = -.50$ or $r = +.50$ would indicate a moderate degree of correlation, and so on.

The second component of Pearson r analysis is to determine if the result obtained for r is different enough from the null-hypothesis r value to suggest that the null hypothesis is probably not true. For our purposes, we will assume that the null-hypothesis r value is typically zero, and that the easiest way to determine whether or not we can reject the null hypothesis is to use Table B.4 in Appendix B. More information on how to do so will be presented in Chapter 13.

Regression Analysis

If the calculated Pearson r is sufficiently high for us to reject the null hypothesis, it can be used to make predictions about the y variable on the basis of values of the x variable. For example, if we found a significant correlation between the amount of snowfall and the number of children having snowball fights, we could use the Pearson r value to predict the number of children having snowball fights for a particular snowfall amount. The following formula, called the **regression equation**, is used to make such predictions

$$Y_{predicted} = mX + b \qquad (12.2)$$

To understand the regression equation, consider Figure 12.1, which shows the relationship between variable x (inches of snowfall) and variable y (number of children having snowball fights).

Notice that the correlation between the number of inches of snowfall and the number of children having snowball fights is positive but not perfect. If the correlation were perfect, the points would fall along a straight line. In fact, Eq. (12.2) is the equation for the **regression line**—the straight line such that the sum of the squared distances of each point from the line is a minimum.

In Eq. (12.2), m is the slope of the regression line; that is, it indicates how the y variable is changing relative to the x variable. If the slope of the line is $+1$, y changes at the same rate and in the same direction as x. If the slope is -1, y changes at the same rate as x, but in the opposite direction. The **slope** of the regression line is calculated using the following formula

$$m = \text{Pearson } r_{calc} \left(\frac{\sigma_y}{\sigma_x} \right) \qquad (12.3)$$

Note that, if the correlation is perfect ($r = 1$), the slope of the regression line will be the ratio of the standard deviation of the y variable to the standard deviation of the x variable.

In Eq. (12.2), b is the **y intercept** of the regression line; that is, it represents the point at which the line touches the vertical axis (where x is zero). The y intercept of the regression line is calculated using the following formula

$$b = \bar{Y} - m\bar{X} \qquad (12.4)$$

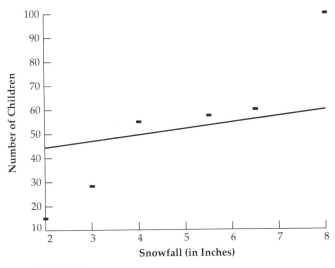

| FIGURE 12.1 | Scatterplot of Snowfall and Number of Children Having Snowball Fights |

Once the regression equation is established, a particular value for the *x* variable can be placed into the equation in order to predict a value for the *y* variable. Thus, using the regression equation, we predict that 53 children would have snowball fights if 5 inches of snow fell. Where in Figure 12.1 would you plot the point for 5 inches of snow and 53 children?

ASIDE ■ See Calculation C.17 in Appendix C for

a detailed example of how the regression equation

is used to make predictions.

T I M E ■ O U T
Take some time to answer this question.

The point would be plotted exactly on the regression line. In other words, the regression line represents the predicted *y* values for each value along the *x* axis.

SPEARMAN *r* ANALYSIS

The logic of the **Spearman *r* analysis** is precisely the same as the logic of the Pearson *r* analysis. However, Spearman *r* analysis is used only when both variables are measured at the ordinal level. Because of the nature of ordinal-level measurement, the sampling distribution used to test the null hypothesis is different and, therefore, the calculated Spearman *r* must be compared to a separate table of critical values (Table B.5 in Appendix B).

The formula for calculating a Spearman r value is illustrated in Calculation C.22 (Appendix C).

RELATIONSHIP BETWEEN THE Z ANALYSIS AND t-TEST ANALYSIS

Consider the following formulas

$$t_{calc} = \frac{\bar{X}_{sample} - \mu_{null\ hypothesis}}{\tilde{\sigma}_{\bar{X}}} \tag{10.4}$$

$$Z_{calc} = \frac{\bar{X}_{sample} - \mu_{null\ hypothesis}}{\tilde{\sigma}_{\bar{X}}} \tag{12.5}$$

$$t_{calc} = \frac{(\bar{X}_{obs_1} - \bar{X}_{obs_2}) - (\mu_{obs_1} - \mu_{obs_2})}{\tilde{\sigma}_{\bar{X}}} \tag{12.6}$$

T I M E ■ O U T

Take some time to study these formulas.

Each of these formulas is different, but they use the same logic.

The difference between Eqs. (12.5) and (10.4) has to do with how the standard deviation of the sample means is estimated. Strictly speaking, Eq. (12.5) should only be used if the sample size is 130 or greater. With large sample sizes, the shape of the sampling distribution is reasonably constant and reasonably close to the normal distribution, and so the table of critical Z values can be used to test the null hypothesis. However, when sample sizes fall below 130, the sampling distribution changes; the smaller the sample, the less it resembles the normal distribution. Under these conditions, it is important to use a slightly different model—and, therefore, slightly different critical values—for each sample size. These critical values are referred to as t values rather than Z values and are compiled in Table B.12 (Appendix B).

ASIDE ■ **Because of the different assumptions regarding between-groups experiments and within-groups experiments (Chapter 11), the variability of the differences between the sample means— the denominator in Eq. (12.6)—is estimated differently for these two types of experiments. Compare Calculations C.25 and C.26 in Appendix C.**

The difference between Eqs. (10.4) and (12.6) has to do with the nature of the null hypothesis. In the case of Eq. (10.4), we are comparing a calculated sample mean to a specific value of a null-hypothesis population mean. In the case of Eq. (12.6), we are comparing the difference between two calculated sample means to a null-hypothesis difference between population means. The null-hypothesis difference between population means is typically zero, because the null hypothesis states that there will be no effect and, therefore, we expect the means of the two different experimental conditions to be the same.

The denominator of Eq. (12.6) is an estimate of how we expect the differences between the sample means to vary under normal circumstances. Therefore, Eq. (12.6), like Eq. (10.4), determines how far an actual observation—in this case, an observed difference between sample means—varies from what we would expect if the null hypothesis were true, and then compares this variance to an estimate of the normally occurring variance.

A more detailed discussion of how to interpret the results of t-test analysis will be presented in Chapter 13.

INFLATED ALPHA

Recall from Chapter 10 that we typically set the alpha level at .05 before testing a null hypothesis. When alpha is set at .05, there is a probability of .05 that we will incorrectly reject the null hypothesis—in other words, that we will make a type-I error. The t-test analysis is designed to compare two sample means at a given alpha level. However, some experiments involve more than two conditions and, therefore, more than a simple comparison between two means. For example, if there were three experimental conditions, three possible comparisons could be made: mean 1 with mean 2; mean 2 with mean 3; and mean 1 with mean 3.

When there is more than one comparison between sample means, it would be inappropriate to use the t-test for each comparison. Under such conditions, the probability of making a type-I error—that is, the probability of incorrectly rejecting at least one of the null hypotheses involved—increases. If, for example, there were three comparisons to be made among three means, and a t-test were used to make each comparison at the standard alpha level of .05, then the true probability of making at least one type-I error would be closer to .14. This is known as **inflated alpha.** Note that the increase in the probability of making a type-I error is not only substantial but difficult to calculate. (See Petrinovich 1969.)

The analysis of variance avoids the problem of inflated alpha, and is much preferable to the use of multiple t-tests when making multiple comparisons.

ANALYSIS OF VARIANCE

The **analysis of variance (ANOVA)**—sometimes referred to as an **F-test**—is used instead of a t-test when more than two experimental conditions are involved and in other circumstances specified in the decision tree. There are several different applications of this analysis, four of which are outlined in Calculations C.1–C.4 (Appendix C). A simplified and generalized version of the formula is as follows

$$F_{calc} = \frac{variance_{sys} + variance_{unsys}}{variance_{unsys}} \tag{12.7}$$

Like the Z formula and the t formula, Eq. (12.7) determines how far an actual observation varies from what we would expect if the null hypothesis were true, and then compares this variance to an estimate of the variance occurring in normal circumstances. In a simple analysis of variance, the numerator of the F formula indicates the amount of variability in the dependent variable that can be attributed to the systematic variation of a particular independent variable; the denominator indicates the amount of variability in the dependent variable that can be attributed to all the factors other than the independent variable. Ideally, if the experiment is well controlled, the independent variable will be the only source of the *systematic variance*, and the sources of the **unsystematic variance** will include such factors as individual differences among the subjects, measurement errors, and moment-to-moment changes in the experimental conditions. The general null hypothesis for an analysis of variance is that the amount of systematic variance will be the same as the amount of unsystematic variance; this would be true if the independent variable had no effect. By comparing the calculated F value to a critical F value (see Table B.13 in Appendix B), we determine whether or not we can reject the null hypothesis.

Any confounds present in the experiment would contribute to the systematic variation. Do you understand why this is so?

T I M E ■ O U T
Take some time to answer this question.

A confound is some variable other than the independent variable that varies systematically among the experimental conditions. For example, if the intended independent variable were room temperature, and a 60° condition was run at 7:00 A.M., while a 70° condition was run at 4:00 P.M., the time of day would be a confound because it would vary systematically along with the temperature of the room. Under such conditions the numerator of the F test would reflect the variation due to both room temperature and time of day. If the systematic variance was found to be significantly greater than the unsystematic variance, we would have to reject the null hypothesis and say that there was a systematic effect. However, it would be impossible to determine whether the effect was due to the room temperature, the time of the day, or a combination of both.

MAIN POINT SUMMARY

The fundamental logic whereby the null hypothesis is tested is the same for the *Z*, *t*, and *F* analyses. All three formulas determine how much an actual observation varies from what we would expect if the null hypothesis were true and then compare this variance to an estimate of the unsystematic variance that occurs normally under uncontrolled conditions.

A more detailed discussion of how to interpret the results of an analysis of variance will be presented in Chapter 13.

LIMITATIONS OF THE ANALYSIS OF VARIANCE

The underlying logic of the *t*-test and the *F*-test (analysis of variance) is the same; however, the conclusions that they support are different. In the case of the *t*-test, only two experimental conditions are compared. Therefore, if we reject the null hypothesis, we can accept the alternative hypothesis, and we will know immediately whether or not our research hypothesis is supported. In the case of the *F*-test, however, more than two experimental conditions are compared. Therefore, if we reject the null hypothesis, we can accept the alternative hypothesis, but we will not know immediately whether or not our research hypothesis is supported.

This difference in interpretation exists because the alternative hypothesis is different for the *t*-test and the *F*-test. In the *t*-test, the alternative hypothesis is essentially identical to the researcher's hypothesis. For example, if the researcher predicts that a 60° group will have a lower average test score than a 70° group, the alternative hypothesis is stated the same way. In the *F*-test, however, the alternative hypothesis is not identical to the researcher's hypothesis. For example, if the researcher predicts that a 70° group will have the highest average of three groups (a 70° group, a 60° group, and a 50° group), the alternative hypothesis will simply state that the amount of systematic variation is significantly greater than the amount of unsystematic variation. In other words, the statement suggests that the independent variable has an effect, but the precise nature of the effect is not indicated. Therefore, rejecting the null hypothesis in an analysis of variance doesn't tell us whether or not the researcher's prediction is correct.

Because of this limitation, if the analysis of variance (ANOVA) allows us to reject the null hypothesis, we must do an additional analysis (a **post-ANOVA analysis**) to determine whether the researcher's prediction is correct. There are many such analyses; in this book, we focus on the Scheffe analysis.

SCHEFFE ANALYSIS

The **Scheffe analysis** makes use of the results of the analysis of variance to determine how large the difference between the means of any two experimental conditions must be in order to reject the null hypothesis for each possible comparison in a given experiment. If there were four experimental conditions, there would be four sample means—one for each condition—and six possible comparisons: mean 1 with mean 2; mean 2 with mean 3; mean 3 with mean 4; mean 1 with mean 3; mean 1 with mean 4; and mean 2 with mean 4. With six possible comparisons there would be six possible null hypotheses; each null hypothesis predicts no difference between the means for that comparison. The Scheffe analysis keeps the alpha level constant (at .05, for example) for the entire group of comparisons and determines how large the difference would have to be in order to reject the null hypothesis for each comparison. The Scheffe formula is stated as follows

$$CD = \pm \sqrt{(df_{\text{sys}})(F_{\text{crit}})(\text{variance}_{\text{unsys}})\left(\frac{1}{n_1} + \frac{1}{n_2}\right)} \qquad (12.8)$$

The Z, t, and F formulas discussed above result in a calculated value, which is then compared to a critical value from a table. The Scheffe formula is different in that it results in a **critical difference** (CD), which is the size of the difference necessary in order to reject the null hypothesis. Thus, the actually observed difference is compared directly to this critical difference.

The components of the formula are as follows:

- df_{sys} denotes the number of degrees of freedom, which is related to the number of conditions in the experiment. (The abbreviation "sys" is for "systematic.") In fact, the number of degrees of freedom is one less than the total number of conditions in the experiment. For example, if there are four conditions then $df_{\text{sys}} = 4 - 1 = 3$.

- F_{crit} is the critical F value used in the initial analysis of variance.

- Variance$_{\text{unsys}}$ denotes the amount of unsystematic variation estimated in the initial analysis of variance.

- n_1 is the number of scores in the first of the two experimental conditions being compared.

- n_2 is the number of scores in the second of the two experimental conditions being compared.

For any given experiment, the df_{sys}, F_{crit}, and variance$_{\text{unsys}}$ values for a particular set of comparisons will be consistent. However, n_1 and n_2 may differ from comparison to comparison. A separate CD must be calculated for each unique set of n_1 and n_2 values. (See Procedure C.20 in Appendix C.)

A more detailed discussion of how to interpret the Scheffe analysis will be presented in Chapter 13.

INTERACTION

We have seen that, when we move from a simple experiment involving only two conditions of one independent variable to an experiment involving three or more conditions of one independent variable, we move from a t-test analysis to an analysis of variance. What happens when we move from an experiment involving only one independent variable to an experiment involving more than one independent variable?

First, consider a simple experiment in which there is only one independent variable (task difficulty) and two conditions (easy task and hard task). The dependent variable is number of errors. One group of subjects is measured under an easy-task condition and a separate group of subjects is measured under a hard-task condition. The researcher predicts that the average number of errors will be significantly greater for the hard-task group. Under these conditions, a t-test for an independent-groups (between-groups) design would be appropriate.

Now consider the addition of another independent variable (motivation) to this experiment. There will be two conditions of motivation (high motivation and low motivation). Half of the easy-task group will now be measured under a high-motivation condition, and the remaining half will be measured under a low-motivation condition. Half of the hard-task group will also be measured under a high-motivation condition, and the remaining half will be measured under a low-motivation condition. Thus, there will be four different experimental conditions: easy task, high motivation; easy task, low motivation; hard task, high motivation; and hard task, low motivation. The researcher's hypothesis is now more complex. She predicts that there will be an increase in the average number of errors when looking at the hard task compared to the easy task for both the high- and low-motivation conditions. More precisely, she predicts that this increase in average number of errors will be greater under high-motivation conditions. This prediction illustrates a general concept known as interaction.

An **interaction** between two independent variables is said to occur when one independent variable has a different effect on the dependent variable under different conditions of some other independent variable. In the above example, the interaction predicted by the researcher is such that one independent variable (task difficulty) would have a greater effect on the number of errors under the high-motivation condition than on the number of errors under the low-motivation condition. Figure 12.2 illustrates this predicted interaction.

Although the concept of interaction may seem quite complex at first sight, it is actually very basic to an understanding of how any behavior is influenced by variables. Certainly, in the case of human behavior, we are never affected by

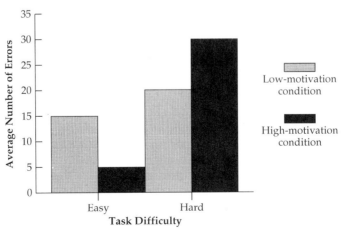

FIGURE 12.2   Interaction between Task Difficulty and Motivation

only one variable in our environment. Instead, our behavior is affected by the interaction of many variables.

Experiments involving more than one independent variable are quite common; they are referred to **factorial experiments** when each possible combination of independent variable conditions is considered as a separate condition. In the previous example, there were two conditions of each of two independent variables and, therefore, four factorial combinations of conditions ($2 \times 2 = 4$). This is referred to specifically as a **2×2 factorial design**. If there were three conditions of one independent variable and two conditions of another independent variable, there would be six factorial combinations and the design would be called a **3×2 factorial**. More generally, both of these designs are referred to as **$A \times B$ factorials**.

To analyze the results of these experiments, a more complex application of the analysis of variance is required.

FACTORIAL ANALYSIS OF VARIANCE

The conceptual formula for the **factorial analysis of variance** is essentially the same as for the simple analysis of variance

$$F_{calc} = \frac{variance_{sys} + variance_{unsys}}{variance_{unsys}} \tag{12.7}$$

However, because there are three separate null hypotheses in a factorial experiment involving two independent variables, this formula must be applied three times. Referring to the two independent variables as variable A and variable B, the three null hypotheses are:

1. The amount of variance due to the systematic effect of variable A will be the same as the amount of unsystematic variance. (In other words, independent variable A will have no overall effect.)

2. The amount of variance due to the systematic effect of variable B will be the same as the amount of unsystematic variance. (In other words, independent variable B will have no overall effect.)

3. The amount of variance due to the systematic combination of variable A and variable B will be the same the amount of unsystematic variance. (In other words, independent variable A will not have a different effect under different conditions of independent variable B; there will be no interaction between independent variable A and independent variable B.)

A separate F is calculated for each of these three null hypotheses and compared to the appropriate critical F from Table B.13 in Appendix B. (See

Chapter 13 and Calculations C.3 and C.4 in Appendix C for more details.) Depending on the number of independent variables, the number of conditions of each independent variable, and the precise nature of the researcher's hypothesis, it may be necessary to do a post-ANOVA analysis as stated previously. (This will be discussed in more detail in Chapter 13.)

COMPLEX EXPERIMENTAL DESIGNS

As you must know by now, several factors can make an experiment more complicated than the simple case characterized by only two conditions of a single independent variable and only one group of subjects for each of the two conditions. These complicating factors are as follows:

- Between-groups versus within-groups design (Chapter 11).
- More than two conditions of a single independent variable.
- More than one independent variable.

The combination of these three complicating factors can lead to some very interesting designs. Consider, for example, a design characterized by two independent variables, one of which is manipulated in between-groups mode, while the other is manipulated in within-groups mode. This would be referred to as a **mixed factorial design**.

Of the vast variety of complicated designs, we confine our attention to those that can be analyzed by the inferential methods in the decision tree included inside the front and back covers of this book: the *two-way ANOVA* and *Mixed ANOVA* analyses. (See Calculations C.3 and C.4 in Appendix C for further discussion.)

SIMPLE CHI SQUARE ANALYSIS

The **simple chi square analysis** is one of the most common inferential analyses. Note from the decision tree that the simple chi square is used in situations where ony one variable is measured and the level of measurement is nominal. Under such conditions, we only have frequency counts of the number of times our observations fall into each of the nominal categories.

For example, a situation in which the researcher is predicting that consumers will prefer one particular color of packaging (red) over two others (blue and green) would be appropriate for a simple chi square analysis. The null hypothesis would be that, if 30 packages are bought, 10 of each color will be chosen—in other words, no color preference.

The chi square formula is as follows:

$$\chi^2_{calc} = \sum \frac{(\text{observed frequency} - \text{expected frequency})^2}{\text{expected frequency}} \qquad (12.9)$$

This formula once again alludes to a familiar logic. The numerator is an index of the difference between what we actually observe and what we would expect to observe if the null hypothesis were true: With increase in this difference, the calculated chi square will also increase. As with the Z, t, and F analyses, the calculated chi square is compared to a critical chi square value taken from a table in Appendix B. (See Chapter 13 and Calculation C.6 in Appendix C for more details.)

Some special considerations regarding simple chi square analysis that are often negelected are as follows:

- The categories must be mutually exclusive. In other words, it is not possible for an observation to fall into more than one of the categories.

- The categories must be exhaustive. In other words, every observation must fall into one of the categories.

- If the null hypothesis is true, then there must be the expectation of at least five observations in each category.

Note that the simple chi square analysis appears in the observation branch of the decision tree. The rationale for this placement is that, in experiments to which the chi square analysis can be applied, only one variable (for example, color preference) is measured and, therefore, there are no true independent and dependent variables. Some authors might argue that there is actually an independent variable (for example, color of the packaging) and a dependent variable (for example, choice of color) and, therefore, that simple chi square analysis belongs in the experiment branch. This is an excellent example of the gray area between research projects that are purely observational and those that are purely experimental.

NONPARAMETRIC ANALYSES

As you know, the first six analyses at the end of the experiment branch in the decision tree are classified as parametric analyses and require that the parametric assumptions be met (Chapter 11). The remaining analyses in this branch (labeled NP) are classified as nonparametric analyses. These analyses are used either because one or more of the parametric assumptions cannot be met, even though the data are at the interval or ratio level, or because the data are not at the interval or ratio level, in which case the parametric assumptions are inapplicable. Notice that there is a nonparametric alternative to each of the parametric analyses corresponding to experiments with only one independent variable, as follows.

Parametric analysis	Nonparametric alternative
t-test (independent groups)	Mann-Whitney *U*
t-test (dependent groups)	Wilcoxin
ANOVA (between-groups)	Kruskal-Wallis
ANOVA (within-groups)	Friedman

Unlike the formulas for parametric analyses, the formulas for nonparametric analyses do not provide a clear illustration of the logic of null-hypothesis testing, and so they are not presented here. These formulas and the corresponding procedures may be found in Appendix C.

SUMMARY

We began by reviewing the logic of hypothesis testing and then related this to the general logic of sampling distributions and inferential analyses. Our primary purpose in this chapter was to show the relationship between this general logic and the formulas for some of the most commonly used inferential analyses: Pearson *r*, Spearman *r*, Z, t, F, Scheffe, and simple chi square. In this context, we also discussed inflated alpha, interaction, and complex designs. Finally, we considered the role of nonparametric analyses.

ASIDE ■ When you need a complete and detailed presentation of a particular analysis, you can refer to Appendix C, which provides comprehensive coverage of each parametric and nonparametric analysis—including calculations—within the context of a specific scenario. Each scenario illustrates a total process approach, beginning with the researcher's motivation to collect the data and ending with a plain English statement relating the results of the statistical analysis to the researcher's hypothesis.

KEY SYMBOLS

$r, Z, m, b, \text{CD}, df, F, t, \chi^2$

KEY TERMS AND CONCEPTS

$+r$ versus $-r$

2×2 factorial

3×2 factorial

$A \times B$ factorial

Analysis of variance (ANOVA)

Calculated statistic

Complex experimental design

Correlation

Critical difference

Critical value

F-test

Factorial analysis of variance

Factorial design

Factorial experiments

General logic of inferential statistics

Inflated alpha

Interaction

Mixed factorial design

Normally occurring variance

Pearson r analysis

Post-ANOVA analysis

Regression analysis

Regression equation

Regression line

Rejecting the null

Scheffe analysis

Simple chi square analysis

Slope

Spearman r analysis

Systematic variance

t-test

Unsystematic variance

Variable x

Variable y

y-intercept

EXERCISES

12.1 In your own words, state the general logic of hypothesis testing. (Be sure to make reference to the concepts of null and alternative hypotheses.)

12.2 In your own words, state the purpose of sampling distributions as they relate to the general logic of hypothesis testing.

12.3 For the following analyses, state the generalized form of the formula and describe the corresponding logic of null-hypothesis testing:

- Pearson r
- Z
- t
- F

12.4 How many possible comparisons between means could you make in each of the following situations?

        A. Three experimental conditions.

        B. Four experimental conditions.

        C. Six experimental conditions.

12.5 In situations A, B, and C above, why would it be inappropriate to use multiple *t*-tests?

12.6 Summarize the factors that add to the complexity of an experimental design.

12.7 What would a 3×3 factorial design be like?

12.8 Describe the problem of inflated alpha. How is this problem solved?

12.9 What does it mean to say that two independent variables interact? Give an example.

12.10 What is the difference between systematic and unsystematic variation?

Interpreting the Results of Inferential Analyses

General Considerations

Information Required

Using the Tables of Critical Values

Stating Statistical Conclusions

Relating Statistical Conclusions to Research Hypotheses

Stating Plain English Conclusions

Interpreting Computer-Generated Outputs

Summary

Key Terms and Concepts

Exercises

OBJECTIVES

After reading and studying Chapter 13 you should understand the following.

- *some key issues regarding the selection and interpretation of inferential analyses.*

- *which information is necessary in order to interpret each of the following commonly used inferential analyses: Pearson r, Spearman r, Z, t, F, Scheffe, simple chi square.*

- *how to use the appropriate table of critical values for each of the commonly used inferential analyses.*

- *how to state the statistical conclusion for each of the commonly used inferential analyses.*

- *how to relate the statistical conclusion to the original research hypothesis.*

- *how to state a plain English conclusion that relates the statistical results to the original hypothesis.*

- *how to interpret the results of computer-generated statistical analyses.*

GENERAL CONSIDERATIONS

Your ability to interpret the results of your analysis is directly related to how well you understand the assumptions and conditions on which the analysis is based. For that reason, you should select an inferential analysis before you collect your data, whenever possible. This enables you to accomplish the following:

- to design your data collection procedure so that the data will easily fit into the analysis.

- to state your null and alternative hypotheses in a form that explicitly matches the analysis.

- to anticipate the general type of conclusion that you will be able to make if you reject the null hypothesis or if you are unable to reject the null hypothesis.

It is very helpful to work closely with the decision tree as you design your strategy for collecting data. Of course, the first question to ask is: Will this be an experiment or an observation?

INFORMATION REQUIRED

You must know certain pieces of information before you can interpret the results of a particular inferential analysis, as follows.

Pearson *r* Analysis

The following information is required:

- the alpha level (usually .05).

- the degrees of freedom (df). For the Pearson r analysis, $df = N_{pairs} - 2$, where N_{pairs} is the total number of pairs of observations. For example, if there are 20 pairs of observations, $df = 18$.

- whether the alternative hypothesis is one-tailed or two-tailed.

- the critical value (or values) of the Pearson r from Table B.4 in Appendix B.

- the calculated Pearson r based upon the data collected.

Spearman *r* Analysis

The following information is required:

- the alpha level (usually .05).

- the number of pairs of observations. (Tables of critical Spearman r values are based upon the number of pairs of observations rather than degrees of freedom.)

- whether the alternative hypothesis is one-tailed or two-tailed.

- the critical value (or values) of the Spearman r from Table B.5 in Appendix B.

- the calculated Spearman r based upon the data collected.

Z Analysis

The following information is required:

- the alpha level (usually .05).
- whether the alternative hypothesis is one-tailed or two-tailed.
- the critical value (or values) of Z from Table B.2 in Appendix B.
- the calculated Z based upon the data collected.

t Analysis

The following information is required:

- the alpha level (usually .05).
- whether the alternative hypothesis is one-tailed or two-tailed.
- the degrees of freedom (df). For the independent-groups t-test, $df = n_{tot} - 2$, where n_{tot} is the total number of subjects in all conditions. For the dependent-groups t-test, if each subject is measured under both experimental conditions, $df = n_{tot}$. If the subjects are matched, $df = N_{pairs} - 1$, where N_{pairs} is the total number of matched pairs.
- the critical value (or values) of t from Table B.12 in Appendix B.
- the calculated t based upon the data collected.

F Analysis (One Independent Variable, Between-Groups)

The following information is required:

- the alpha level (usually .05).
- the degrees of freedom for the systematic source of variance (df_{sys}). In a simple between-groups analysis of variance, $df_{sys} = k - 1$, where k is the number of conditions of the systematic variable. For example, with four conditions of the independent variable in a simple F analysis, there are three degrees of freedom. (The calculation of df may be different for different experimental designs. See Calculations C.2–C.4 in Appendix C for details.)
- the degrees of freedom for the unsystematic source of variance (df_{unsys}). In a simple between-groups analysis of variance, $df_{unsys} = n_{total} - k$, where n_{total} is the total number of subjects in the experiment. The calculation of

df_{unsys} can become complicated if the design is complex. (See Calculations C.3 and C.4 in Appendix C.)

- the critical F from Table B.13 in Appendix B.
- the calculated F based upon the data collected.

Scheffe Analysis

The following information is required:

- the alpha level (usually .05).
- the critical difference (CD) calculated from the corresponding formula.
- the calculated difference based upon the data collected.

Simple Chi Square Analysis

The following information is required:

- the alpha level (usually .05).
- the degrees of freedom (df). For the simple chi square analysis, $df = N_{cat} - 1$, where N_{cat} is the total number of independent categories.
- the critical chi square value from Table B.3 in Appendix B.
- the calulated chi square value based upon the data collected.

Calculations by Computer

Generally speaking, you must have all of the required information before you will be able to interpret the results of the analysis. However, there is one exception to this rule. If you are using a computer program for the analysis, the output of the program may include the exact probability for a given calculated statistic. For example, the output may state

$(t = +4.26; df = 9; p = .00035;$ one-tailed$)$

In such cases you will know immediately whether or not the probability of making a type-I error is less than or equal to .05; in the above example, p is clearly less than .05. When an exact value of p is given, you do not have to compare your calculated statistic to a critical value from a table.

USING THE TABLES OF CRITICAL VALUES

Except when using certain computer programs, you will need to look up a critical value from a table in Appendix B before you can interpret the results of your analysis. Once again, we consider each type of analysis separately.

Pearson *r* Analysis: One-Tailed Alternative Hypothesis

The following steps are required:

- Determine the degrees of freedom (as in the previous discussion).
- Find the critical Pearson *r* value corresponding to the degrees of freedom and the probability value for the given alpha (usually .05) in Table B.4, for the prediction of a positive or negative correlation, as appropriate.

If the alternative hypothesis predicts that the correlation will be positive, the search is in the upper tail of the sampling distribution of Pearson *r* statistics, and the critical Pearson *r* is positive. For $\alpha = .05$ and $df = 18$, the critical Pearson *r* would be $+.3783$.

If the alternative hypothesis predicts that the correlation will be negative, the search is in the lower tail of the sampling distribution of Pearson *r* statistics, and the critical Pearson *r* is negative. For $\alpha = .05$ and $df = 18$, the critical Pearson *r* would be $-.3783$.

Pearson *r* Analysis: Two-Tailed Alternative Hypothesis

Find the corresponding critical Pearson *r* value in Table B.4 for the given alpha level and degrees of freedom.

If the alternative hypothesis simply predicts that there will be a correlation but does not specify the direction of the correlation, then the search will be in both the upper and lower tails of the sampling distribution of Pearson *r* statistics, and there will be two critical Pearson *r* values—one negative and one positive. For $\alpha = .05$ and $df = 18$ the critical Pearson *r* values would be $+.4438$ and $-.4438$.

Z Analysis: One-Tailed Alternative Hypothesis

The following steps are required:

- Find the critical Z value corresponding to the probability value for the given alpha (usually .05) in Table B.2. For example, if $\alpha = .05$, the critical $Z = 1.645$.

■ If the alternative hypothesis requires searching in the upper tail of the distribution, attach a plus sign to the critical Z value.

If the alternative hypothesis predicts that the sample mean will be greater than the population mean, then the predicted difference is positive, the search is in the upper tail, and the critical Z is positive.

■ If the alternative hypothesis requires searching in the lower tail of the distribution, attach a negative sign to the critical Z value.

If the alternative hypothesis predicts that the sample mean will be less than the population mean, then the predicted difference is negative, the search is in the lower tail, and the critical Z is negative.

Z Analysis: Two-Tailed Alternative Hypothesis

In Table B.2, find the critical Z value corresponding to half the probability value for the given alpha level. For example, if $\alpha = .05$, the probability value to be found in Table B.2 is .025. (With a two-tailed test, the alpha probability must be divided equally between the upper and lower tails of the distribution.) The critical Z values would then be $+1.96$ and -1.96

t Analysis: One-Tailed Alternative Hypothesis

The following steps are required:

■ Determine the degrees of freedom, as in the previous discussion (p. 240).
■ Find the critical t value corresponding to the degrees of freedom and the probability value for the given alpha (usually .05) in Table B.12 for the prediction of a positive or negative difference between the first and second sample means, as appropriate.

If the alternative hypothesis predicts that the difference between sample means will be positive, the search is in the upper tail of the sampling distribution of differences, and the critical t would be positive. For $\alpha = .05$ and $df = 18$, the critical t would be $+1.734$.

If the alternative hypothesis predicts that the difference between the sample means will be negative, the search is in the lower tail of the sampling distribution of differences, and the critical t would be negative. For $\alpha = .05$ and $df = 18$, the critical t would be -1.734.

t Analysis: Two-Tailed Alternative Hypothesis

Find the corresponding critical *t* value in Table B.12 for the given alpha level and degrees of freedom.

> If the alternative hypothesis simply predicts that there will be a difference between the sample means but does not specify the direction of the difference, then the search will be in both the upper and lower tails of the sampling distribution of differences, and there will be two critical *t* values—one negative and one positive. For $\alpha = .05$ and $df = 18$, the critical *t* values would be $+2.101$ and -2.101.

F Analysis

The following steps are required:

- Determine the degrees of freedom for the systematic source of variance, as in the previous discussion (p. 240).

- Determine the degrees of freedom for the unsystematic source of variance, as in the previous discussion (pp. 240–241).

- In Table B.13, find the critical *F* value corresponding to the given alpha level, the *df* for the systematic source of variance (df_{sys}), and the *df* for the unsystematic source of variance (df_{unsys}).

For example, if $\alpha = .05$, $df_{sys} = 3$, and $df_{unsys} = 27$, the critical *F* value from Table B.13 is 2.96.

Although the procedure for determining *df* is different for different experimental designs, the procedure for looking up the critical *F* is always the same once the *df* values have been determined for the systematic and unsystematic sources of variance.

The alternative hypothesis usually implied in an analysis of variance is that the variance due to a given systematic source will be greater than the variance due to unsystematic sources. Therefore, the alternative hypothesis in *F* analysis is always one-tailed, in contrast to *t* analysis, in which the alternative hypothesis may be either one-tailed or two-tailed.

Scheffe Analysis

As we already noted, there is no table of critical values for the Scheffe analysis since the analysis itself is designed to provide the critical difference (CD) necessary to reject the null hypothesis.

Chi Square Analysis

The following steps are required:

- Determine the degrees of freedom, as in the previous discussion (p. 241).
- In Table B.3, find the critical chi square value corresponding to the given alpha level and *df* value.

For example, if $\alpha = .05$ and $df = 2$, the critical chi square value from Table B.3 is 5.991.

Nonparametric Analysis Revisited

Typically, once the critical value is obtained from the appropriate table in Appendix B, the calculated value is compared to the critical value: If the calculated value is greater than a positive critical value or less than a negative critical value, this means that the null hypothesis can be rejected at the chosen alpha level.

However, for certain nonparametric analyses—such as the Mann-Whitney *U* analysis—the calculated value must be less than the critical value in order to reject the null hypothesis. This is another example of the obscure logic of nonparametric analyses. I encourage you to study every scenario in Appendix C so that you will understand the subtleties of all the analyses in the decision tree.

STATING STATISTICAL CONCLUSIONS

In inferential analyses, the primary objective is to determine whether or not the null hypothesis can be rejected at a given alpha level. Researchers often set the alpha level at .05, indicating that they are not willing to be wrong more than 5% of the time when rejecting the null hypothesis. At the same time, the researchers know that they probably will make a type-I error 5% of the time when rejecting the null hypothesis at an alpha level of .05. In any case, the primary point of interest in conducting an inferential analysis is the probability of obtaining the given calculated statistic under the assumption that the null hypothesis is true. The following discussion illustrates the reasoning.

For an alpha level of .05 and a one-tailed alternative hypothesis in the upper tail of the normal distribution, the critical Z would be $+1.645$. If the observation resulted in a calculated Z value of $+1.80$, the probability of obtaining such a Z value by chance, if the null hypothesis were true, would be less than .05. Therefore, we reject the null hypothesis, because it is unlikely to be true for this particular observation.

In view of this reasoning, statistical conclusions based on inferential analyses typically include a statement regarding the probability (p) of the calculated statistic. In order to reject the null hypothesis, this p value must be less than the alpha level chosen by the researcher (typically, .05). The corresponding p value can be stated exactly (for example, $p = .034$), as in the case of some computer-generated analyses, or it can be stated in terms of its magnitude relative to alpha (for example, $p < .05$). The results of an inferential analysis are said to be *statistically significant* when the p value is less than the alpha value.

When p is greater than .05, once again, the exact p value may be stated (for example, $p = .263$), or a symbolic statement may be used ($p > .05$). If the p value is greater than the alpha level, you will sometimes see *ns* (not significant).

When reporting the results of our analyses, we assume that the reader understands the reasoning (no matter how lengthy it may be), and we make the statement as brief as possible, in a standard format. Notice that, even though the following statements are brief, they contain all the relevant information regarding the results of the statistical analysis itself—specifically, all the information required to determine whether the null hypothesis can be rejected.

(Pearson $r = +.48$; $df = 11$; $p < .05$; one-tailed)

(Pearson $r = +.50$; $df = 8$; $p > .05$; one-tailed)

(Pearson $r = -.48$; $df = 11$; $p < .05$; one-tailed)

(Pearson $r = -.42$; $df = 35$; $p < .05$; two-tailed)

(Spearman $r = +.63$; $N_{pairs} = 10$; $p < .05$; two-tailed)

(Spearman $r = -.25$; $N_{pairs} = 20$; ns; two-tailed)

(Spearman $r = +.87$; $N_{pairs} = 20$; $p < .05$; one-tailed)

($Z = +1.80$; $p < .05$; one-tailed)

($Z = +.86$; ns; one-tailed)

($Z = +.86$; $p = .1949$; one-tailed)

($Z = +1.84$; $p < .05$; one-tailed)

($t = +1.74$; $df = 26$; ns; one-tailed)

($t = -1.86$; $df = 24$; $p < .05$; one-tailed)

($t = +1.97$; $df = 18$; ns; two-tailed)

($F = 3.46$; $df_{sys} = 3$; $df_{unsys} = 27$; $p < .05$)

($F = 3.46$; $df_{sys} = 3$; $df_{unsys} = 9$; ns)

(Observed diff. $= 4.11$; CD $= 3.56$; $p < .05$)

(Observed diff. $= 5.63$; CD $= 6.52$; ns)

($\chi^3 = 6.37$; $df = 1$; $p < .05$)

($\chi^2 = 3.24$; $df = 2$; ns)

Generally speaking, if the null hypothesis is rejected, the alternative hypothesis is accepted, but we are not necessarily supporting the exact statement of the researcher's hypothesis. For the sake of clarity, it is important to relate statistical summary statements like those cited here to the reseacher's specific prediction.

RELATING STATISTICAL CONCLUSIONS TO RESEARCH HYPOTHESES

It is a fundamental principle of this book that gathering data, interpreting data, and making decisions on the basis of those interpretations are all parts of an integrated process. Intelligent decisions must take into consideration all aspects of the process, beginning with the researcher's original question. As we have seen, the strategy for data collection must be chosen on the basis of an understanding of how inferential statistical analyses work.

Likewise, after the results of the statistical analysis have been obtained, they should be interpreted within the context of the total process. The most important information at that stage is as follows:

- the researcher's initial hypothesis (prediction).

- the null hypothesis, stated for purposes of statistical analysis.

- the alternative hypothesis, stated for purposes of statistical analysis.

- the statistical summary statement obtained after the analysis.

On the basis of this information, we can formulate the final conclusion regarding the researcher's hypothesis.

The following scenario illustrates the total decision-making process.

Type of research:	Experiment
Number of dependent variables:	1
Level of measurement:	Interval/ratio
Assumptions met:	Yes
Number of independent variables:	1
Conditions of independent variable:	2
Type of design:	Between-groups (B-G)
Choice of analysis:	t-test for independent groups

Motivation for Research: A researcher believes that listening to classical music will improve a person's reaction time.

Description of Research: The researcher randomly selects 20 people from the general population and then randomly assigns 10 of these people to a control group and the remaining 10 to an experimental group. In the control group, each of the 10 people is asked to sit in a room for 15 minutes and to try to relax as well as they can. In the experimental group, each of the 10 people is asked to sit in a room for 15 minutes and try to relax by listening to classical music. All subjects in both the experimental and control groups are tested for their reaction time after the 15-minute relaxation period.

Type of Conclusion Possible: The *t*-test for independent groups analysis will allow the researcher to determine if the average reaction time for the experimental group (who listened to classical music) is significantly lower than the average reaction time for the control group.

Comments: If the results of the *t*-test indicate that the mean reaction time is significantly lower for the experimental group, then the researcher may conclude that listening to classical music had the significant effect of improving the reaction times of the subjects.

Assumptions: Suppose that the parametric assumptions are met.

Test Data:

Classical Group		Control Group	
Person	Reaction Time	Person	Reaction Time
1	2.36	11	2.79
2	2.10	12	2.58
3	2.20	13	2.41
4	2.32	14	2.49
5	2.14	15	2.47
6	2.30	16	2.34
7	2.45	17	2.68
8	2.47	18	2.70
9	2.38	19	2.56
10	2.46	20	2.62

Specifics Regarding the *t*-Test for Independent Groups Analysis: The *t*-test for independent groups analysis helps the researcher to determine whether or not two sample means differ significantly from what would be expected on the basis of chance.

Research Hypothesis: The researcher believes that listening to classical music will decrease reaction time. The corresponding alternative hypothesis may be stated symbolically as follows:

$$H_{Alt}: \mu_{classical} < \mu_{control}$$

Translated into plain English, this means that the researcher is predicting that the average reaction time for the classical music group will be significantly lower than the average reaction time for the control group.

Null Hypothesis: If the research hypothesis is incorrect, there will be no difference between the average reaction time for the classical music group and the average reaction time for the control group. That is our null hypothesis. Stated symbolically

H_{Null}: $\mu_{classical} = \mu_{control}$

Organizing Raw Data for the t-Test: When preparing the data for entry into the t-test calculation formula — whether the calculations are by hand or by computer — we must identify the following:

- the independent variable: music, in the present case.
- the two conditions of the experiment: classical music and control group.
- the number of subjects in each condition: 10 and 10.
- the dependent variable: reaction time.

Once the above values are identified, we may enter them into the computer or into the calculation formulas. (A step-by-step example of using the t-test for independent groups formula is provided in Procedure C.25 in Appendix C.)

Testing the t-test Statistic for Significance: The t-test for independent groups calculation results in a specific numerical value for t, which is compared with the critical t from Table B.12 for the alpha level chosen by the researcher. If the calculated t is greater than the critical t, the null hypothesis is rejected and the alternative hypothesis is accepted.

Results of the t-Test Calculations:

Mean for classical condition:	2.12
Mean for control condition:	2.56
Total number of subjects:	20
Degrees of freedom:	18
Alpha:	.05
Critical t:	-1.734 (one-tailed test)
Calculated t:	-4

If the null hypothesis were true, the probability of observing a calculated t of -4 with $df = 18$ would be .00055.

Statistical Conclusion: Because the calculated t of -4 is beyond the critical t of -1.734 for a one-tailed test, we reject the null hypothesis. Note also that, for a one-tailed test, the exact probability of the calculated t is .00055, which is less than .05.

Plain English Conclusion: The average reaction time after listening to classical music is significantly shorter than the average reaction time for the control group, which did not listen to classical music. This supports the researcher's argument that listening to classical music will improve a person's reaction time.

As this scenario illustrates, the results of a statistical analysis can be understood more clearly if the total process is considered — beginning with the initial motivation to do the research and ending with a plain English statement that ties it all together.

STATING PLAIN ENGLISH CONCLUSIONS

Ideally, the final conclusion of a statistical analysis should remind the reader of the researcher's original hypothesis, and should clearly explain the relevance of the results to that hypothesis, without using jargon or confusing language of any kind. Even the word *significantly* in the plain English conclusion of the previous scenario has the potential to confuse the reader, since it could lead to a discussion of what statistical significance means.

An important point here is that those who understand the logic of statistical inference do not need such an explanation, and those who do not understand the logic would not benefit from an explanation at that stage. Always ask yourself if you've given the reader the most concise and accurate statement regarding the results, without adding unnecessary words.

INTERPRETING COMPUTER-GENERATED OUTPUTS

There are many computer software packages designed specifically to perform inferential statistical analyses. Some of the more popular ones are: Statistical Package for the Social Sciences (SPSS), a Statistical Analysis System (SAS), Minitab, and Systat. Because it is relatively easy for computers to process complex statistical formulas, the output from these software packages often includes much more information than the simple summary statements illustrated in our previous examples. You should keep the following points in mind when interpreting such computer-generated outputs:

- Remember that, for most inferential analyses, the main objective is to reject the null hypothesis.

- Look for some indication of the p value and how it relates to an alpha level. It is often given as an exact value (for example, $p = .067$) or in relation to alpha (for example, $p < .05$). Sometimes, information on p may be found as a footnote to the calculated statistic.

- Don't expect to find any indication of the critical value. The computer calculations indicate whether or not you can reject the null hypothesis; you don't need to compare the calculated statistic to a critical value.

- Different software packages may use different conventions. For example, the sample standard deviation may be denoted by s in some packages and by $\tilde{\sigma}$ in others. Be prepared to refer to the manual for the particular package.

- Stay in touch with your data, so that you will have some expectation of what the results should be. Here are two examples of why this is important.

Example 1: If the output indicates that the mean for variable A is 34.71, whereas your measurements for condition A ranged from 3.47 to 8.21, you know that a mistake had been made. It may be that the data were entered incorrectly, or that the wrong information was entered regarding the number of variables, the number of conditions, or some other factor.

Example 2: If the output indicates that the mean for condition A is 62.36 and the mean for condition B is 23.46, would you know which conditions were meant? Does A refer to the experimental group? To the control group?

- Computers will perform calculations in robotic fashion, even if the data were entered incorrectly. Ideally, you should check at least one of the calculations — maybe the mean for one of the conditions — with a calculator to see if you and the computer are getting the same answer.

- When using a computer software package for the first time, you should run an analysis using a textbook example. This will allow you to see the relationship between the computer-generated output and values that you already know to be correct.

SUMMARY

In this chapter, we focused on the general logic that should guide the interpretation of statistical analyses. From the outset, we emphasized that intelligent interpretation of the analysis requires an understanding of the total process, which includes the original motivation for the data collection, the conditions of data collection, and the underlying logic of the chosen statistical analysis.

We itemized the information required to interpret commonly used analyses, and outlined the recommended steps for looking up critical values and the recommended standard formats for stating the statistical results. Finally, we discussed how to make the connection between the statistical results and the researcher's hypothesis and, very importantly, how to state a final conclusion without jargon.

KEY TERMS AND CONCEPTS

ns

One-tailed versus two-tailed

$p < .05$

$p > .05$

Plain English conclusion

Statistical conclusion

EXERCISES

13.1 Look up the critical value and write a concise statistical summary statement using the format recommended in this chapter for each of the following situations (assume that $\alpha = .05$).

A. Alternative hypothesis: mean 1 > mean 2
$n_1 = 10$; $n_2 = 10$
Calculated t for independent groups: $+1.68$

B. Alternative hypothesis: mean 1 > mean 2
$n_1 = 10$; $n_2 = 10$
Calculated t for independent groups: -1.76

C. Alternative hypothesis: mean 1 < mean 2
$n_1 = 15$; $n_{2.} = 15$
Calculated t for independent groups: -1.72

D. Alternative hypothesis: mean 1 ≠ mean 2
$n_1 = 12$; $n_2 = 12$
Calculated t for independent groups: $+2.36$

E. Alternative hypothesis: mean 1 > mean 2
$n_1 = 10$; $n_2 = 10$ (matched-groups design)
Calculated t for dependent groups: $+1.82$

F. Alternative hypothesis: variance$_{systematic}$ > variance$_{unsystematic}$
Number of conditions: 3 (between-groups design)
Number of subjects in each condition: 10
Calculated F: 3.36

G. Alternative hypothesis: Expected frequency not equal to observed frequency
Number of categories: 4
Calculated chi square: 8.1

H. Alternative hypothesis: Variable A and variable B are negatively correlated
Number of pairs of observations: 16
Calculated Pearson r: $-.46$

I. Alternative hypothesis: Variable A and variable B are negatively correlated
   Number of pairs of observations: 16
   Calculated Pearson r: $+.46$

J. Alternative hypothesis: Variable A and variable B are positively correlated
   Number of pairs of observations: 18
   Calculated Pearson r: $+.38$

K. Alternative hypothesis: Variable A and variable B are correlated
   Number of pairs of observations: 19
   Calculated Pearson r: $+.40$

L. Alternative hypothesis: Variable A and variable B are negatively correlated
   Number of pairs of observations: 16
   Calculated Spearman r: $-.46$

M. Alternative hypothesis: Variable A and variable B are negatively correlated
   Number of pairs of observations: 16
   Calculated Spearman r: $+.46$

N. Alternative hypothesis: Variable A and variable B are positively correlated
   Number of pairs of observations: 18
   Calculated Spearman r: $+.38$

O. Alternative hypothesis: Variable A and variable B are correlated
   Number of pairs of observations: 19
   Calculated Spearman r: $+.40$

13.2 For each of the situations in Exercise 13.1:

- create your own variable names.

- state your research hypothesis.

- state your plain English conclusions based upon the statistical results.

13.3 Summarize the important issues regarding the selection and interpretation of statistical analyses.

13.4 Make a clear distinction between one-tailed and two-tailed tests of null hypotheses.

13.5 What is the general relationship between the calculated statistic and the tabulated critical value? What are the important exceptions to this general relationship?

13.6 Generally speaking, when is the null hypothesis rejected?

13.7 Generally speaking, what does it mean to say that the results of the statistical analysis were significant?

13.8 What is a type-I error?

13.9 What is the probability of making a type-I error?

13.10 If alpha is set at .01, how often will you make a type-I error?

13.11 What are some of the general considerations when interpreting computer-generated outputs?

Databases

Body Weights for 1000 People

Rainfall for 1000 Locations

Reaction Times for 1000 People

Hand Strengths for 1000 People

Room Temperature on 1000 Days

Sizes for 1000 T-Shirts Sold

Arm Length (Inches) for 1000 People

Heights (Inches) for 1000 People

DATABASE A.1 BODY WEIGHTS FOR 1000 PEOPLE

$N = 1000$; population mean 140 pounds; population standard deviation 23.77.

117 156 142 136 126 128 137 177 156 193 134 143 171 131 143 142 145 158 135 148 163 135 108 124 133 146 115 164 173 142
168 181 172 132 132 148 142 123 124 160 108 153 150 121 114 144 100 113 109 147 149 147 135 104 145 177 174 112 103 149
135 142 149 143 144 167 152 103 162 134 144 190 126 116 177 110 136 153 103 156 170 142 138 174 171 145 111 154 125 144
175 131 170 143 147 148 138 162 145 148 123 146 112 158 116 139 183 122 121 165 137 115 152 133 147 162 120 148 122 155
140 155 155 138 178 138 163 172 151 195 140 114 120 159 113 154 142 102 145 183 151 141 179 156 119 141 122 196 152 142
118 119 146 151 167 102 106 120 164 145 182 111 136 101 101 150 168 151 122 128 159 102 136 133 142 199 145 81 165 144
129 139 145 124 155 145 109 127 112 104 145 119 175 111 113 152 138 164 102 136 167 124 138 151 163 161 131 155 147 95
150 107 144 157 108 172 135 165 139 144 104 103 152 153 124 168 123 133 150 165 82 131 123 116 133 155 129 124 121 115
173 170 159 163 156 149 173 137 143 109 141 183 126 200 106 109 178 107 159 121 169 150 142 98 176 110 123 115 124 152
172 169 153 119 171 120 127 171 158 130 154 133 158 143 168 150 176 153 125 126 99 92 126 159 132 103 127 167 170 171
132 122 129 110 123 163 155 133 102 152 106 136 114 127 107 133 81 176 147 156 126 110 123 202 175 115 199 161 123 108
186 136 157 86 82 140 129 165 187 115 144 155 131 134 114 156 110 146 157 154 174 139 177 115 174 155 152 143 125 111
154 144 174 138 144 134 154 150 138 127 143 102 106 120 179 122 126 163 149 163 144 129 150 159 129 119 125 174 159 123
155 150 101 145 125 163 155 100 144 106 90 166 142 167 143 164 175 124 137 161 141 123 136 128 130 151 106 107 144 141
156 147 172 136 134 127 142 150 154 156 169 128 127 139 122 157 102 146 132 178 155 155 148 173 164 131 155 137 178 128
124 124 152 169 153 111 126 86 162 183 104 158 106 128 114 154 155 172 120 127 107 175 159 148 107 116 154 169 162 167
148 152 161 114 163 170 138 137 141 189 133 168 193 102 158 152 131 118 132 90 129 133 106 115 146 126 105 152 146 131
102 145 112 179 112 192 173 134 116 103 151 103 110 189 139 129 173 102 187 141 121 135 142 131 134 131 143 159 101 129
152 156 106 159 161 90 125 168 140 160 167 155 127 108 165 144 120 144 165 127 157 116 127 112 153 133 108 180 174 105
107 154 138 124 168 102 145 147 118 151 148 89 142 106 164 141 159 111 161 176 126 133 141 115 124 175 171 132 121 155
173 142 157 138 108 95 104 132 141 144 142 174 157 132 150 124 165 169 189 110 110 115 144 189 137 152 177 171 153 149
110 148 133 102 169 110 120 163 167 103 142 112 100 175 159 143 150 159 120 123 150 108 103 109 100 143 134 110 105 173
124 114 105 100 82 113 137 141 130 123 148 178 179 159 144 155 166 143 147 144 176 150 156 133 101 139 150 102 152 112
150 154 162 159 177 127 128 139 167 156 125 174 171 124 170 160 114 155 152 160 116 131 189 127 80 162 83 179 135 83
130 134 177 149 128 98 170 167 139 152 107 136 117 163 127 147 83 104 140 155 128 154 150 116 154 121 172 143 155 146
139 123 157 162 114 128 117 140 85 181 124 127 148 167 122 178 151 108 118 144 60 105 104 128 134 127 131 125 152 85
110 129 154 133 128 152 199 146 104 151 128 146 143 185 138 127 179 121 194 189 174 98 142 127 121 141 126 134 142 145
109 138 107 139 149 157 120 177 167 167 166 111 120 120 147 165 143 160 137 136 120 152 134 193 161 149 144 159 179 158
149 123 150 142 172 173 154 158 109 126 112 107 151 147 152 118 142 145 177 137 144 145 153 142 155 144 141 136 100 129
126 157 144 155 168 106 163 158 140 140 150 161 169 126 125 133 155 132 140 116 125 159 164 135 177 138 188 141 145 152
143 137 150 130 139 107 178 139 140 131 137 120 145 136 155 147 144 107 139 135 141 136 130 168 135 163 164 130 148 139
152 148 166 130 151 92 156 132 92 165 104 129 176 164 138 128 120 126 129 172 168 153 157 157 152 150 150 113 144 139
167 125 149 130 131 137 149 117 100 159 171 165 133 148 168 157 152 172 154 84 106 128 150 163 121 158 129 121 105 107
168 122 180 164 76 160 159 148 106 167

The following 10 samples were randomly selected from the above database.

1: 128, 103, 102, 175, 145, 137, 144, 102, 144, 147, 174, 173, 144, 154, 173, 148, 155, 153, 124, 108; $N = 20$; $\bar{X} = 141.65$; $S = 23.42$.
2: 144, 111, 163, 131, 155, 107, 123, 136, 145, 174, 152, 127, 149, 141, 121, 175, 155, 136, 138, 161; $N = 20$; $\bar{X} = 142.20$; $S = 18.49$.
3: 159, 171, 143, 150, 83, 192, 122, 115, 110, 167, 144, 138, 102, 99, 115, 132, 147, 165, 134, 154; $N = 20$; $\bar{X} = 137.10$; $S = 26.96$.
4: 127, 170, 157, 112, 148, 106, 129, 120, 133, 100, 152, 114, 178, 128, 179, 152, 86, 175, 115, 115; $N = 20$; $\bar{X} = 134.80$; $S = 26.88$.
5: 100, 131, 131, 148, 155, 136, 138, 148, 123, 136, 134, 170, 171, 102, 103, 127, 189, 111, 113, 167; $N = 20$; $\bar{X} = 136.65$; $S = 24.28$.
6: 160, 154, 169, 168, 154, 141, 137, 121, 174, 162, 132, 174, 174, 112, 157, 132, 125, 141, 145, 83; $N = 20$; $\bar{X} = 145.75$; $S = 23.22$.
7: 165, 147, 144, 149, 138, 152, 122, 90, 131, 138, 123, 176, 127, 171, 128, 171, 140, 133, 107, 134; $N = 20$; $\bar{X} = 139.30$; $S = 20.99$.
8: 128, 161, 154, 190, 161, 144, 175, 136, 124, 110, 127, 158, 104, 90, 110, 92, 173, 127, 126, 144; $N = 20$; $\bar{X} = 136.70$; $S = 27.28$.
9: 131, 120, 163, 172, 110, 110, 154, 143, 122, 119, 152, 122, 171, 156, 92, 155, 145, 117, 148, 151; $N = 20$; $\bar{X} = 137.65$; $S = 21.96$.
10: 179, 152, 141, 157, 182, 156, 161, 163, 177, 120, 122, 139 145, 163, 128, 128, 163, 139, 171, 128; $N = 20$; $\bar{X} = 150.70$; $S = 19.01$.

DATABASE A.2 RAINFALL FOR 1000 LOCATIONS

$N = 1000$; population mean 8.56 inches; population standard deviation 2.80.

```
13.6   9.8 13.3   6.7 10.5   9.6   8.7 11.6   8.6   8.3   8.1   9.7   7.4 13.0   8.6 10.4 12.3   8.1 10.2   6.3   8.3   1.5   8.5 10.9
 7.4   6.8   7.4   7.7   6.5   5.4   8.6   8.7 13.2   2.5   9.0   6.6 10.8 11.5   7.9   6.3   7.8 10.9 11.3   8.5   1.2   6.5 12.7   7.1
 9.5   3.7   8.0 10.2   7.2   8.9   6.3   5.7   7.6   7.9   9.1   8.5   8.2   1.4   7.0   5.6 10.9 12.6   9.8 11.8   9.0   1.1   7.1   5.2
 6.4   8.9 12.4 12.4   6.4 11.8   5.5   9.5 10.6 10.2   8.7   7.9 12.9 11.6   6.6 10.4   9.3   7.7   7.0   7.4 10.1   6.5   6.4   9.8
13.5   7.1   9.7   5.0 10.3   4.2   7.7   7.9   4.2   9.8   8.5   4.5   6.1   4.1   4.1   9.1   8.9   7.3 10.1 12.1 13.0   9.6 12.9 12.2
 9.9   4.5   8.8   5.0   3.0   5.3   7.3 10.3   7.0   6.4   5.6   4.2 11.5 12.8   8.4   5.9   9.1   3.9   9.6   6.9   5.0   4.5   9.9   9.8
 4.1   6.6   8.1   6.3   8.4   8.7 12.4   8.5 12.8   9.4   6.7 12.5 10.1   9.7   4.5 10.9 12.3   6.6   3.8   4.5   9.2 12.7   6.6   8.6
13.3   6.2 10.5 11.8   5.7   4.4 15.4   6.8   9.5 11.3   7.2   4.4 11.2 13.2   9.7 12.6 12.1   9.4   8.9   9.1 11.7 10.1   5.4 10.2
 9.0 12.9   9.5 12.4   8.5   7.9   7.5 13.2   9.0   8.6 13.3   8.2 11.8   9.5   7.5 14.2   7.6   9.1 10.8   9.3 12.7   7.0   3.6   8.6
 7.3 10.9   7.6 11.5 10.2   7.9 11.7   9.3 12.7 10.3   8.0 12.7   4.3   8.5   4.8 10.1   8.0   7.8   3.8   5.8   6.2 10.2   9.3 12.8
 3.0   8.2 11.1   8.8   9.3   7.1   6.9   9.6   8.6 13.7   8.3   9.4 10.6 12.3   9.3 11.7 10.2 13.0   7.8   7.7   6.0 11.0 12.6 10.2
10.9   8.7   7.9   8.0   6.9 12.6   2.5   8.3   6.7   4.6   6.6 12.4   8.0   9.5   4.6   8.4   5.3   9.8   8.8   5.2   7.6 12.1   9.5 11.2
10.8   7.9   9.3 10.4   5.5   9.1 10.8   6.7   5.7   7.3   9.4 10.9   9.1 14.3 11.6   8.2 10.4   6.6 15.2   1.0   7.9   9.9   7.5   3.8
 5.4 10.1   7.4   2.1 13.0   9.6 11.6   8.8   8.5   6.5   8.7   6.8   9.5   6.6   8.3   9.0 12.9   5.5   8.4   7.1   7.6   9.7   7.3   7.2
 7.1 10.5   5.7 12.4 10.9 10.0   4.3 10.6   6.6   6.0 11.0   8.4   8.2   4.1 11.9   6.6   9.5   9.0   8.4   9.7   5.2   5.3   5.2 11.1
12.1 10.2 11.5   5.5   8.1   9.5 12.2   7.8   9.2   7.3 10.7 11.5   6.5 10.5   6.7 10.2 10.2 12.7   3.8   5.0   8.6   7.0 10.9   5.1
 5.7   9.4 13.3   5.6 15.5   9.4 11.4   5.6 10.9   7.4 10.6   9.7 10.8   4.4   8.8   2.0 10.3   3.9   8.3   7.9   8.0   4.1   8.8 10.0
 7.9 10.9   7.7 10.6 10.1   3.8   6.3   5.1   4.2   7.9   3.3 11.6 14.4   3.9   8.9   8.5 12.7 12.7   4.5   2.3   4.6   5.9 10.6   2.9
 4.9   8.9   7.0 11.7   8.7 10.5   6.9   8.6   9.9   8.2   6.8 12.1   7.7 11.7 11.4 11.3   6.7   8.7   8.8 13.1   9.7 10.4   6.3   6.5
 5.8   3.5 10.8   9.6 11.4   7.6   7.4   5.3 10.5   5.7 13.3   8.2   5.8   4.3   4.1 13.3   1.9   5.1   4.1 10.5 10.5   8.9   9.5   9.2
10.2   6.0   3.8   6.2   8.5   4.2   8.1   5.4   9.5   8.9   9.1 12.0 10.6   6.2 12.0   7.1   8.4   6.4   6.3   6.5   5.3   7.0   8.0   6.6
 6.4   6.9   8.2   8.4 10.2 12.4 11.1 10.1   6.6 14.4   8.2 10.1   8.9   8.9   8.6   8.9   9.4   7.6   9.5 12.8   5.1 10.6 10.6   4.4
 7.3   7.5   9.2   7.9   8.4 10.9   6.7   4.3   8.0   6.9 12.6 13.2   5.4   5.2   6.8   6.6 11.9   6.8   6.8   9.4   6.6 14.1   9.9   9.8
10.3   6.3   3.0 10.0   9.5 11.8   5.4   7.2   8.7 14.0   1.6 11.4   5.6   9.8 12.1   9.7 10.8   9.9   4.0 11.6   5.5   7.0   5.7 10.0
 5.4   7.4 12.7   7.1   8.0   9.9   9.9   4.2   9.1 11.4   4.4 14.0 13.1 15.6   5.7   9.5   8.6   7.9 10.5   9.3   9.6   9.9   7.8 11.9
 9.1 11.5   6.5   8.9   6.7   7.7 10.3 13.0 12.8 11.3   6.4   8.4 10.9 14.9   9.4 11.1   7.1   2.2   9.8   5.1   4.7   7.6 11.8 12.4
 3.9 10.4   2.6   7.7   7.7 12.5   5.0   4.7   9.8   8.4   6.6   8.3   7.8 13.0 12.7 13.2 12.1 12.5 13.1   7.4   9.4 10.4   4.8   4.3
 8.5   8.4 10.2   9.2   6.7   7.2   6.5   6.8   3.9   7.3 10.5 13.4 14.6   8.3   2.4 14.9   8.0   7.5   9.5 12.8 10.9 12.0 10.5   9.9
 6.7   6.4   7.1   4.7 12.6   8.2   7.1   7.6   8.9 10.8 10.7   9.2 13.1   4.5   8.0   6.9 13.1 11.9   6.9   7.3   8.6   6.2   4.9   9.6
 4.8 11.1   8.9 11.9   8.1   8.4 10.7   6.2 11.4   9.4 10.8   7.4   6.4 13.9   4.1   5.2 12.4 10.1   5.4 10.3 10.5 10.3   9.3   6.6
 5.4   9.9   9.3 12.2   6.4   3.7   9.2 10.4   9.0   9.9   7.2 12.1   9.5   5.9   6.5   9.7   9.0 12.1 12.5   9.4   5.6   2.8   5.6   2.6
 3.2   8.7   8.5 10.8 12.1   6.7   4.7 11.2 11.7   4.5   7.8   8.1 10.6   5.8   6.4 13.9 12.8   4.7   6.2   7.1   8.3   6.6 10.3   6.6
 6.2   7.9   9.6   6.3 13.0   9.0 14.2   7.4   2.9   9.1   5.8 10.4 10.8   7.1   7.1   6.3   9.5 11.8 11.2 10.2   4.1   6.2   7.2   7.7
 8.6   5.2   9.5   6.9   9.6 10.3   7.7   2.3   6.5   7.2   6.0   9.4   9.0   4.4 13.0   8.6   6.2 10.8   7.5 11.3 10.1   9.6   4.9 10.7
10.7   7.6   5.7   8.3 14.9   7.8 10.8   3.8   7.7   7.8   9.3 10.8 11.4   2.7   7.1   4.0   9.1 11.1 10.6   4.4 11.6   3.8   9.5   6.6
 7.4   7.8   6.7   9.7   9.1   7.9   7.9   9.1   9.1 12.7   6.4 10.6   5.3   0.7 11.8   8.2   6.2   9.8   8.9   7.6   5.7   5.4 10.3   6.7
 8.9   8.9   8.0   5.5 12.5   4.1 13.2   6.9 11.4   5.7   3.4   8.2 11.3 15.1   4.7   5.4 14.9   4.2   9.0 10.8   8.1   6.3   4.0 11.7
10.2 13.3 11.2 13.2   7.6   7.2   6.2   6.0 11.2   5.9   7.9   5.8   6.8   7.3   6.0   5.9   9.2   8.0 10.0 12.4 10.2   9.3   8.5 12.7
 7.9 12.8   8.1   6.4   9.3   5.3 10.5 10.8   5.5   3.9 12.7 10.9 10.2   8.8 10.0   7.3   7.1 10.6   6.3 10.2   9.0 13.1   9.8   1.8
14.0   7.9 12.2   2.3   7.2   6.0   8.3 12.5   8.0 12.3   8.0   6.0 13.6   9.1   8.9   9.3   7.2   8.3   4.1 10.8   9.9   6.7   9.1   8.9
 5.5   6.4 12.7 12.2   8.9   6.7   9.9 12.5 12.9   7.4 13.2   4.0   9.0   3.6 11.7 10.7 10.4   7.1   3.9   8.8   5.8   8.4   9.9   7.0
12.0   6.5 10.2 13.0   7.5 10.9   6.6   9.0 12.8   9.1   8.1   7.7   5.4 12.4   9.1 12.8
```

The following five samples were randomly selected from the above data base.

1: 4.7, 9.4, 9.9, 3.9, 8.6, 9.4, 9.0, 10.6, 6.7, 2.6; $N = 10$; $\bar{X} = 7.48$; $S = 2.67$.
2: 8.6, 11.6, 8.9, 6.0, 12.4, 11.2, 4.5, 11.5, 8.7, 6.8; $N = 10$; $\bar{X} = 9.02$; $S = 2.53$.
3: 11.1, 9.4, 10.6, 6.2, 6.7, 4.5, 6.2, 7.6, 14.0, 3.0; $N = 10$; $\bar{X} = 7.93$; $S = 3.16$.
4: 5.4, 10.5, 11.7, 10.2, 10.5, 11.2, 3.0, 4.5, 3.9, 5.1; $N = 10$; $\bar{X} = 7.60$; $S = 3.30$.
5: 7.3, 9.5, 9.8, 7.6, 8.0, 9.7, 9.5, 5.6, 7.8, 8.0; $N = 10$; $\bar{X} = 8.28$; $S = 1.28$.

$N = 1000$; population mean 2.56 seconds; population standard deviation = 0.23.

2.01	2.95	2.87	2.97	2.77	2.82	3.14	2.17	2.80	2.54	2.71	2.71	2.83	2.32	2.71	2.59	3.01			
2.27	2.77	2.33	2.25	2.50	2.62	2.76	2.30	2.62	2.84	2.64	2.68	2.45	2.71	2.59	2.86	2.41			
2.42	2.40	2.45	2.37	2.73	2.18	2.69	2.75	2.79	2.55	2.42	2.52	2.19	2.40	2.74	2.96	2.95			
3.00	2.62	2.92	2.52	2.49	2.95	2.67	2.50	2.17	2.64	2.08	2.44	2.63	2.67	2.60	2.50	2.55			
2.60	2.58	2.63	2.65	2.62	2.79	2.51	2.18	2.78	2.20	2.39	2.93	2.34	2.54	2.41	2.95	2.52			
2.27	2.74	2.67	2.38	2.38	2.39	3.03	2.39	2.44	2.47	2.57	2.26	2.38	2.37	2.18	3.08	2.64			
2.00	2.52	2.55	2.84	2.64	2.83	2.29	2.59	2.79	2.71	2.25	2.06	2.20	2.39	2.68	2.89	2.30			
2.43	2.66	2.17	2.70	2.67	2.28	2.81	2.51	2.38	2.94	2.42	2.78	2.75	2.09	2.34	2.85	2.86			
2.56	2.61	2.64	2.27	2.62	2.27	2.21	2.75	2.20	2.86	2.72	2.46	2.52	2.70	2.38	3.09	2.63			
2.48	2.44	2.96	2.86	3.01	2.68	2.18	2.44	2.06	2.43	2.19	2.92	2.57	2.36	2.96	2.75	2.91			
2.94	2.69	2.70	2.44	2.31	2.72	2.77	2.70	2.83	2.54	2.65	2.97	2.22	2.50	2.59	2.42	3.10			
2.06	2.79	2.90	2.52	2.04	2.34	2.43	1.90	2.71	2.19	2.22	2.75	2.53	2.38	2.88	2.33	3.08			
2.63	2.74	2.84	2.54	2.59	2.78	2.44	2.69	2.36	2.61	2.23	2.59	2.86	2.78	2.50	2.77	2.56			
2.69	2.57	2.96	2.20	2.96	2.19	2.55	3.06	2.84	2.96	2.74	2.51	2.84	2.80	2.86	2.37	2.49			
2.56	2.19	2.42	2.65	2.40	2.42	2.64	2.90	2.57	2.85	2.58	2.30	2.70	2.45	2.76	2.68	2.49			
2.38	2.64	2.84	2.40	2.82	2.35	2.30	2.41	2.19	2.97	2.52	2.72	2.24	2.87	2.68	2.54	2.73			
2.32	2.74	2.37	2.94	2.62	2.55	2.18	2.60	2.21	2.67	2.40	2.23	2.96	2.27	2.54	2.31	2.49			
2.43	2.53	2.90	2.38	2.95	2.46	2.20	2.59	2.70	2.66	2.75	2.47	2.46	2.52	2.83	2.18	2.46			
2.39	2.54	2.72	2.44	2.63	2.62	2.40	2.31	2.71	2.52	2.69	2.98	2.57	2.83	2.75	2.26	2.81			
2.48	2.93	2.84	2.21	2.67	2.54	2.34	2.45	2.55	2.47	2.69	2.30	2.18	2.43	2.91	2.63	2.69			
2.70	2.54	2.19	2.33	2.19	2.70	2.39	2.33	2.57	2.37	2.56	2.13	2.54	2.52	2.69	2.47	3.17			
2.81	2.67	2.51	3.06	2.79	2.40	2.23	2.89	2.73	2.47	2.62	2.46	2.58	2.18	2.31	2.28	2.69			
3.05	2.66	2.98	3.09	2.59	2.31	2.61	2.74	2.36	2.71	3.00	2.86	2.71	2.63	2.46	2.30	2.80			
2.60	2.48	2.49	2.81	2.73	2.34	2.45	2.25	2.53	2.58	2.53	2.39	2.84	2.66	2.95	2.74	2.47			
2.67	2.25	2.25	2.64	2.86	2.55	2.59	2.95	2.21	2.66	2.71	2.48	2.77	2.60	2.33	2.35	2.29			
2.28	2.65	2.43	2.53	2.57	2.51	2.41	2.43	2.27	2.55	2.64	2.68	2.57	2.36	2.18	2.45	2.62			
2.61	2.68	2.74	2.39	2.55	2.74	2.56	2.26	2.75	2.41	2.39	2.68	2.72	2.65	2.18	3.01	2.68			
2.69	2.79	2.61	2.52	2.43	2.36	2.23	2.71	2.44	2.66	2.55	2.92	2.57	2.61	2.93	2.72	2.52			
2.26	2.63	2.47	2.51	2.82	2.23	2.91	2.41	2.41	2.10	2.29	2.72	2.88	2.64	2.10	2.64	2.62			
2.55	2.47	2.96	2.64	2.47	2.47	2.46	2.19	2.38	2.90	2.54	3.03	2.77	2.48	2.21	2.50	2.67			
2.00	2.57	2.45	2.15	2.37	2.55	2.53	2.23	2.51	2.67	2.75	2.66	2.56	2.24	2.94	2.55	2.29			
2.70	2.33	2.47	2.28	2.22	2.52	2.54	2.35	2.48	2.59	2.36	2.80	3.02	2.74	2.32	2.62	2.77			
2.49	2.31	2.85	2.52	2.59	2.55	2.60	2.77	2.87	2.52	2.32	2.41	2.40	2.73	2.74	2.35	2.56			
2.66	2.48	2.66	2.33	2.58	2.85	3.03	2.28	2.77	2.46	2.38	2.48	2.58	2.27	2.59	2.21	2.51			
2.34	2.56	2.09	2.67	2.33	2.60	2.73	2.86	2.56	2.95	2.36	2.53	2.22	2.26	2.24	2.69	2.38			
2.32	2.58	2.40	2.62	2.67	2.89	2.91	2.37	2.31	2.74	2.35	2.50	2.51	2.84	2.91	2.57	2.62			
2.88	2.56	2.76	2.73	2.70	2.43	2.81	2.41	2.76	2.27	2.57	2.33	2.72	2.57	2.96	2.72	2.37			
2.92	2.41	2.72	2.56	2.68	2.94	2.48	3.00	2.93	2.54	2.57	2.87	2.50	2.67	2.66	2.70	2.67			
2.93	3.00	2.60	2.72	2.54	2.77	2.62	2.62	2.57	2.95	2.24	2.57	2.30	2.85	2.75	2.93	2.65			
2.31	3.15	2.72	2.28	2.74	2.42	2.42	2.39	2.07	2.52	2.65	2.90	2.74	2.87	2.24	2.28	2.56			
2.77	2.28	2.26	2.51	2.52	3.08	2.50	2.52	2.60	2.38	2.20	2.76	2.87	2.66	2.29	2.06	2.71			
2.97	2.93	2.50	2.55	2.52	2.70	2.62	2.66	2.70	2.35	2.36	2.57	2.65	2.72	2.54	2.82	2.62			
2.57	2.83	2.23	2.49	2.56	2.74	2.51	2.81	2.16	2.48	2.32	2.77	2.70	2.55	2.31	2.41	2.50			
2.50	2.26	2.96	2.48	2.50	2.57	2.83	2.07	2.55	2.65	2.65	2.25	2.52	2.71	2.38	2.87	2.54			
2.47	2.64	2.66	2.74	2.31	2.48	2.83	2.86	2.94	2.09	2.46	2.11	2.50	2.62	2.41	2.18	2.54			
2.47	2.49	2.54	2.45	2.62	2.50	2.74	2.91	2.37	2.29	2.43	2.05	2.19	2.24	2.55	2.87	2.58			
2.54	2.85	2.37	2.53	2.20	2.96	2.25	2.25	2.78	2.44	2.65	2.53	2.32	2.44	2.39	2.95	2.63			
2.90	2.19	2.34	2.42	2.39	2.61	2.78	2.69	2.19	2.27	2.80	2.91	2.40	2.51	2.57	2.35	2.48			
2.66	2.87	2.34	2.20	2.42	2.64	2.72	2.92	2.88	2.13	3.09	2.68	2.40	2.53	2.97	2.33	2.61			
2.63	2.44	2.38	2.38	2.41	2.99	2.98	2.64	2.96	2.85	2.95	2.21	2.40	2.97	2.46	2.41	2.42			
2.59	2.41	2.69	2.70	2.68	2.97	2.42	2.48	3.00	2.42	2.46	2.63	2.92	2.95	2.44	2.75	2.55			
1.98	2.72	2.26	2.34	2.44	2.25	2.33	2.19	2.38	2.45	2.68	3.15	2.66	2.37	2.71	2.56	2.41			
2.60	2.71	2.94	2.33	2.87	2.70	3.06	2.85	2.66	2.63	2.55	2.66	2.96	2.56	2.62	2.75	2.27			
2.56	2.42	2.42	2.63	2.50	2.80	2.64	2.22	2.73	2.58	2.41	2.27	2.59	2.50	2.30	3.06	2.34			
2.51	2.44	2.29	2.67	2.64	2.19	2.91	2.31	2.62	2.64	2.40	2.61	2.46	2.62	2.65	2.26	2.42			
2.47	2.91	2.25	2.71	2.79	2.46	2.49	2.85	3.14	2.61	2.86	2.79	2.52	2.81	2.57	2.57	2.65			
2.58	2.51	2.38	2.66	2.20	2.23	2.81	2.25	2.37	3.16	2.38	2.76	3.07	2.56	2.39	2.96	2.31			
2.41	2.65	2.47	2.71	2.64	2.79	2.51	2.86	2.23	2.39	2.59	2.61	2.48	2.50	2.62	2.62	2.55			
2.72	2.78	2.68	2.67	2.83	2.44	2.94	2.53	2.73	2.62	2.56	2.41	2.77							

The following five samples were randomly selected from the above database.

1: 2.64, 2.64, 2.76, 2.33, 2.73, 3.03, 2.92, 2.23, 2.86, 2.61; $N = 10$; $\bar{X} = 2.68$; $S = 0.235$.
2: 2.06, 2.74, 2.19, 2.53, 2.74, 1.98, 2.69, 2.77, 2.62, 2.80; $N = 10$; $\bar{X} = 2.51$; $S = 0.298$.
3: 3.07, 2.32, 2.35, 2.76, 2.14, 2.41, 2.08, 2.80, 2.91, 2.66; $N = 10$; $\bar{X} = 2.55$; $S = 0.319$.
4: 2.42, 1.98, 2.47, 2.34, 2.60, 2.79, 2.64, 2.69, 2.58, 2.57; $N = 10$; $\bar{X} = 2.51$; $S = 0.215$.
5: 2.71, 2.76, 2.44, 2.29, 2.85, 2.16, 2.42, 3.04, 2.97, 2.37; $N = 10$; $\bar{X} = 2.60$; $S = 0.288$.

DATABASE A.4   HAND STRENGTHS FOR 1000 PEOPLE

$N = 1000$; population mean 49.72 kilograms; population standard deviation 11.98.

50	41	42	29	51	51	57	51	40	42	30	35	64	47	47	64	48	61	46	60
42	33	37	60	61	43	51	59	38	41	50	54	56	26	54	53	71	43	36	62
48	65	48	59	64	60	79	69	55	43	32	34	73	61	51	59	54	58	56	30
40	62	44	74	36	32	57	52	46	38	34	42	59	74	55	39	47	56	65	69
54	47	41	35	63	41	27	57	47	31	60	48	57	28	26	44	55	49	37	61
47	35	49	33	33	42	47	52	34	68	49	69	46	37	42	48	24	40	57	64
43	88	58	40	45	46	53	63	49	50	42	60	44	48	58	47	37	65	62	62
42	53	47	34	51	52	56	37	47	63	56	69	32	63	34	35	52	33	65	77
71	49	49	29	66	70	39	52	60	63	45	52	41	76	52	47	37	78	42	40
61	55	49	61	31	56	41	65	59	40	54	52	65	64	41	63	52	72	33	59
36	43	50	40	50	40	66	60	50	37	56	67	55	56	51	41	54	67	33	43
38	54	45	55	59	39	63	31	42	42	26	64	47	50	62	57	59	38	35	57
25	69	30	34	40	42	39	58	38	32	64	39	66	59	43	68	42	53	68	48
39	52	47	34	61	51	46	42	36	58	43	49	49	15	53	57	51	37	62	53
44	24	61	34	44	51	67	49	34	53	54	55	66	46	35	27	65	69	68	58
44	43	47	58	45	47	69	41	65	47	50	52	62	38	67	58	30	46	56	50
59	25	35	47	31	65	47	45	45	44	40	39	31	66	41	34	47	57	30	44
40	50	49	55	61	47	68	57	58	53	35	64	58	63	32	45	32	59	51	50
68	57	39	44	49	50	24	43	50	49	33	44	55	67	64	57	47	53	36	45
28	51	43	38	67	53	71	43	53	63	42	44	49	47	51	69	73	63	35	41
37	69	41	48	74	35	56	33	31	49	52	50	45	54	56	43	58	40	50	62
52	70	62	46	31	68	59	28	49	30	52	49	53	58	43	53	42	56	55	53
65	51	62	57	61	19	78	38	48	50	46	59	33	35	69	66	45	42	51	63
41	53	47	48	47	50	39	45	42	28	56	69	47	46	64	36	38	48	34	50
20	35	42	64	71	43	64	44	48	31	42	51	43	44	44	41	41	38	54	69
42	56	41	17	73	51	47	59	51	51	23	47	59	44	48	61	61	57	59	52
47	45	56	37	50	50	52	45	50	59	23	54	54	59	53	49	34	40	68	41
59	58	79	55	31	48	47	30	31	48	31	32	59	58	49	53	54	65	52	63
44	35	40	57	50	63	41	53	66	79	53	34	54	53	37	63	50	63	54	40
52	52	51	45	42	36	27	54	23	50	42	60	52	57	69	63	49	56	35	56
63	47	47	52	65	73	45	40	31	57	59	44	57	59	52	60	48	56	24	38
22	64	60	58	57	45	58	46	57	42	55	30	43	65	49	35	47	59	64	48
56	39	27	53	32	56	31	59	48	58	38	76	54	64	48	69	44	41	30	32
54	48	66	43	44	52	78	68	54	65	56	44	49	44	54	43	48	50	33	33
73	68	46	47	49	56	50	37	70	56	50	50	40	62	41	58	45	46	64	54
52	47	53	43	50	78	51	69	41	62	58	44	37	50	73	26	30	38	41	32
43	69	46	60	32	48	57	28	68	54	63	43	45	37	51	58	35	41	45	67
38	51	42	53	66	69	62	53	39	36	33	49	66	69	61	45	38	46	42	44
50	50	53	53	57	55	61	52	36	65	57	66	67	55	43	55	37	20	38	69
55	58	43	39	42	47	56	44	50	52	59	50	41	78	52	42	50	47	35	51
53	49	58	36	37	43	63	46	85	47	39	44	25	67	55	47	42	59	58	60
50	32	58	50	37	51	43	30	65	40	47	50	36	64	66	32	43	37	20	54
46	45	65	74	62	54	41	36	46	63	22	60	33	78	43	65	53	46	58	57
52	32	42	55	42	46	59	41	53	72	61	43	46	51	46	54	58	61	51	24
44	70	56	37	37	53	56	37	56	54	65	50	67	68	59	31	64	49	56	47
45	63	41	16	60	53	44	42	41	42	40	56	50	34	42	68	44	67	47	45
49	67	49	40	38	54	57	40	54	50	61	58	40	31	28	37	44	54	47	66
65	32	33	50	32	43	68	57	55	41	69	46	55	47	67	49	32	68	58	65
43	32	58	57	50	69	47	46	48	46	65	56	45	32	32	64	35	54	56	56
56	43	79	32	31	65	53	50	38	68	60	44	51	54	69	64	37	47	63	35

The following five samples were randomly selected from the above database.

1: 53, 39, 47, 56, 62, 40, 58, 73, 65, 63; $N = 10$; $\bar{X} = 55.6$; $S = 10.45$.
2: 32, 55, 59, 16, 63, 62, 48, 52, 54, 45; $N = 10$; $\bar{X} = 48.6$; $S = 13.89$.
3: 45, 76, 59, 64, 58, 57, 47, 68, 59, 56; $N = 10$; $\bar{X} = 58.9$; $S = 8.65$.
4: 59, 54, 58, 53, 50, 48, 50, 59, 55, 44; $N = 10$; $\bar{X} = 53.0$; $S = 4.75$.
5: 52, 37, 60, 43, 49, 53, 69, 42, 72, 62; $N = 10$; $\bar{X} = 53.9$; $S = 11.10$.

DATABASE A.5   ROOM TEMPERATURE ON 1000 DAYS

$N = 1000$; population mean 79°F; population standard deviation 6.02.

```
86  86  75  81  88  82  86  84  70  73  89  77  75  77  79  85  78  73  84  66  75  80  70  66  83  81
83  84  74  80  86  79  82  67  82  86  84  83  81  72  80  77  92  87  75  81  76  73  75  84  79  71
75  82  75  70  79  79  88  72  71  75  88  71  70  86  84  81  70  79  77  81  78  86  75  80  76  84
79  77  81  81  76  65  76  75  74  83  73  72  83  86  77  74  70  79  87  84  71  84  76  76  76  74
84  71  75  88  70  83  70  86  75  88  80  87  75  76  85  74  75  76  76  88  73  79  82  73  89  81
73  80  70  70  83  73  85  80  81  82  81  77  76  76  86  85  91  83  77  67  81  76  78  85  82  66
88  76  92  80  82  83  83  69  87  76  81  87  86  70  76  68  82  89  77  70  85  85  75  84  81  79
76  67  85  78  76  81  79  86  84  79  84  71  87  81  79  83  86  67  91  83  82  86  77  85  86  82
81  69  79  87  82  83  78  66  76  81  77  60  77  77  83  82  89  66  79  79  82  77  73  81  86  79
84  82  75  79  80  89  80  71  80  76  78  73  85  79  84  84  84  70  74  87  80  72  75  78  71  79
84  78  90  72  80  74  89  80  76  84  84  87  79  79  83  79  86  82  65  79  73  75  78  79  83  93
72  77  70  76  84  76  82  85  71  77  81  84  75  85  84  79  77  87  82  86  71  85  68  77  71  73
82  77  84  82  83  85  65  88  70  86  82  73  87  67  73  84  70  72  84  70  71  81  81  75  77  78
81  84  78  80  80  96  75  89  75  84  84  67  84  83  81  74  76  82  79  85  79  69  76  78  78  74
84  72  73  83  87  84  76  84  81  89  79  81  83  79  78  80  87  78  88  83  65  84  76  84  80  83
83  80  82  74  76  79  79  87  76  84  71  75  74  78  84  80  84  80  72  84  71  83  83  82  80  71
79  65  85  77  83  83  77  74  78  70  71  82  70  72  86  74  84  78  83  86  71  82  77  84  72  76
74  71  88  81  67  89  78  79  70  75  81  80  74  77  83  77  85  87  89  71  69  65  87  76  88  92
79  80  83  83  76  86  75  76  77  89  82  77  82  72  85  77  83  90  91  78  79  81  77  72  87  79
71  74  90  84  80  71  81  80  80  74  94  72  71  79  88  85  87  73  80  71  84  80  70  77  93  78
73  79  80  84  85  82  72  80  81  84  86  88  80  65  83  84  76  89  88  86  74  92  85  73  79  75
84  77  93  80  68  71  80  65  80  75  82  84  85  82  89  75  75  76  76  69  89  71  79  88  76  76
75  73  68  89  81  76  74  89  81  77  83  84  78  84  79  84  88  80  78  75  78  66  82  65  78  80
74  81  76  71  83  81  89  81  84  75  76  87  74  79  84  85  82  74  86  70  88  73  82  88  90  77
78  71  74  82  83  83  81  87  82  82  75  75  77  88  71  71  76  78  79  85  87  83  83  78  78  76
83  86  86  76  83  80  87  75  76  88  73  75  81  79  81  81  76  83  88  75  75  80  82  84  71  78
83  80  80  80  76  74  84  81  79  74  73  79  75  83  79  71  87  91  76  85  76  77  84  77  79  86
81  82  82  73  77  80  85  89  74  76  70  75  82  87  87  77  77  66  85  83  73  77  80  85  84  70
94  88  72  82  82  81  91  84  77  78  82  77  71  72  80  73  71  81  73  78  82  84  71  79  65  88
71  71  71  78  84  80  75  78  72  71  75  78  82  75  74  82  75  80  87  71  76  69  82  84  83  84
76  82  76  83  71  70  65  76  76  82  83  81  79  82  85  76  76  90  86  81  61  79  84  84  84  89
73  79  89  68  79  70  82  85  83  75  79  71  85  78  87  73  82  78  70  82  75  79  70  81  80  73
80  84  87  83  88  81  72  88  83  76  65  87  81  74  92  78  75  69  80  82  84  75  75  75  74  81
66  74  69  76  73  72  71  75  75  89  72  84  76  82  81  82  75  84  70  81  82  77  76  82  83  76
87  85  77  92  83  81  81  82  79  82  81  90  88  76  84  80  82  70  76  84  89  75  74  76  71  75
83  87  70  80  76  89  73  77  86  78  81  65  76  79  89  82  71  71  76  77  75  76  72  84  88  68
74  73  83  72  81  78  71  82  80  65  81  67  92  85  75  83  65  89  82  75  76  78  73  78  74  71
77  79  64  86  86  89  84  86  82  77  78  93  79  84  79  86  85  83  87  82  81  75  89  80  78  79
71  79  77  89  87  77  87  75  85  78  78  77
```

The following five samples were randomly selected from the above database.

1: 78, 80, 85, 75, 83, 77, 78, 76, 71, 88; $N = 10$; $\bar{X} = 79.1$; $S = 4.78$.
2: 89, 79, 79, 76, 87, 81, 76, 81, 92, 71; $N = 10$; $\bar{X} = 81.1$; $S = 6.16$.
3: 77, 65, 81, 94, 73, 72, 82, 73, 81, 79; $N = 10$; $\bar{X} = 77.7$; $S = 7.39$.
4: 77, 78, 82, 70, 92, 75, 83, 75, 75, 84; $N = 10$; $\bar{X} = 79.1$; $S = 5.94$.
5: 77, 75, 74, 71, 81, 80, 73, 81, 81, 76; $N = 10$; $\bar{X} = 76.9$; $S = 3.51$.

DATABASE A.6 SIZES FOR 1000 T-SHIRTS SOLD

$N = 1000$; population mode M; population range XS–XL.

L S M S M M S L M L S L S M L XL S L M M L L S M S S M M L S

S L M L XS M M M M M S XS S M S M L M L M L L M M XS M L M M XS

L S S M S M M S S L S S M M L L L S M M L M M L M S M S S M

M M S M S S L L L L XS M M L L M S S M M L S M S M S M M L XS

S M M M S M M M M M M L M M S S M M M M S S S S L S L M M S

XL L L L M L S L M M L S S M M L M L L S S M L M M M S S S L

M L M S XS L M M XL M M M S M L M M M L M L M M S M M M M M M

S XL S L M M XS M M M M M S M M M S S M M M L M M L L L M M

M M M M M L M L S L M L S S XL S XS S L S M S S S M S M S L S

L M M S XS S M L M M L S L M L L S S M S S L M L L L S S L M

S M L M L M S L L M L L S S M M S M M M M M M XL M S S L XS S

M M S L L S M M S S M S S M S M XL M M S L S M L L M M M M L

L S L M S L M L S L S M L S S S M XS S M M M M L L M XS S L M

M M L M S M S M M M XL M S M M S L M M M L M M M M L S M M S

M S L M L S M L L M M L L L XS M M M M M S M M M XL L M M L M

L M M M L M M L L S M L M S M S M S M S M XS S M S L M M S S

S S M L L S M S M S S M L M M M M XS M M M M M L L M L S S S

L M M S L M S M L M L M S S L L S M L M M S M M M L L XL L M

L M M S M M XL S S S XL L S S M M M S M S M L L M M M S S M L

M M M M S M M L L L M S M M L S S L M S M M M M M M M M M L

XS L L M M L S S M M M S M M M M M L M M L M M S L M XS S M M

L M M L S L L L M M L S L M L L M M L M M S S M M S M XL L XL

M M M L M L XS S XL M L L L M M S L S S M M M S XS M L M M S S

XL M M M M M S L M L S L M L M L L S M S L S L S S S S L S L

L S M S L S L S M S L L L L XS M L M S S S M XS L L M M M L XL

S L M M L M L S L L L L L M S XS S M L S S L L L M L L M M M

M M L L L L M S L L L XS M L L M L L S M M XL M L M S M L L M

L M L M M S M M M M L S L L M M S M S L M M S M M S S L M L

L L M S M M L S L M M M L M XL S S S S S L L L M L L M S L M

M L S L S L M S M M L M L L S L M M L M L S L L M S M L S L

S M M L L M L S M S L L S L XL S M L M M M M M M M M L S L L

M M L L M L S L XL M M M XS M XS M S S M S L M S L M M M L M L

M M L S L XL S L S M M M M L L L M L XS L L L L M S S L M S L

L L M S S M L S L M

The following five samples were randomly selected from the above database.

1: L, M, L, L, M, M, S, M, L, M; $N = 10$; mode M; range S–L.
2: S, M, XS, L, M, L, L, L, M, L; $N = 10$; mode L; range XS–L.
3: L, M, L, L, M, M, S, M, L, M; $N = 10$; mode M; range S–L.
4: M, L, M, S, M, XS, L, M, M, L; $N = 10$; mode M; range XS–L.
5: M, XL, S, S, S, L, L, S, L, XS; $N = 10$; mode S; range XS–XL.

DATABASE A.7   ARM LENGTH (INCHES) FOR 1000 PEOPLE

$N = 1000$; population mean 29.6 inches; population standard deviation 3.52.

35	32	28	33	24	32	28	30	27	30	32	30	29	29	30	33	34	27	32	29	28	33	32	27
28	31	32	27	31	25	29	32	34	31	32	28	31	24	31	31	24	29	28	27	30	30	26	24
29	30	25	25	29	32	26	27	38	28	28	23	30	34	32	27	29	32	32	27	24	28	27	31
25	31	30	33	39	22	32	33	25	38	35	29	30	32	22	32	24	30	34	34	29	30	28	33
30	22	36	38	25	33	29	32	31	29	34	34	26	23	33	38	33	26	24	27	30	24	27	28
33	34	32	28	23	25	25	28	24	33	29	27	27	32	32	27	30	27	26	26	34	27	22	21
30	29	32	26	31	28	30	25	28	30	25	35	37	36	31	34	31	27	30	28	31	34	26	30
36	27	23	31	31	35	29	31	30	31	35	38	26	27	34	33	25	32	27	32	21	24	30	32
28	27	33	35	32	35	34	31	34	24	31	30	32	31	26	32	29	28	25	27	27	35	24	27
32	35	27	29	32	31	28	27	26	33	32	30	30	35	35	26	27	24	34	29	28	31	30	32
31	25	34	28	38	27	26	28	24	25	25	25	22	29	27	21	27	32	34	26	32	29	29	29
25	27	24	24	27	34	34	32	27	37	26	24	35	26	27	24	26	33	31	26	37	34	31	29
32	23	31	28	27	33	28	33	27	25	33	29	25	29	24	34	25	32	33	27	31	31	35	31
35	32	31	35	31	24	32	31	24	25	32	29	25.	31	28	24	27	32	28	32	35	30	28	24
29	28	32	29	26	31	35	25	30	27	24	24	28	26	32	24	33	35	32	28	30	38	34	28
32	27	26	30	30	30	29	27	31	30	33	27	32	24	25	30	30	27	30	31	28	30	28	32
31	29	27	32	30	34	30	28	37	33	35	31	31	26	22	24	23	35	30	32	24	21	30	31
24	28	27	35	32	33	32	24	31	30	28	28	27	33	28	26	26	37	30	35	31	34	27	29
34	37	35	29	32	32	26	28	35	30	32	26	34	29	34	34	24	27	31	30	35	30	30	33
29	26	30	25	32	33	28	32	29	33	31	26	30	34	32	37	30	28	31	27	30	34	30	27
26	34	26	29	24	29	23	35	29	34	32	31	31	21	28	35	30	38	30	29	24	36	30	34
30	30	28	35	27	32	27	30	27	28	35	29	29	26	30	25	30	26	28	32	28	29	30	26
32	30	32	28	28	22	25	28	32	25	30	25	32	38	24	27	28	28	32	26	29	26	34	25
29	28	29	38	23	27	34	26	32	32	31	30	33	31	30	35	35	33	28	27	38	32	29	33
29	30	36	27	28	32	34	30	32	28	30	22	28	24	32	34	28	31	24	35	32	29	28	27
23	35	33	32	27	34	26	30	32	22	30	27	28	37	22	30	27	27	33	30	34	27	26	21
33	28	27	34	31	31	32	25	31	27	27	30	31	28	30	30	27	29	27	29	35	34	37	29
29	30	30	34	26	33	25	30	26	30	32	31	26	24	26	27	31	21	27	32	28	29	32	31
27	30	24	25	23	28	27	29	35	25	36	24	29	29	35	29	25	32	32	31	29	29	35	33
29	29	32	24	33	29	25	29	30	24	32	32	33	28	32	21	35	29	30	35	26	29	28	28
28	35	32	27	33	21	30	30	28	30	27	36	40	27	38	24	28	27	30	29	26	27	38	31
29	24	29	27	27	26	27	27	32	32	27	35	33	29	28	27	34	27	28	32	36	27	28	31
29	28	35	27	26	29	27	24	24	27	38	29	24	28	28	21	31	33	34	27	31	30	27	35
27	33	35	34	26	31	29	26	28	30	32	31	33	24	29	35	30	27	29	31	29	30	26	33
28	31	25	31	29	35	28	32	29	29	34	30	28	28	32	24	34	28	31	29	34	29	29	29
35	34	30	30	26	28	31	35	31	31	28	30	29	29	28	34	28	31	27	33	27	30	29	29
27	32	34	26	33	26	31	35	24	34	26	31	32	30	29	29	32	30	36	26	31	29	27	29
33	30	29	28	35	35	35	25	26	21	28	33	27	32	34	33	29	32	29	30	26	32	34	30
28	33	24	28	30	33	35	32	32	30	30	31	34	31	30	31	32	31	35	29	32	32	31	31
32	29	32	27	31	32	25	28	31	24	30	27	24	25	35	28	32	29	31	26	28	30	29	28
37	36	28	30	31	32	32	31	30	31	32	29	24	29	27	28	32	29	27	26	31	35	28	32
30	33	33	27	28	25	29	26	31	32	31	29	29	29	24	29								

The following five samples were randomly selected from the above database.

1: 27, 31, 27, 30, 28, 30, 25, 28, 24, 27; $N = 10$; $\bar{X} = 27.7$; $S = 2.10$.
2: 32, 30, 27, 29, 31, 24, 31, 32, 27, 23; $N = 10$; $\bar{X} = 28.6$; $S = 3.07$.
3: 25, 27, 24, 33, 30, 26, 24, 25, 38, 32; $N = 10$; $\bar{X} = 28.4$; $S = 4.45$.
4: 25, 33, 26, 30, 29, 22, 32, 30, 30, 24; $N = 10$; $\bar{X} = 28.1$; $S = 3.45$.
5: 31, 28, 36, 28, 35, 29, 30, 31, 35, 32; $N = 10$; $\bar{X} = 31.5$; $S = 2.80$.

DATABASE A.8   HEIGHTS (INCHES) FOR 1000 PEOPLE

$N = 1000$; population mean 65.3 inches; population standard deviation 7.08.

60	71	80	63	71	66	54	55	62	82	69	70	60	73	75	59	57	61	60	73	76	71	68	51
55	58	58	65	64	69	70	77	60	62	73	76	57	55	56	64	56	55	83	61	68	68	62	60
66	76	56	77	57	64	62	67	63	61	58	65	76	78	54	68	62	62	61	61	60	62	65	65
67	62	67	65	60	60	61	67	75	65	69	65	69	71	60	70	65	62	60	67	61	56	62	62
56	60	56	49	60	65	71	68	57	61	74	54	62	60	64	61	62	72	78	72	63	57	63	62
58	59	73	77	66	59	62	65	73	62	58	69	65	65	71	55	62	54	72	54	64	67	61	66
70	58	73	64	74	72	51	67	82	65	61	61	56	63	64	56	75	77	77	63	65	54	61	62
76	62	71	74	69	65	63	55	48	54	54	55	58	56	71	64	60	62	57	60	70	67	60	62
66	62	76	70	77	59	68	68	70	70	65	56	65	64	64	68	69	62	58	64	54	60	64	76
69	71	60	68	69	60	60	65	58	60	68	60	64	60	73	71	74	74	70	80	50	69	54	75
68	67	62	68	62	67	67	71	59	75	54	63	64	49	61	55	61	61	66	63	69	55	76	66
67	62	67	65	63	74	74	61	61	62	73	66	68	60	55	74	60	65	74	65	66	69	69	71
59	63	69	70	71	55	64	59	54	66	70	76	59	63	65	76	73	60	77	54	75	71	56	63
59	64	55	77	61	75	62	73	65	54	75	56	63	73	71	68	75	68	58	69	58	61	71	57
74	72	59	76	49	58	63	67	72	71	79	77	54	71	67	55	66	71	57	64	71	66	71	61
56	72	82	65	70	60	73	54	66	64	72	58	72	80	65	78	66	65	61	60	77	66	64	63
68	67	61	71	80	55	55	56	50	50	67	75	56	65	61	59	61	77	52	60	81	57	57	70
79	66	60	62	76	75	53	60	63	65	61	69	61	66	68	60	60	68	57	65	64	59	66	67
67	52	69	58	74	68	65	58	64	74	56	68	70	67	55	56	60	59	63	57	63	62	50	75
77	66	75	44	60	77	64	67	71	70	61	74	71	78	72	69	61	57	72	62	62	63	69	73
65	67	67	74	70	69	76	60	54	66	64	71	63	67	70	54	59	74	70	61	77	54	73	74
60	59	59	70	73	72	71	62	74	76	70	67	59	64	74	64	58	68	63	70	62	67	63	62
58	68	61	61	69	57	56	69	74	71	71	70	73	62	61	58	83	59	59	50	61	66	74	71
68	68	62	54	73	82	64	75	56	60	73	69	54	69	67	61	73	78	59	64	56	67	69	70
66	60	65	83	54	61	68	70	75	57	76	71	56	54	70	65	59	58	63	60	77	56	61	71
73	57	78	69	66	68	63	66	58	59	71	53	57	59	72	81	77	56	62	65	66	66	61	75
76	68	62	79	74	68	74	72	48	68	54	49	65	68	72	68	60	71	66	67	64	71	73	60
67	60	61	62	69	64	64	64	73	61	62	55	54	76	58	76	64	67	75	57	73	64	55	59
75	61	75	74	75	77	55	61	57	68	73	67	60	63	83	60	60	66	62	64	67	74	70	56
75	55	64	55	70	67	65	75	75	67	72	56	63	62	66	67	77	77	57	63	59	71	75	71
65	61	68	72	66	59	77	63	57	57	62	64	70	63	62	66	55	70	53	63	59	67	52	54
70	71	76	80	54	54	73	66	57	66	68	77	59	60	64	70	70	54	58	69	56	69	60	64
53	68	69	61	75	63	61	59	77	56	66	70	69	69	69	71	65	83	56	80	50	77	77	78
65	60	60	62	67	62	72	66	61	65	76	73	75	61	55	64	66	60	71	68	75	57	60	67
67	73	75	65	69	67	61	60	61	65	70	73	64	67	74	63	55	72	62	48	60	69	67	64
63	68	61	60	73	66	71	74	74	77	73	65	69	73	71	64	83	71	75	61	65	62	65	70
63	67	63	63	54	69	70	77	68	69	65	66	65	67	77	58	67	65	74	61	54	58	68	50
76	62	65	76	54	73	46	71	63	68	66	73	70	48	69	57	68	61	64	61	65	56	58	66
50	61	65	59	60	69	64	70	56	69	65	70	66	74	56	63	68	59	65	78	55	61	54	66
66	72	71	66	64	69	68	60	74	58	70	73	57	62	72	75	70	69	48	58	70	64	66	61
59	65	76	65	66	64	57	71	72	59	62	62	62	63	62	60	62	73	63	76	74	64	62	71
62	60	68	76	76	66	64	67	76	62	65	65	62	72	67	50								

The following five samples were randomly selected from the above database.

1: 69, 48, 64, 75, 69, 75, 76, 54, 71, 65; $N = 10$; $\bar{X} = 66.6$; $S = 8.80$.
2: 70, 66, 75, 72, 71, 74, 61, 57, 75, 59; $N = 10$; $\bar{X} = 68.0$; $S = 6.47$.
3: 68, 70, 73, 67, 70, 71, 65, 60, 67, 67; $N = 10$; $\bar{X} = 67.8$; $S = 3.43$
4: 72, 68, 64, 57, 76, 70, 71, 61, 49, 72; $N = 10$; $\bar{X} = 66.0$; $S = 7.85$.
5: 60, 49, 61, 66, 69, 75, 76, 54, 71, 65; $N = 10$; $\bar{X} = 64.6$; $S = 8.31$.

Tables

TABLE B.1 *Z* Values and Corresponding Normal Curve Areas

Z	Decimal area between *Z* Λ and mean	Decimal area beyond *Z*	*Y* value for $X = Z$, mean = 0, standard deviation = 1	Percentage area between *Z*, and mean	Percentage area beyond *Z*
0.01	.0040	.4960	.3989	0.40	49.60
0.02	.0080	.4920	.3989	0.20	49.20
0.03	.0120	.4880	.3988	1.20	48.80
0.04	.0160	.4840	.3986	1.60	48.40
0.05	.0199	.4801	.3984	1.99	48.01
0.06	.0239	.4761	.3982	2.39	47.61
0.07	.0279	.4721	.3980	2.79	47.21
0.08	.0319	.4681	.3977	3.19	46.81
0.09	.0359	.4641	.4642	3.59	46.41
0.10	.0398	.4602	.3970	3.98	46.02
0.11	.0438	.4562	.3965	4.38	45.62
0.12	.0478	.4522	.3961	4.78	45.22
0.13	.0517	.4483	.3956	5.17	44.83
0.14	.0557	.4443	.3951	5.57	44.43
0.15	.0596	.4404	.3945	5.96	44.04
0.16	.0636	.4364	.3939	6.36	43.64
0.17	.0675	.4325	.3932	6.75	43.25
0.18	.0714	.4286	.3925	7.14	42.86
0.19	.0754	.4246	.3918	7.54	42.46
0.20	.0793	.4207	.3910	7.93	42.07
0.21	.0832	.4168	.3902	8.32	41.68
0.22	.0871	.4129	.3894	8.71	41.29
0.23	.0910	.4090	.3885	9.10	40.90
0.24	.0948	.4052	.3876	9.48	40.52
0.25	.0987	.4013	.3867	9.87	40.13
0.26	.1026	.3974	.3857	10.26	39.74
0.27	.1064	.3936	.3847	10.64	39.36
0.28	.1103	.3897	.3836	11.03	38.97
0.29	.1141	.3859	.3825	11.41	38.59
0.30	.1180	.3820	.3814	11.80	38.20
0.31	.1218	.3782	.3802	12.18	37.82
0.32	.1256	.3744	.3790	12.56	37.44
0.33	.1293	.3707	.3778	12.93	37.07
0.34	.1331	.3669	.3765	13.31	36.69
0.35	.1369	.3631	.3752	13.69	36.31
0.36	.1406	.3594	.3739	14.06	35.94
0.37	.1444	.3556	.3725	14.44	35.56
0.38	.1481	.3519	.3711	14.81	35.19
0.39	.1518	.3482	.3697	15.18	34.82
0.40	.1555	.3445	.3683	15.55	34.45
0.41	.1591	.3409	.3668	15.91	34.09
0.42	.1628	.3372	.3653	16.28	33.72
0.43	.1664	.3336	.3637	16.64	33.36
0.44	.1701	.3299	.3621	17.01	32.99
0.45	.1737	.3263	.3605	17.37	32.63
0.46	.1773	.3227	.3589	17.73	32.27

(continued)

Z	Decimal area between Z Λ and mean	Decimal area beyond Z	Y value for X = Z, mean = 0, standard deviation = 1	Percentage area between Z, and mean	Percentage area beyond Z
0.47	.1809	.3191	.3572	18.09	31.91
0.48	.1844	.3156	.3555	18.44	31.56
0.49	.1880	.3120	.3538	18.80	31.20
0.50	.1915	.3085	.3521	19.15	30.85
0.51	.1950	.3050	.3503	19.50	30.50
0.52	.1985	.3015	.3485	19.85	30.15
0.53	.2020	.2980	.3467	20.20	29.80
0.54	.2054	.2946	.3448	20.54	29.46
0.55	.2089	.2911	.3429	20.89	29.11
0.56	.2123	.2877	.3410	21.23	28.77
0.57	.2157	.2843	.3391	21.57	28.43
0.58	.2191	.2809	.3372	21.91	28.09
0.59	.2224	.2776	.3352	22.24	27.76
0.60	.2258	.2742	.3332	22.58	27.42
0.61	.2291	.2709	.3312	22.91	27.09
0.62	.2324	.2676	.3292	23.24	26.76
0.63	.2357	.2643	.3271	23.57	26.43
0.64	.2390	.2610	.3250	23.90	26.10
0.65	.2422	.2578	.3230	24.22	25.78
0.66	.2454	.2546	.3208	24.54	25.46
0.67	.2486	.2514	.3187	24.86	25.14
0.68	.2518	.2482	.3166	25.18	24.82
0.69	.2549	.2451	.3144	25.49	24.51
0.70	.2580	.2420	.3123	25.80	24.20
0.71	.2612	.2388	.3101	26.12	23.88
0.72	.2642	.2358	.3078	26.42	23.58
0.73	.2673	.2327	.3056	26.73	23.27
0.74	.2704	.2296	.3034	27.04	22.96
0.75	.2734	.2266	.3011	27.34	22.66
0.76	.2764	.2236	.2989	27.64	22.36
0.77	.2794	.2206	.2966	27.94	22.06
0.78	.2823	.2177	.2943	28.23	21.77
0.79	.2852	.2148	.2920	28.52	21.48
0.80	.2882	.2118	.2897	28.82	21.18
0.81	.2910	.2090	.2874	29.10	20.90
0.82	.2939	.2061	.2850	29.39	20.61
0.83	.2967	.2033	.2827	29.67	20.33
0.84	.2996	.2004	.2803	29.96	20.04
0.85	.3023	.1977	.2780	30.23	19.77
0.86	.3051	.1949	.2756	30.51	19.49
0.87	.3079	.1921	.2732	30.79	19.21
0.88	.3106	.1894	.2709	31.06	18.94
0.89	.3133	.1867	.2685	31.33	18.67
0.90	.3159	.1841	.2661	31.59	18.41
0.91	.3186	.1814	.2637	31.86	18.14
0.92	.3212	.1788	.2613	32.12	17.88

Z	Decimal area between Z Λ and mean	Decimal area beyond Z	Y value for X = Z, mean = 0, standard deviation = 1	Percentage area between Z, and mean	Percentage area beyond Z
0.93	.3238	.1762	.2589	32.28	17.62
0.94	.3264	.1736	.2565	32.64	17.36
0.95	.3289	.1711	.2540	32.89	17.11
0.96	.3315	.1685	.2516	33.15	16.85
0.97	.3340	.1660	.2492	33.40	16.60
0.98	.3365	.1635	.2468	33.65	16.35
0.99	.3389	.1611	.2444	33.89	16.11
1.00	**.3413**	**.1587**	**.2420**	**34.13**	**15.87**
1.01	.3438	.1562	.2395	34.38	15.62
1.02	.3461	.1539	.2371	34.61	15.39
1.03	.3485	.1515	.2347	34.85	15.15
1.04	.3508	.1492	.2323	35.08	14.92
1.05	.3531	.1469	.2299	35.31	14.69
1.06	.3554	.1446	.2275	35.54	14.46
1.07	.3577	.1423	.2250	35.77	14.23
1.08	.3599	.1401	.2226	35.99	14.01
1.09	.3621	.1379	.2202	36.21	13.79
1.10	.3643	.1357	.2178	36.43	13.57
1.11	.3665	.1335	.2154	36.65	13.35
1.12	.3686	.1314	.2131	36.86	13.14
1.13	.3708	.1292	.2107	37.08	12.92
1.14	.3729	.1271	.2083	37.29	12.71
1.15	.3749	.1251	.2059	37.49	12.51
1.16	.3770	.1230	.2036	37.70	12.30
1.17	.3790	.1210	.2012	37.90	12.10
1.18	.3810	.1190	.1988	38.10	11.90
1.19	.3830	.1170	.1965	38.30	11.70
1.20	.3849	.1151	.1942	38.49	11.51
1.21	.3869	.1131	.1918	38.69	11.31
1.22	.3888	.1112	.1895	38.88	11.12
1.23	.3906	.1094	.1872	39.06	10.94
1.24	.3925	.1075	.1849	39.25	10.75
1.25	.3943	.1057	.1826	39.43	10.57
1.26	.3962	.1038	.1803	39.62	10.38
1.27	.3980	.1020	.1781	39.80	10.20
1.28	.3997	.1003	.1758	39.97	10.03
1.29	.4014	.0986	.1736	40.14	9.86
1.30	.4032	.0968	.1714	40.32	9.68
1.31	.4049	.0951	.1691	40.49	9.51
1.32	.4066	.0934	.1669	40.66	9.34
1.33	.4082	.0918	.1647	40.82	9.18
1.34	.4099	.0901	.1626	40.99	9.01
1.35	.4115	.0885	.1604	41.15	8.85
1.36	.4131	.0869	.1582	41.31	8.69
1.37	.4146	.0854	.1561	41.46	8.54
1.38	.4162	.0838	.1539	41.62	8.38

Z	Decimal area between Z Λ and mean	Decimal area beyond Z	Y value for X = Z, mean = 0, standard deviation = 1	Percentage area between Z, and mean	Percentage area beyond Z
1.39	.4177	.0823	.1518	41.77	8.23
1.40	.4192	.0808	.1497	41.92	8.08
1.41	.4207	.0793	.1476	42.07	7.93
1.42	.4222	.0778	.1456	42.22	7.78
1.43	.4236	.0764	.1435	42.36	7.64
1.44	.4250	.0750	.1415	42.50	7.50
1.45	.4264	.0736	.1394	42.64	7.36
1.46	.4278	.0722	.1374	42.78	7.22
1.47	.4292	.0708	.1354	42.92	7.08
1.48	.4305	.0695	.1334	43.05	6.95
1.49	.4319	.0681	.1315	43.19	6.81
1.50	.4332	.0668	.1295	43.32	6.68
1.51	.4345	.0655	.1276	43.45	6.55
1.52	.4357	.0643	.1257	43.57	6.43
1.53	.4370	.0630	.1238	43.70	6.30
1.54	.4382	.0618	.1219	43.82	6.18
1.55	.4394	.0606	.1200	43.94	6.06
1.56	.4406	.0594	.1181	44.06	5.94
1.57	.4418	.0582	.1163	44.18	5.82
1.58	.4429	.0571	.1145	44.29	5.71
1.59	.4441	.0559	.1127	44.41	5.59
1.60	.4452	.0548	.1109	44.52	5.48
1.61	.4463	.0537	.1091	44.62	5.37
1.62	.4474	.0526	.1074	44.74	5.26
1.63	.4484	.0516	.1057	44.84	5.16
1.64	.4495	.0505	.1040	44.95	5.05
1.645	**.4500**	**.0500**	**.1032**	**45.00**	**5.00**
1.65	.4505	.0495	.1023	45.05	4.95
1.66	.4515	.0485	.1006	45.15	4.85
1.67	.4525	.0475	.0989	46.25	4.75
1.68	.4535	.0465	.0973	45.35	4.65
1.69	.4545	.0455	.0956	45.45	4.55
1.70	.4554	.0446	.0941	45.54	4.46
1.71	.4563	.0437	.0924	45.63	4.37
1.72	.4573	.0427	.0909	45.73	4.27
1.73	.4582	.0418	.0893	45.82	4.18
1.74	.4590	.0410	.0878	45.90	4.10
1.75	.4599	.0401	.0863	45.99	4.01
1.76	.4608	.0392	.0848	46.08	3.92
1.77	.4616	.0384	.0833	46.16	3.84
1.78	.4624	.0376	.0818	46.24	3.76
1.79	.4632	.0368	.0804	46.32	3.68
1.80	.4640	.0360	.0789	46.40	3.60
1.81	.4648	.0352	.0775	46.48	3.52
1.82	.4656	.0344	.0761	46.56	3.44
1.83	.4663	.0337	.0748	46.63	3.37

Z	Decimal area between Z Λ and mean	Decimal area beyond Z	Y value for X = Z, mean = 0, standard deviation = 1	Percentage area between Z, and mean	Percentage area beyond Z
1.84	.4671	.0329	.0734	46.71	3.29
1.85	.4678	.0322	.0721	46.78	3.22
1.86	.4685	.0315	.0707	46.85	3.15
1.87	.4692	.0308	.0694	46.92	3.08
1.88	.4699	.0301	.0681	46.99	3.01
1.89	.4706	.0294	.0669	47.06	2.94
1.90	.4712	.0288	.0656	47.12	2.88
1.91	.4719	.0281	.0644	47.19	2.81
1.92	.4725	.0275	.0632	47.25	2.75
1.93	.4732	.0268	.0620	47.32	2.68
1.94	.4738	.0262	.0608	47.38	2.62
1.95	.4744	.0256	.0596	47.44	2.56
1.96	**.4750**	**.0250**	**.0584**	**47.50**	**2.50**
1.97	.4755	.0245	.0573	47.55	2.45
1.98	.4761	.0239	.0562	47.61	2.39
1.99	.4767	.0233	.0551	47.67	2.33
2.00	**.4772**	**.0228**	**.0540**	**47.72**	**2.28**
2.01	.4777	.0223	.0529	47.77	2.23
2.02	.4783	.0217	.0519	47.83	2.17
2.03	.4788	.0212	.0508	47.88	2.12
2.04	.4793	.0207	.0498	47.93	2.07
2.05	.4798	.0202	.0488	47.98	2.02
2.06	.4803	.0197	.0478	48.03	1.97
2.07	.4807	.0193	.0468	48.07	1.93
2.08	.4812	.0188	.0459	48.12	1.88
2.09	.4817	.0183	.0449	48.17	1.83
2.10	.4821	.0179	.0440	48.21	1.79
2.11	.4825	.0175	.0431	48.25	1.75
2.12	.4830	.0170	.0422	48.30	1.70
2.13	.4834	.0166	.0413	48.34	1.66
2.14	.4838	.0162	.0404	48.38	1.62
2.15	.4842	.0158	.0395	48.42	1.58
2.16	.4846	.0154	.0387	48.46	1.54
2.17	.4850	.0150	.0379	48.50	1.50
2.18	.4853	.0147	.0371	48.53	1.47
2.19	.4857	.0143	.0363	48.57	1.43
2.20	.4861	.0139	.0355	48.61	1.39
2.21	.4864	.0136	.0347	48.64	1.36
2.22	.4868	.0132	.0339	48.68	1.32
2.23	.4871	.0129	.0332	48.71	1.29
2.24	.4874	.0126	.0325	48.74	1.26
2.25	.4877	.0123	.0317	48.77	1.23
2.26	.4881	.0119	.0310	48.81	1.19
2.27	.4884	.0116	.0303	48.84	1.16
2.28	.4887	.0113	.0297	48.87	1.13
2.29	.4890	.0110	.0290	48.90	1.10

Z	Decimal area between Z Λ and mean	Decimal area beyond Z	Y value for X = Z, mean = 0, standard deviation = 1	Percentage area between Z, and mean	Percentage area beyond Z
2.30	.4892	.0108	.0283	48.92	1.08
2.31	.4895	.0105	.0277	48.95	1.05
2.32	.4898	.0102	.0270	48.98	1.02
2.33	.4901	.0099	.0264	49.01	0.99
2.34	.4903	.0097	.0258	49.03	0.97
2.35	.4906	.0094	.0252	49.06	0.94
2.36	.4908	.0092	.0246	49.08	0.92
2.37	.4911	.0089	.0241	49.11	0.89
2.38	.4913	.0087	.0235	49.13	0.87
2.39	.4915	.0085	.0229	49.15	0.85
2.40	.4918	.0082	.0224	49.18	0.82
2.41	.4920	.0080	.0219	49.20	0.80
2.42	.4922	.0078	.0213	49.22	0.78
2.43	.4924	.0076	.0208	49.24	0.76
2.44	.4926	.0074	.0203	49.26	0.74
2.45	.4928	.0072	.0198	49.28	0.72
2.46	.4930	.0070	.0194	49.30	0.73
2.47	.4932	.0068	.0189	49.32	0.68
2.48	.4934	.0066	.0184	49.34	0.66
2.49	.4936	.0064	.0180	49.36	0.64
2.50	.4938	.0062	.0175	49.38	0.62
2.51	.4939	.0061	.0171	49.39	0.61
2.52	.4941	.0059	.0167	49.41	0.59
2.53	.4943	.0057	.0163	49.43	0.57
2.54	.4944	.0056	.0158	49.44	0.56
2.55	.4946	.0054	.0154	49.46	0.54
2.56	.4947	.0053	.0151	49.47	0.53
2.56	.4949	.0051	.0147	49.49	0.51
2.58	**.4950**	**.0050**	**.0143**	**49.50**	**0.50**
2.59	.4952	.0048	.0139	49.52	0.48
2.60	.4953	.0047	.0136	49.53	0.47
2.61	.4954	.0046	.0132	49.54	0.46
2.62	.4956	.0044	.0129	49.56	0.44
2.63	.4957	.0043	.0126	49.57	0.43
2.64	.4958	.0042	.0122	49.58	0.42
2.65	.4959	.0041	.0119	49.59	0.41
2.66	.4961	.0039	.0116	49.61	0.39
2.67	.4962	.0038	.0113	49.62	0.38
2.68	.4963	.0037	.0110	49.63	0.37
2.69	.4964	.0036	.0107	49.64	0.36
2.70	.4965	.0035	.0104	49.65	0.35
2.71	.4966	.0034	.0101	49.66	0.34

Z	Decimal area between Z Λ and mean	Decimal area beyond Z	Y value for X = Z, mean = 0, standard deviation = 1	Percentage area between Z, and mean	Percentage area beyond Z
2.72	.4967	.0033	.0099	49.67	0.33
2.73	.4968	.0032	.0096	49.68	0.32
2.74	.4969	.0031	.0093	49.69	0.31
2.75	.4970	.0030	.0091	49.70	0.30
2.76	.4971	.0029	.0088	49.71	0.29
2.77	.4972	.0028	.0086	49.72	0.28
2.78	.4973	.0027	.0084	49.73	0.27
2.79	.4973	.0027	.0081	49.73	0.27
2.80	.4974	.0026	.0079	49.74	0.26
2.81	.4975	.0025	.0077	49.75	0.25
2.82	.4976	.0024	.0075	49.76	0.24
2.83	.4976	.0024	.0073	49.76	0.24
2.84	.4977	.0023	.0071	49.77	0.23
2.85	.4978	.0022	.0069	49.78	0.22
2.86	.4979	.0021	.0067	49.79	0.21
2.87	.4979	.0021	.0065	49.79	0.21
2.88	.4980	.0020	.0063	49.80	0.20
2.89	.4980	.0020	.0061	49.80	0.20
2.90	.4981	.0019	.0060	49.81	0.19
2.91	.4982	.0018	.0058	49.82	0.18
2.92	.4982	.0018	.0056	49.82	0.18
2.93	.4983	.0017	.0055	49.83	0.17
2.94	.4983	.0017	.0053	49.83	0.17
2.95	.4984	.0016	.0051	49.84	0.16
2.96	.4984	.0016	.0050	49.84	0.16
2.97	.4985	.0015	.0048	49.85	0.15
2.98	.4985	.0015	.0047	49.85	0.15
2.99	.4986	.0014	.0046	49.86	0.14
3.00	**.4986**	**.0014**	**.0044**	**49.86**	**0.14**
3.01	.4987	.0013	.0043	49.87	0.13
3.02	.4987	.0013	.0042	49.87	0.13
3.03	.4988	.0012	.0040	49.88	0.12
3.04	.4988	.0012	.0039	49.88	0.12
3.05	.4988	.0012	.0038	49.88	0.12
3.06	.4989	.0011	.0037	49.89	0.11
3.07	.4989	.0011	.0036	49.89	0.11
3.08	.4989	.0011	.0035	49.89	0.11
3.09	.4990	.0010	.0034	49.90	0.10
3.10	.4990	.0010	.0033	49.90	0.10
3.11	.4990	.0010	.0032	49.90	0.10
3.12	.4991	.0009	.0031	49.91	0.09
3.13	.4991	.0009	.0030	49.91	0.09

Z	Decimal area between Z Λ and mean	Decimal area beyond Z	Y value for X = Z, mean = 0, standard deviation = 1	Percentage area between Z, and mean	Percentage area beyond Z
3.14	.4992	.0008	.0029	49.92	0.08
3.15	.4992	.0008	.0028	49.92	0.08
3.16	.4992	.0008	.0027	49.92	0.08
3.17	.4992	.0008	.0026	49.92	0.08
3.18	.4992	.0008	.0025	49.92	0.08
3.19	.4993	.0007	.0025	49.93	0.07
3.20	.4993	.0007	.0024	49.93	0.07
3.21	.4993	.0007	.0023	49.93	0.07
3.22	.4993	.0007	.0023	49.93	0.07
3.23	.4994	.0006	.0022	49.94	0.06
3.24	.4994	.0006	.0021	49.94	0.06
3.25	.4994	.0006	.0020	49.94	0.06
3.26	.4994	.0006	.0020	49.94	0.06
3.27	.4994	.0006	.0019	49.94	0.06
3.28	.4995	.0005	.0018	49.95	0.05
3.29	.4995	.0005	.0018	49.95	0.05
3.30	.4995	.0005	.0017	49.95	0.05
3.31	.4995	.0005	.0017	49.95	0.05
3.32	.4995	.0005	.0016	49.95	0.05
3.33	.4995	.0005	.0016	49.95	0.05
3.34	.4996	.0004	.0015	49.96	0.04
3.35	.4996	.0004	.0015	49.96	0.04
3.36	.4996	.0004	.0014	49.96	0.04
3.37	.4996	.0004	.0014	49.96	0.04
3.38	.4996	.0004	.0013	49.96	0.04
3.39	.4996	.0004	.0013	49.96	0.04
3.40	.4996	.0004	.0012	49.96	0.04
3.41	.4997	.0003	.0012	49.97	0.03
3.42	.4997	.0003	.0012	49.97	0.03
3.43	.4997	.0003	.0011	49.97	0.03
3.44	.4997	.0003	.0011	49.97	0.03
3.45	.4997	.0003	.0010	49.97	0.03
3.46	.4997	.0003	.0010	49.97	0.03
3.47	.4997	.0003	.0010	49.97	0.03
3.48	.4997	.0003	.0009	49.97	0.03
3.49	.4997	.0003	.0009	49.97	0.03
3.50	.4997	.0003	.0009	49.97	0.03
3.51	.4998	.0002	.0008	49.98	0.02
3.52	.4998	.0002	.0008	49.98	0.02
3.53	.4998	.0002	.0008	49.98	0.02
3.54	.4998	.0002	.0008	49.98	0.02
3.55	.4998	.0002	.0007	49.98	0.02
3.56	.4998	.0002	.0007	49.98	0.02
3.57	.4998	.0002	.0007	49.98	0.02

Z Values and Corresponding Normal Curve Areas

Z	Decimal area between Z ∧ and mean	Decimal area beyond Z	Y value for X = Z, mean = 0, standard deviation = 1	Percentage area between Z, and mean	Percentage area beyond Z
3.58	.4998	.0002	.0007	49.98	0.02
3.59	.4998	.0002	.0006	49.98	0.02
3.60	.4998	.0002	.0006	49.98	0.02
3.61	.4998	.0002	.0006	49.98	0.02
3.62	.4998	.0002	.0006	49.98	0.02
3.63	.4998	.0002	.0005	49.98	0.02
3.64	.4998	.0002	.0005	49.98	0.02
3.65	.4998	.0002	.0005	49.98	0.02
3.66	.4999	.0001	.0005	49.99	0.01
3.67	.4999	.0001	.0005	49.99	0.01
3.68	.4999	.0001	.0005	49.99	0.01
3.69	.4999	.0001	.0004	49.99	0.01
3.70	.4999	.0001	.0004	49.99	0.01
3.71	.4999	.0001	.0004	49.99	0.01
3.72	.4999	.0001	.0004	49.99	0.01
3.73	.4999	.0001	.0004	49.99	0.01
3.74	.4999	.0001	.0004	49.99	0.01
3.75	.4999	.0001	.0004	49.99	0.01
3.76	.4999	.0001	.0003	49.99	0.01
3.77	.4999	.0001	.0003	49.99	0.01
3.78	.4999	.0001	.0003	49.99	0.01
3.79	.4999	.0001	.0003	49.99	0.01
3.80	.4999	.0001	.0003	49.99	0.01
3.81	.4999	.0001	.0003	49.99	0.01
3.82	.4999	.0001	.0003	49.99	0.01
3.83	.4999	.0001	.0003	49.99	0.01
3.84	.4999	.0001	.0003	49.99	0.01
3.85	.4999	.0001	.0002	49.99	0.01
3.86	.4999	.0001	.0002	49.99	0.01
3.87	.4999	.0001	.0002	49.99	0.01
3.88	.4999	.0001	.0002	49.99	0.01
3.89	.4999	.0001	.0002	49.99	0.01
3.90	.4999	.0001	.0002	49.99	0.01
3.91	.4999	.0001	.0002	49.99	0.01
3.92	.4999	.0001	.0002	49.99	0.01
3.93	.4999	.0001	.0002	49.99	0.01
3.94	.4999	.0001	.0002	49.99	0.01
3.95	.4999	.0001	.0002	49.99	0.01
3.96	.4999	.0001	.0002	49.99	0.01
3.97	.5000	.0000	.0002	50.00	0.00
3.98	.5000	.0000	.0001	50.00	0.00
3.99	.5000	.0000	.0001	50.00	0.00
4.00	.5000	.0000	.0001	50.00	0.00

$\alpha = .05$, One-Tailed (Upper Tail)

Null hypothesis: population mean $=$ specific value.

Alternative hypothesis: population mean $>$ specific value.

Reject the null hypothesis and favor the alternative hypothesis if the calculated Z is greater than the critical Z.

Critical $Z = +1.645$.

$\alpha = .05$, One-Tailed (Lower Tail)

Null hypothesis: population mean $=$ specific value.

Alternative hypothesis: population mean $<$ specific value.

Reject the null hypothesis and favor the alternative hypothesis if the calculated Z is less than the critical Z.

Critical $Z = -1.645$.

$\alpha = .05$, Two-Tailed

Null hypothesis: population mean $\neq$ specific value.

Alternative hypothesis: population mean $\neq$ specific value.

Reject the null hypothesis and favor the alternative hypothesis if the calculated Z is less than the lower critical Z or greater than the upper critical Z.

Lower critical $Z = -1.96$.

Upper critical $Z = +1.96$.

$\alpha = .01$, One-Tailed (Upper Tail)

Null hypothesis: population mean $=$ specific value.

Alternative hypothesis: population mean $>$ specific value.

Reject the null hypothesis and favor the alternative hypothesis if the calculated Z is greater than the critical Z.

Critical $Z = +2.33$.

$\alpha = .01$, One-Tailed (Lower Tail)

Null hypothesis: population mean $=$ specific value.

Alternative hypothesis: population mean $<$ specific value.

Reject the null hypothesis and favor the alternative hypothesis if the calculated Z is less than the critical Z.

Critical $Z = -2.33$.

$\alpha = .01$, Two-Tailed

Null hypothesis: population mean $=$ specific value.

Alternative hypothesis: population mean $\neq$ specific value.

Reject the null hypothesis and favor the alternative hypothesis if the calculated Z is less than the lower critical Z or greater than the upper critical Z.

Lower critical $Z = -2.58$.

Upper critical $Z = +2.58$.

Critical Chi Square Values

$\alpha = .05$, One-Tailed (Upper Tail)

Null hypothesis: Expected frequencies and observed frequencies equal.
Alternative hypothesis: Expected frequencies and observed frequencies not equal.
Reject the null hypothesis and favor the alternative hypothesis if the calculated chi square is greater than the critical chi square.

Number of categories	Degrees of freedom	Critical chi square
2	1	3.841
3	2	5.991
4	3	7.815
5	4	9.488
6	5	11.070
7	6	12.592
8	7	14.067
9	8	15.507
10	9	16.919
11	10	18.307

$\alpha = .01$, One-Tailed (Upper Tail)

Null hypothesis: expected frequencies and observed frequencies equal.
Alternative hypothesis: expected frequencies and observed frequencies not equal.
Reject the null hypothesis and favor the alternative hypothesis if the calculated chi square is greater than the critical chi square.

Number of categories	Degrees of freedom	Critical chi square
2	1	6.635
3	2	9.210
4	3	11.341
5	4	13.277
6	5	15.086
7	6	16.812
8	7	18.475
9	8	20.090
10	9	21.666
11	10	23.209

α = .05, One-Tailed (Upper Tail)

Null hypothesis: no correlation in population.
Alternative hypothesis: positive correlation in population.
Reject the null hypothesis and favor the alternative hypothesis if the calculated
   r is greater than or equal to the critical *r*.
Note: N_{pairs} denotes the number of data pairs, and *df* denotes the degrees of freedom.

N_{pairs}	df	Critical r	N_{pairs}	df	Critical r	N_{pairs}	df	Critical r
3	1	+.9877	43	41	+.2542	83	81	+.1818
4	2	+.9000	44	42	+.2514	84	82	+.1807
5	3	+.8054	45	43	+.2483	85	83	+.1796
6	4	+.7293	46	44	+.2457	86	84	+.1785
7	5	+.6694	47	45	+.2429	87	85	+.1775
8	6	+.6215	48	46	+.2403	88	86	+.1765
9	7	+.5822	49	47	+.2379	89	87	+.1755
10	8	+.5494	50	48	+.2354	90	88	+.1746
11	9	+.5214	51	49	+.2330	91	89	+.1736
12	10	+.4971	52	50	+.2308	92	90	+.1727
13	11	+.4762	53	51	+.2285	93	91	+.1717
14	12	+.4575	54	52	+.2263	94	92	+.1706
15	13	+.4409	55	53	+.2242	95	93	+.1697
16	14	+.4259	56	54	+.2222	96	94	+.1689
17	15	+.4124	57	55	+.2202	97	95	+.1680
18	16	+.4000	58	56	+.2182	98	96	+.1671
19	17	+.3888	59	57	+.2163	99	97	+.1663
20	18	+.3783	60	58	+.2146	100	98	+.1655
21	19	+.3687	61	59	+.2126	101	99	+.1647
22	20	+.3599	62	60	+.2109	102	100	+.1639
23	21	+.3516	63	61	+.2092	103	101	+.1631
24	22	+.3438	64	62	+.2076	104	102	+.1623
25	23	+.3365	65	63	+.2060	105	103	+.1615
26	24	+.3297	66	64	+.2042	106	104	+.1607
27	25	+.3233	67	65	+.2027	107	105	+.1599
28	26	+.3173	68	66	+.2012	108	106	+.1592
29	27	+.3114	69	67	+.1998	109	107	+.1585
30	28	+.3060	70	68	+.1984	110	108	+.1577
31	29	+.3009	71	69	+.1968	111	109	+.1570
32	30	+.2959	72	70	+.1954	112	110	+.1562
33	31	+.2912	73	71	+.1941	113	111	+.1555
34	32	+.2867	74	72	+.1928	114	112	+.1549
35	33	+.2825	75	73	+.1915	115	113	+.1542
36	34	+.2785	76	74	+.1902	116	114	+.1535
37	35	+.2747	77	75	+.1888	117	115	+.1529
38	36	+.2710	78	76	+.1876	118	116	+.1522
39	37	+.2673	79	77	+.1864	119	117	+.1516
40	38	+.2638	80	78	+.1853	120	118	+.1509
41	39	+.2605	81	79	+.1841	121	119	+.1503
42	40	+.2573	82	80	+.1829	122	120	+.1496

α = .05, One-Tailed (Lower Tail)

Null hypothesis: no correlation in population.
Alternative hypothesis: negative correlation in population.
Reject the null hypothesis and favor the alternative hypothesis if the calculated
r is less than or equal to the critical *r*.
Note: N_{pairs} denotes the number of data pairs, and *df* denotes the degrees of freedom.

N_{pairs}	df	Critical r	N_{pairs}	df	Critical r	N_{pairs}	df	Critical r
3	1	−.9877	43	41	−.2542	83	81	−.1818
4	2	−.9000	44	42	−.2514	84	82	−.1807
5	3	−.8054	45	43	−.2483	85	83	−.1796
6	4	−.7293	46	44	−.2457	86	84	−.1785
7	5	−.6694	47	45	−.2429	87	85	−.1775
8	6	−.6215	48	46	−.2403	88	86	−.1765
9	7	−.5822	49	47	−.2379	89	87	−.1755
10	8	−.5494	50	48	−.2354	90	88	−.1746
11	9	−.5214	51	49	−.2330	91	89	−.1736
12	10	−.4973	52	50	−.2308	92	90	−.1727
13	11	−.4762	53	51	−.2285	93	91	−.1717
14	12	−.4575	54	52	−.2263	94	92	−.1706
15	13	−.4309	55	53	−.2242	95	93	−.1697
16	14	−.4259	56	54	−.2222	96	94	−.1689
17	15	−.4124	57	55	−.2202	97	95	−.1680
18	16	−.4000	58	56	−.2182	98	96	−.1671
19	17	−.3888	59	57	−.2163	99	97	−.1663
20	18	−.3783	60	58	−.2146	100	98	−.1655
21	19	−.3687	61	59	−.2126	101	99	−.1647
22	20	−.3599	62	60	−.2109	102	100	−.1639
23	21	−.3516	63	61	−.2092	103	101	−.1631
24	22	−.3438	64	62	−.2076	104	102	−.1623
25	23	−.3365	65	63	−.2060	105	103	−.1615
26	24	−.3297	66	64	−.2042	106	104	−.1607
27	25	−.3233	67	65	−.2027	107	105	−.1599
28	26	−.3173	68	66	−.2012	108	106	−.1592
29	27	−.3114	69	67	−.1998	109	107	−.1585
30	28	−.3060	70	68	−.1984	110	108	−.1577
31	29	−.3009	71	69	−.1968	111	109	−.1570
32	30	−.2959	72	70	−.1954	112	110	−.1562
33	31	−.2912	73	71	−.1941	113	111	−.1555
34	32	−.2867	74	72	−.1928	114	112	−.1549
35	33	−.2825	75	73	−.1915	115	113	−.1542
36	34	−.2785	76	74	−.1902	116	114	−.1535
37	35	−.2747	77	75	−.1888	117	115	−.1529
38	36	−.2710	78	76	−.1876	118	116	−.1522
39	37	−.2673	79	77	−.1864	119	117	−.1516
40	38	−.2638	80	78	−.1853	120	118	−.1509
41	39	−.2605	81	79	−.1841	121	119	−.1503
42	40	−.2573	82	80	−.1829	122	120	−.1496

$\alpha = .05$, Two-Tailed

Null hypothesis:　no correlation in population.

Alternative hypothesis:　correlation in population.

Reject the null hypothesis and favor the alternative hypothesis if the calculated
r is less than or equal to the negative critical r or greater than or equal to the positive
critical r.

Note: N_{pairs} denotes the number of data pairs, and df denotes the degrees of freedom.

N_{pairs}	df	Critical r	N_{pairs}	df	Critical r	N_{pairs}	df	Critical r
3	1	$\pm.9969$	43	41	$\pm.3007$	83	81	$\pm.2158$
4	2	$\pm.9500$	44	42	$\pm.2973$	84	82	$\pm.2145$
5	3	$\pm.8783$	45	43	$\pm.2939$	85	83	$\pm.2132$
6	4	$\pm.8114$	46	44	$\pm.2907$	86	84	$\pm.2120$
7	5	$\pm.7545$	47	45	$\pm.2875$	87	85	$\pm.2107$
8	6	$\pm.7067$	48	46	$\pm.2845$	88	86	$\pm.2095$
9	7	$\pm.6664$	49	47	$\pm.2816$	89	87	$\pm.2084$
10	8	$\pm.6319$	50	48	$\pm.2786$	90	88	$\pm.2072$
11	9	$\pm.6021$	51	49	$\pm.2759$	91	89	$\pm.2060$
12	10	$\pm.5760$	52	50	$\pm.2732$	92	90	$\pm.2049$
13	11	$\pm.5529$	53	51	$\pm.2706$	93	91	$\pm.2038$
14	12	$\pm.5324$	54	52	$\pm.2680$	94	92	$\pm.2027$
15	13	$\pm.5139$	55	53	$\pm.2655$	95	93	$\pm.2016$
16	14	$\pm.4973$	56	54	$\pm.2631$	96	94	$\pm.2006$
17	15	$\pm.4821$	57	55	$\pm.2607$	97	95	$\pm.1996$
18	16	$\pm.4683$	58	56	$\pm.2586$	98	96	$\pm.1985$
19	17	$\pm.4555$	59	57	$\pm.2563$	99	97	$\pm.1975$
20	18	$\pm.4438$	60	58	$\pm.2541$	100	98	$\pm.1965$
21	19	$\pm.4329$	61	59	$\pm.2520$	101	99	$\pm.1955$
22	20	$\pm.4227$	62	60	$\pm.2500$	102	100	$\pm.1945$
23	21	$\pm.4133$	63	61	$\pm.2480$	103	101	$\pm.1936$
24	22	$\pm.4044$	64	62	$\pm.2461$	104	102	$\pm.1927$
25	23	$\pm.3961$	65	63	$\pm.2441$	105	103	$\pm.1918$
26	24	$\pm.3883$	66	64	$\pm.2422$	106	104	$\pm.1908$
27	25	$\pm.3809$	67	65	$\pm.2404$	107	105	$\pm.1899$
28	26	$\pm.3740$	68	66	$\pm.2386$	108	106	$\pm.1890$
29	27	$\pm.3673$	69	67	$\pm.2368$	109	107	$\pm.1882$
30	28	$\pm.3609$	70	68	$\pm.2351$	110	108	$\pm.1873$
31	29	$\pm.3550$	71	69	$\pm.2334$	111	109	$\pm.1864$
32	30	$\pm.3494$	72	70	$\pm.2319$	112	110	$\pm.1856$
33	31	$\pm.3439$	73	71	$\pm.2302$	113	111	$\pm.1848$
34	32	$\pm.3388$	74	72	$\pm.2287$	114	112	$\pm.1840$
35	33	$\pm.3338$	75	73	$\pm.2272$	115	113	$\pm.1831$
36	34	$\pm.3291$	76	74	$\pm.2256$	116	114	$\pm.1823$
37	35	$\pm.3246$	77	75	$\pm.2241$	117	115	$\pm.1816$
38	36	$\pm.3202$	78	76	$\pm.2227$	118	116	$\pm.1808$
39	37	$\pm.3159$	79	77	$\pm.2213$	119	117	$\pm.1801$
40	38	$\pm.3120$	80	78	$\pm.2198$	120	118	$\pm.1793$
41	39	$\pm.3080$	81	79	$\pm.2185$	121	119	$\pm.1786$
42	40	$\pm.3044$	82	80	$\pm.2172$	122	120	$\pm.1779$

α = .01, One-Tailed (Upper Tail)

Null hypothesis: no correlation in population.
Alternative hypothesis: positive correlation in population.
Reject the null hypothesis and favor the alternative hypothesis if the calculated
   r is greater than or equal to the critical *r*.
Note: N_{pairs} denotes the number of data pairs, and *df* denotes the degrees of freedom.

N_{pairs}	df	Critical r	N_{pairs}	df	Critical r	N_{pairs}	df	Critical r
3	1	+.9995	43	41	+.3535	83	81	+.2550
4	2	+.9800	44	42	+.3496	84	82	+.2535
5	3	+.9343	45	43	+.3457	85	83	+.2520
6	4	+.8822	46	44	+.3420	86	84	+.2506
7	5	+.8329	47	45	+.3384	87	85	+.2491
8	6	+.7887	48	46	+.3348	88	86	+.2476
9	7	+.7498	49	47	+.3314	89	87	+.2463
10	8	+.7155	50	48	+.3281	90	88	+.2448
11	9	+.6852	51	49	+.3249	91	89	+.2436
12	10	+.6581	52	50	+.3218	92	90	+.2422
13	11	+.6339	53	51	+.3187	93	91	+.2409
14	12	+.6120	54	52	+.3158	94	92	+.2397
15	13	+.5923	55	53	+.3129	95	93	+.2384
16	14	+.5742	56	54	+.3101	96	94	+.2372
17	15	+.5577	57	55	+.3074	97	95	+.2359
18	16	+.5425	58	56	+.3048	98	96	+.2347
19	17	+.5285	59	57	+.3021	99	97	+.2335
20	18	+.5155	60	58	+.2997	100	98	+.2324
21	19	+.5034	61	59	+.2972	101	99	+.2312
22	20	+.4921	62	60	+.2948	102	100	+.2301
23	21	+.4816	63	61	+.2925	103	101	+.2290
24	22	+.4715	64	62	+.2902	104	102	+.2279
25	23	+.4623	65	63	+.2880	105	103	+.2268
26	24	+.4534	66	64	+.2858	106	104	+.2257
27	25	+.4451	67	65	+.2837	107	105	+.2246
28	26	+.4372	68	66	+.2816	108	106	+.2236
29	27	+.4299	69	67	+.2795	109	107	+.2226
30	28	+.4226	70	68	+.2775	110	108	+.2215
31	29	+.4158	71	69	+.2755	111	109	+.2206
32	30	+.4093	72	70	+.2737	112	110	+.2196
33	31	+.4032	73	71	+.2718	113	111	+.2186
34	32	+.3973	74	72	+.2700	114	112	+.2177
35	33	+.3916	75	73	+.2681	115	113	+.2167
36	34	+.3863	76	74	+.2664	116	114	+.2158
37	35	+.3810	77	75	+.2647	117	115	+.2148
38	36	+.3759	78	76	+.2630	118	116	+.2140
39	37	+.3711	79	77	+.2614	119	117	+.2131
40	38	+.3665	80	78	+.2597	120	118	+.2121
41	39	+.3620	81	79	+.2580	121	119	+.2113
42	40	+.3578	82	80	+.2565	122	120	+.2104

$\alpha = .01$, One-Tailed (Lower Tail)

Null hypothesis: no correlation in population.

Alternative hypothesis: negative correlation in population.

Reject the null hypothesis and favor the alternative hypothesis if the calculated *r* is less than or equal to the critical *r*.

Note: N_{pairs} denotes the number of data pairs, and *df* denotes the degrees of freedom.

N_{pairs}	df	Critical r	N_{pairs}	df	Critical r	N_{pairs}	df	Critical r
3	1	−.9995	43	41	−.3535	83	81	−.2550
4	2	−.9800	44	42	−.3496	84	82	−.2535
5	3	−.9343	45	43	−.3457	85	83	−.2520
6	4	−.8822	46	44	−.3420	86	84	−.2506
7	5	−.8329	47	45	−.3384	87	85	−.2491
8	6	−.7887	48	46	−.3348	88	86	−.2476
9	7	−.7498	49	47	−.3314	89	87	−.2463
10	8	−.7155	50	48	−.3281	90	88	−.2448
11	9	−.6852	51	49	−.3249	91	89	−.2436
12	10	−.6581	52	50	−.3218	92	90	−.2422
13	11	−.6339	53	51	−.3187	93	91	−.2409
14	12	−.6120	54	52	−.3158	94	92	−.2397
15	13	−.5923	55	53	−.3129	95	93	−.2384
16	14	−.5742	56	54	−.3101	96	94	−.2372
17	15	−.5577	57	55	−.3074	97	95	−.2359
18	16	−.5425	58	56	−.3048	98	96	−.2347
19	17	−.5285	59	57	−.3021	99	97	−.2335
20	18	−.5155	60	58	−.2997	100	98	−.2324
21	19	−.5034	61	59	−.2972	101	99	−.2312
22	20	−.4921	62	60	−.2948	102	100	−.2301
23	21	−.4816	63	61	−.2925	103	101	−.2290
24	22	−.4715	64	62	−.2902	104	102	−.2279
25	23	−.4623	65	63	−.2880	105	103	−.2268
26	24	−.4534	66	64	−.2858	106	104	−.2257
27	25	−.4451	67	65	−.2837	107	105	−.2246
28	26	−.4372	68	66	−.2816	108	106	−.2236
29	27	−.4299	69	67	−.2795	109	107	−.2226
30	28	−.4226	70	68	−.2775	110	108	−.2215
31	29	−.4158	71	69	−.2755	111	109	−.2206
32	30	−.4093	72	70	−.2737	112	110	−.2196
33	31	−.4032	73	71	−.2718	113	111	−.2186
34	32	−.3973	74	72	−.2700	114	112	−.2177
35	33	−.3916	75	73	−.2681	115	113	−.2167
36	34	−.3863	76	74	−.2664	116	114	−.2158
37	35	−.3810	77	75	−.2647	117	115	−.2148
38	36	−.3759	78	76	−.2630	118	116	−.2140
39	37	−.3711	79	77	−.2614	119	117	−.2131
40	38	−.3665	80	78	−.2597	120	118	−.2121
41	39	−.3620	81	79	−.2580	121	119	−.2113
42	40	−.3578	82	80	−.2565	122	120	−.2104

$\alpha = .01$, Two-Tailed

Null hypothesis: no correlation in population.
Alternative hypothesis: correlation in population.
Reject the null hypothesis and favor the alternative hypothesis if the calculated
   r is less than or equal to the negative critical *r* or greater than or equal to the positive
critical *r*.
Note: N_{pairs} denotes the number of data pairs, and *df* denotes the degrees of freedom.

N_{pairs}	df	Critical r	N_{pairs}	df	Critical r	N_{pairs}	df	Critical r
3	1	±.9999	43	41	±.3885	83	81	±.2813
4	2	±.9900	44	42	±.3842	84	82	±.2796
5	3	±.9587	45	43	±.3800	85	83	±.2779
6	4	±.9172	46	44	±.3760	86	84	±.2764
7	5	±.8745	47	45	±.3721	87	85	±.2748
8	6	±.8343	48	46	±.3682	88	86	±.2732
9	7	±.7977	49	47	±.3646	89	87	±.2718
10	8	±.7646	50	48	±.3610	90	88	±.2702
11	9	±.7348	51	49	±.3574	91	89	±.2687
12	10	±.7079	52	50	±.3541	92	90	±.2673
13	11	±.6835	53	51	±.3508	93	91	±.2658
14	12	±.6614	54	52	±.3476	94	92	±.2643
15	13	±.6411	55	53	±.3444	95	93	±.2630
16	14	±.6226	56	54	±.3414	96	94	±.2617
17	15	±.6055	57	55	±.3385	97	95	±.2603
18	16	±.5897	58	56	±.3356	98	96	±.2590
19	17	±.5751	59	57	±.3327	99	97	±.2577
20	18	±.5614	60	58	±.3301	100	98	±.2564
21	19	±.5487	61	59	±.3275	101	99	±.2552
22	20	±.5368	62	60	±.3248	102	100	±.2540
23	21	±.5256	63	61	±.3222	103	101	±.2527
24	22	±.5151	64	62	±.3197	104	102	±.2515
25	23	±.5051	65	63	±.3173	105	103	±.2503
26	24	±.4958	66	64	±.3150	106	104	±.2491
27	25	±.4869	67	65	±.3127	107	105	±.2480
28	26	±.4785	68	66	±.3103	108	106	±.2468
29	27	±.4706	69	67	±.3081	109	107	±.2457
30	28	±.4629	70	68	±.3059	110	108	±.2445
31	29	±.4556	71	69	±.3038	111	109	±.2435
32	30	±.4487	72	70	±.3017	112	110	±.2424
33	31	±.4419	73	71	±.2997	113	111	±.2413
34	32	±.4357	74	72	±.2977	114	112	±.2403
35	33	±.4296	75	73	±.2957	115	113	±.2393
36	34	±.4238	76	74	±.2938	116	114	±.2382
37	35	±.4182	77	75	±.2919	117	115	±.2373
38	36	±.4126	78	76	±.2900	118	116	±.2362
39	37	±.4075	79	77	±.2882	119	117	±.2352
40	38	±.4026	80	78	±.2864	120	118	±.2343
41	39	±.3977	81	79	±.2846	121	119	±.2334
42	40	±.3932	82	80	±.2830	122	120	±.2324

$\alpha = .05$, One-Tailed (Upper Tail)

Null hypothesis: no correlation in population.

Alternative hypothesis: positive correlation in population.

Reject the null hypothesis and favor the alternative hypothesis if the calculated r_s is greater than or equal to the critical r_s.

Note: N_{pairs} denotes the number of data pairs, and df denotes the degrees of freedom.

N_{pairs}	df	Critical r_s	N_{pairs}	df	Critical r_s	N_{pairs}	df	Critical r_s
3	1	none	43	41	+.254	83	81	+.182
4	2	+1.000	44	42	+.251	84	82	+.181
5	3	+.900	45	43	+.248	85	83	+.180
6	4	+.829	46	44	+.246	86	84	+.179
7	5	+.714	47	45	+.243	87	85	+.178
8	6	+.643	48	46	+.240	88	86	+.177
9	7	+.600	49	47	+.238	89	87	+.176
10	8	+.564	50	48	+.235	90	88	+.175
11	9	+.520	51	49	+.233	91	89	+.174
12	10	+.506	52	50	+.231	92	90	+.173
13	11	+.475	53	51	+.229	93	91	+.172
14	12	+.456	54	52	+.226	94	92	+.171
15	13	+.440	55	53	+.224	95	93	+.170
16	14	+.425	56	54	+.222	96	94	+.169
17	15	+.411	57	55	+.220	97	95	+.168
18	16	+.399	58	56	+.218	98	96	+.167
19	17	+.388	59	57	+.216	99	97	+.166
20	18	+.378	60	58	+.215	100	98	+.166
21	19	+.369	61	59	+.213	101	99	+.165
22	20	+.360	62	60	+.211	102	100	+.164
23	21	+.352	63	61	+.209	103	101	+.163
24	22	+.344	64	62	+.208	104	102	+.162
25	23	+.337	65	63	+.206	105	103	+.162
26	24	+.330	66	64	+.204	106	104	+.161
27	25	+.323	67	65	+.203	107	105	+.160
28	26	+.317	68	66	+.201	108	106	+.159
29	27	+.311	69	67	+.200	109	107	+.159
30	28	+.306	70	68	+.198	110	108	+.158
31	29	+.301	71	69	+.197	111	109	+.157
32	30	+.296	72	70	+.195	112	110	+.156
33	31	+.291	73	71	+.194	113	111	+.156
34	32	+.287	74	72	+.193	114	112	+.155
35	33	+.283	75	73	+.192	115	113	+.154
36	34	+.279	76	74	+.190	116	114	+.154
37	35	+.275	77	75	+.189	117	115	+.153
38	36	+.271	78	76	+.188	118	116	+.152
39	37	+.267	79	77	+.186	119	117	+.152
40	38	+.264	80	78	+.185	120	118	+.151
41	39	+.261	81	79	+.184	121	119	+.150
42	40	+.257	82	80	+.183	122	120	+.150

$\alpha = .05$ One-Tailed (Lower Tail)

Null hypothesis: no correlation in population.
Alternative hypothesis: negative correlation in population.
Reject the null hypothesis and favor the alternative hypothesis if the calculated
   r_s is less than or equal to the critical r_s.
Note: N_{pairs} denotes the number of data pairs, and df denotes the degrees of freedom.

N_{pairs}	df	Critical r_s	N_{pairs}	df	Critical r_s	N_{pairs}	df	Critical r_s
3	1	none	43	41	$-.254$	83	81	$-.182$
4	2	-1.000	44	42	$-.251$	84	82	$-.181$
5	3	$-.900$	45	43	$-.248$	85	83	$-.180$
6	4	$-.829$	46	44	$-.246$	86	84	$-.179$
7	5	$-.714$	47	45	$-.243$	87	85	$-.178$
8	6	$-.643$	48	46	$-.240$	88	86	$-.177$
9	7	$-.600$	49	47	$-.238$	89	87	$-.176$
10	8	$-.564$	50	48	$-.235$	90	88	$-.175$
11	9	$-.520$	51	49	$-.233$	91	89	$-.174$
12	10	$-.506$	52	50	$-.231$	92	90	$-.173$
13	11	$-.475$	53	51	$-.229$	93	91	$-.172$
14	12	$-.456$	54	52	$-.226$	94	92	$-.171$
15	13	$-.440$	55	53	$-.224$	95	93	$-.170$
16	14	$-.425$	56	54	$-.222$	96	94	$-.169$
17	15	$-.411$	57	55	$-.220$	97	95	$-.168$
18	16	$-.399$	58	56	$-.218$	98	96	$-.167$
19	17	$-.388$	59	57	$-.216$	99	97	$-.166$
20	18	$-.378$	60	58	$-.215$	100	98	$-.166$
21	19	$-.369$	61	59	$-.213$	101	99	$-.165$
22	20	$-.360$	62	60	$-.211$	102	100	$-.164$
23	21	$-.352$	63	61	$-.209$	103	101	$-.163$
24	22	$-.344$	64	62	$-.208$	104	102	$-.162$
25	23	$-.337$	65	63	$-.206$	105	103	$-.162$
26	24	$-.330$	66	64	$-.204$	106	104	$-.161$
27	25	$-.323$	67	65	$-.203$	107	105	$-.160$
28	26	$-.317$	68	66	$-.201$	108	106	$-.159$
29	27	$-.311$	69	67	$-.200$	109	107	$-.159$
30	28	$-.306$	70	68	$-.198$	110	108	$-.158$
31	29	$-.301$	71	69	$-.197$	111	109	$-.157$
32	30	$-.296$	72	70	$-.195$	112	110	$-.156$
33	31	$-.291$	73	71	$-.194$	113	111	$-.156$
34	32	$-.287$	74	72	$-.193$	114	112	$-.155$
35	33	$-.283$	75	73	$-.192$	115	113	$-.154$
36	34	$-.279$	76	74	$-.190$	116	114	$-.154$
37	35	$-.275$	77	75	$-.189$	117	115	$-.153$
38	36	$-.271$	78	76	$-.188$	118	116	$-.152$
39	37	$-.267$	79	77	$-.186$	119	117	$-.152$
40	38	$-.264$	80	78	$-.185$	120	118	$-.151$
41	39	$-.261$	81	79	$-.184$	121	119	$-.150$
42	40	$-.257$	82	80	$-.183$	122	120	$-.150$

$\alpha = .05$ Two-Tailed

Null hypothesis: no correlation in population.
Alternative hypothesis: · correlation in population.
Reject the null hypothesis and favor the alternative hypothesis if the calculated
r_s is less than or equal to the negative critical r_s or greater than or equal to the positive
critical r_s.
Note: N_{pairs} denotes the number of data pairs, and df denotes the degrees of freedom.

N_{pairs}	df	Critical r_s	N_{pairs}	df	Critical r_s	N_{pairs}	df	Critical r_s
3	1	none	43	41	$\pm.301$	83	81	$\pm.216$
4	2	none	44	42	$\pm.297$	84	82	$\pm.215$
5	3	±1.000	45	43	$\pm.294$	85	83	$\pm.213$
6	4	$\pm.886$	46	44	$\pm.291$	86	84	$\pm.212$
7	5	$\pm.786$	47	45	$\pm.288$	87	85	$\pm.211$
8	6	$\pm.738$	48	46	$\pm.285$	88	86	$\pm.210$
9	7	$\pm.683$	49	47	$\pm.282$	89	87	$\pm.208$
10	8	$\pm.648$	50	48	$\pm.277$	90	88	$\pm.207$
11	9	$\pm.620$	51	49	$\pm.276$	91	89	$\pm.206$
12	10	$\pm.591$	52	50	$\pm.273$	92	90	$\pm.205$
13	11	$\pm.566$	53	51	$\pm.271$	93	91	$\pm.204$
14	12	$\pm.544$	54	52	$\pm.268$	94	92	$\pm.203$
15	13	$\pm.524$	55	53	$\pm.266$	95	93	$\pm.202$
16	14	$\pm.506$	56	54	$\pm.263$	96	94	$\pm.201$
17	15	$\pm.490$	57	55	$\pm.261$	97	95	$\pm.200$
18	16	$\pm.475$	58	56	$\pm.259$	98	96	$\pm.199$
19	17	$\pm.462$	59	57	$\pm.256$	99	97	$\pm.198$
20	18	$\pm.450$	60	58	$\pm.254$	100	98	$\pm.197$
21	19	$\pm.438$	61	59	$\pm.252$	101	99	$\pm.196$
22	20	$\pm.428$	62	60	$\pm.250$	102	100	$\pm.195$
23	21	$\pm.418$	63	61	$\pm.248$	103	101	$\pm.194$
24	22	$\pm.409$	64	62	$\pm.246$	104	102	$\pm.193$
25	23	$\pm.400$	65	63	$\pm.244$	105	103	$\pm.192$
26	24	$\pm.392$	66	64	$\pm.242$	106	104	$\pm.191$
27	25	$\pm.384$	67	65	$\pm.240$	107	105	$\pm.190$
28	26	$\pm.377$	68	66	$\pm.239$	108	106	$\pm.189$
29	27	$\pm.370$	69	67	$\pm.237$	109	107	$\pm.188$
30	28	$\pm.364$	70	68	$\pm.235$	110	108	$\pm.187$
31	29	$\pm.355$	71	69	$\pm.233$	111	109	$\pm.186$
32	30	$\pm.349$	72	70	$\pm.232$	112	110	$\pm.186$
33	31	$\pm.344$	73	71	$\pm.230$	113	111	$\pm.185$
34	32	$\pm.339$	74	72	$\pm.229$	114	112	$\pm.184$
35	33	$\pm.334$	75	73	$\pm.227$	115	113	$\pm.183$
36	34	$\pm.329$	76	74	$\pm.226$	116	114	$\pm.182$
37	35	$\pm.325$	77	75	$\pm.224$	117	115	$\pm.182$
38	36	$\pm.320$	78	76	$\pm.223$	118	116	$\pm.181$
39	37	$\pm.316$	79	77	$\pm.221$	119	117	$\pm.180$
40	38	$\pm.312$	80	78	$\pm.220$	120	118	$\pm.179$
41	39	$\pm.308$	81	79	$\pm.219$	121	119	$\pm.179$
42	40	$\pm.304$	82	80	$\pm.217$	122	120	$\pm.178$

$\alpha = .01$, One-Tailed (Upper Tail)

Null hypothesis: no correlation in population.
Alternative hypothesis: positive correlation in population.
Reject the null hypothesis and favor the alternative hypothesis if the calculated r_s is greater than or equal to the critical r_s.

N_{pairs}	df	Critical r_s	N_{pairs}	df	Critical r_s	N_{pairs}	df	Critical r_s
3	1	none	43	41	+.354	83	81	+.255
4	2	none	44	42	+.350	84	82	+.254
5	3	+1.000	45	43	+.346	85	83	+.252
6	4	+.943	46	44	+.342	86	84	+.251
7	5	+.893	47	45	+.338	87	85	+.249
8	6	+.833	48	46	+.335	88	86	+.248
9	7	+.783	49	47	+.331	89	87	+.246
10	8	+.745	50	48	+.328	90	88	+.245
11	9	+.709	51	49	+.325	91	89	+.244
12	10	+.671	52	50	+.322	92	90	+.242
13	11	+.648	53	51	+.319	93	91	+.241
14	12	+.622	54	52	+.316	94	92	+.240
15	13	+.604	55	53	+.313	95	93	+.238
16	14	+.582	56	54	+.310	96	94	+.237
17	15	+.566	57	55	+.307	97	95	+.236
18	16	+.550	58	56	+.305	98	96	+.235
19	17	+.535	59	57	+.302	99	97	+.234
20	18	+.520	60	58	+.300	100	98	+.232
21	19	+.508	61	59	+.297	101	99	+.231
22	20	+.496	62	60	+.295	102	100	+.230
23	21	+.486	63	61	+.293	103	101	+.229
24	22	+.476	64	62	+.290	104	102	+.228
25	23	+.466	65	63	+.288	105	103	+.227
26	24	+.457	66	64	+.286	106	104	+.226
27	25	+.448	67	65	+.284	107	105	+.225
28	26	+.440	68	66	+.282	108	106	+.224
29	27	+.433	69	67	+.280	109	107	+.223
30	28	+.425	70	68	+.278	110	108	+.222
31	29	+.416	71	69	+.276	111	109	+.221
32	30	+.409	72	70	+.274	112	110	+.220
33	31	+.403	73	71	+.272	113	111	+.219
34	32	+.397	74	72	+.270	114	112	+.218
35	33	+.392	75	73	+.268	115	113	+.217
36	34	+.386	76	74	+.266	116	114	+.216
37	35	+.381	77	75	+.265	117	115	+.215
38	36	+.376	78	76	+.263	118	116	+.214
39	37	+.371	79	77	+.261	119	117	+.213
40	38	+.367	80	78	+.260	120	118	+.212
41	39	+.362	81	79	+.258	121	119	+.211
42	40	+.358	82	80	+.257	122	120	+.210

$\alpha = .01$, One-Tailed (Lower Tail)

Null hypothesis: no correlation in population.
Alternative hypothesis: positive correlation in population.
Reject the null hypothesis and favor the alternative hypothesis if the calculated
   r_s is greater than or equal to the critical r_s.
Note: N_{pairs} denotes the number of data pairs, and df denotes the degrees of freedom.

N_{pairs}	df	Critical r_s	N_{pairs}	df	Critical r_s	N_{pairs}	df	Critical r_s
3	1	none	43	41	−.354	83	81	−.255
4	2	none	44	42	−.350	84	82	−.254
5	3	−1.000	45	43	−.346	85	83	−.252
6	4	−.943	46	44	−.342	86	84	−.251
7	5	−.893	47	45	−.338	87	85	−.249
8	6	−.833	48	46	−.335	88	86	−.248
9	7	−.783	49	47	−.331	89	87	−.246
10	8	−.745	50	48	−.328	90	88	−.245
11	9	−.709	51	49	−.325	91	89	−.244
12	10	−.671	52	50	−.322	92	90	−.242
13	11	−.648	53	51	−.319	93	91	−.241
14	12	−.622	54	52	−.316	94	92	−.240
15	13	−.604	55	53	−.313	95	93	−.238
16	14	−.582	56	54	−.310	96	94	−.237
17	15	−.566	57	55	−.307	97	95	−.236
18	16	−.550	58	56	−.305	98	96	−.235
19	17	−.535	59	57	−.302	99	97	−.234
20	18	−.520	60	58	−.300	100	98	−.232
21	19	−.508	61	59	−.297	101	99	−.231
22	20	−.496	62	60	−.295	102	100	−.230
23	21	−.486	63	61	−.293	103	101	−.229
24	22	−.476	64	62	−.290	104	102	−.228
25	23	−.466	65	63	−.288	105	103	−.227
26	24	−.457	66	64	−.286	106	104	−.226
27	25	−.448	67	65	−.284	107	105	−.225
28	26	−.440	68	66	−.282	108	106	−.224
29	27	−.433	69	67	−.280	109	107	−.223
30	28	−.425	70	68	−.278	110	108	−.222
31	29	−.416	71	69	−.276	111	109	−.221
32	30	−.409	72	70	−.274	112	110	−.220
33	31	−.403	73	71	−.272	113	111	−.219
34	32	−.397	74	72	−.270	114	112	−.218
35	33	−.392	75	73	−.268	115	113	−.217
36	34	−.386	76	74	−.266	116	114	−.216
37	35	−.381	77	75	−.265	117	115	−.215
38	36	−.376	78	76	−.263	118	116	−.214
39	37	−.371	79	77	−.261	119	117	−.213
40	38	−.367	80	78	−.260	120	118	−.212
41	39	−.362	81	79	−.258	121	119	−.211
42	40	−.358	82	80	−.257	122	120	−.210

$\alpha = .01$, Two-Tailed

Null hypothesis: no correlation in population.
Alternative hypothesis: correlation in population.
Reject the null hypothesis and favor the alternative hypothesis if the calculated
   r_s is less than or equal to the negative critical r_s or greater than or equal to the positive
critical r_s.
Note: N_{pairs} denotes the number of data pairs, and df denotes the degrees of freedom.

N_{pairs}	df	Critical r_s	N_{pairs}	df	Critical r_s	N_{pairs}	df	Critical r_s
3	1	none	43	41	±.389	83	81	±.281
4	2	none	44	42	±.384	84	82	±.280
5	3	none	45	43	±.380	85	83	±.278
6	4	±1.000	46	44	±.376	86	84	±.276
7	5	±.929	47	45	±.372	87	85	±.275
8	6	±.881	48	46	±.368	88	86	±.273
9	7	±.833	49	47	±.365	89	87	±.272
10	8	±.794	50	48	±.361	90	88	±.270
11	9	±.755	51	49	±.357	91	89	±.269
12	10	±.727	52	50	±.354	92	90	±.267
13	11	±.703	53	51	±.351	93	91	±.266
14	12	±.675	54	52	±.348	94	92	±.264
15	13	±.654	55	53	±.344	95	93	±.263
16	14	±.635	56	54	±.341	96	94	±.262
17	15	±.615	57	55	±.339	97	95	±.260
18	16	±.600	58	56	±.336	98	96	±.259
19	17	±.584	59	57	±.333	99	97	±.258
20	18	±.570	60	58	±.330	100	98	±.256
21	19	±.556	61	59	±.328	101	99	±.255
22	20	±.544	62	60	±.325	102	100	±.254
23	21	±.532	63	61	±.322	103	101	±.253
24	22	±.521	64	62	±.320	104	102	±.252
25	23	±.511	65	63	±.317	105	103	±.250
26	24	±.501	66	64	±.315	106	104	±.249
27	25	±.491	67	65	±.313	107	105	±.248
28	26	±.483	68	66	±.310	108	106	±.247
29	27	±.475	69	67	±.308	109	107	±.246
30	28	±.467	70	68	±.306	110	108	±.245
31	29	±.456	71	69	±.304	111	109	±.244
32	30	±.449	72	70	±.302	112	110	±.242
33	31	±.442	73	71	±.300	113	111	±.241
34	32	±.436	74	72	±.298	114	112	±.240
35	33	±.430	75	73	±.296	115	113	±.239
36	34	±.424	76	74	±.294	116	114	±.238
37	35	±.418	77	75	±.292	117	115	±.237
38	36	±.413	78	76	±.290	118	116	±.236
39	37	±.408	79	77	±.288	119	117	±.235
40	38	±.403	80	78	±.286	120	118	±.234
41	39	±.398	81	79	±.285	121	119	±.233
42	40	±.393	82	80	±.283	122	120	±.232

TABLE B.6 Critical Eta Values

$$\alpha = .05$$

Null hypothesis: no correlation in population.
Alternative hypothesis: correlation in population.
Reject the null hypothesis and favor the alternative hypothesis if the calculated eta is greater than or equal to the critical eta.

Number of data pairs	Critical eta for 2 nominal predictor categories	Critical eta for 3 nominal predictor categories	Critical eta for 4 nominal predictor categories	Critical eta for 5 nominal predictor categories
2	.9241	.8796	.8399	.8066
3	.7570	.7132	.6751	.6440
4	.6451	.6100	.5766	.5500
5	.5695	.5399	.5111	.4875
6	.5145	.4896	.4637	.4420
7	.4732	.4508	.4273	.4072
8	.4399	.4205	.3984	.3785
9	.4127	.3948	.3742	.3573
10	.3901	.3735	.3538	.3380
11	.3709	.3559	.3373	.3218
12	.3542	.3402	.3226	.3075
13	.3396	.3260	.3094	.2945
14	.3264	.3139	.2982	.2837
15	.3152	.3028	.2881	.2739
16	.3046	.2926	.2781	.2649
17	.2952	.2838	.2696	.2566
18	.2865	.2757	.2617	.2489
19	.2785	.2682	.2551	.2426
20	.2714	.2612	.2483	.2360

$$\alpha = .01$$

Number of data pairs	Critical eta for 2 nominal predictor categories	Critical eta for 3 nominal predictor categories	Critical eta for 4 nominal predictor categories	Critical eta for 5 nominal predictor categories
2	.9850	.9605	.9330	.9066
3	.8953	.8442	.8016	.7666
4	.8034	.7488	.7053	.6710
5	.7299	.6772	.6355	.6031
6	.6716	.6219	.5826	.5522
7	.6249	.5777	.5408	.5120
8	.5864	.5419	.5067	.4782
9	.5540	.5116	.4783	.4524
10	.5263	.4863	.4543	.4294
11	.5027	.4640	.4331	.4095
12	.4815	.4450	.4150	.3921
13	.4630	.4275	.3991	.3769
14	.4464	.4124	.3855	.3631
15	.4316	.3984	.3716	.3510
16	.4179	.3858	.3602	.3399
17	.4057	.3746	.3496	.3296
18	.3942	.3641	.3403	.3212
19	.3838	.3539	.3312	.3129
20	.3742	.3455	.3227	.3051

$\alpha = .05$, One-Tailed

Null hypothesis: no correlation in population.

Alternative hypothesis: positive correlation in population.

Reject the null hypothesis and favor the alternative hypothesis if the calculated lambda is greater than or equal to the critical lambda.

Number of data pairs	Critical lambda
3	*
4	*
5	*
6	*
7	*
8	*
9	*
10	*
.	*
.	*
.	*
49	*
50	0
.	.
.	.
.	.
120	0

*According to Harshbarger (1977), when using the lambda statistic to estimate the degree of predictability of one particular variable based upon the other, statistical significance can only be determined if the sample size is 50 or greater. With sample sizes that large, the null hypothesis that $\lambda = 0$ can be rejected whenever $\lambda > 0$.

(See Harshbarger, T. R. (1977). *Introductory statistics: A decision map* (pp. 481–482). New York: Macmillan).

$\alpha = .05$, One-Tailed

Null hypothesis: average ranks equal in both conditions.

Alternative hypothesis: average rank greater in condition 1.

Reject the null hypothesis and favor the alternative hypothesis if the calculated U is less than or equal to the critical U.

Note: n_1 and n_2 denote the numbers of ranks in the first and second conditions, respectively.

n_1	n_2	Critical U	n_1	n_2	Critical U	n_1	n_2	Critical U	n_1	n_2	Critical U
5	5	4	9	5	9	13	5	15	17	5	20
5	6	5	9	6	12	13	6	19	17	6	26
5	7	6	9	7	15	13	7	24	17	7	33
5	8	8	9	8	18	13	8	28	17	8	39
5	9	9	9	9	21	13	9	33	17	9	45
5	10	11	9	10	24	13	10	37	17	10	51
5	11	12	9	11	27	13	11	42	17	11	57
5	12	13	9	12	30	13	12	47	17	12	64
5	13	15	9	13	33	13	13	51	17	13	70
5	14	16	9	14	36	13	14	56	17	14	77
5	15	18	9	15	39	13	15	61	17	15	83
5	16	19	9	16	42	13	16	65	17	16	89
5	17	20	9	17	45	13	17	70	17	17	96
5	18	22	9	18	48	13	18	75	17	18	102
5	19	23	9	19	51	13	19	80	17	19	109
5	20	25	9	20	54	13	20	84	17	20	115
6	5	5	10	5	11	14	5	16	18	5	22
6	6	7	10	6	14	14	6	21	18	6	28
6	7	8	10	7	17	14	7	26	18	7	35
6	8	10	10	8	20	14	8	31	18	8	41
6	9	12	10	9	24	14	9	36	18	9	48
6	10	14	10	10	27	14	10	41	18	10	55
6	11	16	10	11	31	14	11	46	18	11	61
6	12	17	10	12	34	14	12	51	18	12	68
6	13	19	10	13	37	14	13	56	18	13	75
6	14	21	10	14	41	14	14	61	18	14	82
6	15	23	10	15	44	14	15	66	18	15	88
6	16	25	10	16	48	14	16	71	18	16	95
6	17	26	10	17	51	14	17	77	18	17	102
6	18	28	10	18	55	14	18	82	18	18	109
6	19	30	10	19	58	14	19	87	18	19	116
6	20	32	10	20	62	14	20	92	18	20	123
7	5	6	11	5	12	15	5	18	19	5	23
7	6	8	11	6	16	15	6	23	19	6	30
7	7	11	11	7	19	15	7	28	19	7	37
7	8	13	11	8	23	15	8	33	19	8	44
7	9	15	11	9	27	15	9	39	19	9	51

(continued)

n_1	n_2	Critical U	n_1	n_2	Critical U	n_1	n_2	Critical U	n_1	n_2	Critical U
7	10	17	11	10	31	15	10	44	19	10	58
7	11	19	11	11	34	15	11	50	19	11	65
7	12	21	11	12	38	15	12	55	19	12	72
7	13	24	11	13	42	15	13	61	19	13	80
7	14	26	11	14	46	15	14	66	19	14	87
7	15	28	11	15	50	15	15	72	19	15	94
7	16	30	11	16	54	15	16	77	19	16	101
7	17	33	11	17	57	15	17	83	19	17	109
7	18	35	11	18	61	15	18	88	19	18	116
7	19	37	11	19	65	15	19	94	19	19	123
7	20	39	11	20	69	15	20	100	19	20	130
8	5	8	12	5	13	16	5	19	20	5	25
8	6	10	12	6	17	16	6	25	20	6	32
8	7	13	12	7	21	16	7	30	20	7	39
8	8	15	12	8	26	16	8	36	20	8	47
8	9	18	12	9	30	16	9	42	20	9	54
8	10	20	12	10	34	16	10	48	20	10	62
8	11	23	12	11	38	16	11	54	20	11	69
8	12	26	12	12	42	16	12	60	20	12	77
8	13	28	12	13	47	16	13	65	20	13	84
8	14	31	12	14	51	16	14	71	20	14	92
8	15	33	12	15	55	16	15	77	20	15	100
8	16	36	12	16	60	16	16	83	20	16	107
8	17	39	12	17	64	16	17	89	20	17	115
8	18	41	12	18	68	16	18	95	20	18	123
8	19	44	12	19	72	16	19	101	20	19	130
8	20	47	12	20	77	16	20	107	20	20	138

$\alpha = .01$, One-Tailed

Null hypothesis: average ranks equal in both conditions.
Alternative hypothesis: average rank greater in condition 1.
Reject the null hypothesis and favor the alternative hypothesis if the calculated U is less than or equal to the critical U.

n_1	n_2	Critical U	n_1	n_2	Critical U	n_1	n_2	Critical U	n_1	n_2	Critical U
5	5	1	9	5	9	13	5	9	17	5	13
5	6	2	9	6	7	13	6	12	17	6	18
5	7	3	9	7	9	13	7	16	17	7	23
5	8	4	9	8	11	13	8	20	17	8	28
5	9	5	9	9	14	13	9	23	17	9	33
5	10	6	9	10	16	13	10	27	17	10	38
5	11	7	9	11	18	13	11	31	17	11	44
5	12	8	9	12	21	13	12	35	17	12	49

n_1	n_2	Critical U	n_1	n_2	Critical U	n_1	n_2	Critical U	n_1	n_2	Critical U
5	13	9	9	13	23	13	13	39	17	13	55
5	14	10	9	14	26	13	14	43	17	14	60
5	15	11	9	15	28	13	15	47	17	15	66
5	16	12	9	16	31	13	16	51	17	16	71
5	17	13	9	17	33	13	17	55	17	17	77
5	18	14	9	18	36	13	18	59	17	18	82
5	19	15	9	19	38	13	19	63	17	19	88
5	20	16	9	20	40	13	20	67	17	20	93
6	5	2	10	5	6	14	5	10	18	5	14
6	6	3	10	6	8	14	6	13	18	6	19
6	7	4	10	7	11	14	7	17	18	7	24
6	8	6	10	8	13	14	8	22	18	8	30
6	9	7	10	9	16	14	9	26	18	9	36
6	10	8	10	10	19	14	10	30	18	10	41
6	11	9	10	11	22	14	11	34	18	11	47
6	12	11	10	12	24	14	12	38	18	12	53
6	13	12	10	13	27	14	13	43	18	13	59
6	14	13	10	14	30	14	14	47	18	14	65
6	15	15	10	15	33	14	15	51	18	15	70
6	16	16	10	16	36	14	16	56	18	16	76
6	17	18	10	17	38	14	17	60	18	17	82
6	18	19	10	18	41	14	18	65	18	18	88
6	19	20	10	19	44	14	19	69	18	19	94
6	20	22	10	20	47	14	20	73	18	20	100
7	5	3	11	5	7	15	5	11	19	5	15
7	6	4	11	6	9	15	6	15	19	6	20
7	7	6	11	7	12	15	7	19	19	7	26
7	8	7	11	8	15	15	8	24	19	8	32
7	9	9	11	9	18	15	9	28	19	9	38
7	10	11	11	10	22	15	10	33	19	10	44
7	11	12	11	11	25	15	11	37	19	11	50
7	12	14	11	12	28	15	12	42	19	12	56
7	13	16	11	13	31	15	13	47	19	13	63
7	14	17	11	14	34	15	14	51	19	14	69
7	15	19	11	15	37	15	15	56	19	15	75
7	16	21	11	16	41	15	16	61	19	16	82
7	17	23	11	17	44	15	17	66	19	17	88
7	18	24	11	18	47	15	18	70	19	18	94
7	19	26	11	19	50	15	19	75	19	19	101
7	20	28	11	20	53	15	20	80	19	20	107
8	5	4	12	5	8	16	5	12	20	5	16
8	6	6	12	6	11	16	6	16	20	6	22
8	7	7	12	7	14	16	7	21	20	7	28

TABLE B.8   Critical Mann-Whitney U Values (*continued*)

n_1	n_2	Critical U	n_1	n_2	Critical U	n_1	n_2	Critical U	n_1	n_2	Critical U
8	8	9	12	8	17	16	8	26	20	8	34
8	9	11	12	9	21	16	9	31	20	9	40
8	10	13	12	10	24	16	10	36	20	10	47
8	11	15	12	11	28	16	11	41	20	11	53
8	12	17	12	12	31	16	12	46	20	12	60
8	13	20	12	13	35	16	13	51	20	13	67
8	14	22	12	14	38	16	14	56	20	14	73
8	15	24	12	15	42	16	15	61	20	15	80
8	16	26	12	16	46	16	16	66	20	16	87
8	17	28	12	17	49	16	17	71	20	17	93
8	18	30	12	18	53	16	18	76	20	18	100
8	19	32	12	19	56	16	19	82	20	19	107
8	20	34	12	20	60	16	20	87	20	20	114

$\alpha = .05$, Two-Tailed

Null hypothesis: average ranks equal in both conditions.
Alternative hypothesis: average ranks not equal in both conditions.
Reject the null hypothesis and favor the alternative hypothesis if the calculated U is less than or equal to the critical U.

n_1	n_2	Critical U	n_1	n_2	Critical U	n_1	n_2	Critical U	n_1	n_2	Critical U
5	5	2	9	5	7	13	5	12	17	5	17
5	6	3	9	6	10	13	6	16	17	6	22
5	7	5	9	7	12	13	7	20	17	7	28
5	8	6	9	8	15	13	8	24	17	8	34
5	9	7	9	9	17	13	9	28	17	9	39
5	10	8	9	10	20	13	10	33	17	10	45
5	11	9	9	11	23	13	11	37	17	11	51
5	12	11	9	12	26	13	12	41	17	12	57
5	13	12	9	13	28	13	13	45	17	13	63
5	14	13	9	14	31	13	14	50	17	14	69
5	15	14	9	15	34	13	15	54	17	15	75
5	16	15	9	16	37	13	16	59	17	16	81
5	17	17	9	17	39	13	17	63	17	17	87
5	18	18	9	18	42	13	18	67	17	18	93
5	19	19	9	19	45	13	19	72	17	19	99
5	20	20	9	20	48	13	20	76	17	20	105
6	5	3	10	5	8	14	5	13	18	5	18
6	6	5	10	6	11	14	6	17	18	6	24
6	7	6	10	7	14	14	7	22	18	7	30
6	8	8	10	8	17	14	8	26	18	8	36
6	9	10	10	9	20	14	9	31	18	9	42

TABLE B.8 Critical Mann-Whitney U Values (*continued*)

n_1	n_2	Critical U	n_1	n_2	Critical U	n_1	n_2	Critical U	n_1	n_2	Critical U
6	10	11	10	10	23	14	10	36	18	10	48
6	11	13	10	11	26	14	11	40	18	11	55
6	12	14	10	12	29	14	12	45	18	12	61
6	13	16	10	13	33	14	13	50	18	13	67
6	14	17	10	14	36	14	14	55	18	14	74
6	15	19	10	15	39	14	15	59	18	15	80
6	16	21	10	16	42	14	16	64	18	16	86
6	17	22	10	17	45	14	17	69	18	17	93
6	18	24	10	18	48	14	18	74	18	18	99
6	19	25	10	19	52	14	19	78	18	19	106
6	20	27	10	20	55	14	20	83	18	20	112
7	5	5	11	5	9	15	5	14	19	5	19
7	6	6	11	6	13	15	6	19	19	6	25
7	7	8	11	7	16	15	7	24	19	7	32
7	8	10	11	8	19	15	8	29	19	8	38
7	9	12	11	9	23	15	9	34	19	9	45
7	10	14	11	10	26	15	10	39	19	10	52
7	11	16	11	11	30	15	11	44	19	11	58
7	12	18	11	12	33	15	12	49	19	12	65
7	13	20	11	13	37	15	13	54	19	13	72
7	14	22	11	14	40	15	14	59	19	14	78
7	15	24	11	15	44	15	15	64	19	15	85
7	16	26	11	16	47	15	16	70	19	16	92
7	17	28	11	17	51	15	17	75	19	17	99
7	18	30	11	18	55	15	18	80	19	18	106
7	19	32	11	19	58	15	19	85	19	19	113
7	20	34	11	20	62	15	20	90	19	20	119
8	5	6	12	5	11	16	5	15	20	5	20
8	6	8	12	6	14	16	6	21	20	6	27
8	7	10	12	7	18	16	7	26	20	7	34
8	8	13	12	8	22	16	8	31	20	8	41
8	9	15	12	9	26	16	9	37	20	9	48
8	10	17	12	10	29	16	10	42	20	10	55
8	11	19	12	11	33	16	11	47	20	11	62
8	12	22	12	12	37	16	12	53	20	12	69
8	13	24	12	13	41	16	13	59	20	13	76
8	14	26	12	14	45	16	14	64	20	14	83
8	15	29	12	15	49	16	15	70	20	15	90
8	16	31	12	16	53	16	16	75	20	16	98
8	17	34	12	17	57	16	17	81	20	17	105
8	18	36	12	18	61	16	18	86	20	18	112
8	19	44	12	19	72	16	19	101	20	19	130
8	20	47	12	20	77	16	20	107	20	20	138

$\alpha = .01$, Two-Tailed

Null hypothesis: average ranks equal in both conditions.
Alternative hypothesis: average ranks not equal in both conditions.
Reject the null hypothesis and favor the alternative hypothesis if the calculated U is less than or equal to the critical U.

n_1	n_2	Critical U	n_1	n_2	Critical U	n_1	n_2	Critical U	n_1	n_2	Critical U
5	5	0	9	5	3	13	5	7	17	5	10
5	6	1	9	6	5	13	6	10	17	6	15
5	7	1	9	7	7	13	7	13	17	7	19
5	8	2	9	8	9	13	8	17	17	8	24
5	9	3	9	9	11	13	9	20	17	9	29
5	10	4	9	10	13	13	10	24	17	10	34
5	11	5	9	11	16	13	11	27	17	11	39
5	12	6	9	12	18	13	12	31	17	12	44
5	13	7	9	13	20	13	13	34	17	13	49
5	14	7	9	14	22	13	14	38	17	14	54
5	15	8	9	15	24	13	15	42	17	15	60
5	16	9	9	16	27	13	16	45	17	16	65
5	17	10	9	17	29	13	17	49	17	17	70
5	18	11	9	18	31	13	18	53	17	18	75
5	19	12	9	19	33	13	19	57	17	19	81
5	20	13	9	20	36	13	20	60	17	20	86
6	5	1	10	5	4	14	5	7	18	5	11
6	6	2	10	6	6	14	6	11	18	6	16
6	7	3	10	7	9	14	7	15	18	7	21
6	8	4	10	8	11	14	8	18	18	8	26
6	9	5	10	9	13	14	9	22	18	9	31
6	10	6	10	10	16	14	10	26	18	10	37
6	11	7	10	11	18	14	11	30	18	11	42
6	12	9	10	12	21	14	12	34	18	12	47
6	13	10	10	13	24	14	13	38	18	13	53
6	14	11	10	14	26	14	14	42	18	14	58
6	15	12	10	15	29	14	15	46	18	15	64
6	16	13	10	16	31	14	16	50	18	16	70
6	17	15	10	17	34	14	17	54	18	17	75
6	18	16	10	18	37	14	18	58	18	18	81
6	19	17	10	19	39	14	19	63	18	19	87
6	20	18	10	20	42	14	20	67	18	20	92
7	5	1	11	5	5	15	5	8	19	5	12
7	6	3	11	6	7	15	6	12	19	6	17
7	7	4	11	7	10	15	7	16	19	7	22
7	8	6	11	8	13	15	8	20	19	8	28
7	9	7	11	9	16	15	9	24	19	9	33
7	10	9	11	10	18	15	10	29	19	10	39
7	11	10	11	11	21	15	11	33	19	11	45

n_1	n_2	Critical U	n_1	n_2	Critical U	n_1	n_2	Critical U	n_1	n_2	Critical U
7	12	12	11	12	24	15	12	37	19	12	51
7	13	13	11	13	27	15	13	42	19	13	57
7	14	15	11	14	30	15	14	46	19	14	63
7	15	16	11	15	33	15	15	51	19	15	69
7	16	18	11	16	36	15	16	55	19	16	74
7	17	19	11	17	39	15	17	60	19	17	81
7	18	21	11	18	42	15	18	64	19	18	87
7	19	22	11	19	45	15	19	69	19	19	93
7	20	24	11	20	48	15	20	73	19	20	99
8	5	2	12	5	6	16	5	9	20	5	13
8	6	4	12	6	9	16	6	13	20	6	18
8	7	6	12	7	12	16	7	18	20	7	24
8	8	7	12	8	15	16	8	22	20	8	30
8	9	9	12	9	18	16	9	27	20	9	36
8	10	11	12	10	21	16	10	31	20	10	42
8	11	13	12	11	24	16	11	36	20	11	48
8	12	15	12	12	27	16	12	41	20	12	54
8	13	17	12	13	31	16	13	45	20	13	60
8	14	18	12	14	34	16	14	50	20	14	67
8	15	20	12	15	37	16	15	55	20	15	73
8	16	22	12	16	41	16	16	60	20	16	79
8	17	24	12	17	44	16	17	65	20	17	86
8	18	26	12	18	47	16	18	70	20	18	92
8	19	28	12	19	51	16	19	74	20	19	99
8	20	30	12	20	54	16	20	78	20	20	105

TABLE B.9   Critical Wilcoxon *T* Values

α = .05, One-Tailed

Null hypothesis: average ranks equal in both conditions.
Alternative hypothesis: average rank greater in condition 1.
Reject the null hypothesis and favor the alternative hypothesis if the calculated Wilcoxon
  T is less than or equal to the critical Wilcoxon *T*.

Number of data pairs with nonzero difference	Degrees of freedom	Critical Wilcoxon *T*
3	1	0
4	2	0
5	3	0
6	4	2
7	5	3
8	6	5
9	7	8
10	8	10
11	9	13
12	10	17
13	11	21
14	12	25
15	13	30
16	14	35
17	15	41
18	16	47
19	17	53
20	18	60
21	19	67
22	20	75
23	21	83
24	22	91
25	23	100
26	24	110
27	25	119
28	26	130
29	27	140
30	28	151
31	29	163
32	30	175
33	31	187
34	32	200
35	33	213
36	34	227
37	35	241
38	36	256
39	37	271
40	38	286
41	39	302
42	40	319
43	41	336
44	42	353
45	43	371
46	44	389
47	45	407
48	46	426
49	47	446
50	48	466

$\alpha = .01$, Two-Tailed

Null hypothesis: average ranks equal in both conditions.

Alternative hypothesis: average rank not equal in both conditions.

Reject the null hypothesis and favor the alternative hypothesis if the calculated Wilcoxon *T* is less than or equal to the critical Wilcoxon *T*.

Number of data pairs with nonzero difference	Degrees of freedom	Critical Wilcoxon *T*
3	1	0
4	2	0
5	3	0
6	4	0
7	5	2
8	6	3
9	7	5
10	8	8
11	9	10
12	10	13
13	11	17
14	12	21
15	13	25
16	14	29
17	15	34
18	16	40
19	17	46
20	18	52
21	19	58
22	20	65
23	21	73
24	22	81
25	23	89
26	24	98
27	25	107
28	26	116
29	27	126
30	28	137
31	29	147
32	30	159
33	31	170
34	32	182
35	33	195
36	34	208
37	35	221
38	36	235
39	37	249
40	38	264
41	39	279
42	40	294
43	41	310
44	42	327
45	43	343
46	44	361
47	45	378
48	46	396
49	47	415
50	48	434

$\alpha = .01$, One-Tailed

Null hypothesis: average ranks equal in both conditions.

Alternative hypothesis: average ranks not equal in both conditions.

Reject the null hypothesis and favor the alternative hypothesis if the calculated Wilcoxon *T* is less than or equal to the critical Wilcoxon *T*.

Number of data pairs with nonzero difference	Degrees of freedom	Critical Wilcoxon *T*
3	1	0
4	2	0
5	3	0
6	4	0
7	5	0
8	6	1
9	7	3
10	8	5
11	9	7
12	10	9
13	11	12
14	12	15
15	13	19
16	14	23
17	15	27
18	16	32
19	17	37
20	18	43
21	19	49
22	20	55
23	21	62
24	22	69
25	23	76
26	24	84
27	25	92
28	26	101
29	27	110
30	28	120
31	29	130
32	30	140
33	31	151
34	32	162
35	33	173
36	34	185
37	35	198
38	36	211
39	37	224
40	38	238
41	39	252
42	40	266
43	41	281
44	42	296
45	43	312
46	44	328
47	45	345
48	46	362
49	47	379
50	48	397

$\alpha = .01$, Two-Tailed

Null hypothesis: average ranks equal in both conditions.
Alternative hypothesis: average ranks not equal in both conditions.
Reject the null hypothesis and favor the alternative hypothesis if the calculated Wilcoxon
  T is less than or equal to the critical Wilcoxon *T*.

Number of data pairs with nonzero difference	Degrees of freedom	Critical Wilcoxon *T*
3	1	0
4	2	0
5	3	0
6	4	0
7	5	0
8	6	0
9	7	1
10	8	3
11	9	5
12	10	7
13	11	9
14	12	12
15	13	15
16	14	19
17	15	23
18	16	27
19	17	32
20	18	37
21	19	42
22	20	48
23	21	54
24	22	61
25	23	68
26	24	75
27	25	83
28	26	91
29	27	100
30	28	109
31	29	118
32	30	128
33	31	138
34	32	148
35	33	159
36	34	171
37	35	182
38	36	194
39	37	207
40	38	220
41	39	233
42	40	247
43	41	261
44	42	276
45	43	291
46	44	307
47	45	322
48	46	339
49	47	355
50	49	373

These critical values are equivalent to chi square critical values. Use this table only if there are five or more data points per condition.

$\alpha = .05$, One-Tailed (Upper Tail)

Null hypothesis: average ranks equal in all conditions.

Alternative hypothesis: average ranks not equal in all conditions.

Reject the null hypothesis and favor the alternative hypothesis if the calculated *H* is greater than or equal to the critical *H*.

Number of categories	Degrees of freedom	Critical Kruskal-Wallis *H*
2	1	3.841
3	2	5.991
4	3	7.815
5	4	9.488
6	5	11.070
7	6	12.592
8	7	14.067
9	8	15.507
10	9	16.919
11	10	18.307

$\alpha = .01$, One-Tailed (Upper Tail)

Null hypothesis: average ranks equal in all conditions.

Alternative hypothesis: average ranks not equal in all conditions.

Reject the null hypothesis and favor the alternative hypothesis if the calculated *H* is greater than or equal to the critical *H*.

Number of categories	Degrees of freedom	Critical Kruskal-Wallis *H*
2	1	6.635
3	2	9.210
4	3	11.341
5	4	13.277
6	5	15.086
7	6	16.812
8	7	18.475
9	8	20.090
10	9	21.666
11	10	23.209

| TABLE B.11 | Critical Friedman Values |

The Friedman analysis results in a specific chi square value. The table of chi square critical values is repeated here for your convenience.

$\alpha = .05$ One-Tailed (Upper Tail)

Null hypothesis: expected frequencies and observed frequencies equal.
Alternative hypothesis: expected frequencies and observed frequencies not equal.
Reject the null hypothesis and favor the alternative hypothesis if the calculated chi square is greater than or equal to the critical chi square.

Number of categories	Degrees of freedom	Critical chi square
2	1	3.841
3	2	5.991
4	3	7.815
5	4	9.488
6	5	11.070
7	6	12.592
8	7	14.067
9	8	15.507
10	9	16.919
11	10	18.307

$\alpha = .01$ One-Tailed (Upper Tail)

Null hypothesis: expected frequencies and observed frequencies equal.
Alternative hypothesis: expected frequencies and observed frequencies not equal.
Reject the null hypothesis and favor the alternative hypothesis if the calculated chi square is greater than or equal to the critical chi square.

Number of categories	Degrees of freedom	Critical chi square
2	1	6.635
3	2	9.210
4	3	11.341
5	4	13.277
6	5	15.086
7	6	16.812
8	7	18.475
9	8	20.090
10	9	21.666
11	10	23.209

Critical *t* Values

α = .05, One-Tailed (Upper Tail)

Null hypothesis: average scores equal for conditions 1 and 2.
Alternative hypothesis: average score greater for condition 1 (positive difference).
Reject the null hypothesis and favor the alternative hypothesis if the calculated *t* is greater
  than or equal to the critical *t*.
Note: *df* denotes degrees of freedom.

df	Critical *t*	df	Critical *t*	df	Critical *t*
1	+6.314	41	+1.683	81	+1.663
2	+2.920	42	+1.683	82	+1.663
3	+2.353	43	+1.681	83	+1.663
4	+2.132	44	+1.680	84	+1.663
5	+2.015	45	+1.679	85	+1.663
6	+1.943	46	+1.679	86	+1.663
7	+1.895	47	+1.678	87	+1.663
8	+1.860	48	+1.677	88	+1.663
9	+1.833	49	+1.677	89	+1.663
10	+1.812	50	+1.676	90	+1.663
11	+1.796	51	+1.675	91	+1.661
12	+1.782	52	+1.675	92	+1.661
13	+1.771	53	+1.675	93	+1.661
14	+1.761	54	+1.674	94	+1.661
15	+1.753	55	+1.673	95	+1.661
16	+1.746	56	+1.673	96	+1.661
17	+1.740	57	+1.673	97	+1.661
18	+1.734	58	+1.671	98	+1.661
19	+1.729	59	+1.671	99	+1.661
20	+1.724	60	+1.671	100	+1.661
21	+1.721	61	+1.671	101	+1.661
22	+1.717	62	+1.671	102	+1.661
23	+1.714	63	+1.669	103	+1.660
24	+1.711	64	+1.669	104	+1.660
25	+1.708	65	+1.669	105	+1.660
26	+1.706	66	+1.669	106	+1.660
27	+1.703	67	+1.669	107	+1.660
28	+1.701	68	+1.667	108	+1.660
29	+1.699	69	+1.667	109	+1.660
30	+1.697	70	+1.667	110	+1.659
31	+1.695	71	+1.667	111	+1.659
32	+1.693	72	+1.667	112	+1.659
33	+1.692	73	+1.667	113	+1.659
34	+1.691	74	+1.665	114	+1.659
35	+1.690	75	+1.665	115	+1.659
36	+1.689	76	+1.665	116	+1.659
37	+1.687	77	+1.665	117	+1.659
38	+1.686	78	+1.665	118	+1.658
39	+1.685	79	+1.664	119	+1.658
40	+1.684	80	+1.664	120	+1.658
				∞	+1.645

α = .05, One-Tailed (Lower Tail)

Null hypothesis: average scores equal for conditions 1 and 2.

Alternative hypothesis: average score greater for condition 2 (negative difference).

Reject the null hypothesis and favor the alternative hypothesis if the calculated *t* is less than or equal to the critical *t*.

Note: *df* denotes degrees of freedom.

df	Critical t	df	Critical t	df	Critical t
1	−6.314	41	−1.683	81	−1.663
2	−2.920	42	−1.683	82	−1.663
3	−2.353	43	−1.681	83	−1.663
4	−2.132	44	−1.680	84	−1.663
5	−2.015	45	−1.679	85	−1.663
6	−1.943	46	−1.679	86	−1.663
7	−1.895	47	−1.678	87	−1.663
8	−1.860	48	−1.677	88	−1.663
9	−1.833	49	−1.677	89	−1.663
10	−1.812	50	−1.676	90	−1.663
11	−1.796	51	−1.675	91	−1.661
12	−1.782	52	−1.675	92	−1.661
13	−1.771	53	−1.675	93	−1.661
14	−1.761	54	−1.674	94	−1.661
15	−1.753	55	−1.673	95	−1.661
16	−1.746	56	−1.673	96	−1.661
17	−1.740	57	−1.673	97	−1.661
18	−1.734	58	−1.671	98	−1.661
19	−1.729	59	−1.671	99	−1.661
20	−1.724	60	−1.671	100	−1.661
21	−1.721	61	−1.671	101	−1.661
22	−1.717	62	−1.671	102	−1.661
23	−1.714	63	−1.669	103	−1.660
24	−1.711	64	−1.669	104	−1.660
25	−1.708	65	−1.669	105	−1.660
26	−1.706	66	−1.669	106	−1.660
27	−1.703	67	−1.669	107	−1.660
28	−1.701	68	−1.667	108	−1.660
29	−1.699	69	−1.667	109	−1.660
30	−1.697	70	−1.667	110	−1.659
31	−1.695	71	−1.667	111	−1.659
32	−1.693	72	−1.667	112	−1.659
33	−1.692	73	−1.667	113	−1.659
34	−1.691	74	−1.665	114	−1.659
35	−1.690	75	−1.665	115	−1.659
36	−1.689	76	−1.665	116	−1.659
37	−1.687	77	−1.665	117	−1.659
38	−1.686	78	−1.665	118	−1.658
39	−1.685	79	−1.664	119	−1.658
40	−1.684	80	−1.664	120	−1.658
				∞	−1.645

$\alpha = .05$, Two-Tailed

Null hypothesis: average scores equal for conditions 1 and 2.
Alternative hypothesis: average scores not equal in conditions 1 and 2.
Reject the null hypothesis and favor the alternative hypothesis if the calculated *t* is less than or equal to the negative critical *t* or greater than or equal to the positive critical *t*.
Note: *df* denotes degrees of freedom.

df	Critical t	df	Critical t	df	Critical t
1	+12.706	41	±2.019	81	±1.989
2	± 4.303	42	±2.018	82	±1.989
3	± 3.182	43	±2.016	83	±1.988
4	± 2.776	44	±2.015	84	±1.988
5	± 2.571	45	±2.014	85	±1.987
6	± 2.447	46	±2.013	86	±1.987
7	± 2.365	47	±2.012	87	±1.987
8	± 2.306	48	±2.010	88	±1.987
9	± 2.262	49	±2.009	89	±1.986
10	± 2.228	50	±2.008	90	±1.986
11	± 2.201	51	±2.007	91	±1.986
12	± 2.179	52	±2.006	92	±1.985
13	± 2.160	53	±2.005	93	±1.985
14	± 2.145	54	±2.004	94	±1.985
15	± 2.131	55	±2.003	95	±1.985
16	± 2.120	56	±2.003	96	±1.984
17	± 2.110	57	±2.002	97	±1.984
18	± 2.101	58	±2.001	98	±1.984
19	± 2.093	59	±2.000	99	±1.984
20	± 2.086	60	±2.000	100	±1.983
21	± 2.080	61	±1.999	101	±1.983
22	± 2.074	62	±1.999	102	±1.983
23	± 2.069	63	±1.998	103	±1.983
24	± 2.064	64	±1.997	104	±1.982
25	± 2.060	65	±1.997	105	±1.982
26	± 2.056	66	±1.996	106	±1.982
27	± 2.052	67	±1.995	107	±1.982
28	± 2.048	68	±1.995	108	±1.981
29	± 2.045	69	±1.994	109	±1.981
30	± 2.042	70	±1.994	110	±1.981
31	± 2.039	71	±1.993	111	±1.981
32	± 2.037	72	±1.993	112	±1.981
33	± 2.034	73	±1.993	113	±1.980
34	± 2.032	74	±1.992	114	±1.980
35	± 2.030	75	±1.991	115	±1.980
36	± 2.028	76	±1.991	116	±1.980
37	± 2.025	77	±1.991	117	±1.980
38	± 2.024	78	±1.990	118	±1.980
39	± 2.022	79	±1.990	119	±1.980
40	± 2.021	80	±1.990	120	±1.980
				∞	±1.960

$\alpha = .01$, One-Tailed (Upper Tail)

Null hypothesis: average scores equal for conditions 1 and 2.
Alternative hypothesis: average score greater for condition 1 (positive difference).
Reject the null hypothesis and favor the alternative hypothesis if the calculated *t* is greater than or equal to the critical *t*.
Note: *df* denotes degrees of freedom

df	Critical t	df	Critical t	df	Critical t
1	+31.821	41	+2.420	81	+2.373
2	+6.965	42	+2.418	82	+2.373
3	+4.541	43	+2.416	83	+2.372
4	+3.747	44	+2.414	84	+2.372
5	+3.365	45	+2.412	85	+2.371
6	+3.143	46	+2.410	86	+2.370
7	+2.998	47	+2.408	87	+2.370
8	+2.896	48	+2.406	88	+2.369
9	+2.821	49	+2.405	89	+2.369
10	+2.764	50	+2.403	90	+2.368
11	+2.718	51	+2.401	91	+2.368
12	+2.681	52	+2.400	92	+2.368
13	+2.650	53	+2.398	93	+2.367
14	+2.624	54	+2.397	94	+2.367
15	+2.602	55	+2.396	95	+2.366
16	+2.583	56	+2.395	96	+2.366
17	+2.567	57	+2.393	97	+2.365
18	+2.552	58	+2.392	98	+2.365
19	+2.539	59	+2.391	99	+2.365
20	+2.528	60	+2.390	100	+2.364
21	+2.518	61	+2.389	101	+2.364
22	+2.508	62	+2.388	102	+2.364
23	+2.500	63	+2.387	103	+2.363
24	+2.492	64	+2.386	104	+2.363
25	+2.485	65	+2.385	105	+2.362
26	+2.479	66	+2.384	106	+2.362
27	+2.473	67	+2.383	107	+2.362
28	+2.467	68	+2.382	108	+2.361
29	+2.462	69	+2.381	109	+2.361
30	+2.457	70	+2.381	110	+2.361
31	+2.453	71	+2.380	111	+2.360
32	+2.449	72	+2.379	112	+2.360
33	+2.445	73	+2.378	113	+2.360
34	+2.442	74	+2.378	114	+2.360
35	+2.437	75	+2.377	115	+2.359
36	+2.434	76	+2.376	116	+2.359
37	+2.431	77	+2.376	117	+2.359
38	+2.428	78	+2.375	118	+2.358
39	+2.425	79	+2.374	119	+2.358
40	+2.423	80	+2.374	120	+2.358
				∞	+2.326

α = .01, One-Tailed (Lower Tail)

Null hypothesis: average score equal for conditions 1 and 2.
Alternative hypothesis: average score less for condition 1 (negative difference).
Reject the null hypothesis and favor the alternative hypothesis if the calculated *t* is less
than or equal to the critical *t*.
Note: *df* denotes degrees of freedom.

df	Critical t	df	Critical t	df	Critical t
1	−31.821	41	−2.420	81	−2.373
2	−6.965	41	−2.418	82	−2.373
3	−4.541	43	−2.416	83	−2.372
4	−3.747	44	−2.414	84	−2.372
5	−3.365	45	−2.412	85	−2.371
6	−3.143	46	−2.410	86	−2.370
7	−2.998	47	−2.408	87	−2.370
8	−2.896	48	−2.406	88	−2.369
9	−2.821	49	−2.405	89	−2.369
10	−2.764	50	−2.403	90	−2.368
11	−2.718	51	−2.401	91	−2.368
12	−2.681	52	−2.400	92	−2.368
13	−2.650	53	−2.398	93	−2.367
14	−2.624	54	−2.397	94	−2.367
15	−2.602	55	−2.396	95	−2.366
16	−2.583	56	−2.395	96	−2.366
17	−2.567	57	−2.393	97	−2.365
18	−2.552	58	−2.392	98	−2.365
19	−2.539	59	−2.391	99	−2.365
20	−2.528	60	−2.390	100	−2.364
21	−2.518	61	−2.389	101	−2.364
22	−2.508	62	−2.388	102	−2.364
23	−2.500	63	−2.387	103	−2.363
24	−2.492	64	−2.386	104	−2.363
25	−2.485	65	−2.385	105	−2.362
26	−2.479	66	−2.384	106	−2.362
27	−2.473	67	−2.383	107	−2.362
28	−2.467	68	−2.382	108	−2.361
29	−2.462	69	−2.381	109	−2.361
30	−2.457	70	−2.381	110	−2.361
31	−2.453	71	−2.380	111	−2.360
32	−2.449	72	−2.379	112	−2.360
33	−2.445	73	−2.378	113	−2.360
34	−2.442	74	−2.378	114	−2.360
35	−2.437	75	−2.377	115	−2.359
36	−2.434	76	−2.376	116	−2.359
37	−2.431	77	−2.376	117	−2.359
38	−2.428	78	−2.375	118	−2.358
39	−2.425	79	−2.374	119	−2.358
40	−2.423	80	−2.374	120	−2.358
				∞	−2.326

$\alpha = .01$, Two-Tailed

Null hypothesis: average scores equal for both conditions.
Alternative hypothesis: average scores not equal for both conditions.
Reject the null hypothesis and favor the alternative hypothesis if the calculated *t* is greater than or equal to the positive critical *t*, or less than or equal to the negative critical *t*.
Note: *df* denotes degrees of freedom.

df	Critical t	df	Critical t	df	Critical t
1	±63.657	41	±2.700	81	±2.638
2	±9.925	41	±2.697	82	±2.637
3	±5.841	43	±2.694	83	±2.636
4	±4.604	44	±2.692	84	±2.636
5	±4.032	45	±2.689	85	±2.635
6	±3.707	46	±2.686	86	±2.634
7	±3.499	47	±2.684	87	±2.634
8	±3.355	48	±2.682	88	±2.633
9	±3.250	49	±2.679	89	±2.632
10	±3.169	50	±2.677	90	±2.631
11	±3.106	51	±2.675	91	±2.630
12	±3.055	52	±2.673	92	±2.629
13	±3.012	53	±2.671	93	±2.629
14	±2.977	54	±2.669	94	±2.629
15	±2.947	55	±2.668	95	±2.628
16	±2.921	56	±2.666	96	±2.627
17	±2.898	57	±2.664	97	±2.627
18	±2.878	58	±2.663	98	±2.626
19	±2.861	59	±2.662	99	±2.626
20	±2.845	60	±2.660	100	±2.625
21	±2.831	61	±2.658	101	±2.625
22	±2.819	62	±2.657	102	±2.624
23	±2.807	63	±2.656	103	±2.624
24	±2.797	64	±2.655	104	±2.623
25	±2.787	65	±2.654	105	±2.623
26	±2.779	66	±2.652	106	±2.622
27	±2.771	67	±2.651	107	±2.622
28	±2.763	68	±2.650	108	±2.621
29	±2.756	69	±2.649	109	±2.621
30	±2.750	70	±2.648	110	±2.621
31	±2.743	71	±2.647	111	±2.620
32	±2.738	72	±2.646	112	±2.620
33	±2.733	73	±2.645	113	±2.620
34	±2.728	74	±2.644	114	±2.619
35	±2.723	75	±2.643	115	±2.619
36	±2.718	76	±2.642	116	±2.618
37	±2.714	77	±2.641	117	±2.618
38	±2.711	78	±2.640	118	±2.618
39	±2.707	79	±2.639	119	±2.618
40	±2.704	80	±2.639	120	±2.617
				∞	±2.576

α = .05 One-Tailed (Upper Tail)

Null hypothesis: The systematic variance is equal to the unsystematic variance.

Alternative hypothesis: The systematic variance is greater than the unsystematic variance.

Reject the null hypothesis and favor the alternative hypothesis if the calculated *F* is greater than or equal to the critical *F*.

Note: df_s and df_u denote the degrees of freedom corresponding to the systematic and unsystematic variance, respectively.

df_s	df_u	F	df_s	df_u	F	df_s	df_u	F	df_s	df_u	F
1	8	5.32	3	8	4.07	5	8	3.69	7	8	3.50
1	9	5.12	3	9	3.86	5	9	3.48	7	9	3.29
1	10	4.96	3	10	3.71	5	10	3.33	7	10	3.14
1	11	4.84	3	11	3.59	5	11	3.20	7	11	3.01
1	12	4.75	3	12	3.49	5	12	3.11	7	12	2.92
1	13	4.67	3	13	3.41	5	13	3.03	7	13	2.84
1	14	4.60	3	14	3.34	5	14	2.96	7	14	2.77
1	15	4.54	3	15	3.29	5	15	2.90	7	15	2.70
1	16	4.49	3	16	3.24	5	16	2.85	7	16	2.66
1	17	4.45	3	17	3.20	5	17	2.81	7	17	2.62
1	18	4.41	3	18	3.16	5	18	2.77	7	18	2.58
1	19	4.38	3	19	3.13	5	19	2.74	7	19	2.55
1	20	4.35	3	20	3.10	5	20	2.71	7	20	2.52
1	21	4.32	3	21	3.07	5	21	2.68	7	21	2.49
1	22	4.30	3	22	3.05	5	22	2.66	7	22	2.47
1	23	4.28	3	23	3.03	5	23	2.64	7	23	2.45
1	24	4.26	3	24	3.01	5	24	2.62	7	24	2.43
1	25	4.24	3	25	2.99	5	25	2.60	7	25	2.41
1	26	4.22	3	26	2.98	5	26	2.59	7	26	2.39
1	27	4.21	3	27	2.96	5	27	2.57	7	27	2.37
1	28	4.20	3	28	2.95	5	28	2.56	7	28	2.36
1	29	4.18	3	29	2.93	5	29	2.55	7	29	2.35
1	30	4.17	3	30	2.92	5	30	2.53	7	30	2.34
1	32	4.15	3	32	2.90	5	32	2.51	7	32	2.32
1	34	4.13	3	34	2.88	5	34	2.49	7	34	2.30
1	36	4.11	3	36	2.86	5	36	2.48	7	36	2.28
1	38	4.10	3	38	2.85	5	38	2.46	7	38	2.26
1	40	4.08	3	40	2.84	5	40	2.45	7	40	2.25
1	42	4.07	3	42	2.83	5	42	2.44	7	42	2.24
1	44	4.06	3	44	2.82	5	44	2.43	7	44	2.23
1	46	4.05	3	46	2.81	5	46	2.42	7	46	2.22
1	48	4.04	3	48	2.80	5	48	2.41	7	48	2.21
1	50	4.03	3	50	2.79	5	50	2.40	7	50	2.20
1	55	4.02	3	55	2.78	5	55	2.38	7	55	2.18
1	60	4.00	3	60	2.76	5	60	2.37	7	60	2.17

df_s	df_u	F	df_s	df_u	F	df_s	df_u	F	df_s	df_u	F
1	65	3.99	3	65	2.75	5	65	2.36	7	65	2.15
1	70	3.98	3	70	2.74	5	70	2.35	7	70	2.14
1	80	3.96	3	80	2.72	5	80	2.33	7	80	2.12
1	100	3.94	3	100	2.70	5	100	2.30	7	100	2.10
2	8	4.46	4	8	3.84	6	8	3.58	8	8	3.44
2	9	4.26	4	9	3.63	6	9	3.37	8	9	3.23
2	10	4.10	4	10	3.48	6	10	3.22	8	10	3.07
2	11	3.98	4	11	3.36	6	11	3.09	8	11	2.95
2	12	3.89	4	12	3.26	6	12	3.00	8	12	2.85
2	13	3.81	4	13	3.18	6	13	2.92	8	13	2.77
2	14	3.74	4	14	3.11	6	14	2.85	8	14	2.70
2	15	3.68	4	15	3.06	6	15	2.79	8	15	2.64
2	16	3.63	4	16	3.01	6	16	2.74	8	16	2.59
2	17	3.59	4	17	2.96	6	17	2.70	8	17	2.55
2	18	3.55	4	18	2.93	6	18	2.66	8	18	2.51
2	19	3.52	4	19	2.90	6	19	2.63	8	19	2.48
2	20	3.49	4	20	2.87	6	20	2.60	8	20	2.45
2	21	3.47	4	21	2.84	6	21	2.57	8	21	2.42
2	22	3.44	4	22	2.82	6	22	2.55	8	22	2.40
2	23	3.42	4	23	2.80	6	23	2.53	8	23	2.38
2	24	3.40	4	24	2.78	6	24	2.51	8	24	2.36
2	25	3.39	4	25	2.76	6	25	2.49	8	25	2.34
2	26	3.37	4	26	2.74	6	26	2.47	8	26	2.32
2	27	3.35	4	27	2.73	6	27	2.46	8	27	2.30
2	28	3.34	4	28	2.71	6	28	2.45	8	28	2.29
2	29	3.33	4	29	2.70	6	29	2.43	8	29	2.28
2	30	3.32	4	30	2.69	6	30	2.42	8	30	2.27
2	32	3.30	4	32	2.67	6	32	2.40	8	32	2.25
2	34	3.28	4	34	2.65	6	34	2.38	8	34	2.23
2	36	3.26	4	36	2.63	6	36	2.36	8	36	2.21
2	38	3.25	4	38	2.62	6	38	2.35	8	38	2.19
2	40	3.23	4	40	2.61	6	40	2.34	8	40	2.18
2	42	3.22	4	42	2.59	6	42	2.32	8	42	2.17
2	44	3.21	4	44	2.58	6	44	2.31	8	44	2.16
2	46	3.20	4	46	2.57	6	46	2.30	8	46	2.14
2	48	3.19	4	48	2.56	6	48	2.30	8	48	2.14
2	50	3.18	4	50	2.56	6	50	2.29	8	50	2.13
2	55	3.17	4	55	2.54	6	55	2.27	8	55	2.11
2	60	3.15	4	60	2.52	6	60	2.25	8	60	2.10
2	65	3.14	4	65	2.50	6	65	2.24	8	65	2.08
2	70	3.13	4	70	2.51	6	70	2.23	8	70	2.07
2	80	3.11	4	80	2.48	6	80	2.21	8	80	2.05
2	100	3.09	4	100	2.46	6	100	2.19	8	100	2.03

α = .01 One-Tailed (Upper Tail)

Null hypothesis: The systematic variance is equal to the unsystematic variance.

Alternative hypothesis: The systematic variance is greater than the unsystematic variance.

Reject the null hypothesis and favor the alternative hypothesis if the calculated *F* is greater than or equal to the critical *F*.

Note: df_s and *ef_u* denote the degrees of freedom corresponding to the systematic and unsystematic variance, respectively.

df_s	df_u	F	df_s	df_u	F	df_s	df_u	F	df_s	df_u	F
1	8	11.26	3	8	7.59	5	8	6.63	7	8	6.19
1	9	10.56	3	9	6.99	5	9	6.06	7	9	5.62
1	10	10.04	3	10	6.55	5	10	5.64	7	10	5.21
1	11	9.65	3	11	6.22	5	11	5.32	7	11	4.88
1	12	9.33	3	12	5.95	5	12	5.06	7	12	4.65
1	13	9.07	3	13	5.74	5	13	4.86	7	13	4.44
1	14	8.86	3	14	5.56	5	14	4.69	7	14	4.28
1	15	8.68	3	15	5.42	5	15	4.56	7	15	4.14
1	16	8.53	3	16	5.29	5	16	4.44	7	16	4.03
1	17	8.40	3	17	5.18	5	17	4.34	7	17	3.93
1	18	8.29	3	18	5.09	5	18	4.25	7	18	3.85
1	19	8.18	3	19	5.01	5	19	4.17	7	19	3.77
1	20	8.10	3	20	4.94	5	20	4.10	7	20	3.71
1	21	8.02	3	21	4.87	5	21	4.04	7	21	3.65
1	22	7.95	3	22	4.82	5	22	3.99	7	22	3.59
1	23	7.88	3	23	4.76	5	23	3.94	7	23	3.54
1	24	7.82	3	24	4.72	5	24	3.90	7	24	3.50
1	25	7.77	3	25	4.68	5	25	3.85	7	25	3.46
1	26	7.72	3	26	4.64	5	26	3.82	7	26	3.42
1	27	7.68	3	27	4.60	5	27	3.79	7	27	3.39
1	28	7.64	3	28	4.57	5	28	3.76	7	28	3.36
1	29	7.60	3	29	4.54	5	29	3.73	7	29	3.33
1	30	7.56	3	30	4.51	5	30	3.70	7	30	3.30
1	32	7.50	3	32	4.46	5	32	3.66	7	32	3.25
1	34	7.44	3	34	4.42	5	34	3.61	7	34	3.21
1	36	7.39	3	36	4.38	5	36	3.58	7	36	3.18
1	38	7.35	3	38	4.34	5	38	3.54	7	38	3.15
1	40	7.31	3	40	4.31	5	40	3.51	7	40	3.12
1	42	7.27	3	42	4.29	5	42	3.49	7	42	3.10
1	44	7.24	3	44	4.26	5	44	3.46	7	44	3.07
1	46	7.21	3	46	4.24	5	46	3.44	7	46	3.05
1	48	7.19	3	48	4.22	5	48	3.42	7	48	3.04
1	50	7.17	3	50	4.20	5	50	3.41	7	50	3.02
1	55	7.12	3	55	4.16	5	55	3.37	7	55	2.98
1	60	7.08	3	60	4.13	5	60	3.34	7	60	2.95
1	65	7.04	3	65	4.10	5	65	3.31	7	65	2.93

Critical *F* Values (*continued*)
$\alpha = .01$ One Tailed (Upper Tail)

df_s	df_u	F	df_s	df_u	F	df_s	df_u	F	df_s	df_u	F
1	70	7.01	3	70	4.08	5	70	3.29	7	70	2.91
1	80	6.96	3	80	4.04	5	80	3.25	7	80	2.87
1	100	6.90	3	100	3.98	5	100	3.20	7	100	2.82
2	8	8.65	4	8	7.01	6	8	6.37	8	8	6.03
2	9	8.02	4	9	6.42	6	9	5.80	8	9	5.47
2	10	7.56	4	10	5.99	6	10	5.39	8	10	5.06
2	11	7.21	4	11	5.67	6	11	5.07	8	11	4.74
2	12	6.93	4	12	5.41	6	12	4.82	8	12	4.50
2	13	6.70	4	13	5.21	6	13	4.62	8	13	4.30
2	14	6.51	4	14	5.04	6	14	4.46	8	14	4.14
2	15	6.36	4	15	4.89	6	15	4.32	8	15	4.00
2	16	6.23	4	16	4.77	6	16	4.20	8	16	3.89
2	17	6.11	4	17	4.67	6	17	4.10	8	17	3.79
2	18	6.01	4	18	4.58	6	18	4.01	8	18	3.71
2	19	5.93	4	19	4.50	6	19	3.94	8	19	3.63
2	20	5.85	4	20	4.43	6	20	3.87	8	20	3.56
2	21	5.78	4	21	4.37	6	21	3.81	8	21	3.51
2	22	5.72	4	22	4.31	6	22	3.76	8	22	3.45
2	23	5.66	4	23	4.26	6	23	3.71	8	23	3.41
2	24	5.61	4	24	4.22	6	24	3.67	8	24	3.36
2	25	5.57	4	25	4.18	6	25	3.63	8	25	3.32
2	26	5.53	4	26	4.14	6	26	3.59	8	26	3.29
2	27	5.49	4	27	4.11	6	27	3.56	8	27	3.26
2	28	5.45	4	28	4.07	6	28	3.53	8	28	3.23
2	29	5.42	4	29	4.04	6	29	3.50	8	29	3.20
2	30	5.39	4	30	4.02	6	30	3.47	8	30	3.17
2	32	5.34	4	32	3.97	6	32	3.42	8	32	3.12
2	34	5.29	4	34	3.93	6	34	3.38	8	34	3.08
2	36	5.25	4	36	3.89	6	36	3.35	8	36	3.04
2	38	5.21	4	38	3.86	6	38	3.32	8	38	3.02
2	40	5.18	4	40	3.83	6	40	3.29	8	40	2.99
2	42	5.15	4	42	3.80	6	42	3.26	8	42	2.96
2	44	5.12	4	44	3.78	6	44	3.24	8	44	2.94
2	46	5.10	4	46	3.76	6	46	3.22	8	46	2.92
2	48	5.08	4	48	3.74	6	48	3.20	8	48	2.90
2	50	5.06	4	50	3.72	6	50	3.18	8	50	2.88
2	55	5.01	4	55	3.68	6	55	3.15	8	55	2.85
2	60	4.98	4	60	3.65	6	60	3.12	8	60	2.82
2	65	4.95	4	65	3.62	6	65	3.09	8	65	2.79
2	70	4.92	4	70	3.60	6	70	3.07	8	70	2.77
2	80	4.88	4	80	3.56	6	80	3.04	8	80	2.74
2	100	4.82	4	100	3.51	6	100	2.99	8	100	2.69

```
8 1 0 3 6 0 1 7 4 6 4 3 0 6 8 9 1 7 6 5 5 9 2 3 8
7 3 4 4 1 5 9 0 1 8 6 0 5 2 7 9 9 3 8 3 5 7 4 6 3
9 6 7 7 4 4 8 0 6 5 1 8 1 0 8 1 8 3 6 8 2 0 7 3 5
6 2 4 8 3 4 2 2 1 8 0 5 2 2 3 0 5 4 8 3 2 5 0 4 0
9 2 1 2 0 7 5 8 9 7 0 1 5 5 7 3 4 2 2 3 1 5 8 5 6
3 0 3 0 7 9 4 4 2 4 0 7 0 2 7 2 8 1 5 9 1 7 2 0 6
4 3 4 6 3 7 3 8 9 8 3 1 5 1 7 2 1 1 9 1 8 2 4 1 9
3 6 8 5 0 1 7 8 9 2 4 8 2 9 8 9 4 5 2 5 8 2 5 0 1
6 9 5 7 3 1 1 0 8 6 4 9 3 9 3 7 6 9 5 2 3 5 7 8 6
7 2 6 6 6 7 7 9 3 6 2 2 0 5 3 4 3 5 0 0 6 5 4 5 0
8 8 1 5 2 7 7 6 9 8 4 0 1 4 7 2 4 9 7 3 9 8 4 0 4
4 9 2 2 6 0 5 9 2 7 0 0 6 7 9 9 4 0 9 9 1 2 6 2 1
3 5 1 3 0 4 1 4 4 0 3 1 2 5 1 5 8 7 0 3 8 4 5 6 0
8 0 3 3 3 2 7 6 9 8 4 0 5 0 1 1 6 6 5 0 7 7 0 7 7
9 4 9 1 8 6 0 1 1 7 0 3 7 0 2 9 9 7 6 2 4 7 5 3 7
3 4 1 0 7 2 6 5 6 0 8 3 4 5 3 0 9 5 4 0 1 4 0 0 9
8 3 5 2 2 5 6 4 6 6 2 8 7 7 5 2 4 1 4 0 7 5 7 7 6
6 4 3 0 5 1 6 6 9 6 9 7 9 2 5 2 6 5 6 5 2 7 6 6 0
6 6 0 7 3 6 6 7 2 6 3 9 9 5 1 9 1 9 3 1 4 6 3 6 5
9 7 3 7 0 2 2 1 2 1 7 3 3 3 7 6 2 9 5 1 3 2 0 2 4
9 3 0 1 8 9 3 2 3 6 1 0 9 2 8 4 8 2 2 5 9 4 9 3 5
8 6 6 1 2 1 5 8 7 5 4 1 9 0 6 1 8 1 3 8 7 1 3 6 5
8 9 3 9 5 9 4 2 1 1 6 5 2 4 7 6 5 2 4 5 2 2 5 2 6
6 0 7 1 0 1 9 0 6 9 5 4 2 1 5 4 0 8 7 2 0 5 9 6 1
5 7 0 1 2 4 2 5 5 2 2 7 8 3 3 6 8 4 3 8 5 8 4 2 1
8 9 2 2 7 4 8 6 3 6 5 5 6 8 8 4 9 6 6 2 7 7 2 0 4
2 3 8 9 6 1 1 6 2 3 9 7 9 8 6 2 5 6 1 3 2 0 5 8 7
9 9 4 0 7 2 6 4 0 5 6 1 8 0 1 7 9 7 9 1 0 7 4 9 5
5 9 1 9 1 8 8 6 3 1 8 5 3 0 2 1 4 5 4 0 7 2 8 1 0
6 8 9 7 8 0 3 1 9 4 0 0 8 0 0 1 0 1 4 6 6 9 8 8 9
5 2 4 7 7 0 4 3 8 2 9 3 1 4 7 5 7 1 4 8 7 1 7 7 5
0 9 2 8 2 3 1 1 3 0 5 8 7 4 5 9 6 1 7 6 7 6 3 9 8
3 6 1 3 8 4 9 0 3 7 2 5 5 7 9 7 6 7 2 5 5 4 8 7 4
0 7 4 4 6 9 7 7 1 7 5 7 7 1 1 8 0 3 8 8 1 8 3 3 1
4 5 4 6 4 1 9 1 6 8 6 8 2 5 6 2 5 0 1 8 7 8 5 1 4
2 9 6 6 5 9 5 5 8 4 3 6 6 9 7 9 9 4 8 9 0 9 0 9
4 3 7 9 4 8 9 0 2 6 9 2 7 9 8 6 2 1 5 7 5 3 3 0 6
7 4 5 1 1 3 4 3 5 7 0 5 1 9 3 2 5 7 9 6 3 7 1 3 3
6 2 6 2 6 1 3 2 9 8 6 8 7 2 8 6 8 9 9 8 3 6 9 7
3 6 5 4 4 2 4 4 0 5 9 4 7 2 7 9 2 4 8 8 7 7 1 9
6 0 8 1 7 9 6 1 9 3 2 7 4 6 8 8 8 2 5 1 1 2 0 1 3
4 5 0 3 4 1 9 7 4 2 8 3 2 2 8 3 9 4 1 5 5 6 2 8 1
6 4 1 5 5 2 0 4 2 4 5 6 3 6 0 0 4 6 7 0 4 3 9 9 2
8 0 5 4 5 3 1 6 4 3 7 9 7 6 4 2 2 9 5 4 6 8 4 0 7
5 8 9 1 9 4 0 9 4 9 1 5 1 1 8 2 2 0 9 8 1 3 0 3 9
6 3 5 0 3 0 3 3 0 5 8 1 2 0 6 3 2 4 2 7 4 1 8 2
5 9 1 1 2 4 3 2 8 0 6 8 0 4 6 0 9 2 7 3 9 2 0 9
0 2 9 6 0 2 8 3 8 0 5 8 2 3 8 6 8 9 7 2 8 5 5 4 0
6 5 7 5 5 0 2 7 4 5 3 3 3 1 1 9 9 5 8 9 3 3 8 8 7
2 7 1 8 0 6 5 9 8 0 9 0 4 2 8 2 8 2 1 3 3 8 8 7 0
```

Calculations and Analysis Scenarios

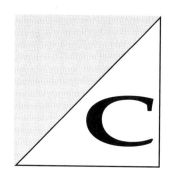

Calculation C.1 Analysis of Variance
(One Independent Variable, Between Groups)

Type of research:	Experiment
Number of dependent variables:	1
Level of measurement:	Interval/ratio
Assumptions met:	Yes
Number of independent variables:	1
Conditions of independent variable:	3
Type of design:	Between-groups (B-G)
Choice of analysis:	B-G ANOVA, then Scheffe

Motivation for Research: A researcher believes that listening to classical music will improve a person's reaction time.

Description of Research: The researcher randomly selects 30 people from the general population and then randomly assigns 10 of these people to a control group; 10 to a 15-minute experimental condition; and the remaining 10 to a 30-minute experimental condition. In the control group, each of the 10 people is asked to sit in a room for 15 minutes and to try to relax. In the 15-minute experimental condition, each of the 10 people is asked to sit in a room for 15 minutes and to try to relax by listening to classical music. In the 30-minute experimental condition, each of the 10 people is asked to sit in a room for 30 minutes and to try to relax by listening to classical music. All subjects in each of the three groups are tested for their reaction times after the relaxation period.

Type of Conclusion Possible: The analysis of variance (ANOVA) will allow the researcher to determine if the mean reaction times for the three conditions of the experiment differ in any way. If the ANOVA indicates that there is some difference—in other words, that the three means are not equal—then the researcher may draw the general conclusion that listening to music does have an effect on reaction time.

In order to be more specific about the effect, the researcher will then have to conduct a Scheffe analysis, which permits the comparison of pairs of means: the mean of the control group versus the mean of the 15-minute group; the mean of the control group versus the mean of the 30-minute group; and the mean of the 15-minute group versus the mean of the 30-minute group.

Comments: If the results of the Scheffe analysis indicate that the mean reaction time is significantly lower for the 15-minute group than for the control group, and that the mean reaction time is significantly lower for the 30-minute group than for the 15-minute group, the researcher may conclude that listening to classical music had the significant effect of improving the reaction times of the subjects, and that the effect increased as the subjects listened longer (up to 30 minutes).

Assumptions: Suppose that the parametric assumptions have been met.

Test Data:

Control group		15-minute group		30-minute group	
Person	Reaction time	Person	Reaction time	Person	Reaction time
1	2.69	11	2.56	21	2.35
2	2.72	12	2.58	22	2.46
3	2.56	13	2.41	23	2.43
4	2.53	14	2.49	24	2.39
5	2.60	15	2.47	25	2.42
6	2.58	16	2.34	26	2.21
7	2.79	17	2.68	27	2.54
8	2.86	18	2.70	28	2.58
9	2.58	19	2.56	29	2.63
10	2.68	20	2.62	30	2.59

Specifics Regarding the Analysis: The ANOVA analysis helps the researcher to determine whether or not the variability between two or more groups is greater than what would be expected by chance.

Research Hypothesis: The researcher believes that listening to classical music will decrease the subjects' reaction times, and that a longer listening period will produce a greater decrease in reaction times. Symbolically, the research hypothesis—the alternative hypothesis—appears as follows

$$H_{alt}: \mu_{30min} < \mu_{15min} < \mu_{control}$$

In plain English, the researcher is predicting that the average reaction time after listening to classical music for 30 minutes will be significantly lower than the average reaction of the 15-minute group, which, in turn, will be significantly lower than the average reaction time of the control group.

ANOVA Alternative Hypothesis: The ANOVA is an analysis of *variance*. Although the alternative hypothesis stated here represents the researcher's prediction, the ANOVA does not directly test this hypothesis. Instead, the alternative hypothesis for the ANOVA predicts that the variance between the groups will be significantly greater than the variance within the groups—that is, that the variability in the dependent variable due to the independent variable will be greater than the random variability in the dependent variable that we expect in the absence of the independent variable. Symbolically

$$H_A: \sigma^2_{independent\ variable} > \sigma^2_{random}$$

If the above hypothesis is true, then the following hypothesis *might* also be true:

$$H_{alt}: \mu_{30min} < \mu_{15min} < \mu_{control}$$

If the means for the groups are not all equal, then the variance due to the independent variable will be greater than the normal variability of the dependent variable. However, since there is more than one way for the means of the groups to be unequal, the first of these symbolic statements is not necessarily true even if the second is. For this reason, it is necessary to do an additional analysis after the ANOVA to test the researcher's hypothesis more exactly.

Null Hypothesis: As we noted in Chapter 9, we state the null hypothesis, for the sake of argument, on the assumption that our research hypothesis is incorrect. In the present case, the null hypothesis is that there is *no difference between the average reaction times of all three groups*. Symbolically

$$H_{null}: \mu_{30min} = \mu_{15min} = \mu_{control}$$

ANOVA Null Hypothesis: Although the null hypothesis stated here is correct, the ANOVA does not directly test this hypothesis. Instead, the null hypothesis for the ANOVA predicts that the variance between the groups will be equal to the variance within the groups—that is, that the variability in the dependent variable due to the independent variable will be the same as the random variability in the dependent variable that we expect in the absence of the independent variable. Symbolically

$$H_0: \sigma^2_{independent\ variable} = \sigma^2_{random}$$

Organizing the Raw Data: When you prepare the data for entry into the ANOVA calculation formula—whether you do the calculations by hand or by computer—you must identify the following:

- the independent variable: duration of music, in the present example.
- the conditions of the experiment: 30 minutes, 15 minutes, and control.
- the number of subjects in each condition: 10, 10, and 10.
- the dependent variable: reaction time.

ANOVA Calculation: Once these values have been identified, you may enter them into the computer or use the calculation formula as follows.

Step 1. List your data.

The test data have already been tabulated.

Step 2. Square each data value (each X) and place the result (X^2) next to the original data value (Table C.1.1).

Step 3. Sum the X values and the X^2 values for each group (Table C.1.1).

TABLE C.1.1   Results of Squaring and Summing

	Control group		15-minute group		30-minute group	
	X	X^2	X	X^2	X	X^2
	2.69	7.2361	2.56	6.5536	2.35	5.5225
	2.72	7.3984	2.58	6.6564	2.46	6.0516
	2.56	6.5536	2.41	5.8081	2.43	5.9049
	2.53	6.4009	2.49	6.2001	2.39	5.7121
	2.60	6.7600	2.47	6.1009	2.42	5.8564
	2.58	6.6564	2.34	5.4756	2.21	4.8841
	2.79	7.7841	2.68	7.1824	2.54	6.4516
	2.86	8.1796	2.70	7.2900	2.58	6.6564
	2.58	6.6564	2.56	6.5536	2.63	6.9169
	2.68	7.1824	2.62	6.8644	2.59	6.7081
Sum	26.59	70.8079	25.41	64.6851	24.60	60.6646

Step 4. Determine the *total sum of squares* using the following formula

$$SS_{total} = \sum X_{all}^2 - \frac{\left(\sum X_{all}\right)^2}{N_{total}} \tag{C.1.1}$$

The first term in Eq. (C.1.1) requires that you square each of the scores in the entire data set and then sum all of these squared values (30 in the present case).

$$\sum X_{all}^2 = 2.69^2 + 2.72^2 + \cdots + 2.59^2$$
$$= 7.2361 + 7.3984 + \cdots + 6.7081$$

Since we already squared all 30 data values in step 2, we can obtain the sum of all 30 squared data values by summing the corresponding column totals from Table C.1.1

$$\sum X_{all}^2 = 70.8079 + 64.6851 + 60.6646$$
$$= 196.1576$$

The second term in Eq. (C.1.1) requires that you sum all the data points first, square the result, and then divide by the total number of data points (N_{total}). Since we already summed the data points for each condition in step 3, we can obtain the sum of all the data points by summing the corresponding column totals from Table C.1.1

$$\sum X_{all} = 26.59 + 25.41 + 24.60$$
$$= 76.60$$

Now we square this sum

$$\left(\sum X_{all}\right)^2 = 76.60^2 = 5867.56$$

Now we divide this squared sum by N_{total}

$$\frac{\left(\sum X_{\text{all}}\right)^2}{N_{\text{total}}} = \frac{5867.56}{30} = 195.5853$$

Finally, we substract this term from $\sum X_{\text{all}}{}^2$

$$SS_{\text{total}} = 196.1576 - 195.5853 = 0.5723$$

Step 5. Determine the *between-groups sum of squares* by means of the following formula

$$SS_{\text{B-G}} = \frac{\left(\sum X_1\right)^2}{n_1} + \frac{\left(\sum X_2\right)^2}{n_2} + \frac{\left(\sum X_3\right)^2}{n_3} - \frac{\left(\sum X_{\text{all}}\right)^2}{N_{\text{total}}} \tag{C.1.2}$$

To calculate the first three terms, the sum of the scores for each of the groups is obtained from Table C.1.1, squared, and divided by the number of data values in the appropriate group. The last term in Eq. (C.1.2) is the same as in Eq. (C.1.1). Thus

$$\begin{aligned}
SS_{\text{B-G}} &= \frac{26.59^2}{10} + \frac{25.41^2}{10} + \frac{24.6^2}{10} - 195.5853 \\
&= \frac{707.0281}{10} + \frac{645.6681}{10} + \frac{605.16}{10} - 195.5853 \\
&= 70.70281 + 64.56681 + 60.516 - 195.5853 \\
&= 195.78562 - 195.5853 \\
&= 0.20032
\end{aligned}$$

Step 6. Determine the *within-groups sum of squares* by means of the following formula

$$SS_{\text{w-g}} = \sum\left(X_{\text{all}}{}^2\right) - \left[\frac{\left(\sum X_1\right)^2}{n_1} + \frac{\left(\sum X_2\right)^2}{n_2} + \frac{\left(\sum X_3\right)^2}{n_3}\right] \tag{C.1.3}$$

Each term in this formula has already been determined. Thus

$$\begin{aligned}
SS_{\text{w-g}} &= 196.1576 - [70.70281 + 64.56681 + 60.516] \\
&= 196.1576 - 195.78562 \\
&= 0.37198
\end{aligned}$$

Step 7. Determine the degrees of freedom for each identifiable source of variance—in the present example, total-data, between-groups, and within-groups variance.

ASIDE ■ In Chapter 10, the concepts of systematic and unsystematic variance were discussed. In a simple between-groups analysis of variance, the systematic source of variance can also be referred to as between-groups variance, because the independent variable is varied systematically between the groups of the experiment, and the unsystematic source of variance can be referred to as within-groups variance, because the variation of the measurements within the groups is unsystematic.

For the variance due to the total data in the experiment

$$df_{total} = N_{total} - 1 \tag{C.1.4}$$

In the present case

$$df_{total} = 30 - 1 = 29$$

For the between-groups variance

$$df_{B-G} = K - 1 \text{ where } K = \text{number of conditions} \tag{C.1.5}$$

In the present case

$$df_{B-G} = 3 - 1 = 2$$

For the within-groups variance

$$df_{w-g} = N_{total} - K \tag{C.1.6}$$

In the present case

$$df_{w-g} = 30 - 3 = 27$$

Step 8. Determine the *mean square* (MS) for each of the systematic and unsystematic sources of variance

$$MS = \frac{SS}{df} \tag{C.1.7}$$

In the present case

$$MS_{B-G} = \frac{SS_{B-G}}{df_{B-G}}$$

$$= \frac{0.200,32}{2} = 0.100,16$$

$$MS_{w-g} = \frac{SS_{w-g}}{df_{w-g}}$$

$$= \frac{0.371,98}{27} = 0.013,78$$

Step 9. Determine the F ratio for each systematic source of variance

$$F = \frac{MS_{B-G}}{MS_{w-g}} \tag{C.1.8}$$

In the present case

$$F = \frac{0.100,16}{0.013,78} = 7.27$$

Step 10. Look in a standard F table (Table B.13) to determine the critical F value for each of the F ratios calculated. Be sure to use the appropriate alpha level and the correct degrees of freedom for the systematic and unsystematic sources of variance.
For $\alpha = .05$, $df_{sys} = 2$, and $df_{unsys} = 27$, the critical F from Table B.13 is 3.35.

Step 11. For each F ratio, identify the result of step 10 as the critical F value.
We may state our result formally as follows

$$(F_{crit} = 3.35; df_{sys} = 2; df_{unsys} = 27; \alpha = .05)$$

Step 12. Compare each calculated F value to the corresponding critical F value. If the calculated F is equal to or greater than the critical F, you must reject the null hypothesis; otherwise, you may not reject the null hypothesis.

The calculated F for our data (7.27) is greater than the critical F (3.35); therefore, we reject the null.

Step 13. State your conclusion in a standard statistical format using appropriate symbols.

An appropriate statement is as follows

$$(F_{calc} = 7.27; \, df_{sys} = 2; \, df_{unsys} = 27; \, p < .05)$$

Step 14. State your statistical conclusion in words.

If the null hypothesis were true, the probability of arriving at a calculated F of 7.27 with 2 and 27 degrees of freedom would be less than .05. Therefore, the null hypothesis is *probably* not true, and the alternative hypothesis is a better bet.

Step 15. State your final conclusion in plain English.

Given the data and the statistical conclusion, it is reasonable to argue that listening to classical music had *an effect* on reaction time.

This concludes the analysis of variance. However, it will be necessary to analyze these data further, using a *Scheffe analysis*, in order to determine if the researcher's specific hypothesis regarding the means of the conditions can be supported.

SCHEFFE ANALYSIS

As we noted, if the ANOVA results are significant, we must conduct an additional analysis to test the researcher's hypothesis more exactly. The Scheffe analysis is one such post-ANOVA analysis.

Specifics Regarding the Analysis: Having rejected the ANOVA null hypothesis, you know that the group means are not all equal. The Scheffe analysis allows you to determine whether or not the group means differ exactly in accordance with your initial prediction. As we discussed earlier (p. 225), it would be inappropriate to do multiple t-tests because of the inflated alpha problem.

Research Hypotheses: As before, the research (alternative) hypothesis may be stated symbolically as follows

$$H_{alt}: \mu_{30min} < \mu_{15min} < \mu_{control}$$

In plain English, the researcher is predicting that the average reaction time after listening to classical music for 30 minutes will be significantly lower than the average reaction after 15 minutes, which, in turn, will be significantly lower than the average reaction time for the control group. Thus, we could break this research hypothesis down into three separate hypotheses

$$H_{alt\,1}: \mu_{30min} < \mu_{15min}$$

$$H_{alt\,2}: \mu_{15min} < \mu_{control}$$

$$H_{alt\,3}: \mu_{30min} < \mu_{control}$$

Null Hypotheses: As before, the null hypothesis may be stated symbolically as follows

$$H_{null}: \mu_{30min} = \mu_{15min} = \mu_{control}$$

In plain English, if the research hypothesis is incorrect, we would expect no difference between the averages of the three conditions. Thus, we could break this null hypothesis into three separate null hypotheses

$$H_{null\,1}: \mu_{30\,min} = \mu_{15\,min}$$

$$H_{null\,2}: \mu_{15\,min} = \mu_{control}$$

$$H_{null\,3}: \mu_{30\,min} = \mu_{control}$$

Organizing the Raw Data: When you prepare the data for entry into the Scheffe calculation formula—whether you do the calculations by hand or by computer—you must identify the following:

- the independent variable: duration of music.

- the conditions of the experiment: 30 minutes, 15 minutes, and control group.

- the number of subjects in each condition: 10, 10, and 10.

- the dependent variable: reaction time.

- the alpha level: .05, unless otherwise stated.

This information was obtained already in the ANOVA.

Scheffe Calculation: Once these values have been identified, you may enter them into the computer or use the following calculation formula

$$\text{CD} = \pm \sqrt{df_s F_{\text{crit}}(\text{MS}_u)\left(\frac{1}{n_1} + \frac{1}{n_2}\right)} \qquad\qquad \text{(C.1.9)}$$

The calculation procedure is as follows.

Step 1. Obtain the relevant degrees of freedom for the systematic source of variance from the ANOVA results.
   In the present case

$$df_{\text{B}-\text{G}} = 2$$

Step 2. Obtain the relevant critical F for the systematic source of variance. You already have this from the analysis of variance.
   In the present case

$$F_{\text{crit}} = 3.35$$

Step 3. Obtain the relevant variance for the unsystematic source from the ANOVA results.
   In the present case

$$\text{MS}_u = 0.013,77$$

Step 4. Obtain the number of data values for each group being compared.
   In the present case

$$n_1 = 10$$
$$n_2 = 10$$

Step 5. Enter each of these values in Eq. (C.1.9), to obtain the corresponding critical difference (CD).
   In the present case

$$\text{CD} = \left[(2)(3.35)(0.013,77)\left(\frac{1}{10} + \frac{1}{10}\right)\right]$$
$$= \sqrt{0.018,451,8}$$
$$= 0.1358$$

Step 6. Determine whether additional CD values will have to be calculated. [A separate CD must be calculated for each unique set of n_1 and n_2 values. Since all the n values are equal in the present example, only one CD has to be calculated.]

Step 7. Calculate the means for each pair of conditions to be compared.
In the present case

$$\mu_{control} = 2.659$$
$$\mu_{15min} = 2.541$$
$$\mu_{30min} = 2.460$$

Step 8. Calculate the difference between the means for each alternative hypothesis, and then compare this difference to CD.

Three comparisons are required in the present case.

1. For the first hypothesis (one-tailed, positive difference)

$$H_{alt1}: \mu_{control} > \mu_{15min}$$

the calculated difference is

$$2.659 - 2.541 = +0.1180$$

which is less than CD ($+0.1358$); therefore, we cannot reject the null hypothesis.

2. For the second hypothesis (one-tailed, positive difference)

$$H_{alt2}: \mu_{control} > \mu_{30min}$$

the calculated difference is

$$2.659 - 2.460 = +0.1990$$

which is greater than CD ($+0.1358$); therefore, we reject the null hypothesis ($p < .05$).

3. For the third hypothesis (one-tailed, positive difference)

$$H_{alt3}: \mu_{15min} > \mu_{30min}$$

the calculated difference is

$$2.541 - 2.460 = +0.010$$

which is less than CD ($+0.1358$); therefore, we cannot reject the null hypothesis.

Step 9. State your statistical conclusion regarding each alternative hypothesis using appropriate symbols.
In the present case

$$(\mu_{control} - \mu_{15min}; ns)$$
$$(\mu_{control} - \mu_{30min}; p < .05)$$
$$(\mu_{15min} - \mu_{30min}; ns)$$

Step 10. State your plain English conclusion regarding each of the alternative hypotheses.

1. Listening to classical music for 15 minutes *did not* result in a significant improvement in reaction time when compared to the control group. The researcher's hypothesis regarding these two groups is *not* supported.

2. Listening to classical music for 30 minutes *did* result in a significant improvement in reaction time when compared to the control group. The researcher's hypothesis regarding these two groups *is* supported.

3. Listening to classical music for 30 minutes *did not* result in a significant improvement in reaction time when compared to the 15-minute group. The researcher's hypothesis regarding these two groups *is not* supported.

Step 11. State a plain English conclusion that summarizes the findings of all comparisons as they relate to the researcher's hypothesis.

It appears that 15 minutes of listening to classical music is not enough to make a difference in reaction times. However, listening for 30 minutes did result in a significant improvement. The researcher's hypothesis is supported only if the length of time is sufficient.

Calculation C.2 Analysis of Variance (One Independent Variable, Within Groups)

Type of research:	Experiment
Number of dependent variables:	1
Level of measurement:	Interval/ratio
Assumptions met:	Yes
Number of independent variables:	1
Conditions of independent variables:	3
Type of design:	Within-groups (w-g)
Choice of analysis:	w-g ANOVA, then Scheffe

Motivation for Research: A researcher believes that listening to classical music will improve a person's reaction time.

Description of Research: The researcher randomly selects 10 people from the general population. All 10 people are first measured for their reaction times on a standard task. Then, each of these 10 people is asked to sit in a room for 15 minutes and try to relax by listening to classical music. After this 15-minute relaxation period, all 10 people are measured again for their reaction times on the same standard task. Then, on the following day, each of these 10 people is asked to sit in a room for 30 minutes and try to relax by listening to classical music. After this 30-minute relaxation period, all 10 people are measured again for their reaction times on the same standard task.

Type of Conclusion Possible: The within-groups ANOVA analysis will allow the researcher to determine if the mean reaction times for the three experimental conditions differ in any way. If the ANOVA indicates that there is some difference—in other words, that the three means are not equal—the researcher may draw the general conclusion that listening to music does have an effect on reaction time.

In order to be more specific about the effect, the researcher will then have to conduct a Scheffe analysis, which permits the comparison of pairs of means: the mean of the control condition versus the mean of the 15-minute condition; the mean of the control group versus the mean of the 30-minute condition; and the mean of the 15-minute condition versus the mean of the 30-minute condition.

Comments: If the results of the Scheffe analysis indicate that the mean reaction time is significantly lower for the 15-minute experimental condition than for the control condition and that the mean reaction time is significantly lower for the 30-minute experimental condition than for the 15-minute experimental condition, the researcher may conclude that listening to classical music had the significant effect of improving the reaction times of the subjects, and that the effect increased as the subjects listened longer (up to 30 minutes).

Assumptions: Suppose that the *parametric assumptions* have been met.

Test Data: Note that the same people are considered in each condition.

	Control condition		15-minute condition		30-minute condition	
Person	Reaction time	Person	Reaction time	Person	Reaction time
1	2.69	1	2.55	1	2.37
2	2.72	2	2.57	2	2.43
3	2.56	3	2.40	3	2.42
4	2.53	4	2.48	4	2.38
5	2.60	5	2.46	5	2.41
6	2.58	6	2.33	6	2.25
7	2.79	7	2.67	7	2.58
8	2.86	8	2.71	8	2.53
9	2.58	9	2.54	9	2.66
10	2.68	10	2.61	10	2.56

Specifics Regarding the Analysis: The ANOVA analysis helps the researcher to determine whether or not the variability between two or more groups is greater than would be expected by chance.

Research Hypothesis: The researcher believes that listening to classical music will decrease the subjects' reaction times and that a longer listening period will produce a greater decrease in reaction times. Symbolically, the research hypothesis—the alternative hypothesis—is as follows

$H_{alt}: \mu_{30\ min} < \mu_{15\ min} < \mu_{control}$

In plain English, the researcher is predicting that the average reaction time after listening to classical music for 30 minutes will be significantly lower than the average reaction time after listening for 15 minutes, which, in turn, will be significantly lower than the average reaction time measured for the control condition (without listening to music).

ANOVA Alternative Hypothesis: The ANOVA is an analysis of *variance*. Although the alternative hypothesis stated here represents the researcher's prediction, the ANOVA does not directly test this hypothesis. Instead, the alternative hypothesis for the ANOVA predicts that the variance between the groups will be significantly greater than the variance within the groups—that is, that the variability in the dependent variable due to the independent variable will be greater than the random variability in the dependent variable that we expect in the absence of the independent variable. Symbolically

$H_A: \sigma^2_{independent\ variable} > \sigma^2_{random}$

If the above hypothesis is true, then the following hypothesis *might* also be true:

$H_{alt}: \mu_{30min} < \mu_{15min} < \mu_{control}$

If the means for the groups are not all equal, then the variance due to the independent variable will be greater than the normal variability of the dependent variable. However, since there is more than one way for the means of the groups to be unequal, the first of these symbolic statements is not necessarily true even if the second is. For this reason, it is necessary to do an additional analysis after the ANOVA to test the researcher's hypothesis more exactly.

Null Hypothesis: As we noted in Chapter 9, we state the null hypothesis, for the sake of argument, on the assumption that our research hypothesis is incorrect. In the present case, the null hypothesis is that there are *no differences among the average reaction times of all three groups.* Symbolically

$H_{null}: \mu_{30min} = \mu_{15min} = \mu_{control}$

ANOVA Null Hypothesis: Although the null hypothesis stated here is correct, the ANOVA does not directly test this hypothesis. Instead, the null hypothesis for the ANOVA predicts that the variance between the groups will be equal to the variance within the groups—that is, that the variability in the dependent variable due to the independent variable will be the same as the random variability in the dependent variable that we expect in the absence of the independent variable. Symbolically

$$H_0: \sigma^2_{\text{independent variable}} = \sigma^2_{\text{random}}$$

Organizing the Raw Data: When you prepare the data for entry into the ANOVA calculation formula—whether you do the calculations by hand or by computer—you must identify the following:

- the independent variable: duration of music, in the present case.

- the conditions of the experiment: 30 minutes, 15 minutes, and control.

- the number of subjects in each condition: 10, 10, and 10.

- the dependent variable: reaction time.

ANOVA Calculation: Once these values have been identified, you may enter them into the computer or use the calculation formula as follows.

Step 1. List your data.
          The test data have already been tabulated.

Step 2. Square each data value (each X) and place the result (X^2) next to the original data value (Table C.2.1).

Step 3. Sum the X values and the X^2 values for each group (Table C.2.1).

TABLE C.2.1   Results of Squaring and Summing

Person	Control condition X	Control condition X^2	15-minute condition X	15-minute condition X^2	30-minute condition X	30-minute condition X^2	$\sum X_{\text{subj}}$
1	2.69	7.2361	2.55	6.5025	2.37	5.6169	7.61
2	2.72	7.3984	2.57	6.6049	2.43	5.9049	7.72
3	2.56	6.5536	2.40	5.7600	2.42	5.8564	7.38
4	2.53	6.4009	2.48	6.1504	2.38	5.6644	7.39
5	2.60	6.7600	2.46	6.0516	2.41	5.8081	7.47
6	2.58	6.6564	2.33	5.4289	2.25	5.0625	7.16
7	2.79	7.7841	2.67	7.1289	2.58	6.6564	8.04
8	2.86	8.1796	2.71	7.3441	2.53	6.4009	8.10
9	2.58	6.6564	2.54	6.4516	2.66	7.0756	7.78
10	2.68	7.1824	2.61	6.8121	2.56	6.5536	7.85
Sum	26.59	70.8079	25.32	64.2350	24.59	60.5997	

Step 4. Determine the *total sum of squares* using the following formula

$$SS_{\text{total}} = \sum X_{\text{all}}^2 - \left[\frac{(\sum X_{\text{all}})^2}{N_{\text{total}}} \right] \tag{C.2.1}$$

The first term in Eq. (C.2.1) requires that you square each of the scores in the entire data set (30 in the present example) and then sum all of these squared values

$$\sum X_{\text{all}}^2 = 2.69^2 + 2.72^2 + \cdots + 2.56^2$$
$$= 7.2361 + 7.3984 + \cdots + 6.5536$$

Since we already squared all 30 data values in step 2, we can obtain the sum of all 30 squared data values by summing the corresponding column totals from Table C.2.1.

$$\sum X_{all}^2 = 70.8079 + 64.2350 + 60.5997$$
$$= 195.6426$$

The second term in Eq. (C.2.1) requires that you sum all the data points first, then square the result, and then divide by the total number of data points (N_{total}). Since we already summed the data points for each condition in step 3, we can obtain the sum of all the data points by summing the corresponding column totals from Table C.2.1

$$\sum X_{all} = 26.59 + 25.32 + 24.59$$
$$= 76.50$$

Now we square this sum

$$(\sum X_{all})^2 = 76.50^2 = 5852.25$$

Now we divide this squared sum by N_{total}

$$\frac{(\sum X_{all})^2}{N_{total}} = \frac{5852.25}{30} = 195.075$$

Finally, we substract this term from $\sum X_{all}^2$

$$SS_{total} = 195.6426 - 195.075 = 0.5676$$

Step 6. Determine the *sum of squares between subject groups* by means of the following formula

$$SS_{B\text{-}subj\text{-}G} = \frac{(\sum X_{subj\,1})^2}{n_{subj\,1}} + \frac{(\sum X_{subj\,2})^2}{n_{subj\,2}} + \cdots + \frac{(\sum X_{subj\,10})^2}{n_{subj\,10}} - \frac{(\sum X_{all})^2}{N_{total}} \tag{C.2.2}$$

The sum of the scores for each subject (each person) is obtained from Table C.2.1, then squared, and divided by the number of data values for each subject. In this case, there are three data values for each subject. The last term is the same as in Eq. (C.2.1).
The results of applying Eq. (C.2.2) are

$$SS_{B\text{-}subj\text{-}G} = \frac{7.61^2}{3} + \frac{7.72^2}{3} + \frac{7.38^2}{3} + \frac{7.39^2}{3} + \frac{7.47^2}{3} + \frac{7.16^2}{3} + \frac{8.04^2}{3} + \frac{8.10^2}{3}$$
$$+ \frac{7.78^2}{3} + \frac{7.85^2}{3} - 195.075$$

$$= \frac{57.9121}{3} + \frac{59.5984}{3} + \frac{54.4644}{3} + \frac{54.6121}{3} + \frac{55.8009}{3} + \frac{51.2656}{3} + \frac{64.6416}{3}$$
$$+ \frac{65.6100}{3} + \frac{60.5284}{3} + \frac{61.6225}{3} - 195.075$$

$$= 19.3040 + 19.8661 + 18.1548 + 18.2040 + 18.6003 + 17.0885 + 21.5472$$
$$+ 21.8700 + 20.1761 + 20.5408 - 195.075$$
$$= 195.3518 - 195.075$$
$$= 0.2768$$

Step 7. Determine the *sum of squares between time groups* by means of the following formula

$$SS_{B\text{-}time\text{-}G} = \frac{(\sum X_{time\,1})^2}{n_{time\,1}} + \frac{(\sum X_{time\,2})^2}{n_{time\,2}} + \frac{(\sum X_{time\,3})^2}{n_{time\,3}} - \frac{(\sum X_{all})^2}{N_{total}} \tag{C.2.3}$$

The sum of the scores for each of the three time conditions (0, 15 minutes, 30 minutes) is obtained from Table C.2.1, then squared, and divided by the number of data values in each condition. In this case, there are 10 data values in each time condition. The last term in Eq. (C.2.3) is the same as in Eq. (C.2.1).

The results of applying Eq. (C.2.3) are

$$SS_{B-time-G} = \frac{26.59^2}{10} + \frac{25.32^2}{10} + \frac{24.59^2}{10} - 195.075$$

$$= \frac{707.0281}{10} + \frac{641.1024}{10} + \frac{604.6681}{10} - 195.075$$

$$= 70.7028 + 64.1102 + 60.4668 - 195.075$$

$$= 195.2799 - 195.0750$$

$$= 0.2049$$

Step 8. Determine the *sum of squares error* by means of the following formula

$$SS_{error} = SS_{total} - SS_{B-subj-G} - SS_{B-time-G} \qquad (C.2.4)$$

Each of the terms in Eq. (C.2.4) has already been obtained. Thus

$$SS_{error} = 0.5676 - 0.2768 - 0.2049$$

$$= 0.0859$$

Step 9. Determine the degrees of freedom for each identifiable source of variance—in the present example, total-data, between-subject-groups, between-time-groups, and error variance.

For the variance due to the total data in the experiment

$$df_{total} = N_{total} - 1 \qquad (C.2.5)$$

In the present case

$$df_{total} = 30 - 1 = 29$$

For the between-subject-groups variance

$$df_{B-subj-G} = N_{subj} - 1 \qquad (C.2.6)$$

where N_{subj} is the number of subjects. In the present case

$$df_{B-subj-G} = 10 - 1 = 9$$

For the between-time-groups variance

$$df_{B-time-G} = N_{time} - 1 \qquad (C.2.7)$$

where N_{time} is the number of time conditions. In the present case

$$df_{B-time-G} = 3 - 1 = 2$$

For the error variance

$$df_{error} = df_{B-subj-G} \times df_{B-time-G} \qquad (C.2.8)$$

In the present case

$$df_{error} = 9 \times 2 = 18$$

Step 10. Determine the *mean squares* (MS) for the independent variable and for the error

$$MS = \frac{SS}{df} \tag{C.2.9}$$

For the independent variable

$$MS_{B-time-G} = \frac{SS_{B-time-G}}{df_{B-time-G}}$$
$$= 0.2049/2 = 0.1025$$

For the error

$$MS_{error} = \frac{SS_{error}}{df_{error}}$$
$$= \frac{0.0859}{18} = 0.0048$$

Step 11. Determine the *F ratio* for the independent variable source of variance

$$F = \frac{MS_{B-time-G}}{MS_{error}} \tag{C.2.10}$$

In the present case

$$F = \frac{0.1025}{0.0048} = 21.354$$

Step 12. Look in a standard F table (Table 8.13) to determine the corresponding critical F value. Be sure to use the appropriate alpha level and the correct degrees of freedom for the systematic and unsystematic sources of variance.

For $\alpha = .05$, $df_s = df_{B-time-G} = 2$, and $df_u = df_{error} = 18$, the critical F from Table B.13 is 3.55.

Step 13. State the result of step 12 in standard format.

An appropriate statement is as follows

$$(F_{crit} = 3.55; df_{time} = 2; df_{error} = 18; \alpha = .05)$$

Step 14. Compare the calculated F value to the critical F value. If the calculated F is equal to or greater than the critical F, you must reject the null hypothesis; otherwise, you cannot reject the null hypothesis.

In the present case, the calculated F (21.81) is greater than the critical F (3.55); therefore, we reject the null.

Step 15. State your conclusion in a standard statistical format using appropriate symbols.

In the present case

$$(F_{calc} = 21.81; df_{time} = 2; df_{error} = 18; p < .05)$$

Step 16. State your statistical conclusion in words.

If the null hypothesis were true, the probability of arriving at a calculated F of 21.81 with 2 and 18 degrees of freedom would be less than .05. Therefore, the null hypothesis is *probably* not true, and the alternative hypothesis is a better bet.

Step 17. State your final conclusion in plain English.

   Given the data and the statistical conclusion, it is reasonable to argue that listening to classical music had *an effect* on reaction time.

This concludes the analysis of variance. However, it will be necessary to analyze these data further using a *Scheffe analysis,* as in Calculation C.1, in order to determine whether the researcher's specific hypothesis regarding the means of the conditions can be supported.

Calculation C.3 Analysis of Variance (Two Independent Variables, Between Groups)

Type of research:	Experiment
Number of dependent variables:	1
Level of measurement:	Interval/ratio
Assumptions met:	Yes
Number of independent variables:	2
Conditions of first independent variable:	2
Conditions of second independent variable:	2
Type of design:	2×2 factorial, both independent variables B-G
Choice of analysis:	Two-way ANOVA, then Scheffe

Motivation for Research: A researcher believes that listening to classical music will improve a person's reaction time. However, the researcher also believes that the improvement will be reduced if the person is uncomfortable while listening to the music.

Description of Research: The researcher randomly selects 40 people from the general population and then randomly assigns 20 of these people to a comfortable condition and the remaining 20 to an uncomfortable condition. Within the comfortable condition, 10 of the 20 people are assigned to a control condition, and the remaining 10 to a 15-minute experimental condition. Within the uncomfortable condition, 10 of the 20 people are assigned to a control condition, and the remaining 10 to a 15-minute experimental condition. For all 20 people in the comfortable condition, the room temperature is maintained at 74°F. For all 20 people in the uncomfortable condition, the room temperature is maintained at 64°F. Each of the 20 people in the two control conditions (10 in the uncomfortable control condition and 10 in the comfortable control condition) is asked to sit in the room for 15 minutes and to try to relax. Each of the 20 people in the two 15-minute experimental conditions (10 in the uncomfortable 15-minute condition and 10 in the comfortable 15-minute condition) is asked to sit in the room for 15 minutes and to try to relax while listening to classical music. All subjects in each of the four conditions are tested for their reaction time after the relaxation period.

Type of Conclusion Possible: The two-way ANOVA analysis will allow the researcher to answer three primary questions:

   1. Is there a main effect of the duration of classical music (0 versus 15 minutes)?

   2. Is there a main effect of the comfort of the room (64° versus 74°F)?

   3. Is there an interactive effect of music duration and room temperature? In other words, is the effect of the music duration different under different conditions of room temperature?

Comments: The primary hypothesis for the researcher is that listening to classical music will have more of an effect if the person is comfortable. This is a hypothesis regarding the interaction between two independent variables. The analysis of variance can only determine whether or not there is a statistically significant interaction. In order to test the more specific hypothesis, the researcher will have to use the Scheffe analysis to make appropriate comparisons among the means in the four experimental conditions.

Assumptions: Suppose that the *parametric assumptions* have been met.

Test Data:

Control group (64°)		Control group (74°)		15-minute group (64°)		15-minute group (74°)	
Person	Reaction time	Person	Reaction time	Person	Reaction time	Person	Reaction time
1	2.61	11	2.21	21	2.64	31	2.07
2	2.58	12	2.28	22	2.55	32	2.04
3	2.74	13	2.59	23	2.70	33	2.48
4	2.81	14	2.36	24	2.85	34	2.22
5	2.90	15	2.42	25	2.80	35	2.30
6	2.68	16	2.39	26	2.78	36	2.18
7	2.59	17	2.60	27	2.69	37	2.00
8	2.48	18	2.58	28	2.38	38	1.99
9	2.83	19	2.30	29	2.73	39	2.06
10	3.01	20	2.19	30	3.20	40	1.91

Specifics Regarding the Analysis: The two-way ANOVA analysis helps the researcher to determine whether or not each of two independent variables had an effect on the dependent variable *and* whether or not there was an interaction between the two independent variables. (In the case of interaction, the effect of one independent variable on the dependent variable is different under different conditions of the other independent variable.)

Research Hypotheses: The researcher believes that listening to classical music will decrease reaction time. Symbolically, the research hypothesis—alternative hypothesis—appears as follows

$$H_{alt_1}: \mu_{15\,min_{74}} < \mu_{0min_{74}}$$

In plain English, the researcher is predicting that the average reaction time after listening to classical music for 15 minutes in a 74° room will be significantly lower than the average reaction time of the control group.

However, the researcher is also predicting that listening to music will have less effect on the reaction time if the temperature of the room is 64° instead of 74°. This is a hypothesis regarding the interaction between two variables: duration of music and room temperature. Symbolically

$$H_{alt_2}: (\mu_{15min_{74}} - \mu_{0min_{74}}) > (\mu_{15min_{64}} - \mu_{0min_{64}})$$

Two-Way ANOVA Alternative Hypothesis: The ANOVA is an analysis of *variance*. Although the alternative hypothesis stated here represents the researcher's prediction, the ANOVA does not directly test this hypothesis. Instead, the alternative hypothesis for the ANOVA predicts that the variance due to the interaction between the independent variables will be significantly greater than the variance within the groups—that is, that the variability in the dependent variable due to the interaction between the two independent variables will be greater than the random variability in the dependent variable that we expect in the absence of interaction. Symbolically

$$H_A: \sigma^2_{A \times B} > \sigma^2_{random}$$

If this hypothesis is true, the researcher's specific hypothesis regarding the interaction *might* also be true. However, it is necessary to do an additional Scheffe analysis after the ANOVA to test the researcher's hypothesis more exactly.

Individual Hypotheses Regarding the Independent Variables: When using a factorial design, the researcher's primary hypothesis pertains to the interaction between the two independent variables. The two-way ANOVA automatically provides a test of two other hypotheses regarding the main effects of the two independent variables, as follows

$$H_A: \sigma^2_A > \sigma^2_{random}$$
$$H_B: \sigma^2_B > \sigma^2_{random}$$

These hypotheses pertain to the main effect of independent variable A and the main effect of independent variable B respectively. In a factorial design, the main effect of each independent variable is determined by grouping the scores only on the basis of that independent variable and temporarily ignoring the other. For example, all of the control subjects are considered as one group, regardless of the temperature condition; and all of the 15-minute subjects are considered as one group, regardless of the temperature condition.

In the present case, the main effect hypotheses may be stated as follows:

H_A: $\sigma^2_{music} > \sigma^2_{random}$

H_B: $\sigma^2_{temperature} > \sigma^2_{random}$

Null Hypotheses: As we noted in Chapter 9, we state the null hypothesis, for the sake of argument, on the assumption that our research hypothesis is incorrect. In the present case, we will need three null hypotheses, one for the main effect of the music variable, one for the main effect of the temperature variable, and one for the interaction

H_{null_A}: $\mu_{15min} = \mu_{0min}$

H_{null_B}: $\mu_{74} = \mu_{64}$

$H_{null_{A \times B}}$: $(\mu_{15 min_{74}} - \mu_{0min_{74}}) = (\mu_{15 min_{64}} - \mu_{0min_{64}})$

ANOVA Null Hypotheses: Although the null hypotheses stated here are correct, the ANOVA does not directly test them. Instead, the null hypotheses for the ANOVA predict that the variance due to the independent variables or interactions between the independent variables will be equal to the variance within the groups—that is, that the variability in the dependent variable due to the independent variables or the interaction between the independent variables will be the same as the random variability in the dependent variable that we expect in the absence of the independent variables. Symbolically

H_{null_A}: $\sigma^2_A = \sigma^2_{random}$

H_{null_B}: $\sigma^2_B = \sigma^2_{random}$

$H_{null_{A \times B}}$: $\sigma^2_{A \times B} = \sigma^2_{random}$

Two-way ANOVA Null Hypothesis: In a two-way analysis, things get pretty complicated. Just as with the simple ANOVA, rejecting the ANOVA null hypothesis does not necessarily mean that the researcher's alternative hypotheses are correct. The general null hypothesis for the *interaction* between the two independent variables in the two-way ANOVA is that the two independent variables *do not* interact. In other words, if there is no interaction between the two independent variables, then one independent variable will have the same effect—or lack of effect—on the dependent variable regardless of the conditions of the other independent variables.

Organizing the Raw Data: When you prepare the data for entry into the two-way ANOVA calculation formula—whether you do the calculations by hand or by computer—you must identify the following:

- the first independent variable: duration of music, in the present case.
- the second independent variable: room temperature.
- the conditions of the experiment: 15 minutes, 64°; 15 minutes, 74°; control, 64°; control, 74°.
- the number of subjects in each condition: 10, 10, 10, and 10.
- the dependent variable: reaction time.

Two-Way ANOVA Calculation: Once these values have been identified, you may enter them into the computer or use the calculation formula as follows.

Step 1. List your data. [The test data have already been tabulated.]

Step 2. Square each data value (each X) and place the result (X^2) next to the original data value (Table C.3.1).

Step 3. Sum the X values and the X^2 values for each group (Table C.3.1).

TABLE C.3.1 Results of Squaring and Summing

	64° Control		74°	
	X	X²	X	X³
	2.61	6.8121	2.21	4.8841
	2.58	6.6564	2.28	5.1984
	2.74	7.5076	2.59	6.7081
	2.81	7.8961	2.36	5.5696
	2.90	8.4100	2.42	5.8564
	2.68	7.1824	2.39	5.7121
	2.59	6.7081	2.60	6.7600
	2.48	6.1504	2.58	6.6564
	2.83	8.0089	2.30	5.2900
	3.01	9.0601	2.19	4.7961
Sum:	27.23	74.3921	23.92	57.4312

15-minute condition

	64°		74°	
	X	X²	X	X²
	2.64	6.9696	2.07	4.2849
	2.55	6.5025	2.04	4.1616
	2.70	7.2900	2.48	6.1504
	2.85	8.1225	2.22	4.9284
	2.80	7.8400	2.30	5.2900
	2.78	7.7284	2.18	4.7524
	2.69	7.2361	2.00	4.0000
	2.38	5.6644	1.99	3.9601
	2.73	7.4529	2.06	4.2436
	3.20	10.2400	1.91	3.6481
Sum:	27.32	75.0464	21.25	45.4195

Group summaries	N	$\sum X$	$\sum X^2$
Control, 64°	10	27.23	74.3921
Control, 74°	10	23.92	57.4312
15-minute, 64°	10	27.32	75.0464
15-minute, 74°	10	21.25	45.4195
Control (combined)	20	51.15	131.8233
15-minute (combined)	20	48.57	120.4659
64° (combined)	20	54.55	149.4385
74° (combined)	20	45.17	102.8507

Step 4. Determine the *total sum of squares* by means of the following formula

$$SS_{total} = \sum X_{all}^2 - \frac{\left(\sum X_{all}\right)^2}{N_{total}}$$ (C.3.1)

The first term in Eq. (C.3.1) requires that you square each of the scores in the entire data set (in the present case, 40 scores) and then sum all of these squared values

$$\sum X_{all}^2 = 2.61^2 + 2.58^2 + \cdots + 1.91^2$$

$$= 6.8121 + 6.6564 + \cdots + 3.6481$$

Since we already squared all 40 of the data values in step 2, we can obtain the sum of all 40 squared data values by summing the corresponding column totals from Table C.3.1 as follows

$$\sum X_{all}^2 = 74.3921 + 57.4312 + 75.0464 + 45.4195$$
$$= 252.2892$$

The second term in Eq. (C.3.1) requires that you sum all the data points first, square the result, and then divide by the total number of data points (N_{total}). Since we already summed the data points for each condition in step 3, we can obtain the sum of all the data points by summing the corresponding column totals from Table C.3.1 as follows

$$\sum X_{all} = 27.23 + 23.92 + 27.32 + 21.25 = 99.72$$

Now we square this sum

$$\left(\sum X_{all}\right)^2 = 99.72^2 = 9944.078$$

Now we divide this squared sum by N_{total}

$$\frac{\left(\sum X_{all}\right)^2}{N_{total}} = \frac{9944.0780}{40} = 248.6020$$

Finally, we subtract this term from $\sum X_{all}^2$

$$SS_{total} = 252.2892 - 248.6020 = 3.6872$$

Step 5. Determine the *between-all-groups sum of squares* by means of the following formula

$$SS_{B-all-G} = \frac{\left(\sum X_1\right)^2}{n_1} + \frac{\left(\sum X_2\right)^2}{n_2} + \frac{\left(\sum X_3\right)^2}{n_3} + \frac{\left(\sum X_4\right)^2}{n_4} - \frac{\left(\sum X_{all}\right)^2}{N_{total}} \tag{C.3.2}$$

The sum of the scores for each group is obtained from Table C.3.1, then squared, and divided by the number of data values in the appropriate groups. In the present example, there are 10 data values in each group. The last term in Eq. (C.3.2) is the same as in Eq. (C.3.1). The results of applying Eq. (C.3.2) are as follows

$$SS_{B-all-G} = \frac{27.23^2}{10} + \frac{23.92^2}{10} + \frac{27.32^2}{10} + \frac{21.25^2}{10} - 248.6020$$

$$= \frac{741.4729}{10} + \frac{572.1664}{10} + \frac{746.3824}{10} + \frac{451.5625}{10} - 248.6020$$

$$= 74.1473 + 57.2166 + 74.6382 + 45.1563 - 248.6020$$

$$= 2.5564$$

Step 6. Determine the *between-A-groups sum of squares* by means of the following formula

$$SS_{B-A-G} = \frac{\left(\sum X_{A_1}\right)^2}{n_{A_1}} + \cdots + \frac{\left(\sum X_{A_j}\right)^2}{n_{A_j}} - \frac{\left(\sum X_{all}\right)^2}{N_{total}} \tag{C.3.3}$$

where j is the number of conditions of the independent variable A.

In the present example, variable A is the duration of the music. There are two conditions of this variable. Thus, Eq. (C.3.3) translates into the following

$$SS_{B-music-G} = \frac{\left(\sum X_{0min}\right)^2}{n_{0min}} + \frac{\left(\sum X_{15min}\right)^2}{n_{15min}} - \frac{\left(\sum X_{all}\right)^2}{N_{total}}$$

The sum of the scores for each of the music groups is obtained from Table C.3.1, then squared, and divided by the number of data values in each group. In the present example, there are 20 data values in each of the two classical music conditions. The last term in Eq. (C.3.3) is the same as in Eq. (C.3.1). The results of applying Eq. (C.3.3) are as follows

$$SS_{B\text{-music-G}} = \frac{51.15^2}{20} + \frac{48.57^2}{20} - 248.6020$$

$$= \frac{2616.3225}{20} + \frac{2359.0449}{20} - 248.6020$$

$$= 130.8161 + 117.9523 - 248.6020$$

$$= 0.1663$$

Step 7. Determine the *between-B-groups sum of squares* by means of the following formula

$$SS_{B\text{-}B\text{-}G} = \frac{(\sum X_{B_1})^2}{n_{B_1}} + \cdots + \frac{(\sum X_{B_k})^2}{n_{B_k}} - \frac{(\sum X_{all})^2}{N_{total}} \qquad (C.3.4)$$

where k is the number of conditions of the independent variable B.

In the present example, the variable B is the room temperature. There are two conditions of this variable. Thus, Eq. (C.3.4) translates into the following

$$SS_{B\text{-temp-G}} = \frac{(\sum X_{64})^2}{n_{64}} + \frac{(\sum X_{74})^2}{n_{74}} - \frac{(\sum X_{all})^2}{N_{total}}$$

The sum of the scores for each of the temperature groups is obtained from Table C.3.1, then squared, and divided by the number of data values in each temperature group. In the present example, there are 20 data values in each of the two temperature conditions. The last term in Eq. (C.3.4) is the same as in Eq. (C.3.1). The results of applying Eq. (C.3.4) are as follows

$$SS_{B\text{-temp-G}} = \frac{54.55^2}{20} + \frac{45.17^2}{20} - 248.6020$$

$$= \frac{2975.7025}{20} + \frac{2040.3289}{20} - 248.6020$$

$$= 148.7851 + 102.0164 - 248.6020$$

$$= 2.1995$$

Step 8. Determine the *between-(A × B)-groups sum of squares* by means of the following formula

$$SS_{A \times B} = SS_{B\text{-all-G}} - SS_{B\text{-}A\text{-}G} - SS_{B\text{-}B\text{-}G} \qquad (C.3.5)$$

In the present case

$$SS_{music \times temp} = SS_{B\text{-all-G}} - SS_{B\text{-music-G}} - SS_{B\text{-temp-G}}$$

Each term in this formula has already been determined. Thus

$$SS_{music \times temp} = 2.5564 - 0.1663 - 2.1995$$

$$= 0.1906$$

Step 9. Determine the *within-groups (error) sum of squares* by means of the following formula

$$SS_{error} = SS_{total} - SS_{B\text{-all-G}} \qquad (C.3.6)$$

Each term in Eq. (C.3.6) has already been determined. Thus

$$SS_{error} = 3.6872 - 2.5564$$
$$= 1.1308$$

Step 10. Determine the degrees of freedom for each of the following sources of variance: *all-groups, A, B, A × B, total-data,* and *error* variance.

For the all-groups variance

$$df_{all} = g - 1 \tag{C.3.7}$$

where g is the total number of conditions in the experiment. In the present case

$$df_{all} = 4 - 1 = 3$$

For the A variance

$$df_A = j - 1 \tag{C.3.8}$$

where j is the number of conditions of A. In the present case

$$df_{music} = 2 - 1 = 1$$

For the B variance

$$df_B = k - 1 \tag{C.3.9}$$

where k is the number of conditions of B. In the present case

$$df_{temp} = 2 - 1 = 1$$

For the $A \times B$ variance

$$df_{A \times B} = df_A \times df_B \tag{C.3.10}$$

In the present case

$$df_{music \times temp} = 1 \times 1 = 1$$

For the variance due to the total-data in the experiment

$$df_{total} = N_{total} - 1 \tag{C.3.11}$$

where N_{total} is the total number of data values in the experiment. In the present case

$$df_{total} = 40 - 1 = 39$$

For the error variance

$$df_{error} = df_{total} - df_{all} = 39 - 3 = 36 \tag{C.3.12}$$

Step 11. Determine the *mean squares* (MS) for each of the following sources of variance: *all-groups, A, B, A × B,* and *error* variance.

For the all-groups variance

$$MS_{all} = \frac{SS_{all}}{df_{all}} \tag{C.3.13}$$

In the present case

$$MS_{all} = \frac{2.5564}{3} = 0.8521$$

For the A variance

$$MS_A = \frac{SS_A}{df_A} \qquad\qquad (C.3.14)$$

In the present case

$$MS_{music} = \frac{0.1663}{1} = 0.1663$$

For the B variance

$$MS_B = \frac{SS_B}{df_B} \qquad\qquad (C.3.15)$$

In the present case

$$MS_{temp} = \frac{2.1995}{1} = 2.1995$$

For the $A \times B$ variance

$$MS_{A \times B} = \frac{SS_{A \times B}}{df_{A \times B}} \qquad\qquad (C.3.16)$$

In the present case

$$MS_{music \times temp} = \frac{0.1906}{1} = 0.1906$$

Because $df = 1$ in these three examples, it may seem that calculation of MS is an unnecessary step. However, it will not always be the case that $df = 1$, since in some experiments there will be more than two conditions of a particular independent variable.
For the error variance

$$MS_{error} = \frac{SS_{error}}{df_{error}} \qquad\qquad (C.13.17)$$

In the present case

$$MS_{error} = \frac{1.1308}{36} = 0.0314$$

Step 12. Determine the F ratio for each of the following sources of variance: *all-groups*, A, B, and $A \times B$ variance.
For the all-groups variance

$$F_{all} = \frac{MS_{all}}{MS_{error}} \qquad\qquad (C.3.18)$$

In the present case

$$F_{all} = \frac{0.8521}{0.0314} = 2.7133$$

For the A variance

$$F_A = \frac{MS_A}{MS_{error}} \qquad \text{(C.3.19)}$$

In the present case

$$F_{music} = \frac{0.1663}{0.0314} = 5.2962$$

For the B variance

$$F_B = \frac{MS_B}{MS_{error}} \qquad \text{(C.3.20)}$$

In the present case

$$F_{temp} = \frac{2.1995}{0.0314} = 70.0478$$

For the $A \times B$ variance

$$F_{A \times B} = \frac{MS_{A \times B}}{MS_{error}} \qquad \text{(C.3.21)}$$

In the present case

$$F_{music \times temp} = \frac{0.1906}{0.0314} = 6.0701$$

Step 13. Look in a standard F table (Table B.13) to determine the critical F value for each of the F ratios calculated. [Be sure to use the appropriate alpha level and the correct degrees of freedom for the systematic and unsystematic sources of variance. In an $A \times B$ factorial experiment with between-groups manipulation of both independent variables, the systematic sources of variance are A, B, and $A \times B$, and the unsystematic source of variance is the error.]

For $\alpha = .05$, $df_s = 1$, and $df_u = 36$, the critical F value from Table B.13 is 4.11.

In the present example, all systematic sources of variance have $df = 1$; therefore, the critical F will be the same for each of these sources of variance.

Step 14. Formally identify the result of step 13 for each F ratio as a critical F value.

In the present case, appropriate statements are as follows

$(F_{music_{crit}} = 4.11; df_{music} = 1; df_{error} = 36; \alpha = .05)$

$(F_{temp_{crit}} = 4.11; df_{temp} = 1; df_{error} = 36; \alpha = .05)$

$(F_{music \times temp_{crit}} = 4.11: df_{music \times temp} = 1; df_{error} = 36; \alpha = .05)$

Step 15. Compare each calculated F value to the corresponding critical F value. If the calculated F is equal to or greater than the critical F, you must reject the null hypothesis; otherwise, you cannot reject the null hypothesis.

In the present case, since

$(F_{music} = 5.2962) < (F_{crit} = 4.11)$

we must reject the null hypothesis regarding the duration of music. Since

$$(F_{temp} = 70.0478) > (F_{crit} = 4.11)$$

we must reject the null hypothesis regarding the room *temperature*. Finally, since

$$(F_{music \times temp} = 6.0701) > (F_{crit} = 4.11)$$

we must reject the null hypothesis regarding the interaction between the duration of music and room temperature.

Step 16. State your conclusion in standard statistical format for each calculated F.
In the present case

$$(F_{music} = 5.2962; df_s = 1; df_u = 36; p < .05)$$
$$(F_{temp} = 70.0478; df_s = 1; df_u = 36; p < .05)$$
$$(F_{music \times temp} = 6.0701; df_s = 1; df_u = 36; p < .05)$$

Step 17. State your statistical conclusion in words for each calculated F.

1. If the null hypothesis regarding the duration of music were true, the probability of arriving at a calculated F of 5.2962 with 1 and 36 degrees of freedom would be less than .05. Therefore, the null hypothesis is *probably not* true, and the alternative hypothesis is probably true.

2. If the null hypothesis regarding the room temperature were true, the probability of arriving at a calculated F of 70.0478 with 1 and 36 degrees of freedom would be less than .05. Therefore, the null hypothesis is *probably* not true, and the alternative hypothesis probably is true.

3. If the null hypothesis regarding the interaction between the duration of music and the room temperature were true, the probability of arriving at a calculated F of 6.0701 with 1 and 36 degrees of freedom would be less than .05. Therefore, the null hypothesis is *probably* not true, and the alternative hypothesis probably is true.

Step 18. State your final conclusion regarding each systematic source of variance in plain English.
Given the data and the statistical conclusions, it is reasonable to argue that:

1. When the different temperature conditions (64° and 74°F) were combined, listening to classical music for 15 minutes *did* have an overall effect on reaction time.

2. When the different music conditions (control and 15 minutes) were combined, the room temperature did have an overall effect.

3. The effect of listening to classical music for 15 minutes was different under the different temperature conditions.

This concludes the analysis of variance. However, in order to test the researcher's specific hypothesis regarding the means of the conditions, it will be necessary to use a *Scheffe analysis*.

SCHEFFE ANALYSIS

Specifics Regarding the Analysis: If the result of the two-way ANOVA allowed you to reject the null hypothesis regarding the interaction between the two independent variables, then you know that there is an interaction. The Scheffe analysis helps you to determine whether or not the means of the groups differ in exactly the way your hypothesis predicted.

Research Hypotheses: The researcher predicted that listening to classical music will improve reaction time more when the subject is comfortable than when the subject is uncomfortable. In order for this to be the case, the following hypothesis would have to be true

$$H_{alt2}: (\mu_{15min_{74}} - \mu_{0min_{74}}) > (\mu_{15min_{64}} - \mu_{0min_{64}})$$

The Scheffe analysis allows us to test this hypothesis indirectly by testing a series of separate hypotheses regarding the means of the four experimental conditions

$H_{alt_2 1}$: $\mu_{0min_{64}} > \mu_{15min_{64}}$

$H_{alt_2 2}$: $\mu_{0min_{74}} > \mu_{15min_{74}}$

$H_{alt_2 3}$: $\mu_{15min_{64}} > \mu_{15min_{74}}$

If the researcher's specific hypothesis regarding the interaction between the two independent variables (H_{Alt_2}) is correct, these three hypotheses must also be correct, as well as the following

$H_{Alt_2 4}$: $\sigma^2_{music \times temp} > \sigma^2_{error}$

H_5: $(\bar{X}_{0min_{64}} - \bar{X}_{0min_{74}}) < (\bar{X}_{15min_{64}} - \bar{X}_{15min_{74}})$

We already know from the analysis of variance that the fourth hypothesis is correct.

Notice that the fifth hypothesis is not stated as an alternative hypothesis and that it is stated in terms of sample means rather than population means. The reason for this is that we do not need to demonstrate that the relationship stated in the fifth hypothesis is statistically significant. If the first four hypotheses are true, then any results that agree with the fifth hypothesis will be sufficient to support the researcher's primary hypothesis regarding the interaction between the two independent variables.

Null Hypotheses: We need only test the following three null hypotheses with the Scheffe analysis:

H_{null1}: $\mu_{0min_{64}} = \mu_{15min_{64}}$

H_{null2}: $\mu_{0min_{74}} = \mu_{15min_{74}}$

H_{null3}: $\mu_{15min_{64}} = \mu_{15min_{74}}$

These correspond to the first three alternative hypotheses.

Organizing the Raw Data: When you prepare the data for entry into the Scheffe calculation formula—whether you do the calculatlions by hand or by computer—you need to identify the following:

- the independent variables: the duration of music and room temperature, in the present case.
- the conditions of the experiment: 15 minutes, 64°; 15 minutes, 74°; control, 64°; control, 74°.
- the number of subjects in each condition: 10, 10, 10, 10.
- the dependent variable: reaction time (accurate to one-hundredth of a second).
- the alpha level: .05, unless otherwise stated.

All this information was obtained in the ANOVA, but must be organized before doing the Scheffe.

Scheffe Calculation: Once these values have been identified, you may enter them into the computer or use the following calculation formula.

$$CD = \pm \sqrt{df_s F_{crit} (MS_u) \left(\frac{1}{n_1} + \frac{1}{n_2} \right)} \tag{C.3.22}$$

The procedure is as follows.

Step 1. Look at the original ANOVA and obtain the degrees of freedom for the *systematic* source of variance related to the researcher's hypothesis.
In the present case

$df_{B\text{-all-G}} = 3$

This is the appropriate source of variance because we are now making comparisons among the four separate groups.

Step 2. Obtain the critical F for the *systematic* source of variance related to the researcher's hypothesis.

The critical F will be based upon $df_{\text{B-all-G}}$ and df_{error} for the two-way ANOVA. For $\alpha = .05$, $df_s = df_{\text{B-all-G}} = 3$, $df_u = df_{\text{error}} = 36$, the critical F from Table B.13 is 2.86.

Step 3. Obtain the MS_u related to the researcher's hypothesis from the ANOVA. (MS_u may also be referred to as MS_{error} here.)

In the present case

$$MS_u = 0.0314$$

Step 4. Obtain the number of data values for each group being compared.

In the present case

$$n_{0\min_{64}} = 10$$

$$n_{0\min_{74}} = 10$$

$$n_{15\min_{64}} = 10$$

$$n_{15\min_{74}} = 10$$

Step 5. Enter each of these values in the Scheffe formula, to obtain the corresponding critical difference (CD).

In the present case

$$CD = \sqrt{\left[3 \times 2.84 \times .0314 \times \left(\frac{1}{10} + \frac{1}{10}\right)\right]}$$

$$= \sqrt{0.0539}$$

$$= 0.0232$$

Step 6. Determine if additional CD values will have to be calculated.

A separate CD must be calculated for each unique set of n_1 and n_2 values. Since all the n values are equal in the present example, only one CD has to be calculated.

Step 7. Calculate the means for each pair of conditions to be compared.

In the present case

$$\mu_{0\min_{64}} = 2.723$$

$$\mu_{0\min_{74}} = 2.392$$

$$\mu_{15\min_{64}} = 2.732$$

$$\mu_{15\min_{74}} = 2.125$$

Step 8. Calculate the difference between the means for each alternative hypothesis, and then compare this difference to CD.

Three comparisons are required in the present case.

1. For the first hypothesis (one-tailed, positive difference)

$$H_{\text{alt}_2 1}: \mu_{0\min_{64}} > \mu_{15\min_{64}}$$

the calculated difference is

$$2.723 - 2.732 = -0.009$$

which is less than CD ($+0.0232$); therefore, we cannot reject the null hypothesis.

2. For the second hypothesis (one-tailed, positive difference)

$H_{alt_2 2}$: $\mu_{0min_{74}} > \mu_{15min_{74}}$

the calculated difference is

$2.392 - 2.125 = +0.267$

which is greater than CD ($+0.0232$); therefore, we reject the null hypothesis ($p < .05$).

3. For the third hypothesis (one-tailed, positive difference)

$H_{alt_2 3}$: $\mu_{15min_{64}} > \mu_{15min_{74}}$

the calculated difference is

$2.732 - 2.125 = +0.607$

which is greater than CD ($+0.0232$); therefore, we reject the null hypothesis ($p < .05$).

Step 9. State your statistical conclusion regarding each alternative hypothesis using appropriate symbols. In the present case

$(\mu_{0min_{64}} - \mu_{15min_{64}};$ ns$)$

$(\mu_{0min_{74}} - \mu_{15min_{74}}; p < .05)$

$(\mu_{15min_{64}} - \mu_{15min_{74}}; p < .05)$

Step 10. State your plain English conclusion regarding each of these three alternative hypotheses.

1. If the subjects were in a room at 64°F, listening to classical music for 15 minutes did not result in a significant improvement in reaction time compared to a control group that was also in the 64° room but did not listen to classical music.

2. If the subjects were in a room at 74°F, listening to classical music for 15 minutes did result in a significant improvement in reaction time compared to a control group that was also in the 74° room but did not listen to classical music.

3. Of the two groups who listened to classical music for 15 minutes, the group in the 74° room had a significantly shorter average reaction time.

Step 11. State a plain English conclusion that summarizes the findings of all comparisons as they relate to the researcher's primary hypothesis.

The data support the researcher's argument that listening to classical music would be more effective in improving reaction times when the subjects were comfortable. In fact, the subjects at the more comfortable temperature (74°) showed a significant improvement in average reaction time after listening to the classical music, while the subjects at the less comfortable temperature (64°) did not show a significant improvement.

Calculation C.4 Analysis of Variance (Two Independent Variables; One Between Groups, One Within Groups)

Type of research:	Experiment
Number of dependent variables:	1
Level of measurement:	Interval/ratio
Assumptions met:	Yes
Number of independent variables:	2
Conditions of first independent variable:	2
Conditions of second independent variable:	2
Type of design:	2 × 2 factorial, 1 B-G independent variable, 1 w-g independent variable
Choice of analysis:	Two-way mixed ANOVA, then Scheffe

Motivation for Research: A researcher believes that listening to classical music will improve a person's reaction time. However, the researcher also believes that the improvement will be reduced if the person is uncomfortable while listening to the music.

Description of Research: The researcher randomly selects 20 people from the general population and then randomly assigns 10 of these people to a comfortable condition and the renamining 10 to an uncomfortable condition. Within the comfortable condition each of the 10 people is first measured for reaction time on a standard task. Then, each of these 10 people is asked to sit for 15 minutes in a room maintained at a temperature of 74°F and to try to relax by listening to classical music. After this relaxation period, each of the 10 people is measured for reaction time again on the same standard task. Within the uncomfortable condition, each of the 10 people is treated the same way, except that the room is kept at 64°F.

Type of Conclusion Possible: The two-way ANOVA analysis will allow the researcher to answer three primary questions:

1. Is there a main effect of the duration of classical music (0 versus 15 minutes)?
2. Is there a main effect of the comfort of the room (64° versus 74°F)?
3. Is there an interactive effect of music duration and room comfort? In other words, is the effect of the music duration different under different conditions of room temperature?

Comments: The researcher's primary hypothesis is that listening to classical music will have more of an effect if the person is comfortable. This is a hypothesis regarding the interaction between two independent variables. The analysis of variance can only determine whether or not there is a statistically significant interaction. In order to test the more specific hypothesis, the researcher will have to use the Scheffe analysis to make appropriate comparisons among the means in the four experimental conditions.

Assumptions: Suppose that the *parametric assumptions* have been met.

Test Data:

Control condition (64°)		Control condition (74°)		15-minute condition (64°)		15-minute condition (74°)	
Person	Reaction time	Person	Reaction time	Person	Reaction time	Person	Reaction time
1	2.60	11	2.22	1	2.63	11	2.10
2	2.59	12	2.29	2	2.53	12	2.11
3	2.72	13	2.57	3	2.74	13	2.52
4	2.83	14	2.34	4	2.87	14	2.36
5	2.94	15	2.41	5	2.84	15	2.42
6	2.62	16	2.35	6	2.79	16	2.29
7	2.58	17	2.62	7	2.65	17	2.14
8	2.49	18	2.59	8	2.33	18	2.05
9	2.80	19	2.35	9	2.74	19	2.18
10	3.04	20	2.14	10	3.18	20	2.00

Specifics Regarding the Analysis: The two-way ANOVA analysis helps the researcher to determine whether or not each of two independent variables—one characterized by between-groups manipulation and the other by within-groups manipulation—had an effect on the dependent variable and whether or not there was an interaction between the two independent variables. (In the case of interaction, the effect of one independent variable on the dependent variable is different under different conditions of the other independent variable.)

Research Hypotheses: The researcher believes that listening to classical music will decrease reaction time. Symbolically, the research hypothesis—the alternative hypothesis—appears as follows

$$H_{alt_1}: \mu_{15min_{74}} < \mu_{0min_{74}}$$

In plain English, the researcher is predicting that the average reaction time after listening to classical music for 15 minutes in a 74° room will be significantly lower than the average reaction time of the control condition.

However, the researcher is also predicting that listening to music will have less effect on the reaction time if the temperature of the room is 64° instead of 74°. This is a hypothesis regarding the interaction between two variables: duration of music and room temperature. Symbolically

$$H_{alt_2}: (\mu_{15min_{74}} - \mu_{0min_{74}}) > (\mu_{15min_{64}} - \mu_{0min_{64}})$$

Two-Way ANOVA Alternative Hypothesis: The ANOVA is an analysis of *variance*. Although the alternative hypothesis stated here represents the researcher's prediction, the ANOVA does not directly test this hypothesis. Instead, the alternative hypothesis for the two-way ANOVA predicts that the variance due to the interaction between the independent variables will be significantly greater than the variance within the groups—that is, that the variability in the dependent variable due to the interaction between the two independent variables will be greater than the random variability in the dependent variable that we expect to occur in the absence of interaction. Symbolically

$$H_A: \sigma^2_{A \times B} > \sigma^2_{random}$$

If this hypothesis is true, the researcher's specific hypothesis regarding the interaction *might* also be true. However, it is necessary to do an additional Scheffe analysis after the ANOVA to test the researcher's hypothesis more exactly.

Mixed Two-Way ANOVA: The analysis will be more complex in a mixed factorial design, where one independent variable is manipulated between groups and the other is manipulated within groups. Each subject is measured more than once in the within-group manipulation and, therefore, becomes an identifiable source of variance. Also, there are different subjects in each of the between-groups manipulations. As a result, there is a confounding of subjects with the between-groups independent variable. Consequently, it is necessary to identify a separate source of unsystematic (error) variance for the between-groups independent variable, on the one hand, and for the within-groups variable and the interaction between the two independent variables, on the other hand. The step-by-step calculations for this analysis will indicate how to calculate these separate sources of unsystematic variance.

Individual Hypotheses Regarding the Independent Variables: When using a factorial design, the researcher's primary hypothesis pertains to the interaction between the two independent variables. The two-way ANOVA automatically provides a test of two other hypotheses regarding the main effects of the two independent variables, as follows

$$H_A: \sigma^2_A > \sigma^2_{random}$$

$$H_B: \sigma^2_B > \sigma^2_{random}$$

These hypotheses pertain to the main effect of independent variable A and the main effect of independent variable B respectively. In a factorial design, the main effect of each independent variable is determined by grouping the scores only on the basis of that independent variable and temporarily ignoring the other. For example, all of the control subjects are considered as one group, regardless of the temperature condition; and all of the 15-minute subjects are considered as one group, regardless of the temperature condition.

In the present case, the main effect hypotheses may be stated as follows

$$H_A: \sigma^2_{music} > \sigma^2_{random}$$

$$H_B: \sigma^2_{temperature} > \sigma^2_{random}$$

Null Hypotheses: As we noted in Chapter 9, we state the null hypothesis, for the sake of argument, on the assumption that our research hypothesis is incorrect. In the present case, we will need three null hypotheses, one for the main effect of the music variable, one for the main effect of the temperature variable, and one for the interaction

$$H_{null_A}: \mu_{15min} = \mu_{0min}$$

$$H_{null_B}: \mu_{74} = \mu_{64}$$

$H_{A \times B}$: $(\mu_{15min_{74}} - \mu_{0min_{74}}) = (\mu_{15min_{64}} - \mu_{0min_{64}})$

ANOVA Null Hypothesis: Although the null hypotheses stated here are correct, the ANOVA does not directly test them. Instead, the null hypotheses for the ANOVA predict that the variance due to the independent variables or interactions between the independent variables will be equal to the variance within the groups—that is, that the variability in the dependent variable due to the independent variables or the interaction between the independent variables will be the same as the random variability in the dependent variable which we expect in the absence of the independent variables. Symbolically

H_{null_A}: $\sigma^2_A = \sigma^2_{random}$

H_{null_B}: $\sigma^2_B = \sigma^2_{random}$

$H_{null_{A \times B}}$: $\sigma^2_{A \times B} = \sigma^2_{random}$

Two-Way ANOVA Null Hypothesis: In a two-way analysis things get pretty complicated. Just as with the simple ANOVA, rejecting the ANOVA null hypothesis does not necessarily mean that the researcher's alternative hypotheses are correct. The general null hypothesis for the *interaction* between the two independent variables in the two-way ANOVA is that the two independent variables *do not* interact. In other words, if there is no interaction between the two independent variables, then the one independent variable will have the same effect—or lack of effect—on the dependent variable regardless of the conditions of the other independent variable.

Organizing the Raw Data: When you prepare the data for entry into the two-way ANOVA calculation formula—whether you do the calculations by hand or by computer—you must identify the following:

- the first independent variable: duration of music, in the present case.

- the second independent variable: room temperature.

- the conditions of the experiment: 15 minutes, 64°; 15 minutes, 74°; control, 64°; control, 74°.

- the number of subjects in each condition: 10, 10, 10, and 10.

- the dependent variable: reaction time.

Two-Way ANOVA Calculation: Once these values have been identified you may enter them into the computer or use the calculation formula as follows.

Step 1. List your data. [The test data have already been tabulated.]

Step 2. Square each data value (each X) and place the result (X^2) next to the original data value (Table C.4.1).

TABLE C.4.1 Results of Squaring and Summing

| | \multicolumn{2}{c}{Control} | | |
| | 64° | | 74° | |
	X	X^2	X	X^2
	2.60	6.7600	2.22	4.9284
	2.59	6.7081	2.29	5.2441
	2.72	7.3984	2.57	6.6049
	2.83	8.0089	2.34	5.4756
	2.94	8.6436	2.41	5.8081
	2.62	6.8644	2.35	5.5225
	2.58	6.6564	2.62	6.8644
	2.49	6.2001	2.59	6.7081
	2.80	7.8400	2.35	5.5225
	3.04	9.2416	2.14	4.5796
Sum:	27.21	74.3215	23.88	57.2582

TABLE C.4.1 Results of Squaring and Summing (Continued)

| | 15-minute condition | | | |
| | 64° | | 74° | |
	X	X^2	X	X^2
	2.63	6.9169	2.10	4.4100
	2.53	6.4009	2.11	4.4521
	2.74	7.5076	2.52	6.3504
	2.87	8.2369	2.36	5.5696
	2.84	8.0656	2.42	5.8564
	2.79	7.7841	2.29	5.2441
	2.65	7.0225	2.14	4.5796
	2.33	5.4289	2.05	4.2025
	2.74	7.5076	2.18	4.7524
	3.18	10.1124	2.00	4.0000
Sum:	27.30	74.9834	22.17	49.4171

Group summaries	N	$\sum X$	$\sum X^2$
Control, 64°	10	27.21	74.3215
Control, 74°	10	23.88	57.2582
15-minute, 64°	10	27.30	74.9834
15-minute, 74°	10	22.17	49.4171
Control (combined)	20	51.09	Not needed
15-minute (combined)	20	49.47	Not needed
64° (combined)	20	54.51	Not needed
75° (combined)	20	46.05	Not needed

Source of variance	Number of data values per subject	Sum
Subject 1	2	5.23
Subject 2	2	5.12
Subject 3	2	5.46
Subject 4	2	5.70
Subject 5	2	5.78
Subject 6	2	5.41
Subject 7	2	5.23
Subject 8	2	4.82
Subject 9	2	5.54
Subject 10	2	6.22
Subject 11	2	4.32
Subject 12	2	4.40
Subject 13	2	5.09
Subject 14	2	4.70
Subject 15	2	4.83
Subject 16	2	4.64
Subject 17	2	4.76
Subject 18	2	4.64
Subject 19	2	4.53
Subject 20	2	4.14

Note: Because each subject is measured more than once, the subjects may now be identified as a source of variance. The sum of the scores for each subject will be required in the calculation.

Step 3. Sum the X values and the X^2 values for each group (Table C.4.1).

Step 4. Determine the *total sum of squares* by means of the following formula

$$SS_{total} = \sum X_{all}^2 - \frac{\left(\sum X_{all}\right)^2}{N_{total}} \qquad (C.4.1)$$

The first term in Eq. (C.4.1) requires that you square each of the scores in the entire data set (in the present case, 40 scores) and then sum all of these squared values.

$$\sum X_{all}^2 = 2.60^2 + 2.59^2 + \cdots + 2.00^2$$
$$= 6.7600 + 6.7081 + \cdots + 4.0000$$

Since we already squared all 40 of the data values in step 2, we can obtain the sum of all 40 squared data values by summing the corresponding column totals from Table C.4.1 as follows

$$\sum X_{all}^2 = 74.3215 + 57.2582 + 74.9834 + 49.4171$$
$$= 255.9802$$

The second term in Eq. (C.4.1) requires that you sum all the data points first, then square the result, and divide by the total number of data points (N_{total}). Since we already summed the data points for each condition in step 3, we can obtain the sum of all the data points by summing the column totals from Table C.4.1 as follows

$$\sum X_{all} = 27.21 + 23.88 + 27.30 + 22.17 = 100.56$$

Now we square this sum

$$\left(\sum X_{all}\right)^2 = 100.56^2 = 10,112.313$$

Now we divide this squared sum by N_{total}

$$\frac{\left(\sum X_{all}\right)^2}{N_{total}} = \frac{10,112.313}{40} = 252.8078$$

Finally, we substract this term from $\sum X_{all}^2$

$$SS_{total} = 255.9802 - 252.8078 = 3.1724$$

Step 5. Determine the *between-all-groups sum of squares* by means of the following formula

$$SS_{B\text{-}all\text{-}G} = \frac{\left(\sum X_1\right)^2}{n_1} + \frac{\left(\sum X_2\right)^2}{n_2} + \frac{\left(\sum X_3\right)^2}{n_3} + \frac{\left(\sum X_4\right)^2}{n_4} - \frac{\left(\sum X_{all}\right)^2}{N_{total}} \qquad (C.4.2)$$

The sum of the scores for each group is obtained from Table C.4.1, then squared, and divided by the number of data values in the appropriate group. In the present example, there are 10 data values in each group. The last term in Eq. (C.4.2) is the same as in Eq. (C.4.1). The results of applying Eq. (C.4.2) are as follows

$$SS_{B\text{-}all\text{-}G} = \frac{27.21^2}{10} + \frac{23.88^2}{10} + \frac{27.30^2}{10} + \frac{22.17^2}{10} - 252.8078$$

$$= \frac{740.3841}{10} + \frac{570.2544}{10} + \frac{745.2900}{10} + \frac{491.5089}{10} - 252.8078$$

$$= 74.0384 + 57.0254 + 74.5290 + 49.1509 - 252.8078$$

$$= 254.7437 - 252.8078$$

$$= 1.9359$$

Step 6. Determine the *between-A-groups sum of squares* (where A is the within-groups independent variable) by means of the following formula

$$SS_{B-A-G} = \frac{\left(\sum X_{A_1}\right)^2}{n_{A_1}} + \cdots + \frac{\left(\sum X_{A_j}\right)^2}{n_{A_j}} - \frac{\left(\sum X_{all}\right)^2}{N_{total}} \qquad (C.4.3)$$

where j is the number of conditions of the independent variable A.

In the present example the variable A is the duration of the music. There are two conditions of this variable. Thus, Eq. (C.4.3) translates into the following

$$SS_{B-music-G} = \frac{\left(\sum X_{0min}\right)^2}{n_{0min}} + \frac{\left(\sum X_{15min}\right)^2}{n_{15min}} - \frac{\left(\sum X_{all}\right)^2}{N_{total}}$$

The sum of the scores for each of the music groups is obtained from Table C.4.1, then squared, and divided by the number of data values in each group. In the present example there are 20 data values in each of the two classical music conditions. The last term in Eq. (C.4.3) is the same as in Eq. (C.4.1). The results of applying Eq. (C.4.3) are as follows

$$SS_{B-music-G} = \frac{51.09^2}{20} + \frac{49.47^2}{20} - 252.8078$$

$$= \frac{2610.1881}{20} + \frac{2447.2809}{20} - 252.8078$$

$$= 130.5094 + 122.3640 - 252.8078$$

$$= 252.8734 - 252.8078$$

$$= 0.0656$$

Step 7. Determine the *between-B-groups sum of squares* (where B is the between-groups independent variable) by means of the following formula:

$$SS_{B-B-G} = \frac{\left(\sum X_{B_1}\right)^2}{n_{B_1}} + \cdots + \frac{\left(\sum X_{B_k}\right)^2}{n_{B_k}} - \frac{\left(\sum X_{all}\right)^2}{N_{total}} \qquad (C.4.4)$$

where k is the number of conditions of the independent variable B.

In the present example the variable B is the room temperature. There are two conditions of this variable. Thus, Eq. (C.4.4) translates into the following

$$SS_{B-temp-G} = \frac{\left(\sum X_{64}\right)^2}{n_{64}} + \frac{\left(\sum X_{74}\right)^2}{n_{74}} - \frac{\left(\sum X_{all}\right)^2}{N_{total}}$$

The sum of the scores for each of the temperature groups is obtained from Table C.4.1, then squared, and divided by the number of data values in each group. In the present example there are 20 data values in each of the two temperature conditions. The last term in Eq. (C.4.4) is the same as in Eq. (C.4.1). The results of applying Eq. (C.4.4) are as follows

$$SS_{B-temp-G} = \frac{54.51^2}{20} + \frac{46.05^2}{20} - 252.8078$$

$$= \frac{2971.3401}{20} + \frac{2120.6025}{20} - 252.8078$$

$$= 148.5670 + 106.0301 - 252.8078$$

$$= 254.5971 - 252.8078$$

$$= 1.7893$$

Step 8. Determine the *between-(A × B)-groups sum of squares* by means of the following formula

$$SS_{A \times B} = SS_{B\text{-all-}G} - SS_{B\text{-}A\text{-}G} - SS_{B\text{-}B\text{-}G} \qquad (C.4.5)$$

In the present case

$$SS_{music \times temp} = SS_{B\text{-all-}G} - SS_{B\text{-min-}G} - SS_{B\text{-temp-}G}$$

Each of the terms in this formula has already been determined. Thus

$$SS_{music \times temp} = 1.9359 - 0.0656 - 1.7893$$
$$= 0.0810$$

Step 9. Determine the *sum of squares for subjects* by means of the following formula

$$SS_{subj} = \frac{\left(\sum X_{subj_1}\right)^2}{n_{subj_1}} + \cdots + \frac{\left(\sum X_{subj_m}\right)^2}{n_{subj_m}} - \frac{\left(\sum X_{all}\right)^2}{N_{total}} \qquad (C.4.6)$$

where m is the number of subjects in the experiment.

The sum of the scores for each of the subjects is obtained from Table C.4.1, then squared, and divided by the number of data values in each subject group. In the present example there are two data values for each subject. The last term in Eq. (C.4.6) is the same as in Eq. (C.4.1). The results of applying Eq. (C.4.6) are as follows

$$SS_{subj} = \frac{5.23^2}{2} + \frac{5.12^2}{2} + \cdots + \frac{4.14^2}{2} - 252.8078$$

$$= \frac{27.3529}{2} + \frac{26.2144}{2} + \cdots + \frac{17.1396}{2} - 252.8078$$

$$= 13.6765 + 13.1072 + \cdots + 8.5698 - 252.8078$$

$$= 255.619 - 252.8078$$

$$= 2.8112$$

Step 10. Determine the *sum of squares for the error variance* associated with the between-groups independent variable by means of the following formula

$$SS_{error(B\text{-}B\text{-}G)} = SS_{subj} - SS_{B\text{-}B\text{-}G} \qquad (C.4.7)$$

For the present case

$$SS_{error(B\text{-temp-}G)} = SS_{subj} - SS_{B\text{-temp-}G}$$

Each term in this formula has already been determined. Thus

$$SS_{error(B\text{-temp-}G)} = 2.8112 - 1.7893$$
$$= 1.0219$$

Step 11. Determine the *sum of squares for the interaction between the subjects and the within-groups independent variable* by means of the following formula

$$SS_{A \times subj} = SS_{total} - SS_A - SS_{subj} \qquad (C.4.8)$$

Each term in this formula has already been determined. Thus

$$SS_{A \times subj} = 3.1724 - 0.0656 - 2.8112$$
$$= 0.2956$$

Step 12. Determine the *sum of squares for the error variance* associated with the within-groups independent variable by means of the following formula

$$SS_{error(B-A-G)} = SS_{A \times subj} - SS_{B \times A}$$ (C.4.9)

Each term in this formula has already been determined. Thus

$$SS_{error(B-A-G)} = 0.2956 - 0.0810$$

$$= 0.2146$$

Step 13. Determine the degrees of freedom for each of the following sources of variance: *all groups, A, B, A × B, total* data, error associated with variable *A*, and error associated with variable *B*. For the all-groups variance

$$df_{all} = g - 1$$ (C.4.10)

where g is the total number of conditions in the experiment. In the present case

$$df_{all} = 4 - 1 = 3$$

For the *A* variance

$$df_A = j - 1$$ (C.4.11)

where j is the number of conditions of *A*. In the present case

$$df_{music} = 2 - 1 = 1$$

For the *B* variance

$$df_B = k - 1$$ (C.4.12)

where k is the number of conditions of *B*. In the present case

$$df_{temp} = 2 - 1 = 1$$

For the *A × B* variance

$$df_{A \times B} = df_A \times df_B$$ (C.4.13)

In the present case

$$df_{music \times temp} = 1 \times 1 = 1$$

For the variance due to the total data in the experiment

$$df_{total} = N_{total} - 1$$ (C.4.14)

where N_{total} is the total number of data values in the experiment. In the present case

$$df_{total} = 40 - 1 = 39$$

For the variance due to the error associated with variable *A*

$$df_{error(B-A-G)} = df_{subj} - df_A$$ (C.4.15)

In the present case

$$df_{error(B\text{-}music\text{-}G)} = 19 - 1 = 18$$

For the variance due to the error associated with variable B

$$df_{error(B\text{-}B\text{-}G)} = df_{subj} - df_B \qquad (C.4.16)$$

In the present case

$$df_{error(B\text{-}temp\text{-}G)} = 19 - 1 = 18$$

Step 14. Determine the *mean squares* (MS) for each of the following sources of variance: *all groups, A, B, A × B*, error associated with variable A, and error associated with variable B.

For the all-groups variance

$$MS_{all} = \frac{SS_{all}}{df_{all}} \qquad (C.4.17)$$

In the present case

$$MS_{all} = \frac{1.9359}{3} = 0.6453$$

For the A variance

$$MS_A = \frac{SS_A}{df_A} \qquad (C.4.18)$$

In the present case

$$MS_{music} = \frac{0.0656}{1} = 0.0656$$

For the B variance

$$MS_B = \frac{SS_B}{df_B} \qquad (C.4.19)$$

In the present case

$$MS_{temp} = \frac{1.7893}{1} = 1.7893$$

For the A × B variance

$$MS_{A \times B} = \frac{SS_{A \times B}}{df_{A \times B}} \qquad (C.4.20)$$

In the present case

$$MS_{music \times temp} = \frac{0.0810}{1} = 0.0810$$

Because $df = 1$ in these three examples, it may seem that calculation of MS is an unnecessary step. However, it will not always be the case that $df = 1$, since in some experiments there will be more than two conditions of a particular independent variable.

For the variance due to the error associated with variable A

$$MS_{error(B-A-G)} = \frac{SS_{error(B-A-G)}}{df_{error(B-A-G)}} \qquad (C.4.21)$$

In the present case

$$MS_{error(B-music-G)} = \frac{0.2146}{18} = 0.0119$$

For the variance due to the error associated with variable B

$$MS_{error(B-B-G)} = \frac{SS_{error(B-B-G)}}{df_{error(B-B-G)}} \qquad (C.4.22)$$

In the present case

$$MS_{error(B-temp-G)} = \frac{1.0219}{18} = 0.0568$$

Step 15. Determine the F *ratio* for each of the following sources of variance: *all groups, A, B,* and $A \times B$.

For the all-groups variance

$$F_{all} = \frac{MS_{all}}{MS_{error(B-A-G)}} \qquad (C.4.23)$$

In the present case

$$F_{all} = \frac{0.6453}{0.0119} = 54.2269$$

For the A variance

$$F_A = \frac{MS_A}{MS_{error(B-A-G)}} \qquad (C.4.24)$$

In the present case

$$F_{music} = \frac{0.0656}{0.0119} = 5.5126$$

For the B variance

$$F_B = \frac{MS_B}{MS_{error(B-B-G)}} \qquad (C.4.25)$$

In the present case

$$F_{temp} = \frac{1.7893}{0.0568} = 31.5018$$

For the $A \times B$ variance

$$F_{A \times B} = \frac{MS_{A \times B}}{MS_{error}} \qquad (C.4.26)$$

In the present case

$$F_{music \times temp} = \frac{0.0810}{0.0119} = 6.8067$$

Step 16. Look in a standard F table (Table B.13) to determine the critical F value for each of the F ratios calculated.

Be sure to use the appropriate alpha level and the correct degrees of freedom for the systematic and unsystematic sources of variance. In an $A \times B$ factorial experiment when one independent variable is manipulated between groups and the other independent variable is manipulated within groups, the systematic sources of variance are A, B, and $A \times B$, and the unsystematic sources of variance are the errors associated with variables A and B.

For $\alpha = .05$, $df_s = 1$ and $df_u = 18$, the critical F value from Table B.13 is 4.41.

In the present example all systematic sources of variance have $df = 1$ and all unsystematic sources of variance have $df = 18$; therefore, the critical F will be the same for each of these sources of variance.

Step 17. Formally identify the result of step 16 for each F ratio as a critical F value.

In the present case, appropriate statements are as follows

$(F_{music_{crit}} = 4.41; df_{music} = 1; df_{error} = 18; \alpha = .05)$

$(F_{temp_{crit}} = 4.41; df_{temp} = 1; df_{error} = 18; \alpha = .05)$

$(F_{music \times temp_{crit}} = 4.41; df_{music \times temp} = 1; df_{error} = 18; \alpha = .05)$

Step 18. Compare each calculated F value with the corresponding critical F value. If the calculated F is equal to or greater than the critical F, you must reject the null hypothesis; otherwise, you cannot reject the null hypothesis.

In the present case, since

$(F_{music} = 5.5126) > (F_{crit} = 4.41)$

we must reject the null hypothesis regarding the duration of music. Since

$(F_{temp} = 31.5018) > (F_{crit} = 4.41)$

we must reject the null hypothesis regarding the room temperature. Finally, since

$(F_{music \times temp} = 6.8067) > (F_{crit} = 4.41)$

we must reject the null hypothesis regarding the interaction between the duration of music and room temperature.

Step 19. State your conclusion in standard statistical format for each calculated F.

In the present case

$(F_{music} = 5.5126; df_s = 1; df_u = 18; p < .05)$

$(F_{temp} = 31.5018; df_s = 1; df_u = 18; p < .05)$

$(F_{music \times temp} = 6.8067; df_s = 1; df_u = 18; p < .05)$

Step 20. State your statistical conclusion using words for each calculated F.

1. If the null hypothesis regarding the duration of music were true, the probability of arriving at a calculated F of 5.5126 with 1 and 18 degrees of freedom would be less than .05. Therefore, the null hypothesis is *probably* not true, and the alternative hypothesis is probably true.

2. If the null hypothesis regarding the room temperature were true, the probability of arriving at a calculated F of 31.5018 with 1 and 18 degrees of freedom would be less than

.05. Therefore, the null hypothesis is *probably* not true, and the alternative hypothesis probably is true.

3. If the null hypothesis regarding the interaction between duration of music and room temperature were true, the probability of arriving at a calculated F of 6.8067 with 1 and 18 degrees of freedom would be less than .05. Therefore, the null hypothesis is *probably* not true, and the alternative hypothesis probably is true.

Step 21. State your final conclusion regarding each systematic source of variance in plain English. Given the data and the statistical conclusion, it is reasonable to argue that:

1. When the different temperature conditions (64° and 74°F) were combined, listening to classical music for 15 minutes did have an overall effect on reaction time.

2. When the different music conditions (control and 15 minutes) were combined, the temperature of the room did have an overall main effect.

3. The effect of listening to classical music for 15 minutes was different under the different temperature conditions.

This concludes the analysis of variance. However, in order to test the researcher's specific hypothesis regarding the means of the conditions, it will be necessary to use a *Scheffe analysis*.

SCHEFFE ANALYSIS

Specifics Regarding the Analysis: If the results of the two-way ANOVA allowed you to reject the null hypothesis regarding the interaction between the two independent variables, you know that there is an interaction. The Scheffe analysis helps you to determine whether or not the means of the groups differ in exactly the way your hypothesis predicted.

Research Hypotheses: The researcher predicted that listening to classical music will improve reaction time more when the subject is comfortable than when the subject is uncomfortable. In order for this to be the case, the following hypothesis would have to be true

$$H_{alt_2}: (\mu_{15min_{74}} - \mu_{0min_{74}}) > (\mu_{15min_{64}} - \mu_{0min_{64}})$$

The Scheffe analysis allows us to test this hypothesis indirectly by testing a series of separate hypotheses regarding the means of the four experimental conditions

$$H_{alt_21}: \mu_{0min_{64}} > \mu_{15min_{64}}$$

$$H_{alt_22}: \mu_{0min_{74}} > \mu_{15min_{74}}$$

$$H_{alt_23}: \mu_{15min_{64}} > \mu_{15min_{74}}$$

If the researcher's specific hypothesis regarding the interaction between the two independent variables is correct, these three hypotheses must also be correct, as well as the following

$$H_{alt_24}: \sigma^2_{music \times temp} > \sigma^2_{error}$$

$$H_5: (\bar{X}_{0min_{64}} - \bar{X}_{0min_{74}}) < (\bar{X}_{15min_{64}} - \bar{X}_{15min_{74}})$$

We already know from the analysis of variance that the fourth hypothesis is correct.

Notice that the fifth hypothesis is not stated as an alternative hypothesis and that it is stated in terms of sample means rather than population means. The reason for this is that we do not need to demonstrate that the relationship stated in the fifth hypothesis is statistically significant. If the first four hypotheses are true, any results that agree with the fifth hypothesis will be sufficient to support the researcher's primary hypothesis regarding the interaction between the two independent variables.

Null Hypotheses: We need only test the following three null hypotheses with the Scheffe analysis

H_{null1}: $\mu_{0min_{64}} = \mu_{15min_{64}}$

H_{null2}: $\mu_{0min_{74}} = \mu_{15min_{74}}$

H_{null3}: $\mu_{15min_{64}} = \mu_{15min_{74}}$

These correspond to the first three alternative hypotheses.

Organizing the Raw Data: When you prepare the data for entry into the Scheffe calculation formula—whether you do the calculations by hand or by computer—you need to identify the following:

- the independent variables: the duration of music and room temperature, in the present case.

- the conditions of the experiment: 15 minutes, 64°; 15 minutes, 74°; control, 64°; control, 74°.

- the number of subjects in each condition: 10, 10, 10, 10.

- the dependent variable: reaction time (accurate to one-hundredth of a second).

- the alpha level: .05, unless otherwise stated.

All this information was obtained in the ANOVA, but must be organized before doing the Scheffe.

Scheffe Calculation: Once these values have been identified, you may enter them into the computer or use the following calculation formula

$$CD = \pm \sqrt{df_s F_{crit}(MS_u)\left(\frac{1}{n_1} + \frac{1}{n_2}\right)}$$ (C.4.27)

The procedure is as follows.

Step 1. Look at the original ANOVA and obtain the degrees of freedom for the *systematic* source of variance related to the researcher's hypothesis.
In the present case

$df_{B-all-G} = 3$

This is the appropriate source of variance because we are now making comparisons among the four separate groups.

Step 2. Obtain the critical F for the *systematic* source of variance related to the researcher's hypothesis.
The critical F will be based upon the $df_{B-all-G}$ and the $df_{error(B-A-G)}$ for the two-way ANOVA. For $\alpha = .05$, $df_s = df_{B-all-G} = 3$, $df_u = df_{error(B-A-G)} = 18$, the critical F from Table B.13 is 3.16.

Step 3. Obtain the MS_u related to the researcher's hypothesis from the ANOVA.
In the present case

$MS_{error(B-A-G)} = 0.0119$

Step 4. Obtain the number of data values for each group being compared.
In the present case

$n_{0min_{64}} = 10$

$n_{0min_{74}} = 10$

$n_{15min_{64}} = 10$

$n_{15min_{74}} = 10$

Step 5. Enter each of these values in the Scheffe formula, to obtain the corresponding critical difference (CD).

In the present case

$$CD = [3 \times 3.16 \times 0.0119 \times (\tfrac{1}{10} + \tfrac{1}{10})]$$

$$= \sqrt{0.0226}$$

$$= 0.1503$$

Step 6. Determine if additional CD values will have to be calculated.

A separate CD must be calculated for each unique set of n_1 and n_2 values. Since all the n values are equal in the present example, only one CD has to be calculated.

Step 7. Calculate the means for each pair of conditions to be compared.

In the present case

$$\mu_{0min_{64}} = 2.721$$

$$\mu_{0min_{74}} = 2.388$$

$$\mu_{15min_{64}} = 2.730$$

$$\mu_{15min_{74}} = 2.217$$

Step 8. Calculate the difference between the means for each alternative hypothesis, and then compare this difference to CD.

Three comparisons are required in the present case.

1. For the first hypothesis (one-tailed, positive difference)

$$H_{alt_21}: \mu_{0min_{64}} > \mu_{15min_{64}}$$

the calculated difference is

$$2.721 - 2.730 = -0.009$$

which is less than CD ($+0.1503$); therefore, we cannot reject the null hypothesis.

2. For the second hypothesis (one-tailed, positive difference)

$$H_{alt_22}: \mu_{0min_{74}} > \mu_{15min_{74}}$$

the calculated difference is

$$2.388 - 2.217 = +0.171$$

which is greater than CD ($+0.1503$); therefore, we reject the null hypothesis ($p < .05$).

3. For the third hypothesis (one-tailed, positive difference)

$$H_{alt_23}: \mu_{15min_{64}} > \mu_{15min_{74}}$$

the calculated difference is

$$2.730 - 2.127 = +0.513$$

which is greater than CD ($+0.1503$); therefore, we reject the null hypothesis ($p < .05$).

Step 9. State your statistical conclusion regarding each alternative hypothesis using appropriate symbols.

In the present case

$$(\mu_{0\min_{64}} - \mu_{15\min_{64}}; ns)$$

$$(\mu_{0\min_{74}} - \mu_{15\min_{74}}; p < .05)$$

$$(\mu_{15\min_{64}} - \mu_{15\min_{74}}; p < .05)$$

Step 10. State your plain English conclusion regarding each alternative hypothesis.

1. If the subjects were in a room at 64°F, listening to classical music for 15 minutes, this did result in a significant improvement in reaction time compared to the control measurement at 64°.

2. If the subjects were in a room at 74°F, listening to classical music for 15 minutes, this did result in a significant improvement in reaction time compared to the control measurement at 74°.

3. Of the two groups who listened to classical music for 15 minutes, the group that was in the 74° room had a significantly shorter average reaction time.

4. As predicted, the difference between the reaction times measured after 15 minutes of classical music for the 64° and 74° groups is greater than the difference between the reaction times measured before listening to music (the control measurements) for the 64° and 74° groups. Recall that this comparison is important in order to support the researcher's hypothesis.

Step 11. State a plain English conclusion that summarizes the findings of all comparisons as they relate to the researcher's primary hypothesis.

The data support the researcher's argument that listening to classical music would be more effective in improving reaction times when the subjects were comfortable.

Calculation C.5 Binomial Test

Type of research:	Observation
Number of variables:	1
Level of measurement:	Nominal
Number of nominal categories:	2
Choice of analysis:	Binomial

Motivation for Research: A researcher believes that by practicing, a person flipping a coin will be able to land the coin on the preselected side (heads, for example) more often.

Description of Research: The researcher asks a person randomly selected from the general population to practice flipping a dime for 30 minutes on each of five consecutive days. At the end of the five-day period, the researcher asks the person to flip nine different dimes. Before each flip, the person is asked to state the side (heads or tails) that the coin will land on. After each flip, the result is recorded as either correct or incorrect, depending upon whether the coin landed on the intended side.

Type of Conclusion Possible: The binomial analysis will allow the researcher to determine if the number of correct outcomes of the coin tossing was significantly greater than would be expected by chance.

Comments: This is another good example of a scenario that falls into the gray area between uncontrolled observation and controlled experiment. Note that there is no true independent variable. The researcher has selected a single person for observation, and no measurement was taken before the five days of practice. This cannot be considered a controlled experiment.

If the number of correct coin toss outcomes is significantly greater than what would be expected by chance, the researcher might cautiously infer that there is some relationship between practicing to flip the coin and having the coin land on the intended side.

Because there are only two nominal categories—correct and incorrect—we have the option of using a chi square analysis or a binomial analysis. If there were more than two nominal categories, the chi square analysis would still be appropriate, but it would not be possible to use the binomial analysis.

Test Data:

Toss	Outcome
1	Correct
2	Incorrect
3	Correct
4	Correct
5	Correct
6	Correct
7	Correct
8	Correct
9	Correct

Specifics Regarding the Analysis: The binomial analysis helps the researcher to determine whether or not a particular series of outcomes differs significantly from what would be expected by chance.

Research Hypothesis: The researcher believes that practicing to flip the coin will increase the number of correct predictions of the coin toss. Symbolically, the research hypothesis—the alternative hypothesis—appears as follows

H_{alt}: (number correct)$_{a.p.}$ > (number correct)$_{chance}$

In plain English, the researcher is predicting that the number of correct predictions after practicing (a.p.) will be greater than the number of correct predictions expected by chance.

Null Hypothesis: As we noted in Chapter 9, we state the null hypothesis, for the sake of argument, on the assumption that our research hypothesis is incorrect. In the present case, the null hypothesis is that there is *no difference between the number of correct predictions made after practicing and the number of correct predictions expected by chance*. Symbolically

H_{null}: (number correct)$_{a.p.}$ = (number correct)$_{chance}$

Organizing the Raw Data: When you prepare the data for entry into the binomial formula—whether you do the calculations by hand or by computer—you need only identify the following values:

- the outcome of interest: correct prediction, in the present case.

- the number of trials: 9.

- the chance probability of the outcome of interest: .5.

Binomial Calculation: Once these values have been identified you may enter them into the computer or use the calculation formula as follows:

Step 1. List your data.
   The test data have already been tabulated.

Step 2. Count the number of times the outcome of interest occurred.
   In the present case, the person was correct on eight of the nine trials.

Step 3. Use the binomial formula to calculate the probability of being correct *at least* as many times as the person was correct.
   In this case, we calculate the probability of being correct on at least eight trials. We will have to calculate the probability of being correct on eight trials and the probability of being correct on nine trials, and then add the two probabilities together.
   For the calculations you will need to know the following three rules:

1. Factorialization is a mathematical operation (denoted by an exclamation point) in which the specified integer is multiplied successively by every smaller integer (down to 1). For example, consider four factorial: $4! = 4 \times 3 \times 2 \times 1$.

2. Zero factorial always equals 1: $0! = 1$.

3. Any number raised to the power of zero equals 1. For example, $3° = 1$.

Step 3a. Determine the probability of being correct on eight out of nine trials using the binomial formula

$$P = {}_NC_r p^r q^{N-r}$$
(C.5.1)

In the present case, the total number of trials is nine

$$N = 9$$

For this particular calculation we are finding the probability of being correct on eight of nine trials; therefore

$$r = 8$$

The probability of being correct on any given trial is .5

$$p = .5$$

The probability of being incorrect on any given trial is .5

$$q = .5$$

Let's first work with ${}_NC_r$

$${}_NC_r = \frac{N!}{r!(N-r)!}$$

In the present case

$${}_9C_8 = \frac{9!}{8! \times 1!}$$

$$= \frac{9 \times 8 \times 7 \times 6 \times 5 \times 4 \times 3 \times 2 \times 1}{(8 \times 7 \times 6 \times 5 \times 4 \times 3 \times 2 \times 1) \times 1}$$

$$= 9$$

This indicates that there are nine different ways to be correct on eight out of nine trials. Turning to $p^r q^{N-r}$

$$p^r q^{N-r} = .5^8 \times .5^1$$

$$= .003,906,25 \times .5$$

$$= .001,953,125$$

Rounding to five decimal places

$$p^r q^{N-r} = .00195$$

Combining the two parts of the formula

$${}_9P_8 = 9 \times .001,95 = .017,55$$

This is the probability of being correct on eight of nine trials.

Step 3b. Determine the probability of being correct on nine out of nine trials using the binomial formula in Eq. (C.5.1).

In this case

$$r = 9$$

The variables N, p, and q remain the same. Once again, let's first work with $_NC_r$

$$_9C_9 = \frac{9!}{9! \times 0!}$$

$$= \frac{9 \times 8 \times 7 \times 6 \times 5 \times 4 \times 3 \times 2 \times 1}{(9 \times 8 \times 7 \times 6 \times 5 \times 4 \times 3 \times 2 \times 1) \times 1}$$

$$= 1$$

This indicates that there is only one way to be correct on nine out of nine trials.

Turning to $p^r q^{N-r}$

$$p^r q^{N-r} = .5^9 \times .5^0$$

$$= .001,953,125 \times 1$$

$$= .001,953,125$$

Rounding to five decimal places

$$p^r q^{N-r} = .001,95$$

Combining the two parts of the formula

$$_9P_9 = 1 \times .001,95 = .001,95$$

This is the probability of being correct on nine out of nine trials.

Step 3c. Determine the probability of being correct on at least eight out of nine trials.
We must add the probabilities calculated in steps 3a and 3b

$$P(r \geqslant 8) = {}_8P_9 + {}_9P_9$$

$$= .017,55 + .001,95$$

$$= .0195$$

Step 4. Determine the alpha level that you will use to test the null hypothesis.
We assume .05, unless otherwise indicated

$$\alpha = .05$$

Step 5. Compare the probability calculated in step 3c to the alpha level. If the probability is less than the alpha level, reject the null hypothesis.
In this case, the probability is .0195, which is less than .05, and therefore, we reject the null hypothesis.

Step 6. State your conclusion in a standard statistical format using appropriate symbols.
In this case

$$P(r \geqslant 8) < .05$$

Step 7. State your statistical conclusion in words.
On the assumption that *the null hypothesis is true,* the probability that the number of correct responses would be greater than or equal to eight is less than .05. Therefore, the null hypothesis is *probably* not true, and the alternative hypothesis probably is true.

Step 8. State your final conclusion in plain English.
Given the data and the statistical conclusion, it is reasonable to argue that practice at coin flipping increased the likelihood that the coin would land as predicted.

This concludes the binomial analysis. As we already noted, the researcher's chosen procedure was not a controlled experiment and the sample was very small. Accordingly, the result should be regarded with considerable caution.

Calculation C.6 Simple Chi Square (One Nominal Variable)

Type of research: Observation
Number of variables: 1
Level of measurement: Nominal
Number of nominal categories: 3
Choice of analysis: Simple chi square

Motivation for Research: A researcher believes that the color of a package will affect the purchasing selections of the public.

Description of Research: The researcher places packages having identical contents and appearance—except for the color of the package—on display in a shopping mall. Three different colors are used: red, yellow, and green. The researcher makes sure that an equal number of each of the three colors is visible to the potential buyers at all times.

Type of Conclusion Possible: The simple chi square analysis will allow the researcher to determine if the numbers of red, yellow, and green packages differed significantly from what would be expected by chance.

Comments: This is yet another scenario that falls into the gray area between uncontrolled observation and controlled experiment. Note that there is no true independent variable.
     Because there are three nominal categories—red, yellow, and green—*binomial* analysis is not an option.

Test Data:

Purchase	Color
1	Red
2	Yellow
3	Red
4	Red
5	Green
6	Yellow
7	Red
8	Green
9	Red
10	Red
11	Yellow
12	Red
13	Green
14	Red
15	Red
16	Yellow
17	Red
18	Red
19	Red
20	Green
21	Red

Specifics Regarding the Analysis: The chi square analysis helps the researcher to determine whether or not a particular series of outcomes differs significantly from what would be expected by chance.

Research Hypothesis. The researcher believes that the color of the packaging will make a difference in consumer choice. Symbolically, the research hypothesis—the alternative hypothesis—appears as follows

H_{alt}: frequency$_{observed}$ ≠ frequency$_{chance}$

In plain English, the researcher is predicting that the number (frequency) of choices observed in each of the color categories will not be equal to the number (frequency) of choices in each category expected by chance.

Null Hypothesis: As we noted in Chapter 9, we state the null hypothesis, for the sake of argument, on the assumption that our research hypothesis is incorrect. In the present case, the null hypothesis is that there is *no difference between the number of choices in each color category and the number of choices expected by chance.* Symbolically

H_{null}: frequency$_{observed}$ = frequency$_{chance}$

Organizing the Raw Data: When you prepare the data for entry into the chi square calculation formula—whether you do the calculations by hand or by computer—you must identify the following:

- the categories of interest: red, yellow, green, in the present case.
- the number of trials: 21.
- the chance expectation for the number of occurrences in each category: red, 7; yellow, 7; green, 7.
- the observed number of occurrences in each category: red, 13; yellow, 4; green, 4.

Next you must determine the degrees of freedom (*df*). This is calculated by subtracting one from the total number of categories: in this case, $3 - 1 = 2$.

Chi Square Calculation: Once these values have been identified, you may enter them into the computer or use the following calculation formula

$$\chi^2 = \sum \frac{(O - E)^2}{E} \tag{C.6.1}$$

In this formula, *O* denotes the observed frequency, and *E* denotes the expected frequency. The procedure is as follows.

Step 1. List your data.
   The test data have already been tabulated.

Step 2. Identify the nominal categories.
   In this case, the categories are red, yellow, and green.

Step 3. Identify the number of nominal categories.
   There are three nominal categories in the present case.

Step 4. Count the observed frequency of occurrence in each category.
   For red, $O = 13$; for yellow, $O = 4$; for green, $O = 4$.

Step 5. Identify the total number of observations.
   The total number of observations is 21.

Step 6. Identify the expected frequency of occurrence in each category. This is the frequency that you would expect if the null hypothesis were true.
   If the null hypothesis were true we would expect the frequencies to be distributed equally across the three color categories. Thus, for red, $E = 7$; for yellow, $E = 7$; for green, $E = 7$.
   Note that each expected frequency value must be 5 or greater in order to conduct a valid chi square analysis.

Step 7. Subtract the expected frequency from the observed frequency in each category.
For red

$$O - E = 13 - 7 = +6$$

For yellow

$$O - E = 4 - 7 = -3$$

For green

$$O - E = 4 - 7 = -3$$

Notice the minus values when an expected frequency is larger than an observed frequency.

Step 8. Square the results of step 7 for each category.
For red

$$(O - E)^2 = +6^2 = +36$$

For yellow

$$(O - E)^2 = (-3)^2 = +9$$

For green

$$(O - E)^2 = (-3)^2 = +9$$

Notice that when you square a negative value the result is a positive value.

Step 9. For each category, divide the results of step 8 by the expected frequency for that category.
For red

$$\frac{(O - E)^2}{E} = \frac{36}{7} = 5.13$$

For yellow

$$\frac{(O - E)^2}{E} = \frac{9}{7} = 1.29$$

For green

$$\frac{(O - E)^2}{E} = \frac{9}{7} = 1.29$$

Step 10. Sum the results of step 9 across all categories. This completes the calculation of chi square according to Eq. (C.6.1).
In the prsent example

$$\chi^2 = \sum \frac{(O - E)^2}{E} = 5.14 + 1.29 + 1.29 = 7.72$$

Step 11. State your alpha level.
As usual, we assume

$$\alpha = .05$$

Step 12. Determine if you are doing a one-tailed or two-tailed test of your null hypothesis.

In this case, a one-tailed test is required. The alternative hypothesis states that the observed frequencies will differ from the expected frequencies but does not specify a direction. Although the alternative hypothesis does not specify a direction, the critical chi square values are in the upper tail of the chi square distribution. This occurs because the formula for chi square involves squaring the observed minus expected frequencies in the numerator, resulting in all positive chi square values.

Step 13. Look in a standard chi square table (Table B.3) to determine the critical chi square value for a one-tailed test with $\alpha = .05$ and two degrees of freedom.

We find that

$$(\chi^2_{critical} = 5.99; df = 2; \alpha = .05; \text{one-tailed})$$

Step 14. Compare the calculated chi square from step 10 to the critical chi square. If the calculated chi square is beyond the critical chi square, you should reject the null hypothesis.

The calculated chi square (7.72) is greater than the critical value (5.99), and we reject the null hypothesis.

Step 15. State your conclusion in a standard statistical format using appropriate symbols.

In the present case, an appropriate statement is as follows

$$(\chi^2_{calc} = 7.72; df = 2; p < .05; \text{one-tailed})$$

Step 16. State your statistical conclusion in words.

If the null hypothesis were true, the probability of arriving at a calculated chi square of 7.72—with two degrees of freedom and a one-tailed test—would be less than .05. Therefore, the null hypothesis *probably* isn't true, and the alternative hypothesis is a better bet.

Step 17. State your final conclusion in plain English.

Given the data and the statistical conclusion, it is reasonable to argue that the color of the package is a significant factor in consumer preference.

Calculation C.7 Complex Chi Square (Test of Independence)

Type of research: Experiment
Number of dependent variables: 1
Level of measurement: Nominal
Number of nominal categories: 2
Number of independent variables: 1
Choice of analysis: Chi square test of independence

Motivation for Research: A researcher believes that the ability to pass a test of hand steadiness will be improved by listening to classical music.

Description of Research: The researcher randomly selects 40 people from the general population and then randomly assigns 20 of these people to a control group and the remaining 20 to an experimental group. In the control group, each of the 20 people is asked to sit in a room for 15 minutes and to try to relax. In the experimental group, each of the 20 people is asked to sit in a room for 15 minutes and to try to relax by listening to classical music. All subjects in both the experimental and control groups are tested for their hand steadiness after the 15-minute relaxation period. The test is such that they either complete the task (pass) or fail to complete the task (fail).

Type of Conclusion Possible: The chi square test of independence will allow the researcher to determine if the ratio of passes to failures was significantly different for the experimental group who listened to classical music and the control group.

Comments: If the results of the chi square test of independence indicate that the ratio of passes to failures was significantly different for the two conditions, the researcher may conclude that listening to classical music had a significant effect on this ratio. If the percentage of passes is greater in the experimental group than in the control group, the researcher may conclude that listening to classical music significantly improved the percentage of passes for the experimental group.

Test Data:

| Music group | | Control group | |
Person	Test result	Person	Test result
1	Pass	21	Fail
2	Fail	22	Fail
3	Pass	23	Pass
4	Fail	24	Fail
5	Pass	25	Pass
6	Pass	26	Pass
7	Pass	27	Fail
8	Pass	28	Fail
9	Pass	29	Fail
10	Pass	30	Fail
11	Pass	31	Fail
12	Fail	32	Fail
13	Pass	33	Pass
14	Fail	34	Fail
15	Pass	35	Pass
16	Pass	36	Pass
17	Pass	37	Fail
18	Pass	38	Fail
19	Pass	39	Fail
20	Pass	40	Fail

Specifics Regarding the Analysis: The chi square test for independent groups helps the researcher to determine whether the proportion of measurements that fall into certain nominal categories in two separate samples differs significantly from what would be expected by chance.

Research Hypothesis: The researcher believes that listening to classical music will improve a person's ability to pass a test of hand steadiness. Symbolically, the research hypothesis—the alternative hypothesis—appears as follows:

H_{alt}: (pass rate)$_{music}$ > (pass rate)$_{control}$

In plain English, the researcher is predicting that the proportion of subjects passing the hand steadiness test in the classical music group will be significantly higher than the proportion of subjects passing the test in the control group.

Null Hypothesis: As we noted in Chapter 9, we state the null hypothesis, for the sake of argument, on the assumption that our research hypothesis is incorrect. In the present case, the null hypothesis is that there is *no difference between the proportion of subjects passing the hand steadiness test in the classical music group and the proportion passing the test in the control group.* Symbolically

H_{null}: (pass rate)$_{music}$ = (pass rate)$_{control}$

Organizing the Raw Data: When you prepare the data for entry into the chi square formula—whether you do the calculations by hand or by computer—you need to identify the following:

- the independent variable: music, in the present case.
- the two conditions of the experiment: classical music and control group.
- the number of subjects in each condition: 20 and 20.
- the dependent variable: performance on hand steadiness test (pass, fail)

Chi Square Test of Independence Calculation: Once these characteristics have been identified, you must count the number of subjects in each group that fall into the dependent variable categories (pass and fail). Then you may enter them into the computer or use the following calculation formula

$$\chi^2 = \sum \frac{(O - E)^2}{E} \tag{C.7.1}$$

In this formula, O denotes the observed frequency, and E denotes the expected frequency.
The calculation procedure is as follows.

Step 1. List your data.
   The test data have already been tabulated.

Step 2. Identify the separate conditions of the independent variable.
   There are two separate conditions of the independent variable: music and control.

Step 3. Identify the separate nominal categories of the dependent variable.
   There are two separate nominal categories of the dependent variable: pass and fail.

Step 4. Count the observed frequency of occurrence for each of the nominal categories of the dependent variable in each of the conditions of the independent variable and create a summary table.
   The observed frequencies are summarized in Table C.7.1.

Step 5. Sum the frequencies for the independent variable conditions and the dependent variable categories.
   The corresponding sums are also shown in Table C.7.1.

TABLE C.7.1 **Summary of Observed Fequencies**

		Dependent variable		Sum
		Pass	Fail	
Independent variable	Music	16	4	20
	Control	6	14	20
	Sum	22	18	

Step 6. Identify the total number of observations.
   In the present case, there are 40 observations altogether.

Step 7. Identify each unique combination of independent and dependent variable categories as a cell.
   In the present case, there are four cells: music pass, music fail, control pass, and control fail.

Step 8. Identify each row total and each column total by an appropriate label.
   There are two row totals

$$\sum\nolimits_{music} = 20$$
$$\sum\nolimits_{control} = 20$$

   There are two column totals

$$\sum\nolimits_{pass} = 22$$
$$\sum\nolimits_{fail} = 18$$

Step 9. Calculate an expected frequency corresponding to each observed frequency by dividing the appropriate column total by the total number of observations (N_{total}) and multiplying this result by the appropriate row total.
   For music pass

$$E_{MP} = \frac{\sum_{pass}}{N_{total}} \times \sum_{music}$$

$$= \frac{22}{40} \times 20$$

$$= 0.55 \times 20$$

$$= 11$$

For control pass

$$E_{CP} = \frac{\sum_{pass}}{N_{total}} \times \sum_{control}$$

$$= \frac{22}{40} \times 20$$

$$= 0.55 \times 20$$

$$= 11$$

For music fail

$$E_{MF} = \frac{\sum_{fail}}{N_{total}} \times \sum_{music}$$

$$= \frac{18}{40} \times 20$$

$$= 0.45 \times 20$$

$$= 9$$

For control fail

$$E_{CF} = \frac{\sum_{fail}}{N_{total}} \times \sum_{control}$$

$$= \frac{18}{40} \times 20$$

$$= 0.45 \times 20$$

$$= 9$$

Step 10. Create a summary table of the expected frequencies. Note that each expected frequency must be 5 or greater in order to use the chi square analysis.

The expected frequencies for the present example are summarized in Table C.7.2. Note that the row and column sums remain the same for the observed frequencies and the expected frequencies.

TABLE C.7.2 **Summary of Expected Frequencies**

| | | Dependent variable | | |
		Pass	Fail	Sum
Independent	Music	11	9	20
variable	Control	11	9	20
	Sum	22	18	

Step 11. Apply the observed and expected frequencies to Eq. (C.7.1) to obtain the calculated chi square.

In the present case

$$\chi^2 = \sum \frac{(O - E)^2}{E}$$

$$= \frac{(16 - 11)^2}{11} + \frac{(4 - 9)^2}{9} + \frac{(6 - 11)^2}{11} + \frac{(14 - 9)^2}{9}$$

$$= \frac{+5^2}{11} + \frac{-5^2}{9} + \frac{-5^2}{11} + \frac{+5^2}{9}$$

$$= \frac{25}{11} + \frac{25}{9} + \frac{25}{11} + \frac{25}{9}$$

$$= 2.2727 + 2.7778 + 2.2727 + 2.7778$$

$$= 10.101$$

Step 12. State your alpha level.
As usual, we assume

$$\alpha = .05$$

Step 13. Determine the degrees of freedom by means of the following formula

$$df = (R - 1) \times (C - 1) \tag{C.7.2}$$

where R denotes the number of rows in the frequency table, and C denotes the numbers of columns. In the present case

$$df = (2 - 1) \times (2 - 1)$$

$$= 1 \times 1$$

$$= 1$$

Step 14. Look in a standard chi square table (Table B.3) to determine the critical chi square for the given alpha level and degrees of freedom.
We find that

$$(\chi^2_{crit} = 3.841; df = 1; \alpha = .05)$$

Step 15. Compare the calculated chi square to the critical chi square. If the calculated chi square is beyond the critical chi square, you must reject the null hypothesis.
In the present case, the calculated chi square (10.101) is greater than the critical value (3.841), and we reject the null hypothesis.

Step 16. State your statistical conclusion using a standard format and appropriate symbols.
An appropriate statement is as follows

$$(\chi^2_{calc} = 10.101; df = 1; p < .05)$$

Step 17. State your statistical conclusion in words.
If the null hypothesis were true, the probability of arriving at a calculated chi square value of 10.101 with one degree of freedom would be less than .05. Therefore, the null hypothesis probably is not true, and the alternative hypothesis probably is true. In the present case, this means that the proportion of people passing the hand steadiness test was significantly higher in the group who listened to classical music.

Step 18. State your final conclusion in plain English.
Given the data and the statistical conclusion, it is reasonable to argue that listening to classical music significantly increased the number of people who passed the hand steadiness test.

Calculation C.8 Eta (Correlation Coefficient)

Type of research: Observation
Number of variables: 2
Levels of measurement: Predictor variable: nominal
                          Predicted variable: interval/ratio
Choice of analysis: Eta

Motivation for Research: A researcher believes that a person's political perspective in the senior year of college can be used to predict his or her yearly income five years after graduation.

Description of Research: The researcher randomly selects 20 students from the population of seniors in college. All 20 students are asked to choose which of two labels—liberal or conservative—is most appropriate to describe their political perspective. Five years later, these same students are contacted and asked to state their yearly income.

Type of Conclusion Possible: The eta analysis will allow the researcher to determine if the political perspective of students in their senior year is correlated with their yearly income five years after graduation. If there is a sufficiently high degree of correlation, the researcher may conclude that political perspective in senior year—as operationally defined in this study—may be used to predict the students' yearly incomes five years after graduation.

Comments: One of the variables being measured—political perspective—is at the nominal level. The other variable—yearly income—is at the ratio level. Neither the Pearson r nor the Spearman r analysis is appropriate.
    In the present example, there are only two conditions of the nominal variable—liberal and conservative. If there were more than three levels of the nominal variable, the interpretation of the analysis would be more complex.

Test Data:

Person	Political perspective	Income (Thousands of $)
1	Liberal	25
2	Liberal	40
3	Conservative	50
4	Liberal	30
5	Conservative	45
6	Conservative	15
7	Liberal	28
8	Conservative	60
9	Conservative	90
10	Liberal	18
11	Conservative	80
12	Conservative	75
13	Conservative	110
14	Liberal	50
15	Conservative	60
16	Conservative	78
17	Conservative	90
18	Liberal	20
19	Conservative	150
20	Liberal	60

Specifics Regarding the Analysis: The eta analysis helps the researcher to determine whether or not there is a significant correlation between two variables when the predictor variable is at the nominal level and the predicted variable is at the interval or ratio level. These two variables must represent a pair of observed measurements for each of the subjects or items in the observation. In the present study, each of the 20 people is characterized by a pair of observed measurements: political perspective and income. For person 13, for example, the observed measurements are: conservative and $110,000.
    The calculations result in a single eta value ranging from 0 to +1.00. Higher eta corresponds

to greater correlation between the two variables. In the present example, the research hypothesis predicts a correlation such that conservatives would tend to have higher incomes than liberals.

Research Hypothesis: The researcher believes that political philosophy is a factor in predicting a person's income. Note, however, that this is *not* an experiment in which political philosophy is manipulated as an independent variable and income measured as a dependent variable. Instead, political philosophy and income are each simply measured for each of the 20 subjects in the study. Therefore, the research hypothesis here is that the measured political philosophy (variable at the nominal level) will be correlated with the measured income (variable at the interval or ratio level). Symbolically, the research hypothesis—the alternative hypothesis—appears as follows

$$H_{alt}: \eta_{P,I} > 0$$

In plain English, the researcher is predicting that the correlation between measured political philosophy (P) and measured income (I) will be greater than zero in the population from which the sample was drawn.

Null Hypothesis: As we noted in Chapter 9, we state the null hypothesis, for the sake of argument, on the assumption that our research hypothesis is incorrect. In the present case, the null hypothesis is that there is *no correlation between political philosophy and income.*

$$H_{null}: \eta_{P,I} = 0$$

Organizing the Raw Data: When you prepare the data for entry into the eta calculation formula—whether you do the calculations by hand or by computer—you must first label one of the variables as the X variable and the other as the Y variable. The X variable should be the variable that could logically be used to predict the Y variable. In the present case, the intention is to predict the income of a person on the basis of that person's political philosophy. Therefore, political philosophy—operationally defined by categorization as either conservative or liberal—is identified as the X variable, and income—operationally defined as income reported on an income tax statement—is identified as the Y variable.

After determining which is the X variable and which is the Y variable, you need to identify the X value and Y value for each observation in the sample. There is one pair of X, Y values for each of the 20 people in this observation. Each X value and each Y value can be subscripted for identification. For example, X_5, Y_5 correspond to person 5 in our sample and, thus, according to the test data

$$X_5 = \text{conservative}$$

$$Y_5 = \$45,000$$

Eta Calculation: Once the X and Y values have been identified, you may enter the data into the computer or use the calculation formula as follows.

Step 1. Group your data according to the categories of the predictor variable.
　　　　In the present case, the test data may be grouped as follows:

Liberal	Conservative
25	50
40	45
30	15
28	60
18	90
50	80
20	75
60	110
	60
	78
	90
	150

Step 2. Square each data value (each X) and place the result (X^2) next to the original data value (Table C.8.1).

Step 3. Sum the X values and the X^2 values for each group (Table C.8.1).

TABLE C.8.1 **Results of Squaring and Summing**

	Liberal		Conservative	
	X	X^2	X	X^2
	25	625	50	2500
	40	1600	45	2025
	30	900	15	225
	28	784	60	3600
	18	324	90	8100
	50	2500	80	6400
	20	400	75	5625
	60	3600	110	12,100
			60	3600
			78	6084
			90	8100
			150	22,500
Sum	271	10,733	903	80,859

Step 4. Determine the *total sum of squares* by means of the following formula

$$SS_{total} = \sum X_{all}^2 - \frac{\left(\sum X_{all}\right)^2}{N_{total}}$$ (C.8.1)

The first term in Eq. (C.8.1) requires that you square each of the scores in the entire data set (20 scores, in the present case), and then sum all of these squared values

$$\sum X_{all}^2 = 25^2 + 40^2 + \cdots + 150^2$$
$$= 625 + 1600 + \cdots + 22,500$$

Since we already squared all 20 of the data values in step 2, we can obtain the sum of all 20 squared data values by summing the corresponding column totals from Table C.8.1

$$\sum X_{all}^2 = 10,733 + 80,859$$
$$= 91,592$$

The second term in Eq. (C.8.1) requires that you sum all the data points first, square the result, and then divide by the total number of data points (N_{total}). Since we already summed the data points for each condition in step 3, we can obtain the sum of all the data points by summing the corresponding column totals from Table C.8.1

$$\sum X_{all} = 271 + 903$$
$$= 1174$$

Now we square this sum

$$\left(\sum X_{all}\right)^2 = 1174^2 = 1,378,276$$

We divide this squared sum by N_{total}

$$\frac{(\sum X_{all})^2}{N_{total}} = \frac{1,378,276}{20} = 68,913.8$$

Finally, we substract this term from the first term

$$SS_{total} = 91,592 - 68,913.8$$
$$= 22,678.2$$

Step 5. Determine the *between-groups sum of squares* by means of the following formula

$$SS_{B-G} = \frac{(\sum X_L)^2}{n_L} + \frac{(\sum X_C)^2}{n_C} - \frac{(\sum X_{all})^2}{N_{total}} \qquad \text{(C.8.2)}$$

The sum of the scores for each of the groups is obtained from Table C.8.1, then squared, and divided by the number of data values in the appropriate group. The last term in Eq. (C.8.2) is the same as in Eq. (C.8.1). The results of applying Eq. (C.8.2) are as follows

$$SS_{B-G} = \frac{271^2}{8} + \frac{903^2}{12} - 68,913.8$$

$$= \frac{73,441}{8} + \frac{81,5409}{12} - 68,913.8$$

$$= 9180.125 + 67,950.75 - 68,913.8$$

$$= 77,130.875 - 68,913.8$$

$$= 8217.075$$

Step 6. Determine the *within-groups sum of squares* by means of the following formula

$$SS_{w-g} = SS_{total} - SS_{B-G} \qquad \text{(C.8.3)}$$

In the present case

$$SS_{w-g} = 22,678.2 - 8217.075$$
$$= 14,461.13$$

Step 7. Determine the degrees of freedom for the following sources of variance: total-data, between-groups, and within-groups variance.
For the total-data variance

$$df_{total} = N_{total} - 1 \qquad \text{(C.8.4)}$$

In the present case

$$df_{total} = 20 - 1 = 19$$

For the between-groups variance

$$df_{B-G} = K - 1 \qquad \text{(C.8.5)}$$

where K is the number of conditions. In the present case

$$df_{B-G} = 2 - 1 = 1$$

For the within-groups variance

$$df_{w-g} = N_{total} - K \tag{C.8.6}$$

In the present case

$$df_{w-g} = 20 - 2 = 18$$

Step 8. Determine the *mean square* (MS) for each source of variance from the general formula

$$MS = \frac{SS}{df} \tag{C.8.7}$$

For the total-data variance

$$MS_{total} = \frac{SS_{total}}{df_{total}} = \frac{22,678.2}{19}$$
$$= 1193.589$$

For the between-groups variance

$$MS_{B-G} = \frac{SS_{B-G}}{df_{B-G}} = \frac{8217.075}{1}$$
$$= 8217.075$$

For the within-groups variance

$$MS_{w-g} = \frac{SS_{w-g}}{df_{w-g}} = \frac{14,461.13}{18}$$
$$= 803.3961$$

Step 9. Calculate the eta coefficient by means of the following formula

$$\eta = \sqrt{\frac{MS_{total} - MS_{w-g}}{MS_{total}}} \tag{C.8.8}$$

In the present case

$$\eta = \sqrt{\frac{390.1929}{1193.589}}$$
$$= \sqrt{0.326,907}$$
$$= .571,758$$

Step 10. Determine you alpha level.
$\qquad$ We assume .05 unless otherwise specified

$$\alpha = .05$$

Step 11. Look in a standard eta table (Table B.6) to determine the critical eta. Be sure to use the appropriate alpha level, number of pairs of data, and number of nominal categories for the predictor variable. For an alpha level of .05, twenty pairs of data, and two nominal categories for the predictor variable, the critical eta value is .2714.

$$\eta_{crit} = .2714$$

Step 12. Compare the calculated eta value to the corresponding critical eta value. If the calculated value is equal to or greater than the critical value, you must reject the null hypothesis; otherwise, you may not reject the null hypothesis.

In the present case, the calculated eta (.571,758) is greater than the critical eta (.4399); therefore, we reject the null.

Step 13. State your conclusion in a standard statistical format using appropriate symbols.

An appropriate statement is as follows

$(\eta_{calc} = .571,758$; two predictor categories; twenty pairs; $p < .05)$

Step 14. State your statistical conclusion in words.

If the null hypothesis were true, the probability of arriving at a calculated eta of .571,758 with two predictor categories would be less than .05. Therefore, the null hypothesis is *probably* not true, and the alternative hypothesis is a better bet.

Step 15. State your final conclusion in plain English.

Given the data and the statistical conclusion, it is reasonable to argue that political perspective as a college senior is significantly correlated with yearly income five years later. This supports the researcher's argument that a person's political perspective in the senior year of college can be used to predict his or her yearly income five years after graduation.

Calculation C.9 Friedman (Nonparametric, Within Groups)

Type of research:	Experiment
Number of dependent variables:	1
Level of measurement:	Interval/ratio
Assumptions met:	No
Number of independent variables:	1
Conditions of independent variable:	3
Type of design:	Within-groups (w-g)
Choice of analysis:	Friedman

Motivation for Research: A researcher believes that listening to classical music will improve a person's reaction time.

Description of Research: The researcher randomly selects 10 people from the general population. The reaction time of each person is first measured on a standard task. Then, each person is asked to sit in a room for 15 minutes and to try to relax by listening to classical music. At the end of the 15-minute relaxation period, the reaction time of each person is measured again on the same standard task. On the following day, each of these 10 people is asked to sit in a room for 30 minutes and to try to relax by listening to classical music. After the 30-minute relaxation period, the reaction time of each person is again measured on the same standard task.

Type of Conclusion Possible: The Friedman within-groups analysis will allow the researcher to determine if the ranked reaction times for the three conditions of the experiment differ significantly in any way. If the Friedman analysis indicates that there is some difference—in other words, that the rankings for the three groups are not equal—the researcher may draw the general conclusion that listening to music does have an effect on reaction time.

Comments: If we obtain significant results in an ANOVA for within-groups or matched-groups experiments, which is the parametric equivalent of the nonparametric Friedman, we may follow up with an additional analysis—for example, a Scheffe—in order to make more specific comparisons between the means of the separate experimental conditions. The corresponding post-Friedman analysis is the Nemenyi analysis, which allows the researcher to make all possible comparisons between any two conditions of the experiment. The Nemenyi analysis is beyond the scope of this book.

Assumptions: Suppose that the parametric assumptions cannot be met.

Person	Control group Reaction time	Person	15-minute condition Reaction time	Person	30-minute condition Reaction time
1	2.69	1	2.55	1	2.37
2	2.72	2	2.57	2	2.43
3	2.56	3	2.40	3	2.42
4	2.53	4	2.48	4	2.38
5	2.60	5	2.46	5	2.41
6	2.33	6	2.58	6	2.25
7	2.79	7	2.67	7	2.58
8	2.86	8	2.53	8	2.71
9	2.58	9	2.54	9	2.66
10	2.68	10	2.61	10	2.56

Specifics Regarding the Analysis: The Friedman analysis helps the researcher to determine whether or not the variability between two or more groups is greater than would be expected by chance.

Research Hypothesis: The researcher believes that a person's reaction time will be shorter after longer periods of listening to classical music. Symbolically, the research hypothesis—the alternative hypothesis—appears as follows

$$H_{alt}: \mu_{ranks_{30min}} < \mu_{ranks_{15min}} < \mu_{ranks_{control}}$$

In plain English, the researcher is predicting that the average rank of the reaction times after listening to classical music for 30 minutes will be significantly lower than the average rank of the reaction times after 15 minutes, which, in turn, will be significantly lower than the average rank of the reaction times in the control.

Null Hypothesis: As we noted in Chapter 9, we state the null hypothesis, for the sake of argument, on the assumption that our research hypothesis is incorrect. In the present case, the null hypothesis is that there is *no difference between the average ranks of the reaction times of all three groups*. Symbolically

$$H_{null}: \mu_{ranks_{30min}} = \mu_{ranks_{15min}} = \mu_{ranks_{control}}$$

Organizing the Raw Data: When you prepare the data for entry into the Friedman test formula—whether you do the calculations by hand or by computer—it is necessary to identify the following:

- the independent variable: music, in the present case.

- the conditions of the experiment: control, 15 minutes, and 30 minutes.

- the number of subjects in each condition: 10.

- the dependent variable: reaction time.

Friedman Test Calculation: Once these values have been identified, you may enter them into the computer or use the calculation formula as follows.

Step 1. List your data.

The test data have already been tabulated.

Step 2. Rank each subject's scores from low (1) to high (k), where k is the total number of conditions. Then sum the ranks for each condition.

The results of ranking and summing the test data are shown in Table C.9.1.

TABLE C.9.1 Ranks of Individual Scores in Three Conditions

Person	Control	15-minute condition	30-minute condition
1	3	2	1
2	3	2	1
3	3	1	2
4	3	2	1
5	3	2	1
6	2	3	1
7	3	2	1
8	3	2	1
9	2	1	3
10	3	2	1
Sum:	28	19	13

Grand sum of all ranks: 60

Step 3. Calculate the *sum of squares for independent variable conditions* by means of the following formula

$$SS_{B-iv-C} = \frac{\left(\sum R_1\right)^2}{N_1} + \frac{\left(\sum R_2\right)^2}{N_2} + \cdots + \frac{\left(\sum R_k\right)^2}{N_k} - \frac{\left(\sum R_{all}\right)^2}{N_{total}} \qquad (C.9.1)$$

In the present case

$$SS_{B-iv-C} = \frac{28^2}{10} + \frac{19^2}{10} + \frac{13^2}{10} - \frac{60^2}{30}$$

$$= \frac{784}{10} + \frac{361}{10} + \frac{169}{10} - \frac{3600}{30}$$

$$= 78.4 + 36.1 + 16.9 - 120$$

$$= 131.4 - 120$$

$$= 11.4$$

Step 4. Calculate the *within-subject sum of squares* by means of the following formula

$$SS_{w-s} = R_2^2 + R_2^2 + \cdots + R_N^2 - j\frac{\left(\sum TPR\right)^2}{k} \qquad (C.9.2)$$

where j is the total number of subjects; $\sum TPR$ is the sum of the total possible ranks for a given subject.

In the present case

$$j = 10$$

$$\sum TPR = 1 + 2 + 3 = 6$$

$$SS_{w\text{-}g} = 3^2 + 3^2 + \cdots + 1^2 - 10 \times \frac{6^2}{3}$$

$$= 9 + 9 + \cdots + 1 - 10 \times \frac{36}{3}$$

$$= 140 - 10 \times 12$$

$$= 140 - 120$$

$$= 20$$

Step 5. Compute the Friedman chi square value by means of the following formula

$$\chi^2 = \frac{j(k-1)SS_{B\text{-}iv\text{-}C}}{SS_{w\text{-}s}} \tag{C.9.3}$$

In the present case

$$\chi^2 - \frac{10(3)11.4}{20}$$

$$= \frac{342}{20}$$

$$= 11.4$$

Step 6. Determine the degrees of freedom using the following formula

$$df = k - 1$$

In the present case

$$df = 3 - 1 = 2$$

Step 7. Determine your alpha level.
We assume .05, unless otherwise specified

$$\alpha = .05$$

Step 8. Look up the critical chi square value in a standard chi square table (Table B.3).
With two degrees of freedom and an alpha level of .05, the critical chi square value is 5.99.

Step 9. Compare the calculated chi square value to the critical chi square value. If the calculated value is greater than or equal to the critical value, you must reject the null hypothesis; otherwise, you must reject the null hypothesis.
In the present case, the calculated chi square (11.4) is greater than the critical value (5.99); therefore, we reject the null.

Step 10. State your conclusion in a standard statistical format using appropriate symbols.
An appropriate statement is as follows

$$(\chi^2_{calc} = 11.4;\ df = 2;\ p < .05)$$

Step 11. State your statistical conclusion in words.

If the null hypothesis were true, the probability of arriving at a calculated chi square of 11.4 with two degrees of freedom would be less than .05. Therefore, the null hypothesis is *probably* not true, and the alternative hypothesis probably is true.

Step 12. State your final conclusion in plain English.

Given the data and the statistical conclusion, it is reasonable to argue that listening to classical music had an effect on the reaction times of the subjects.

Calculation C.10 Grouped Frequency Distributions

In this section, we consider two separate procedures, for integer measurements and decimal measurements. Although these are very lengthy, it is important to go through both of them if you really want to understand the logic by which group frequency distributions are constructed. It is also important to recognize the difference between the limits established with decimal measurements and with integer measurements.

Part A. Grouped Frequency Distribution (Integer Measurements): The sample data for these calculations, originally presented in Table 3.3, are listed again in Table C.10.1, for your convenience.

TABLE C.10.1 Measured Body Weights (to the Nearest Pound) for 20 People (Randomly selected from Database A.1)

| 164 | 111 | 163 | 131 | 155 | 107 | 123 | 136 | 145 | 174 |
| 152 | 127 | 149 | 141 | 121 | 175 | 155 | 136 | 138 | 161 |

Here are the steps you should follow when creating a grouped frequency distribution.

Step 1. Find the highest-valued data point in our data set.

For the data in Table C.10.1, the highest-valued data point is 175.

Step 2. Find the lowest-valued data point in your data set.

For the data in Table C.10.1, the lowest-valued data point is 107.

Step 3. Determine the degree of precision for the most precise data point in your data set.

All the data points in Table C.10.1 are whole numbers and have the same degree of precision. The degree of precision is units of 1.

Step 4. Calculate the precision range for your data. The precision range is simply the total number of possible score values that you would find by counting upward from the lowest-valued data point—in units corresponding to the highest degree of precision for your data set—until you reach the highest-valued data point.

The precision range can be calculated, without counting, by the following procedure.

1. Subtract the lowest-valued data point from the highest-valued data point.
2. Add one unit of the highest degree of precision for your data.
3. Divide by one unit of the highest degree of precision for your data.

For the data in Table C.10.1, the degree of precision is units of 1, and thus:

1. $175 - 107 = 68$.
2. $68 + 1 = 69$.
3. $\frac{69}{1} = 69$.

The precision range is 69. If you started with the score 107 and counted upward in increments of 1 (the highest degree of precision for your data) until you reached 175, you would count 69 possible score values.

Step 5. Select a class interval size such that the total number of class intervals will be at least 7 and at most 17.

If you are considering a class interval size less than 10, sizes of 3, 5, or 7 are recommended. These odd-sized class intervals have the advantage that it is easy to find the middle of the interval.

If you are considering a class interval size of 10 or more, multiples of 10 are recommended: for example, 10, 20, 30, 40, 50, 60, 70, 100.

To estimate the number of class intervals resulting from a given class interval size, divide the precision range by the intended class interval size. To estimate the class interval size resulting from a given number of class intervals, divide the precision range by the intended number of class intervals.

For the data in Table C.10.1, the number of class intervals resulting from a possible class interval size of 3 would be

$$\frac{69}{3} = 23$$

Since 23 is greater than 17, which is the maximum recommended number of class intervals, we try the next recommended class interval size of 5

$$\frac{69}{5} = 13.8$$

We round this result to 14. Since 14 is greater than 7, which is the minimum recommended number of class intervals, and less than 17, the maximum recommended number of class intervals, a class interval size of 5 would be an appropriate choice.

If we chose to have 12 class intervals, the class interval size would be

$$\frac{69}{12} = 5.75$$

We round this result to 6. Since 6 is not one of the recommended class interval sizes, we can either go down to 5 or up to 7. As we already know, choosing a class interval size of 5 results in 14 class intervals, which is within the recommended range, and we conclude that a class interval size of 5 would be an appropriate choice.

Notice that, in selecting an appropriate class interval size, you must consider both the desired approximate total number of class intervals and the desired approximate class interval size. Then you may divide the precision range by either of these approximations to estimate the other. After a few attempts, you should be able to zero in on a class interval size and a total number of class intervals that are acceptable.

On the basis of our estimates, let's select a class interval size of 5 for the data in Table C.10.1.

Step 6. Find the values that will mark the beginning and the end of each of the class intervals.

The beginning of the first class interval is simply the lowest-valued data point.

For the data in Table C.10.1, the lowest-valued data point is 107; therefore, begin the lowest class interval with 107. This will be referred to hereafter as the **lower apparent limit of the lowest class interval**.

Step 7. After finding the beginning of the lowest class interval, determine the value that will mark the end of the lowest class interval, by the following procedure.

1. Determine the unit of highest precision. (This was already done in step 3.)
2. Determine the class interval size. (This was already done in step 5.)
3. Subtract the unit of highest precision from the class interval size.
4. Add the result to the lower apparent limit. This will be referred to hereafter as the **upper apparent limit of the lowest class interval**.

For the data in Table C.10.1:

1. The unit of highest precision is 1.
2. The class interval size is 5.
3. $5 - 1 = 4$.
4. $107 + 4 = 111$.

Thus, the upper apparent limit of the lowest class interval is 111. Now we know that the upper and lower apparent limits of the lowest class interval are

107–111

Note that, if you start with the lower apparent limit and count up in increments of the unit of highest precision until you reach the upper apparent limit, you will have counted the number of score values corresponding to the class interval size. For the data in Table C.10.1

$107 + 1 = 108$

$108 + 1 = 109$

$109 + 1 = 110$

$110 + 1 = 111$

Thus, five score values are included in this class interval

107, 108, 109, 110, 111

The class interval size is 5.

Step 8. After finding the upper and lower apparent limits of the lowest class interval, find the upper and lower apparent limits for each successively higher class interval until all of your class intervals are completed. This is done simply by adding the class interval size to each apparent limit.

For the data in Table C.10.1

$107 + 5 = 112$

$111 + 5 = 116$

Now we've established two class intervals

112–116

107–111

The next class interval is obtained in the same way

$112 + 5 = 117$

$116 + 5 = 121$

Thus, we have established three class intervals

117–121

112–116

107–111

We continue in this way until we have identified all 14 class intervals.

Make sure, when you finish, that the lowest class interval includes your lowest-valued data point and your highest class interval includes your highest-valued data point.

For the data in Table C.10.1, the class intervals are as follows

172–176

167–171

162–166

157–161

152–156

147–151

142–146

137–141

132–136

127–131

122–126

117–121

112–116

107–111

and we note that the lowest-valued data point (107) falls in the lowest class interval, while the highest-valued data point (175) falls in the highest class interval.

Step 9. After finding the upper and lower apparent limits for all of your class intervals the next step is to find the upper and lower real limits, as follows.

1. Determine the unit of highest precision. (This was accomplished in step 3.)
2. Divide the unit of highest precision by 2.
3. Subtract half the unit of highest precision from each lower apparent limit to determine each lower real limit.
4. Add half the unit of highest precision to each upper apparent limit to determine each upper real limit.

For the data in Table C.10.1, we proceed as follows.

1. The unit of highest precision is 1.
2. $1/2 = 0.5$.
3. $107 - 0.5 = 106.5$. The lower real limit for lowest class interval is 106.5.
4. $111 + .5 = 111.5$. The upper real limit for the highest class interval is 111.5.

After completing this procedure for all class intervals, we obtain the following results for the data in Table C.10.1

171.5–176.5

166.5–171.5

161.5–166.5

156.5–161.5

151.5–156.5

146.5–151.5

141.5–146.5

136.5–141.5

131.5–136.5

126.5–131.5

121.5–126.5

116.5–121.5

111.5–116.5

106.5–111.5

Note that upper real limit for each class interval is identical to the lower real limit of the class interval immediately above it. This is intentional: the real limits are established so that there are no gaps between the class intervals.

Step 10. After establishing real limits for all of the class intervals, the next step is to count the number of data points in your data set that fall into each of the class intervals, as follows.

1. Count the number of data points in your data set that fall between the upper and lower real limits of your lowest class interval. (Write this frequency count next to the class interval.)
2. Count the number of data points in your data set that fall between the upper and lower real limits of your next highest class interval.
3. Continue until all data points have been accounted for.

For the data in Table C.10.1, we proceed as follows.

1. Two data points—107 and 111—fall between the upper and lower real limits of 106.5 and 111.5.
2. No data points fall between the upper and lower real limits of 111.5 and 116.5.
3. One data point—121—falls between the upper and lower real limits of 116.5 and 121.5.

After completing this procedure for all the class intervals, we obtain the following results for the data in Table C.10.1

Real class intervals	Frequency
171.5–176.5	2
166.5–171.5	0
161.5–166.5	2
156.5–161.5	1
151.5–156.5	3
146.5–151.5	1
141.5–146.5	1
136.5–141.5	2
131.5–136.5	2
126.5–131.5	2
121.5–126.5	1
116.5–121.5	1
111.5–116.5	0
106.5–111.5	2

Note that these results are the same as in Table 3.8, except that Table 3.8 uses the apparent limits of the class intervals.

Step 11. It is often useful to determine cumulative frequencies for each of the class intervals in a grouped frequency distribution. The cumulative frequency is simply the accumulated frequency count for all the class intervals below and including the class interval in question. Proceed as follows.

1. The cumulative frequency count for the lowest class interval is simply the frequency count for that interval, since the lowest class interval has no other class intervals below it.
2. To determine the cumulative frequency for the next highest class interval, add the frequency value for that interval to the cumulative frequency that you have just calculated.
3. Continue in this way for all the class intervals.

For the data in Table C.10.1, this procedure is as follows.

1. The frequency count for the lowest class interval (106.5–111.5) is 2; therefore, the cumulative frequency for the lowest class interval is also 2.

Real class intervals	Frequency	Cumulative frequency
106.5–111.5	2	2

2. The frequency value for the next highest class interval 111.5–116.5 is 0. Add this to the cumulative frequency that you have just determined: $2 + 0 = 2$. This is the cumulative frequency for class interval 111.5–116.5.

Real class intervals	Frequency	Cumulative frequency
111.5–116.5	0	2
106.5–111.5	2	2

3. The frequency value for the next highest class interval 116.5–121.5 is 1. Add this to the cumulative frequency that you have just determined: $1 + 2 = 3$. This is the cumulative frequency for class interval 116.5–121.5.

Real class intervals	Frequency	Cumulative frequency
116.5–121.5	1	3
111.5–116.5	0	2
106.5–111.5	2	2

After completing this procedure for all the class intervals, we obtain the following results for the data in Table C.10.1.

Real class intervals	Frequency	Cumulative frequency
171.5–176.5	2	20
166.5–171.5	0	18
161.5–166.5	2	18
156.5–161.5	1	16
151.5–156.5	3	15
146.5–151.5	1	12
141.5–146.5	1	11
136.5–141.5	2	10
131.5–136.5	2	8
126.5–131.5	2	6
121.5–126.5	1	4
116.5–121.5	1	3
111.5–116.5	0	2
106.5–111.5	2	2

Finally, the complete grouped frequency distribution is shown in Table C.10.2.

TABLE C.10.2 Complete Grouped Frequency Distribution for 20 Body Weights
(Data from Table C.10.1)

Real class intervals	Apparent class intervals	Frequency	Cumulative frequency
171.5–176.5	172–176	2	20
166.5–171.5	167–171	0	18
161.5–166.5	162–166	2	18
156.5–161.5	157–161	1	16
151.5–156.5	152–156	3	15
146.5–151.5	147–151	1	12
141.5–146.5	142–146	1	11
136.5–141.5	137–141	2	10
131.5–136.5	132–136	2	8
126.5–131.5	127–131	2	6
121.5–126.5	122–126	1	4
116.5–121.5	117–121	1	3
111.5–116.5	112–116	0	2
106.5–111.5	107–111	2	2

Part B. Grouped Frequency Distribution (Decimal Measurements): The data for these calculations, originally presented in Table 3.11, are listed again in Table C.10.3 for your convenience.

TABLE C.10.3 Measured Annual Rainfall
(to Nearest Tenth of an Inch)
for 20 Geographic Locations
(Randomly selected from Database C.1)

8.1	10.8	6.6	8.2	10.7	7.8	9.3	9.9
9.7	9.3	10.3	12.4	7.8	4.6	5.7	7.2
9.6	8.9	5.1	9.5				

Here are the steps you should follow when creating a complete grouped frequency distribution for these data.

Step 1. Find the highest-valued data point in your data set.
      For the data in Table C.10.3, the highest valued data point is 12.4.

Step 2. Find the lowest-valued data point in your data set.
      For the data in Table C.10.3, the lowest-valued data point is 4.6.

Step 3. Determine the degree of precision for the most precise data point in your data set.
      All the data points in Table C.10.3 have the same degree of precision. The degree of precision is units of 0.1.

Step 4. Calculate the precision range for your data. The precision range is simply the total number of possible score values that you would find by counting upward from the lowest-valued data point—in units corresponding to the highest degree of precision for your data set—until you reach the highest-valued data point.
      The precision range can be calculated, without counting, by the following procedure.

1. Subtract the lowest-valued data point from the highest-valued data point.
2. Add one unit of the highest degree of precision for your data.
3. Divide by one unit of the highest degree of precision for your data.

For the data in Table C.10.3, the degree of precision is units of 0.1, and thus we proceed as follows.

1. $12.4 - 4.6 = 7.8$

2. $7.8 + 0.1 = 7.9$.

3. $\dfrac{7.9}{0.1} = 79$

The precision range is 79. If you started with the score 4.6 and counted upward in increments of 0.1 (the highest degree of precision for your data) until you reached 12.4, you would count 79 possible score values.

Step 5. Select a class interval size such that the total number of class intervals will be at least 7 and at most 17.

If you are considering a class interval size less than 10, sizes of 3, 5, or 7 are recommended. These odd-sized class intervals have the advantage that it is easy to find the middle of the interval.

If you are considering a class interval size of 10 or more, multiples of 10 are recommended: for example, 10, 20, 30, 40, 50, 60, 70, 100.

To estimate the number of class intervals resulting from a given class interval size, divide the precision range by the intended class interval size. To estimate the class interval size resulting from a given number of class intervals, divide the precision range by the intended number of class intervals.

For the data in Table C.10.3, the number of class intervals resulting from a possible class interval size of 3 would be

$$\dfrac{79}{3} = 26.33$$

We round this to 26. Since 26 is greater than 17, the maximum recommended number of class intervals, we try the next recommended class interval size of 5

$$\dfrac{79}{5} = 15.8$$

We round this to 16. Since 16 is greater than 7, the minimum recommended number of class intervals, and less than 17, the maximum recommended number of class intervals, a class interval size of 5 would be an appropriate choice.

If we chose to have 12 class intervals, the class interval size would be

$$\dfrac{79}{12} = 6.58$$

We round this to 7, which is one of the recommended class interval sizes. Let's see how many class intervals we would have if we chose a class interval size of 7

$$\dfrac{79}{7} = 11.28$$

We round this to 11. Since 11 is greater than 7, the minimum recommended number of class intervals, and less than 17, the maximum recommended number of class intervals, a class interval size of 7 would also be an appropriate choice.

Notice that, in selecting an appropriate class interval size, you must consider both the desired approximate total number of class intervals and the desired approximate class interval size. Then you may divide the precision range by either of these approximations to estimate the other. After a few attempts, you should be able to zero in on a class interval size and a total number of class intervals that are acceptable.

On the basis of our estimates, let's select a class interval size of 5 for the data in Table C.10.3.

Step 6. Find the values that will mark the beginning and end of each of the class intervals.

Begin by simply using the whole-number part of the lowest-valued data point. (If the lowest valued data point is less than 1, use the lowest valued data point itself.)

For the data in Table C.10.3, the lowest-valued data point is 4.6; therefore, we begin the lowest class interval with 4. This will be referred to hereafter as the lower apparent limit of the lowest class interval.

Step 7. After finding the beginning of the lowest class interval, determine the value that will mark the end of the lowest class interval, as follows.

1. Determine the unit of highest precision. (This was already done in step 3.)
2. Determine the class interval size. (This was already done in step 5).
3. Multiply the class interval size by the unit of highest precision.
4. Take this result and subtract the unit of highest precision.
5. Add this result to the lower apparent limit. This will be referred to hereafter as the upper apparent limit of the lowest class interval.

For the data in Table C.10.3, we proceed as follows:

1. The unit of highest precision is 0.1.
2. The class interval size is 5.
3. $5 \times 0.1 = 0.5$.
4. $0.5 - 0.1 = 0.4$.
5. $4 + 0.4 = 4.4$.

Thus, the upper apparent limit of the lowest class interval is 4.4. Now we know that the upper and lower apparent limits of the lowest class interval are

4.0–4.4

Note that, if you start with the lower apparent limit and count up in increments of the unit of highest precision until you reach the upper apparent limit, you will have counted the number of score values corresponding to the class interval size.
For the data in Table C.10.3

$4.0 + 0.1 = 4.1$

$4.1 + 0.1 = 4.2$

$4.2 + 0.1 = 4.3$

$4.3 + 0.1 = 4.4$

Thus, five score values are included in this class interval

4.0, 4.1, 4.2, 4.3, 4.4

The class interval size is 5.

Step 8. After finding the upper and lower apparent limits of the lowest class interval, find upper and lower apparent limits for each successively higher class interval until all of your class intervals are completed. This is done simply by adding the class interval size (stated in appropriate units of precision) to each apparent limit.
For the data in Table C.10.3, the class interval size of 5 is multiplied by 0.1, because 0.1 is the appropriate unit of precision.

T I M E ∎ O U T

Take some time to think about why this is so.

For the second class interval

$4.0 + .5 = 4.5$

$4.4 + .5 = 4.9$

Now we've established two class intervals

4.5–4.9

4.0–4.4

The next class interval is obtained the same way

$4.5 + .5 = 5.0$

$4.9 + .5 = 5.4$

Now we have established three class intervals

5.0–5.4

4.5–4.9

4.0–4.4

We continue in this way until we have identified all 17 class intervals.

Make sure, when you finish, that the class intervals include your lowest-valued data point and your highest-valued data point.

For the data in Table C.10.3, the class intervals are as follows

12.0–12.4

11.5–11.9

11.0–11.4

10.5–10.9

10.0–10.4

9.5–9.9

9.0–9.4

8.5–8.9

8.0–8.4

7.5–7.9

7.0–7.4

6.5–6.9

6.0–6.4

5.5–5.9

5.0–5.4

4.5–4.9

4.0–4.4

and we note that the lowest-valued data point (4.6) is in the second lowest class interval, while the highest-valued data point (12.4) is in the highest class interval.

Step 9. After finding the upper and lower apparent limits for all of your class intervals, the next step is to find the upper and lower real limits, as follows.

1. Determine the unit of highest precision. (This was already accomplished in step 3.)
2. Divide the unit of highest precision by 2.
3. Subtract half the unit of highest precision from each lower apparent limit to determine each lower real limit.
4. Add half the unit of precision to each upper apparent limit to determine each upper real limit.

For the data in Table C.10.3, we proceed as follows.

1. The unit of highest precision is 0.1.
2. $0.1/2 = 0.05$
3. $4.0 - 0.05 = 3.95$. The lower real limit for the lowest class interval is 3.95.
4. $4.4 + 0.05 = 4.45$. The upper real limit for the lowest class interval is 4.45.

After completing this procedure for all the class intervals, we obtain the following results for the data in Table C.10.3

11.95–12.45	8.95–9.45	5.95–6.45
11.45–11.95	8.45–8.95	5.45–5.95
10.95–11.45	7.95–8.45	4.95–5.45
10.45–10.95	7.45–7.95	4.45–4.95
9.95–10.45	6.95–7.45	3.95–4.45
9.45–9.95	6.45–6.95	

Note that the upper real limit for each class interval is identical to the lower real limit of the class interval immediately above it. This is intentional: The real limits are established so that there are no gaps between the class intervals.

Step 10. After establishing real limits for all of the class intervals, the next step is to count the number of data points in your data set that fall into each of the class intervals, as follows.

1. Count the number of data points in your data set that fall between the upper and lower real limits of your lowest class interval. (Write this frequency count next to the class interval.)
2. Count the number of data points in your data set that fall between the upper and lower real limits of your next highest class interval.
3. Continue until all data points have been accounted for.

For the data in Table C.10.3, we proceed as follows.

1. No data points fall between the upper and lower real limits of 3.95 and 4.45.
2. One data point—4.6—falls between the upper and lower real limits of 4.45 and 4.95.
3. One data point—5.1—falls between the upper and lower real limits of 4.95 and 5.45.

After completing this procedure for all the class intervals, we obtain the following results for the data in Table C.10.3.

Real class intervals	Frequency	Real class intervals	Frequency
11.95–12.45	1	7.45–7.95	2
11.45–11.95	0	6.95–7.45	1
10.95–11.45	0	6.45–6.95	1
10.45–10.95	2	5.95–6.45	0
9.95–10.45	1	5.45–5.95	1
9.45–9.95	4	4.95–5.45	1
8.95–9.45	2	4.45–4.95	1
8.45–8.95	1	3.95–4.45	0
7.95–8.45	2		

Note that the frequency values are the same as in Table 3.14, except that Table 3.14 uses the apparent limits of the class intervals.

Step 11. It is often useful to determine cumulative frequencies for each of the class intervals in a grouped frequency distribution. The cumulative frequency is simply the accumulated frequency count for all the class intervals below and including the class interval in question. Proceed as follows.

1. The cumulative frequency count for the lowest class interval is simply the frequency count for that interval, since the lowest class interval has no other class intervals below it.
2. To determine the cumulative frequency for the next highest class interval, add the frequency value for that interval to the cumulative frequency that you have just calculated.

3. Continue in this way for all the class intervals.

For the data in Table C.10.3, we proceed as follows.

1. The frequency count for the lowest class interval (3.95–4.45) is 0; therefore, the cumulative frequency for the lowest class interval is also 0.

Real class intervals	Frequency	Cumulative frequency
3.95–4.45	0	0

2. The frequency value for the next highest class interval 4.45–4.95 is 1. Add this to the cumulative frequency that you have just determined: $1 + 0 = 1$. This is the cumulative frequency for class interval 4.45–4.95.

Real class intervals	Frequency	Cumulative frequency
4.45–4.95	1	1
3.95–4.45	0	0

3. The frequency value for the next highest class interval 4.95–5.45 is 1. Add this to the cumulative frequency that you have just determined: $1 + 1 = 2$. This is the cumulative frequency for class interval 4.95–5.45.

Real class intervals	Frequency	Cumulative frequency
4.95–5.45	1	2
4.45–4.95	1	1
3.95–4.45	0	0

After completing this procedure for all the class intervals, we obtain the following results for the data in Table C.10.3.

Real class intervals	Frequency	Cumulative frequency
11.95–12.45	1	20
11.45–11.95	0	19
10.95–11.45	0	19
10.45–10.95	2	19
9.95–10.45	1	17
9.45–9.95	4	16
8.95–9.45	2	12
8.45–8.95	1	10
7.95–8.45	2	9
7.45–7.95	2	7
6.95–7.45	1	5
6.45–6.95	1	4
5.95–6.45	0	3
5.45–5.95	1	3
4.95–5.45	1	2
4.45–4.95	1	1
3.95–4.45	0	0

Finally, the complete grouped frequency distribution is shown in Table C.10.4.

TABLE C.10.4 Complete Grouped Frequency Distribution for 20 Measured Rainfall Amounts
(Data from Table C.10.3)

Real class intervals	Apparent class intervals	Frequency	Cumulative frequency
11.95–12.45	12.0–12.4	1	20
11.45–11.95	11.5–11.9	0	19
10.95–11.45	11.0–11.4	0	19
10.45–10.95	10.5–10.9	2	19
9.95–10.45	10.0–10.4	1	17
9.45–9.95	9.5–9.9	4	16
8.95–9.45	9.0–9.4	2	12
8.45–8.95	8.5–8.9	1	10
7.95–8.45	8.0–8.4	2	9
7.45–7.95	7.5–7.9	2	7
6.95–7.45	7.0–7.4	1	5
6.45–6.95	6.5–6.9	1	4
5.95–6.45	6.0–6.4	0	3
5.45–5.95	5.5–5.9	1	3
4.95–5.45	5.0–5.4	1	2
4.45–4.95	4.5–4.9	1	1
3.95–4.45	4.0–4.4	0	0

Calculation C.11 Kruskal-Wallis (Nonparametric, Between Groups)

Type of Research	Experiment
Number of dependent variables	1
Level of measurement:	Interval/ratio
Assumptions met:	No
Number of independent variables:	1
Conditions of independent variables:	3
Type of design:	Between-groups (B-G)
Choice of analysis:	Kruskal-Wallis

Motivation for Research: A researcher believes that listening to classical music will improve a person's reaction time.

Description of Research: The researcher randomly selects 30 people from the general population and then randomly assigns 10 of these people to a control group, 10 to a 15-minute experimental condition, and the remaining 10 to a 30-minute experimental condition. In the control group, each of the 10 people is asked to sit in a room for 15 minutes and to try to relax. In the 15-minute experimental condition, each of the 10 people is asked to sit in a room for 15 minutes and to try to relax by listening to classical music. In the 30-minute experimental condition, each of the 10 people is asked to sit in a room for 30 minutes and to try to relax by listening to classical music. All subjects in each of the three groups are tested for their reaction time after the relaxation period.

Type of Conclusion Possible: The Kruskal-Wallis analysis will allow the researcher to determine if the ranked reaction times for the three conditions of the experiment differ significantly in any way. If the Kruskal-Wallis analysis indicates that there is some difference—in other words, that the three means for the ranks are not equal—the researcher may draw the general conclusion that listening to music does have an effect on reaction time.

Comments: If we obtain significant results in a between-groups ANOVA, which is the parametric equivalent of the nonparametric Kruskal-Wallis, we may follow up with an additional analysis — for example, a Scheffe — in order to make more specific comparisons between the means of the separate experimental conditions. When using the Kruskal-Wallis analysis, however, there is no corresponding post–Kruskal-Wallis analysis that is within the scope of this book.

Assumptions: Suppose that the parametric assumptions cannot be met.

Test Data:

Control group		15-minute group		30-minute group	
Person	Reaction time	Person	Reaction time	Person	Reaction time
1	2.69	11	2.55	21	2.37
2	2.72	12	2.57	22	2.43
3	2.56	13	2.40	23	2.42
4	2.53	14	2.48	24	2.38
5	2.60	15	2.46	25	2.41
6	2.58	16	2.33	26	2.25
7	2.79	17	2.67	27	2.58
8	2.86	18	2.71	28	2.53
9	2.58	19	2.54	29	2.66
10	2.68	20	2.61	30	2.56

Specifics Regarding the Analysis: If your data are at the interval or ratio level but you cannot meet the parametric assumptions, as in the present case, you must rank your data prior to analysis. The Kruskal-Wallis analysis is appropriate in that case. The Kruskal-Wallis analysis is also appropriate if you have ordinal data. The analysis helps the researcher determine whether the variability between two or more conditions is greater than would be expected by chance.

Research Hypothesis: The researcher believes that a person's reaction time will be shorter after longer periods of listening to classical music. The research hypothesis — the alternative hypothesis — symbolically appears as follows.

H_{alt}: $\mu_{ranks_{30min}} < \mu_{ranks_{15min}} < \mu_{ranks_{control}}$

In plain English, the researcher is predicting that the average rank of the reaction times after listening to classical music for 30 minutes will be significantly lower than the average rank of the reaction times after 15 minutes, which, in turn, will be significantly lower than the average rank of the reaction times of the control condition.

Null Hypothesis: As we noted in Chapter 9, we state the null hypothesis for the sake of argument, on the assumption that our research hypothesis is incorrect. In the present case, the null hypothesis is that there are *no differences among the average ranks of the reaction times of all three groups.* Symbolically

H_{null}: $\mu_{ranks_{30min}} = \mu_{ranks_{15min}} = \mu_{ranks_{control}}$

Organizing the Raw Data: When you prepare the data for entry into the Kruskal-Wallis formula — whether you do the calculations by hand or by computer — it is necessary to identify the following:

- the independent variable: music, in the present case.

- the conditions of the experiment: control, 15 minutes, and 30 minutes.

- the number of subjects in each condition: 10.

- the dependent variable: reaction time.

Once these values have been identified, you may enter them into the computer or use the calculation formula as follows.

Kruskal-Wallis Calculation

We proceed as follows.

Step 1. List your data.

> The test data have already been tabulated.

Step 2. Combine all data values into one group and sort from lowest to highest. Then assign ranks, beginning with the rank of 1 for the lowest data value.

> When two or more data values are equal, assign the average of the next available ranks to each data value. This procedure for tied ranks is illustrated in the present data set where person 4 has the same reaction time score (2.53) as person 28. These two scores are thus tied for the ranks 11 and 12, and each is assigned the average of these two ranks (11.5).
> The complete ranking is shown in Table C.11.1.

Step 3. Sum the ranks for each condition, and square each of the resulting sums.

> The corresponding sums and squares are also shown in Table C.11.1.

TABLE C.11.1 Ranks for Reaction Time Measures

| Control group | | 15-minute group | | 30-minute group | |
Person	Reaction time	Person	Reaction time	Person	Reaction time
1	26	11	14	21	3
2	28	12	17	22	8
3	15.5	13	5	23	7
4	11.5	14	10	24	4
5	21	15	9	25	6
6	19	16	2	26	1
7	29	17	24	27	19
8	30	18	27	28	11.5
9	19	19	13	29	23
10	25	20	22	30	15.5
Sum	224		143		98
Squared sum	50,176		20,449		9604

Step 4. Calculate the Kruskal-Wallis H value by means of the following formula

$$H = \frac{12}{N(N+1)}\left[\frac{\left(\sum R^2{}_1\right)}{N_1} + \frac{\left(\sum R^2{}_2\right)}{N_2} + \cdots + \frac{\left(\sum R^2{}_k\right)}{N_k}\right] - 3(N+1) \tag{C.11.1}$$

where N is the total number of ranks; k is the total number of conditions; $\left(\sum R\right)^2$ is the square of the summed ranks for each condition; and subscripts 1 through k denote the corresponding experimental group.

In the present case

$$N = 30$$

$$k = 3$$

$$H = \frac{12}{30(31)}\left(\frac{50,176}{10} + \frac{20,449}{10} + \frac{9604}{10}\right) - 3(30+1)$$

$$= \frac{12}{930}(5017.6 + 2044.9 + 960.4) - 3(31)$$

$$= 0.0129(8022.9) - 93$$

$$= 103.4954 - 93$$

$$= 10.4954$$

Step 5. Determine the degrees of freedom by means of the following formula

$$df = k - 1 \tag{C.11.2}$$

In the present case

$$df = 3 - 1 = 2$$

Step 6. Determine your alpha level. [We assume .05, unless otherwise specified]

$$\alpha = .05$$

Step 7. You must now determine the critical value of H. Since the Kruskal-Wallis H value is interpreted as a chi square value, you may look in a table of critical H values (Table B.10) or a standard chi square table (Table B.3) to determine the corresponding critical value.

The critical H value (or critical chi square value) for $\alpha = .05$ and two degrees of freedom is 5.99.

Step 8. Compare the calculated H value to the critical value. If the calculated H value is greater than or equal to the critical value, you must reject the null hypothesis; otherwise, you cannot.

In the present case, the calculated value (10.4954) is greater than the critical value (5.99); therefore, we reject the null.

Step 9. State your conclusion in a standard statistical format using appropriate symbols.

An appropriate statement is as follows

$$(H_{calc} = 10.4954; df = 2; p < .05)$$

Step 10. State your statistical conclusion in words.

If the null hypothesis were true, the probability of arriving at a calculated H of 10.4954 with two degrees of freedom would be less than .05. Therefore, the null hypothesis is *probably* not true, and the alternative hypothesis probably is true.

Step 11. State your final conclusion in plain English.

Given the data and the statistical conclusion, it is reasonable to argue that listening to classical music had an effect on the reaction times of the subjects.

Calculation C.12 Lambda (Correlation Coefficient)

Type of research: Observation
Number of variables: 2
Levels of measurement: Predictor variable: interval/ratio
                          Predicted variable: nominal
Choice of analysis: Lambda

Motivation for Research: A researcher believes that a person's economic status in the senior year of college can be used to predict his or her political perspective five years after graduation. More specifically, the researcher believes that a person of higher economic class will be more likely to identify as a conservative five years after graduation.

Description of Research: The researcher randomly selects 20 students from the population of seniors in college. Each of these 20 students is asked to state the combined yearly income of his or her parents. Five years later these same students are contacted and asked to choose which of two labels—liberal or conservative—is most appropriate to describe his or her political perspective.

Type of Conclusion Possible: The lambda analysis will allow the researcher to determine whether the parental income of a college senior is correlated with that person's political perspective five years after graduation. If there is a sufficiently strong correlation, the researcher may conclude that economic status in the senior year—as operationally defined in this study—may be used to predict a person's political perspective five years after graduation, as here defined.

Comments: One of the variables being measured—political perspective—is at the nominal level; this is the predicted variable. The other variable—yearly income—is at the ratio level; this is the predictor variable. There are only two conditions of the nominal variable—liberal and conservative. If there were more than three levels of the nominal variable, the interpretation of the analysis would be more complex.

Test Data:

Person	Parents' combined income ($)	Political perspective	Person	Parents' combined income ($)	Political perspective
1	80,000	Conservative	26	31,000	Liberal
2	45,000	Liberal	27	40,000	Liberal
3	56,000	Liberal	28	52,000	Conservative
4	74,000	Conservative	29	74,000	Liberal
5	99,000	Conservative	30	43,000	Liberal
6	84,000	Conservative	31	101,000	Conservative
7	36,000	Liberal	32	51,000	Liberal
8	63,000	Liberal	33	58,000	Liberal
9	88,000	Conservative	34	33,000	Liberal
10	41,000	Conservative	35	43,000	Liberal
11	56,000	Liberal	36	39,000	Conservative
12	40,000	Liberal	37	92,000	Conservative
13	94,000	Conservative	38	67,000	Liberal
14	50,000	Liberal	39	66,000	Conservative
15	120,000	Conservative	40	38,000	Liberal
16	48,000	Liberal	41	48,000	Liberal
17	65,000	Liberal	42	76,000	Conservative
18	72,000	Liberal	43	59,000	Conservative
19	38,000	Liberal	44	35,000	Liberal
20	87,000	Conservative	45	61,000	Liberal
21	84,000	Conservative	46	79,000	Conservative
22	44,000	Liberal	47	125,000	Conservative
23	47,000	Liberal	48	37,000	Liberal
24	81,000	Liberal	49	62,000	Liberal
25	98,000	Conservative	50	54,000	Liberal

Specifics Regarding the Analysis: The lambda analysis helps the researcher to determine whether or not there is a significant correlation between two variables when the predictor variable is at the interval or ratio level and the predicted variable is at the nominal level. These two variables must represent a pair of observed measurements for each of the subjects or items in the observation. In the present study, the two observed measurements for each of the 20 subjects are: the combined income of the subject's parents at the time of his or her senior year of college; and the person's subsequent political perspective. For person 13, for example, the observed measurements are: $94,000 and conservative.

The calculations result in a single lambda value ranging from 0 to +1.00. Higher lambda corresponds to greater correlation between the two variables. In the present example, the research hypothesis predicts a correlation such that college seniors whose parents had relatively high combined incomes would tend to have conservative political philosophies five years after college, whereas those whose parents had relatively low incomes would tend to have liberal views.

Research Hypothesis: The researcher believes that economic class is a factor in predicting a person's political philosophy. Note, however, that this is *not* an experiment in which economic class is manipulated as an independent variable and political philosophy measured as a dependent variable. Instead, combined parental income and political philosophy are each simply measured for each of the 20 subjects in the study. Therefore, the research hypothesis is that the measured combined parental income (ratio level variable) will be correlated with the measured political philosophy (nominal level variable). Symbolically, the research hypothesis — the alternative hypothesis — appears as follows

H_{alt}: $\lambda_{I,P} > 0$

In plain English, the researcher is predicting that the correlation between measured parental income (I) and measured political philosophy (P) will be greater than zero in the population from which the sample was drawn.

Null Hypothesis: As we noted in Chapter 9, we state the null hypothesis, for the sake of argument, on the assumption that our research hypothesis is incorrect. In the present case, the null hypothesis is that there is *no correlation between parental income and political philosophy*. Symbolically

H_{null}: $\lambda_{I,P} = 0$

Organizing the Raw Data: When you prepare the data for entry into the lambda calculation formula — whether you do the calculations by hand or by computer — you must first label one of the variables as the X variable and the other as the Y variable. The X variable should be the variable that could logically be used to predict the Y variable. For example, in the present case, the intention is to predict the person's political philosophy on the basis of the income of the person's parents. Therefore, political philosophy — operationally defined as either conservative or liberal — is identified as the Y variable, and parental income — operationally defined as income reported on income tax statement — is identified as the X variable.

After determining which is the X variable and which is the Y variable, you must identify the X value and Y value for each observation in the sample. There is one pair of X, Y values for each of the 20 people in this observation. Each X value and each Y value can be subscripted for identification. For example, X_5, Y_5 correspond to person 5 in our sample and, thus, according to the test data

$X_5 = \$99,000$

$Y_5 = $ conservative

Once the X and Y values have been identified, you need to make sure that both variables are at the nominal level of measurement. In the present case, since income is at the ratio level, it must be placed into nominal categories. We do this as follows.

Category 1: $110,000–129,000
Category 2:   90,000–109,000
Category 3:   70,000–89,999
Category 4:   50,000–69,999
Category 5:   30,000–49,999

Lambda Calculation

Once these categories have been established, you may enter the data into the computer or use the calculation formulas as follows.

Step 1. List your data.
        The test data have already been tabulated.

Step 2. Count the number of subjects for each possible combination of categories of the predictor and predicted variable and summarize in tabular form.

The corresponding data for the present example are shown in Table C.12.1.

Step 3. Sum the frequencies for each category.

The corresponding sums are also shown in Table C.12.1. Adding the column sums or the row sums, we find that the grand sum of frequencies (GSF) is 50.

TABLE C.12.1 **Frequencies for Combined Categories**

| | Political perspective | | |
	Conservative	Liberal	Sum
$110,000–129,000	2	0	2
90,000–109,999	5	0	5
70,000–89,999	8	3	11
50,000–69,999	3	11	14
30,000–49,999	2	16	18
Sum	20	30	

Step 4. Determine the predicted category that has the highest column total. Label this the **overall modal predicted category**. Then determine the *column total for the overall modal predicated category* (CTOMPC).

In the present case, the liberal column has the highest total: CTOMPC = 30.

Step 5. For each category of the predictor variable, determine which category of the predicted variable occurs most frequently. Label this the **modal predicted category**. You will have one modal predicted category for each category of the predictor variable.

The modal predicted categories for the present example are as follows.

Predictor category	Modal predicted category
$110,000–129,000	Conservative
90,000–109,999	Conservative
70,000–89,999	Conservative
50,000–69,999	Liberal
30,000–49,999	Liberal

Step 6. Determine the actual frequency value for each *modal predicted category*, and then make a summary table including the frequency values and the *sum of the frequencies in the modal predicated categories (SFMPC)*.

The corresponding frequencies are shown in Table C.12.2.

Step 7. Calculate the lambda value by means of the following formula

$$\lambda = \frac{\text{SFMPC} - \text{CTOMPC}}{\text{GSF} - \text{CTOMPC}}$$
(C.12.1)

	TABLE C.12.2	Modal Predicted Frequencies	

Predictor category	Modal predicted category	Frequency in modal predicted category
$110,000–129,000	Conservative	2
90,000–109,999	Conservative	5
70,000–89,999	Conservative	8
50,000–69,999	Liberal	11
30,000–49,999	Liberal	16
SFMPC		42

In the present case

$$\lambda = \frac{42 - 30}{50 - 30}$$

$$= \frac{12}{20}$$

$$= .60$$

Step 8. Determine the predictor category that has the highest frequency in the modal predicted category. Label this the **target predictor row** (TPR).

Looking at Table C.12.2, we see that the highest frequency is 16, and the TPR is 30,000–49,999.

Step 9. For each column of predicted categories, determine whether the frequency in the TPR is also the highest frequency in each column. Identify any frequency that meets this criterion as a *highest column frequency for the TPR* (HCFTPR).

In Table C.12.2, the frequency of 16 for the liberal column in the 30,000–49,999 row is the only one that qualifies.

Step 10. Sum all of the HCFTPR values, and call this the SHCFTPR.

In the present case, SHCFTPR = 16.

Step 11. Calculate a Z value for the data by means of the following formula

$$Z = \frac{\lambda_{calc} - \lambda_{null}}{\sqrt{\frac{(GSF - SFMPC)[SFMPC + CTOMPC - 2(SHCFTPR)]}{(GSF - CTOMPC)^3}}} \tag{C.12.2}$$

For the data in Table C.12.2

$$Z = \frac{.6 - 0}{\sqrt{\frac{(50 - 42)[42 + 30 - 2(16)]}{(50 - 30)^3}}}$$

$$= \frac{0.6}{\sqrt{\frac{(8)(72 - 32)}{(20)^3}}}$$

$$= \frac{0.6}{\sqrt{\dfrac{(8)(40)}{8000}}}$$

$$= \frac{0.6}{\sqrt{\dfrac{320}{8000}}}$$

$$= \frac{0.6}{\sqrt{0.04}}$$

$$= \frac{0.6}{0.2}$$

$$= 3.00$$

Step 12. Determine whether your alternative hypothesis is one-tailed or two-tailed.
In the present case, the alternative hypothesis is one-tailed.

Step 13. Determine your alpha level. [We assume .05 unless otherwise specified]

$\alpha = .05$

Step 14. Determine the critical Z value from a standard table (Table B.2).
For $\alpha = .05$, with a one-tailed alternative hypothesis

$Z_{crit} = 1.645$

Step 15. Compare the calculated Z value with the critical Z value. If the calculated Z is greater than or equal to the critical Z, you must reject the null hypothesis.
In the present case, the calculated Z (3.00) is greater than the critical Z (1.645); therefore, we reject the null hypothesis.

Step 16. State your conclusion in a standard statistical format using appropriate symbols.
An appropriate statement is as follows

$(Z_{calc} = 3.00; p < .05;$ one-tailed)

Step 17. State your statistical conclusion in words.
If the null hypothesis were true, the probability of arriving at a calculated Z of 3.00 would be less than .05. Therefore, the null hypothesis is *probably* not true, and the alternative hypothesis probably is true.

Step 18. State your final conclusion in plain English.
Given the data and the statistical conclusion, it is reasonable to argue that economic status and political perspective are significantly correlated. This supports the researcher's argument that a college senior's economic status, as measured by parental income, can be used to predict that person's political perspective five years after graduating.

Note: Lambda can be interpreted as a percent value indicating the percentage reduction in errors achieved by using the predictor variable to estimate the predicted variable. In the present case, use of the predictor variable reduces errors by 60%. Harshbarger (1977) implies that if the sample size is greater than or equal to 50, and we are predicting only in one direction — for example, only predicting political philosophy using parents' income, and not the reverse — then we can reject the null hypothesis $\lambda = 0$ whenever the calculated λ is not zero. This reasoning is reflected in Table B.7 *Critical Lambda Values*. The Z formula stated in step 11 is a translation of Harshbarger's equation (17–36). Based on his discussion (see Harshbarger [1977] pp. 481–482), the Z calculation is assumed to be a more accurate alternative for determining statistical significance.

Calculation C.13 Mean

A. SAMPLE MEAN

We compute the mean for a sample from the formula

$$\bar{X} = \frac{\sum X}{n}$$

The sample mean ($\bar{X}$) equals the sum of the scores divided by the number of scores in the sample.

Use the following procedure.

Step 1. List your data.

Consider the following sample: 3, 6, 2, 9.

Step 2. Determine n.

In the present case, $n = 4$.

Step 3. Sum the scores.

In the present case, $3 + 6 + 2 + 9 = 20$.

Step 4. Divide the sum of the scores by n.

The mean of our sample is $20/4 = 5$.

B. POPULATION MEAN

The formula for the population mean is

$$\mu = \frac{\sum X}{N_{pop}}$$

The population mean (μ) equals the sum of the scores divided by the number of scores in the population.

The calculation procedure is the same as for a sample mean.

Calculation C.14 Median

The median of a sample is determined by finding the middle point in a given set of data values. The corresponding procedure is as follows.

Step 1. List your data.

Consider the following two samples

1) 3, 6, 2, 9, 7
2) 6, 9, 1, 4

Step 2. Sort your data from the lowest to the highest value.

Sorting our samples gives

1) 2, 3, 6, 7, 9
2) 1, 4, 6, 9

Step 3. Determine n.

For sample 1, $n = 5$.
For sample 2, $n = 4$.

Step 4. Determine if the n is odd or even.

For sample 1, n is odd.
For sample 2, n is even.

Step 5. If n is odd, the median is the middle score of the sorted data set. If n is even, the median is the average of the two middle scores of the sorted data set.

For sample 1, the median is 6.

For sample 2, the median is $(4 + 6)/2 = 10/2 = 5$.

Calculation C.15 Mode

The mode for a sample is determined by finding the data value that occurs most frequently in a data set.

Step 1. List your data.

Consider the following sample

3, 6, 2, 9, 7, 6, 8, 6

Step 2. Count the number of times each data value occurs.

For our sample, the frequency values are as follows.

Data value	Frequency
9	1
8	1
7	1
6	3
3	1
2	1

Step 3. Check to make sure that the sum of the frequency values is equal to the total number of data values in the set (n).

For our sample, $n = 8$, and the sum of the frequency values is also 8.

Step 4. Label the most frequently occurring data value as the mode.

For our sample, the mode is 6.

In some cases, two or more data values may be tied for the highest frequency. In such cases, it can be said that the data set is bimodal (two modes) or trimodal (three modes). However, the use of these terms should be limited to data sets large enough for this to make sense. As an extreme example, consider the following data set

4, 6, 6, 4, 7

The data values of 4 and 6 each occur twice and, strictly speaking, are tied for the highest frequency of occurrence, but it would not be useful to say that such a small data set was bimodal.

Calculation C.16 Mann-Whitney *U* (Nonparametric, Between Groups)

Type of research: Experiment
Number of dependent variables: 1
Level of measurement: Ordinalized interval/ratio
Assumptions met: No
Number of independent variables: 1
Conditions of independent variable: 2
Type of design: Between-groups (B-G)
Choice of analysis: Mann-Whitney *U*

Motivation for Research: A researcher believes that listening to classical music will improve a person's reaction time.

Description of Research: The researcher randomly selects 20 people from the general population and then randomly assigns 10 of these people to a control group and the remaining 10 to an experimental group. In the control group, each of the 10 people is asked to sit in a room for 15 minutes and to try to relax. In the experimental group, each of the 10 people is asked to sit in a room for 15 minutes and to try to relax by listening to classical music. All subjects in both the experimental and control groups are tested for their reaction time after the 15-minute relaxation period.

Type of Conclusion Possible: The Mann-Whitney *U* analysis will allow the researcher to determine if the ranked reaction times for the experimental group (who listened to classical music) are systematically lower than the ranked reaction times for the control group.

Comments: If the results of the Mann-Whitney *U* analysis indicate that the ranks are systematically lower for the experimental group, the researcher may conclude that listening to classical music had the significant effect of improving the ranked reaction times of the subjects.

Assumptions: Suppose that the parametric assumptions cannot be met.

Test Data:

Classical music group		Control group	
Person	Reaction time	Person	Reaction time
1	2.36	11	2.79
2	2.10	12	2.58
3	2.20	13	2.41
4	2.32	14	2.49
5	2.14	15	2.47
6	2.30	16	2.34
7	2.45	17	2.68
8	2.47	18	2.70
9	2.38	19	2.56
10	2.46	20	2.62

Specifics Regarding the Analysis: The Mann-Whitney *U* test is appropriate if, as in the present case, the researcher is beginning with data at the interval or ratio level but cannot meet the parametric assumptions for some other reason. It is also appropriate if the initial data are at the ordinal level.

The Mann-Whitney *U* test for independent groups helps the researcher to determine whether or not two samples differ significantly, with respect to the ordinal ranks, from what would be expected by chance.

Research Hypothesis: The researcher believes that listening to classical music will decrease reaction time. Stated symbolically, the research hypothesis — the alternative hypothesis — appears as follows

$$H_{alt}: \mu_{ranks_{music}} < \mu_{ranks_{control}}$$

In plain English, the researcher is predicting that the average rank of the reaction times for the classical music condition will be significantly lower than the average rank of the reaction times for the control group.

Null Hypothesis: As we noted in Chapter 9, we state the null hypothesis, for the sake of argument, on the assumption that our research hypothesis is incorrect. In the present case, the null hypothesis is that there is *no difference between the average rank of the reaction times for the classical music group and the average rank of the reaction times for the control group.* Symbolically

$$H_{null}: \mu_{ranks_{music}} = \mu_{ranks_{control}}$$

Organizing the Raw Data: When you prepare the data for entry into the Mann-Whitney U test formula — whether you do the calculations by hand or by computer — you need to identify the following:

- the independent variable: music, in the present case.

- the two conditions of the experiment: classical music and control.

- the number of subjects in each condition: 10 and 10.

- the dependent variable: reaction time.

Mann-Whitney U Test Calculation

Once these values have been identified, you may enter them into the computer or use the calculation formula as follows.

Step 1. List your data.
    The test data have already been tabulated.

Step 2. Combine all the data values into one group and sort them from lowest to highest. Then assign ranks, beginning with the rank of 1 for the lowest data value.
    When two or more data values are equal, assign the average of the next available ranks to each data value. This procedure for tied ranks is illustrated in the present data set, where person 15 has the same reaction time score (2.47) as person 8. These two scores are thus tied for the ranks 12 and 13, and each is assigned the average of these two ranks (12.5).
    The complete ranking is shown in Table C.16.1.

TABLE C.16.1 Ranks for Rection Time Measures

Classical music group			Control group		
Person	Reaction time	Rank	Person	Reaction time	Rank
1	2.36	7	11	2.79	20
2	2.10	1	12	2.58	16
3	2.20	3	13	2.41	9
4	2.32	5	14	2.49	14
5	2.14	2	15	2.47	12.5
6	2.30	4	16	2.34	6
7	2.45	10	17	2.68	18
8	2.47	12.5	18	2.70	19
9	2.38	8	19	2.56	15
10	2.46	11	20	2.62	17
		63.5			146.5

Step 3. Sum the ranks for each condition.

The sums of the ranks are also shown in Table C.16.1.

Step 4. Calculate two U values by means of the following formulas

$$U_1 = (n_1 n_2) + \frac{n_1(n_1 + 1)}{2} - \sum R_1 \tag{C.16.1}$$

$$U_2 = (n_1 n_2) + \frac{n_2(n_2 + 1)}{2} - \sum R_2 \tag{C.16.2}$$

where n_1 is the number of ranks in the first condition; $\sum R_1$ is the sum of the ranks for the first condition; n_2 is the number of ranks in the second condition; and $\sum R_2$ is the sum of the ranks for the second condition.

For the classical music group

$$U_1 = (10 \times 10) + \frac{10(10 + 1)}{2} - 63.5$$

$$= 100 + \frac{10(11)}{2} - 63.5$$

$$= 100 + \frac{110}{2} - 63.5$$

$$= (100) + 55 - 63.5$$

$$= 155 - 63.5$$

$$= 91.5$$

For the control group

$$U_2 = (10 \times 10) + \frac{10(10 + 1)}{2} - 146.5$$

$$= 100 + \frac{10(11)}{2} - 146.5$$

$$= 155 - 146.5$$

$$= 8.5$$

Step 5. Select the lower of the two U values and refer to it as the calculated Mann-Whitney U value. In the present case, the calculated Mann-Whitney U value is

$$U = 8.5$$

Step 6. Determine your alpha level. [We assume .05 unless otherwise specified]

$$\alpha = .05$$

Step 7. Determine the number of tails for the alternative hypothesis.

In the present case, the alternative hypothesis specifies a direction, and so it is a one-tailed hypothesis.

Step 8. Look up the critical Mann-Whitney U value in a standard table (Table B.8). Be sure to identify n_1, n_2, α, and the number of tails in the alternative hypothesis.

With $n_1 = 10$, $n_2 = 10$, $\alpha = .05$, and a one-tailed hypothesis, the critical U value is 27

$$U_{crit} = 27$$

Step 9. Compare the critical U value to the calculated U value. If the calculated U is less than or equal to the critical U, you must reject the null hypothesis; otherwise, you cannot. Usually we reject the null hypothesis when the calculated value is greater than or equal to the critical value. The Mann-Whitney U is an exception to this general rule.

In the present case, the calculated U (8.5) is less than the critical U (27); therefore, we reject the null hypothesis.

Step 10. State your conclusion in a standard statistical format using appropriate symbols.

An appropriate statement is as follows

$$(U_{calc} = 8.5; n_1 = 10; n_2 = 10; p < .05; \text{one-tailed})$$

Step 11. State your statistical conclusion in words.

If the null hypothesis were true, the probability of arriving at a calculated U of 8.5 for $n_1 = 10$ and $n_2 = 10$ would be less than .05. Therefore, the null hypothesis is *probably* not true, and the alternative hypothesis probably is true.

Step 12. State your final conclusion in plain English.

Given the data and the statistical conclusion, it is reasonable to argue that the ranks of the group who listened to classical music are systematically lower than the ranks of the control group. This supports the researcher's prediction that listening to classical music will improve reaction time.

Calculation C.17 Pearson *r* Correlation Coefficient

Type of research: Observation
Number of variables: 2
Levels of measurement: Interval/ratio (both variables)
Choice of analysis: Pearson *r*

Motivation for Research: A researcher believes that exercise contributes to a person's ability to cope with difficult life situations. This researcher would like to determine the degree to which exercise might predict the level of depression measured in clinical patients.

Description of Research: The researcher randomly selects 20 patients who have been diagnosed with acute depression resulting from acute stress. Using a combination of interview and paper-and-pencil inventories, the level of depression is measured for each patient and assigned a numerical value in the range from 10 (low depression) to 100 (extremely high depression). Each patient is also interviewed to determine the approximate average number of minutes per week he or she spent exercising during the six months prior to the initial diagnosis of depression.

Type of Conclusion Possible: The Pearson *r* analysis will allow the researcher to determine if the amount of exercise is correlated with the level of depression. If there is a sufficiently high degree of correlation, the researcher may conclude that the amount of exercise, as measured in this study, may be used to predict the level of depression, as measured in this study.

Test Data:

Patient	Exercise (minutes)	Depression	Patient	Exercise (minutes)	Depression
1	110	13	11	10	75
2	0	50	12	0	84
3	20	40	13	70	55
4	0	85	14	10	86
5	10	92	15	240	35
6	5	82	16	20	78
7	50	60	17	5	80
8	80	20	18	30	56
9	0	90	19	0	87
10	15	88	20	5	84

Specifics Regarding the Analysis: The Pearson r analysis helps the researcher to determine whether or not there is a significant correlation between two variables when both are at the interval or ratio level and when these two variables represent a pair of observed measurements for each of the subjects or items in the observation. In the present study, the two observed measurements for each of the 20 subjects are an exercise measure (average minutes of exercise per week) and a depression rating. For patient 17, for example, the observed measurements are: 5 (relatively little exercise) and 80 (fairly highly depressed).

The Pearson r calculations result in a single r value ranging from -1.00 to $+1.00$. The sign of the r value (plus or minus) indicates the direction of the correlation. A plus sign indicates a positive correlation: High values of one variable tend to be associated with high values of the other. A minus sign indicates a negative correlation: High values of one variable tend to be associated with low values of the other. In the present example, the research hypothesis predicts a negative correlation such that high values of depression would tend to be associated with low values of exercise. In other words, the research hypothesis predicts a negative Pearson r value.

The Pearson r value is referred to as a test statistic: It is a *statistic* because it is based upon *sample* data fed into the Pearson r calculation formula. However, research hypotheses and null hypotheses make predictions regarding the populations from which the samples are drawn. The population *parameter* that corresponds to the Pearson r statistic is denoted by ρ.

Research Hypothesis: The researcher believes that exercise is a factor in predicting depression. Note, however, that this is *not* an experiment in which exercise is manipulated as an independent variable and depression measured as a dependent variable. Instead, exercise and depression are simply measured for each of the 20 subjects in the experiment. Therefore, the research hypothesis being tested here is that the measured amount of exercise (a variable at the interval or ratio level) will be negatively correlated with the measured amount of depression (a variable at the interval or ratio level). Symbolically, the research hypothesis—the alternative hypothesis—appears as follows

$$H_{alt}: \rho_{E.D} < 0$$

In plain English, the researcher is predicting that the correlation between measured amount of exercise (E) and measured degree of depression (D) would be less than zero (negative) in the population from which the sample was drawn.

Null Hypothesis: As we saw in Chapter 9, we state the null hypothesis, for the sake of argument, on the assumption that our research hypothesis is incorrect. In the present case, the null hypothesis is that there is *no correlation between exercise and depression*. Symbolically

$$H_{null}: \rho_{E.D} = 0$$

Organizing the Raw Data: When you prepare the data for entry into the Pearson r calculation formula—whether you do the calculations by hand or by computer—you must first label one of the variables as the X variable and the other as the Y variable. The X variable should be the variable that could logically be used to predict the Y variable. In the present example, the intention is to predict a person's level of depression on the basis of that person's amount of exercise. Therefore, amount of exercise is identified as the X variable and level of depression as the Y variable.

After determining which is the X variable and which is the Y variable, you must identify the X value and Y value for each observation in the sample. In the present example, there are 20 pairs of X, Y values, one pair for each of the 20 patients in the sample. Each X value and each Y value can be subscripted for identification. For example, X_3, Y_3 correspond to patient 3 in our sample and thus, according to our test data

$$X_3 = 20$$

$$Y_3 = 40$$

Pearson r Calculation

Once the X and Y values have been identified you may enter the data into the computer or use the following calculation formula

$$r = \frac{N\Sigma(XY) - [(\Sigma X)(\Sigma Y)]}{\sqrt{[N\Sigma X^2 - (\Sigma X)^2][N\Sigma Y^2 - (\Sigma Y)^2]}}$$ (C.17.1)

Note that the square brackets and parentheses indicate the order in which these operations should be carried out. For example, $[(\Sigma X)(\Sigma Y)]$ indicates that the X values are summed and the Y values are summed before the results are multiplied. This is in contrast to $\Sigma(XY)$, in which the X and Y values in each pair are first multiplied, and then the sum of these products is taken.

The calculation procedure is as follows.

Step 1. List your data.

The test data have already been tabulated.

Step 2. Identify the X variable and the Y variable.

We have already decided that amount of exercise is the X variable and degree of depression is the Y variable.

Step 3. Square each of the X values.

In the present case, we obtain the following results.

Patient	X	X^2	Patient	X	X^2
1	110	12,100	11	10	100
2	0	0	12	0	0
3	20	400	13	70	4900
4	0	0	14	10	100
5	10	100	15	240	57,600
6	5	25	16	20	400
7	50	2500	17	5	25
8	80	6400	18	30	900
9	0	0	19	0	0
10	15	225	20	5	25

Step 4. Square each of the Y values.

We obtain the following results.

Patient	Y	Y^2	Patient	Y	Y^2
1	13	169	11	75	5625
2	50	2500	12	84	7056
3	40	1600	13	55	3025
4	85	7225	14	86	7396
5	92	8464	15	35	1225
6	82	6724	16	78	6084
7	60	3600	17	80	6400
8	20	400	18	56	3136
9	90	8100	19	87	7569
10	88	7744	20	84	7056

Step 5. Multiply each X value by each Y value.
Our results are as follows.

X	Y	XY
110	13	1430
0	50	0
20	40	800
0	85	0
10	92	920
5	82	410
50	60	3000
80	20	1600
0	90	0
15	88	1320
10	75	750
0	84	0
70	55	3850
10	86	860
240	35	8400
20	78	1560
5	80	400
30	56	1680
0	87	0
5	84	420

Step 6. Identify N, the total number of observations.
In the present case, $N = 20$.

Step 7. Sum all of the X values.
We find that

$$\sum X = 110 + 0 + 20 + \cdots + 5 = 680$$

Step 8. Sum all of the Y values.
In the present case

$$\sum Y = 13 + 50 + 40 + \cdots + 84 = 1340$$

Step 9. Sum all of X^2 values.
For our data

$$\sum (X^2) = 12,100 + 0 + 400 + \cdots + 25 = 85,800$$

Step 10. Sum all of the Y^2 values.
We find that

$$\sum (Y^2) = 169 + 2500 + 1600 + \cdots + 7056 = 101,098$$

Step 11. Sum all of the XY values.
In the present case

$$\sum (XY) = 1430 + 0 + 800 + \cdots + 420 = 27,400$$

Step 12. Square the sum of the X values.

For our data

$$\left(\sum X\right)^2 = 680^2 = 462,400$$

Step 13. Square the sum of the Y values.
We find that

$$\left(\sum Y\right)^2 = 1340^2 = 1,795,600$$

After completing these operations, you will have calculated all the basic elements in Eq. (C.17.1).

Step 14. Multiply N by the sum of the XY values.
In the present case

$$N\sum(XY) = 20 \times 27,400 = 548,000$$

Step 15. Multiply the sum of the X values by the sum of the Y values.
For our data

$$\left(\sum X\right)\left(\sum Y\right) = 680 \times 1340 = 911,200$$

Step 16. Subtract the result of step 15 from the result of step 14.
We find that

$$N\sum XY - \left[\left(\sum X\right)\left(\sum Y\right)\right] = 548,000 - 911,200$$
$$= -363,200$$

The minus sign here is very important since it will indicate that there is a negative correlation for the data.
We have now calculated the numerator of Eq. (C.17.1).

Step 17. Multiply N by the sum of the squared X values.
In the present case

$$N\sum(X^2) = 20 \times 85,800 = 1,716,000$$

Step 18. Subtract $\left(\sum X\right)^2$ from the results of step 17.
We find that

$$N\sum(X^2) - \left(\sum X\right)^2 = 1,716,000 - 462,400$$
$$= 1,253,600$$

Step 19. Multiply N by the sum of the square Y values.
For our data

$$N\sum(Y^2) = 20 \times 101,098 = 2,021,960$$

Step 20. Subtract $\left(\sum Y\right)^2$ from the results of step 19.
We find that

$$N\sum(Y^2) - \left(\sum Y\right)^2 = 2,021,960 - 1,795,600$$
$$= 226,360$$

Step 21. Multiply the result of step 18 by the results of step 20.
In the present case

$$\left[N\sum X^2 - \left(\sum X\right)^2\right]\left[N\sum Y^2 - \left(\sum Y\right)^2\right] = 1,253,600 \times 226,360$$
$$= 283,764,896,000$$

Step 22. Take the square root of the result of step 21.
We find that

$$\sqrt{\left[N\sum X^2 - \left(\sum X\right)^2\right]\left[N\sum Y^2 - \left(\sum Y\right)^2\right]} = \sqrt{283{,}764{,}896{,}000}$$
$$= 532{,}695{,}876$$

We have now calculated the denominator of Eq. (C.17.1).

Step 23. Divide the result of step 16 by the result of step 22, to obtain the calculated Pearson r value.
Finally, we have

$$r_{calc} = \frac{N\sum(XY) - \left[\left(\sum X\right)\left(\sum Y\right)\right]}{\sqrt{\left[N\sum X^2 - \left(\sum X\right)^2\right]\left[N\sum Y^2 - \left(\sum Y\right)^2\right]}} = \frac{-363{,}200}{532{,}695.876}$$
$$= -.681{,}81 \text{ round to } -.6818$$

Step 24. State your alpha level.
As usual, we assume an alpha level of .05

$$\alpha = .05$$

Step 25. Determine whether you are doing a one-tailed or two-tailed test of your null hypothesis.
The alternative hypothesis for the Pearson r in the present case predicts a negative correlation. Because the alternative hypothesis specifies the direction of the correlation, we set a criterion in only one tail of the sampling distribution of r.

Step 26. Determine the degrees of freedom, by means of the formula

$$df = N - 2$$

where N is the total number of pairs of observations.
In the present case

$$df = 20 - 2 = 18$$

Step 27. Look in a standard Pearson r table (Table B.4) to determine the critical value for a one-tailed test with $\alpha = .05$ and 18 degrees of freedom.
From Table B.4

$$r_{crit} = .3783$$

Step 28. Determine the appropriate sign for the critical Pearson r value.
At this point, we must refer back to our alternative hypothesis. We are predicting a negative correlation, and so the critical r value is located in the left tail of the distribution and will have a negative value.
We state our result formally as follows

$$(r_{crit} = -.3783; \ df = 18; \ \alpha = .05; \text{ one-tailed})$$

Step 29. Compare the calculated Pearson r value to the critical Pearson r value. If the calculated value is at or beyond the critical value, then you should reject the null hypothesis. If the calculated value is not beyond the critical value, then you *should not* reject the null hypothesis.
To say that one value is beyond another means that, regardless of its sign, its magnitude is greater. In the present case, the calculated Pearson r $(-.681{,}88)$ is beyond the critical value $(-.3783)$; therefore, we reject the null hypothesis. (Another way to think about it is to visualize the r value of

−.681,88 as further out in the left tail of the sampling distribution of r values than the critical r value of −.3783.)

Step 30. State your conclusion in a standard statistical format using appropriate statistical symbols.

An appropriate statement is as follows

$$(r_{calc} = -.681.88; df = 18; p < .05; \text{one-tailed})$$

Step 31. State your statistical conclusion in words.

If the null hypothesis were true, the probability of arriving at a calculated Pearson r of −.681.88, with 18 degrees of freedom and a one-tailed test, would be less than .05. Therefore, the null hypothesis *probably* isn't true, and the alternative hypothesis is a better bet.

Step 32. State your final conclusion in plain English.

Given the data and the statistical conclusion, it is reasonable to argue that the degree of depression, as measured in this observation, tends to be lower for people who exercise more, in terms of the measurements made in this observation. In other words, higher levels of exercise tend to be associated with lower levels of depression.

Calculation C.18 Range

There are two methods of computing the range for a set of data. The corresponding formulas are as follows

$$\text{Range} = \frac{(\text{highest data value}) - (\text{lowest data value})}{\text{unit of change}} \qquad (C.18.1)$$

$$\text{Range} = \frac{(\text{highest data value}) - (\text{lowest data value})}{\text{unit of change}} + 1 \qquad (C.18.2)$$

Thus, in the first method, we subtract the lowest data value in the data set from the highest data value, and divide the result by the unit of change for the data set.

In the second method, we proceed exactly as before, but then we add 1 to the result.

In both methods, the basic procedure is the same.

Step 1. List your data.

Step 2. Determine the smallest unit of change for the data set.

Step 3. Determine the highest data value in the data set.

Step 4. Determine the lowest data value in the data set.

Step 5. Substitute these values into the appropriate formula.

Consider the following sample

3, 6, 2, 9

The smallest unit of change is 1, the highest data value is 9, and the lowest data value is 2.

By method 1

$$\text{Range} = \frac{9 - 2}{1} = \frac{7}{1} = 7$$

By method 2, the range is $7 + 1 = 8$.

Now consider the following sample

1.6, 9.3, 8.7, 3.2

The smallest unit of change is 0.1, the highest data value is 9.3, and the lowest data value is 1.6.
By method 1

$$\text{Range} = \frac{9.3 - 1.6}{0.1} = \frac{7.7}{0.1} = 77$$

By method 2, the range is $77 + 1 = 78$.

Calculation C.19 Real Limits of Class Intervals

The real limits for a given class interval may be calculated by means of the following formulas. For the upper real limit (URL)

$$URL_i = UAL_i + \frac{LAL_{i+1} - UAL_i}{2}$$

For the lower real limit (LRL)

$$LRL_i = LAL_i - \frac{LAL_{i+1} - UAL_i}{2}$$

Thus, the upper real limit of a particular class interval (i) is equal to the upper apparent limit (UAL) of that interval plus one-half of the difference between the upper apparent limit of the class interval and the lower apparent limit (LAL) of the class interval immediately above ($i + 1$).

The lower real limit of a particular class interval (i) is equal to the lower apparent limit of that interval minus one-half of the difference between the upper apparent limit of the class interval and the lower apparent limit of the class interval immediately above ($i + 1$).

The corresponding procedure is as follows.

Step 1. Identify the apparent limits of the class intervals.
Consider the following two intervals.

Interval number	Class interval
2	96–100
1	91–95

The lower apparent limit of the first interval is 91: $LAL_1 = 91$.
The upper apparent limit of the first interval is 95: $UAL_1 = 95$.
The lower apparent limit of the second interval is 96: $LAL_2 = 96$.
The upper apparent limit of the second interval is 100: $UAL_2 = 100$.

Step 2. Substitute the values from step 1 into the appropriate formulas for each class interval in your data.
For interval 1

$$URL_1 = UAL_1 + \frac{LAL_2 - UAL_1}{2}$$

$$= 95 + \frac{96 - 95}{2}$$

$$= 95 + 0.5$$

$$= 95.5$$

$$\text{LRL}_1 = \text{LAL}_1 - \frac{\text{LAL}_2 - \text{UAL}_1}{2}$$

$$= 91 - \frac{96 - 95}{2}$$

$$= 91 - 0.5$$

$$= 90.5$$

Step 3. Restate all the class intervals using the real limits.

Applying the same logic to class interval 2, we state the results as follows.

Interval number	Class interval
2	95.5–100.5
1	90.5–95.5

Calculation C.20 Scheffe

Type of research: Experiment
Number of dependent variables: 1
Level of measurement: Interval/ratio
Assumptions met: Yes

The Scheffe is a post-ANOVA analysis and is considered in the discussion of the corresponding ANOVA procedures: one independent variable, between-groups design (Calculation C.1); one independent variable, within-groups design (Calculation C.2); two independent variables, between-groups design (Calculation C.3), and two independent variables, one between-groups and one within groups (Calculation C.4).

Calculation C.21 Sign Test

Type of research: Experiment
Number of dependent variables: 1
Level of measurement: Ordinal
Number of independent variables: 1
Conditions of independent variable: 2
Type of design: Within-groups (w-g)
Choice of analysis: Sign test

Motivation for Research: A researcher believes that listening to classical music will improve a person's reaction time.

Description of Research: The researcher randomly selects 12 people from the general population. The reaction time of each person is first measured in some way. Then, each person is asked to sit in a room for 15 minutes and to try to relax by listening to classical music. At the end of the 15-minute relaxation period, the reaction time of each person is measured again. The only information that the researcher has after this second measurement is whether each person was faster or slower after the

15-minute relaxation period.

Type of Conclusion Possible: The sign test analysis will allow the researcher to determine if the number of subjects who improved their reaction time after the relaxation period is significantly greater than the number of subjects who did not.

Comments: If the results of the sign test analysis indicate that the number of subjects who improved their reaction time is significantly greater than the number who did not, then the researcher may conclude that listening to classical music had the significant effect of improving the reaction times of the subjects.

Test Data:

Person	Score
1	Faster
2	Slower
3	Faster
4	Faster
5	Faster
6	Faster
7	Faster
8	Slower
9	Faster
10	Faster
11	Faster
12	Slower

Specifics Regarding the Analysis: The sign test helps the researcher to determine whether or not there is a significant change from the first to the second of two measurements beyond what would be expected by chance.

Research Hypothesis: The researcher believes that listening to classical music will decrease reaction time. Symbolically, the research hypothesis—alternative hypothesis—appears as follows:

H_{alt}: Number faster > number slower

In plain English, the researcher is predicting that the number of subjects who were faster after listening to classical music will be significantly greater than the number of subjects who were slower.

Null Hypothesis: As we noted in Chapter 9, we state the null hypothesis, for the sake of argument, on the assumption that our research hypothesis is incorrect. In the present case, the null hypothesis is that there is *no difference between the number who are faster and the number who are slower.* Symbolically

H_{null}: Number faster = number slower

Organizing the Raw Data: When you prepare the data for the sign test calculation, you need to identify the following:

- the independent variable: music, in the present case.
- the two conditions of the experiment: before and after.
- the number of subjects in each condition: 12 and 12.
- the dependent variable: reaction time.

Sign Test Calculation

Once these values have been identified, you must find the difference between each pair of before and after scores. Then you simply count the number of subjects whose scores show improvement in reaction time and the number whose after scores are no better than their before scores. You enter these frequency counts in the calculation formulas for the binomial analysis. (See Calculation C.5.)

Testing the Sign Test Statistic for Significance: The sign test calculation is actually a version of the binomial test: To determine whether the null hypothesis can be rejected, the frequency of the event of interest is compared with a criterion based on the binomial model.

Results of the Sign Test Calculation: In the present case, nine subjects are found to be faster after the relaxation period, and three are slower. The binomial probability that at least nine out of 12 will be faster is .073. As usual, we assume an alpha level of .05.

Statistical Conclusion: Since .073 is greater than .05, we cannot reject the null hypothesis.

Plain English Conclusion: Listening to classical music did not improve the reactions times of the subjects.

Calculation C.22 Spearman *r* Correlation Coefficient

Type of research: Observation
Number of variables: 2
Levels of measurement: Ordinal (both variables)
Choice of analysis: Spearman *r*

Motivation for Research: A researcher believes that a boy's height in the freshman year of high school is negatively correlated with his degree of aggressiveness.

Description of Research: The researcher randomly selects 20 students from the population of freshman high school males. Each student is asked to join in a contest in which participants stand in a circle and try to push each other out; they all agree to participate. Each student is ranked on the basis of when he is pushed out of the circle: first, second, and so on. After the contest, all 20 students are asked to line up by height; their height ranks are also recorded, from tallest (first) to shortest (last).

Type of Conclusion Possible: The Spearman *r* analysis will allow the researcher to determine if the aggressiveness of each participant—as measured by his finishing position in the push-out contest—is correlated with his height—as measured by ranking from tallest (first) to shortest (last). If there is a sufficiently high degree of correlation, then the researcher may conclude that the relative height—as operationally defined in this study—may be used to predict the degree of aggressiveness—as measured in this study.

Comments: Both of the variables being measured—height ranked and pushed-out rank—are at the ordinal level of measurement. In this case, the Spearman *r* analysis is appropriate, rather than the Pearson *r* analysis, which requires that both variables be at the interval or ratio level.

Because the researcher is predicting a positive correlation between height and aggressiveness, the correlation between height rank and pushed-out rank should be negative. In other words, it is predicted that the pushed-out rank will be lower for shorter students. The shortest person, with the 20th height rank, is most likely to be pushed out first.

This illustrates that the direction of the correlation—positive versus negative—is incidental. If the short students were ranked lowest (ascribing the first rank to the shortest person and so on), a positive correlation would be predicted.

In determining the ranks, use the procedure outlined in Calculation C.11 (p. 389) to deal with tied ranks. However, if more than a third of the ranks are tied, use the Pearson *r* formula for greater accuracy.

Test Data:

Boy	Height rank	Pushed-out rank
1	4	15
2	11	8
3	3	17
4	12	10
5	2	20
6	20	4
7	19	5
8	10	9
9	15	3
10	5	13
11	16	19
12	13	6
13	14	2
14	6	7
15	1	18
16	7	12
17	18	1
18	9	11
19	17	16
20	8	14

Specifics Regarding the Analysis: The Spearman r analysis helps the researcher to determine whether or not there is a significant correlation between two variables at the ordinal level that represent a pair of observed measurements for each of the subjects or items in the observation. In the present study, the two observed measurements for each of the 20 subjects are a height rank and a push-out rank. For boy 15, for example, the observed ranks are: 1 (he was the tallest in the sample) and 18 (he was one of the last to be pushed out of the circle).

The calculations result in a single Spearman r value ranging from -1.00 to $+1.00$. The sign of the r value (plus or minus) indicates the direction of the correlation. A plus sign indicates a positive correlation: High values of one variable tend to be associated with high values of the other. A minus sign indicates a negative correlation: High values of one variable tend to be associated with low values of the other. In the present example, the research hypothesis predicts a negative correlation such that high rankings on height (that is, short boys) would tend to be associated with low push-out rankings (supposing that the first person to be pushed out is the least aggressive). In other words, the research hypothesis predicts a negative Spearman r.

The Spearman r value is referred to as a test statistic: It is a *statistic* because it is based upon *sample* data fed into the Spearman r calculation formula. However, research hypotheses and null hypotheses make predictions regarding the populations from which the samples are drawn. The population *parameter* that corresponds to the Spearman r statistic is denoted by ρ.

Research Hypothesis: The researcher believes that height is a factor in predicting aggressiveness. Note, however, that this is *not* an experiment in which height is manipulated as an independent variable and aggressiveness is measured as a dependent variable. Instead, height and aggressiveness are each simply measured for each of the 20 subjects in the observation. Therefore, the research hypothesis being tested here is that the ranked height (a variable at the ordinal level) will be negatively correlated with the order in which people are pushed out of the circle (a variable at the ordinal level). Symbolically, the research hypothesis—the alternative hypothesis—appears as follows

$H_{alt}: \rho_{H,PO} < 0$

In plain English, the researcher is predicting that the correlation between height rank (H) and pushed-out rank (PO) would be less than zero (negative) in the population from which the sample was drawn.

Null Hypothesis: As we noted in Chapter 9, we state the null hypothesis, for the sake of argument, on the assumption that our research hypothesis is incorrect. In the present case, the null hypothesis is that there is *no correlation between ranked height and the order in which people are pushed out of the circle.* Symbolically

$$H_{null}: \rho_{H,PO} = 0$$

Organizing the Raw Data: When you prepare the data for entry into Spearman r calculation formula—whether you do the calculations by hand or by computer—you must first label one of the variables as the X variable and the other as the Y variable. The X variable should be the variable that could logically be used to predict the Y variable. In the present case, the intention is to predict a boy's aggressiveness on the basis of his height. Therefore, height—operationally defined by height rank (the tallest ranks first)—is identified as the X variable, and aggressiveness—operationally defined by the order in which the boy is pushed out of the circle (the least aggressive is the first pushed out) is identified as the Y variable.

After determining which is the X variable and which is the Y variable, you need to identify the X value and Y value for each observation in the sample. There is one pair of X, Y values for each of the 20 people in this observation. Each X value and each Y value can be subscripted for identification. For example, X_5, Y_5 correspond to the fifth boy in our sample and thus, according to our test data

$$X_5 = 2$$
$$Y_5 = 20$$

indicating that he was the second tallest boy and the 20th to be pushed out of the circle (more precisely, the last left standing in the circle).

Having identified the X and Y values, you must make sure that both the X variable and the Y variable are at the ordinal level of measurement. In the present example, both variables are already at the ordinal level.

Spearman r Calculation

Having confirmed that the X and Y values are at the ordinal level, you may enter the data into the computer or use the calculation formula as follows.

Step 1. List your data.
  The test data have already been tabulated.

Step 2. Identify the X variable and the Y variable.
  We have already decided that height in the freshman year of high school is the X variable, and aggressiveness is the Y variable.

Step 3. Rank the data for each variable, if they are not already ranked. Then find the difference between the ranks in each pair. Square these differences and sum the squared differences.
  The results of these operations are shown in Table C.22.1.

Step 4. Compute the Spearman r by means of the formula

$$r_s = 1 - \frac{6 \sum (D^2)}{N(N^2 - 1)} \tag{C.22.1}$$

where N is the total number of pairs of ranks. In the present case

$$r_{S_{calc}} = 1 - \frac{6(2162)}{20(20^2 - 1)}$$

$$= 1 - \frac{12,972}{20(399)}$$

TABLE C.22.1 Ranks and Differences between Ranks

Height rank	Pushed-out rank	Difference (D)	D^2
4	15	−11	121
11	8	3	9
3	17	−14	196
12	10	2	4
2	20	−18	324
20	4	16	256
19	5	14	196
10	9	1	1
15	3	12	144
5	13	−8	64
16	19	−3	9
13	6	7	49
14	2	12	144
6	7	−1	1
1	18	−17	289
7	12	−5	25
18	1	17	289
9	11	−2	4
17	16	1	1
8	14	−6	36
Sum			2162

$$= 1 - \frac{12{,}972}{7980}$$

$$= 1 - 1.6256$$

$$= -.6256$$

Step 5. State your alpha level. [We assume .05, unless otherwise stated]

$\alpha = .05$

Step 6. Determine whether you are doing a one-tailed or a two-tailed test of your null hypothesis.
In the present case, the alternative hypothesis specifies the direction of the correlation; therefore, we are doing a one-tailed test.

Step 7. Determine the degrees of freedom by means of the following formula

$df = N - 2$

$(C.22.2)$

In the present case

$df = 20 - 2 = 18$

Step 8. Look in the Spearman r table (Table B.5) to determine the critical Spearman r value for a one-tailed test with $\alpha = .05$ and 18 degrees of freedom.
We find that the critical Spearman r for $\alpha = .05$ with 18 degrees of freedom and a one-tailed alternative hypothesis predicting a negative correlation is $-.378$. We state our

result formally as follows

$$(r_{S_{crit}} = -.378; df = 18; \alpha = .05; \text{one-tailed})$$

You will have noticed that, in Table B.5, the critical r values for positive and negative correlations are given with the corresponding sign. However, most standard tables do not indicate the sign of the critical r. You must determine the sign on the basis of your alternative hypothesis.

Step 9. Compare the calculated Spearman r to the critical Spearman r.

In the case of a negative critical value, you must reject the null hypothesis if the calculated value is less than or equal to the critical value. In the case of a positive negative value, you must reject the null if the calculated value is greater than or equal to the null.

In the present case, the calculated r ($-.6256$) is less than the negative critical value ($-.378$); therefore, we reject the null hypothesis.

Step 10. State your conclusion in a standard statistical format using appropriate statistical symbols.

An appropriate statement is as follows

$$(r_{S_{calc}} = -.6256; df = 18; p < .05; \text{one-tailed})$$

Step 11. State your statistical conclusion in words.

If the null hypothesis were true, the probability of arriving at a calculated Spearman r of $-.6256$ with 18 degrees of freedom and a one-tailed alternative hypothesis would be less than .05. Therefore, the null hypothesis *probably* isn't true, and the alternative hypothesis probably is true.

Step 12. State your final conclusion in plain English.

Given the data and the statisical conclusion, it is reasonable to argue that there is a correlation between a boy's height in the freshman year of high school and his aggressiveness: Tall boys tend to be more aggressive.

Calculation C.23 Standard Deviation

The calculation formula for the standard deviation is as follows

$$\text{Standard deviation} = \sqrt{\frac{\sum (X^2) - \frac{(\sum X)^2}{N}}{N}} \qquad (C.23.1)$$

The sample data for the present calculation, originally stated in Table 4.23, are the measured arm lengths (in inches) for five people (randomly selected from Database A.7)

34, 27, 31, 28, 24

Here are the steps you should follow when calculating the standard deviation for a set of data.

Step 1. Square each of the data values in the data set.

The results for our data are shown in Table C.23.1.

Step 2. Sum all of the squared data values obtained in step 1.

In the present case

$$\sum (X^2) = 1156 + 729 + 961 + 784 + 576 = 4206$$

Step 3. Sum all of the data values.

For our data

$$\sum X = 34 + 27 + 31 + 28 + 24 = 144$$

TABLE C.23.1	Results of Squaring the Data
X	X²
34	1156
27	729
31	961
28	784
24	576

Step 4. Square the sum of the X values.
We find that

$$(\sum X)^2 = 144^2 = 20{,}736$$

Step 5. Divide the result of step 4 by the total number of data values in the data set (N).
In the present case, $N = 5$, and

$$\frac{(\sum X)^2}{N} = \frac{20{,}736}{5} = 4147.2$$

Step 6. Subtract the result of step 5 from the result of step 2.
For our data

$$\sum (X^2) - \frac{(\sum X)^2}{N} = 4206 - 4147.2 = 58.8$$

This step completes the numerator of Eq. (C.23.1).

Step 7. Divide the result of step 6 by the total number of data values in the data set.
In the present case

$$\frac{\sum (X^2) - \frac{(\sum X)^2}{N}}{N} = \frac{58.8}{5} = 11.76$$

We have now calculated the part of the formula within the square root sign. This is actually the variance for the data set.

Step 8. Take the square root of the result of step 7.
We find that

$$\sqrt{11.76} = 3.43$$

This is the final result.

Step 9. Refer to the final result in the following ways.
If all the data values in a sample were used in Eq. (C.23.1), as in the present case, the result is the standard deviation of a sample and may be stated symbolically as follows

$$s = 3.43$$

This is a statistic.

If all the data values in a population were used in Eq. (C.23.1), the result is the standard deviation of the population and may be stated symbolically as follows

$$\sigma = 3.43$$

This is a parameter.

If you do not know whether the data are a sample or a population, the result can be stated generically as follows

Standard deviation = 3.43

$$\text{S.D.} = 3.43$$

Calculation C.24 Standard Score

The conceptual formula for calculating the standard score of a data set is as follows

$$\text{Standard score} = \frac{(\text{raw score}) - (\text{mean})}{\text{standard deviation}}$$

If you are working with the sample mean and the sample standard deviation, this formula takes the form

$$Z = \frac{X - \bar{X}}{s} \qquad (C.24.1)$$

If you are working with the population mean and the population standard deviation, the appropriate form is

$$Z = \frac{X - \mu}{\sigma} \qquad (C.24.2)$$

If you are working with the population mean and an unbiased estimate of the population standard deviation, the correct notation is as follows

$$Z = \frac{X - \mu}{\tilde{\sigma}} \qquad (C.24.3)$$

Finally, if you are working with the sample mean and an unbiased estimate of the population standard deviation, the formula looks like this

$$Z = \frac{X - \bar{X}}{\tilde{\sigma}} \qquad (C.24.4)$$

The calculation procedure is as follows.

Step 1. List your data and identify the raw score for which you wish to calculate the standard score.
Suppose that we have the following data

4, 7, 3, 8, 6, 5, 4, 4, 3, 9

We choose 6 as the raw score for our calculation

$$X = 6$$

Step 2. Square each data value. Determine the sum of the data values. Determine the sum of the squared data values. Summarize the results.
Our results are summarized in Table C.24.1.

Step 3. Calculate the mean for the data
For our data

$$\bar{X} = \frac{53}{10} = 5.3$$

TABLE C.24.1 Results of Squaring and Summing

X	X²
4	16
7	49
3	9
8	64
6	36
5	25
4	16
4	16
3	9
9	81
Sum 53	321

Step 4. Calculate the standard deviation for the data.

Usually, when you compute a standard score, you are assuming that the raw score is coming from a population that is normally distributed. Under such circumstances, it is reasonable to estimate the standard deviation of that population and to use this estimate in the calculation of the standard score. The corresponding formula is as follows (see Chapter 6, p. 128)

$$\tilde{\sigma} = \sqrt{\frac{\sum (X^2) - \frac{\left(\sum X\right)^2}{n}}{n-1}}$$

We find that

$$\tilde{\sigma} = \sqrt{\frac{321 - \frac{(53)^2}{10}}{9}}$$

$$= \sqrt{\frac{321 - \frac{2809}{10}}{9}}$$

$$= \sqrt{\frac{321 - 280.9}{9}}$$

$$= \sqrt{\frac{40.1}{9}}$$

$$= \sqrt{4.455}$$

$$= 2.11$$

Step 5. Enter the results into the appropriate formula for the standard score.

Thus, in the present case, the standard score is

$$Z = \frac{X - \bar{X}}{\hat{\sigma}}$$

$$= \frac{6 - 5.3}{2.11}$$

$$= \frac{0.7}{2.11}$$

$$= 0.3317$$

Calculation C.25 *t*-Test for Independent Groups (Between Groups)

Type of research: Experiment
Number of dependent variables: 1
Level of measurement: Interval/ratio
Assumptions met: Yes
Number of independent variables: 1
Conditions of independent variables: 2
Type of design: Between-groups (B-G)
Choice of analysis: *t*-test for independent groups

Motivation for Research: A researcher believes that listening to classical music will improve a person's reaction time.

Description of Research: The researcher randomly selects 20 people from the general population and then randomly assigns 10 of these people to a control group and the remaining 10 to an experimental group. In the control group, each of the 10 people is asked to sit in a room for 15 minutes and to try to relax. In the experimental group, each of the 10 people is asked to sit in a room for 15 minutes and to try to relax by listening to classical music. All subjects in both the experimental and control groups are tested for their reaction times after the 15-minute relaxation period.

Type of Conclusion Possible: The *t*-test for independent groups analysis will allow the researcher to determine if the average reaction time for the experimental group (who listened to classical music) is significantly lower than the average reaction time for the control group.

Comments: If the results of the *t*-test indicate that the mean reaction time is significantly lower for the experimental group, the researcher may conclude that listening to classical music had the significant effect of improving the reaction times of the subjects.

Assumptions: Suppose that the parametric assumptions are met.

Test Data:

Classical music group		Control group	
Person	Reaction time	Person	Reaction time
1	2.36	11	2.79
2	2.10	12	2.58
3	2.20	13	2.41
4	2.32	14	2.49
5	2.14	15	2.47
6	2.30	16	2.34
7	2.45	17	2.68
8	2.47	18	2.70
9	2.38	19	2.56
10	2.46	20	2.62

Specifics Regarding the Analysis: The *t*-test for independent groups helps the researcher to determine whether or not two sample means differ significantly from what would be expected by chance.

Research Hypothesis: The researcher believes that listening to classical music will decrease reaction time. Symbolically, the research hypothesis—the alternative hypothesis—appears as follows

$$H_{alt}: \mu_{music} < \mu_{control}$$

In plain English, the researcher is predicting that the average reaction time for the classical music condition will be significantly lower than the average reaction time for the control group.

Null Hypothesis: As we noted in Chapter 9, we state the null hypothesis, for the sake of argument, on the assumption that our research hypothesis is incorrect. In the present case, the null hypothesis is that there is *no difference between the average reaction time for the classical music group and the average reaction time for the control group*. Symbolically

$$H_{null}: \mu_{music} = \mu_{control}$$

Organizing the Raw Data: When you prepare the data for entry into the *t*-test formula—whether you do the calculations by hand or by computer—you need to identify the following:

- the independent variable: music, in the present case.
- the two conditions of the experiment: classical music and control group.
- the number of subjects in each condition: 10 and 10.
- the dependent variable: reaction time.

t-Test Calculation

Once these values have been identified, you may enter them into the computer or use the following calculation formula

$$t = \frac{(\bar{X}_1 - \bar{X}_2) - (\mu_1 - \mu_2)}{\sqrt{\left(\dfrac{\{\sum X_1^2 - [(\sum X_1)^2/N_1]\} + \{\sum X_2^2 - [(\sum X_2)^2/N_2]\}}{N_1 + N_2 - 2}\right)\left(\dfrac{1}{N_1} + \dfrac{1}{N_2}\right)}} \tag{C.25.1}$$

The calculation procedure is as follows.

Step 1. List your data.
  The test data have already been tabulated.

Step 2. Identify the conditions of the experiment.
  In the present case, we have the classical music condition (condition 1) and the control condition, with no music (condition 2).

Step 3. Calculate the mean for condition 1.
  The mean of the scores for the classical music group is 2.32. Thus

$$\bar{X}_1 = 2.32$$

Step 4. Calculate the mean for condition 2.
  The mean of the scores for the control group is 2.56. Thus

$$\bar{X}_2 = 2.56$$

Step 5. Calculate the difference between the means for conditions 1 and 2.
  In the present case

$$\bar{X}_1 - \bar{X}_2 = 2.32 - 2.56 = -0.24$$

Step 6. Determine the null-hypothesis difference between the population mean for condition 1 and the population mean for condition 2.

If the null hypothesis were true, the difference between the population mean for the classical music group and the population mean for the control group would be zero. Thus

$$\mu_1 - \mu_2 = 0$$

Step 7. Subtract the result of step 6 from the result of step 5.

We find that

$$(\bar{X}_1 - \bar{X}_2) - (\mu_1 - \mu_2) = -0.24 - 0$$
$$= -0.24$$

We have now calculated the numerator of Eq. (C.25.1).

Step 8. Square each of the scores for condition 1, and then find the sum of all these squared scores.

The sum of the squared scores for the classical music condition is 53.89. Thus

$$\sum X_1{}^2 = 53.89$$

Step 9. Sum all the scores for condition 1, and then square this sum.

The squared sum of scores for the classical music condition is 537.31. Thus

$$\left(\sum X_1\right)^2 = 537.31$$

Step 10. Divide the result of step 9 by the number of scores in condition 1 (N_1).

For our data

$$\frac{\left(\sum X_1\right)^2}{N_1} = \frac{537.31}{10} = 53.73$$

Step 11. Subtract the result of step 10 from the result of step 8.

In the present case

$$\sum X_1{}^2 - \frac{\left(\sum X_1\right)^2}{N_1} = 53.89 - 53.73 = 0.16$$

Step 12. Square each of the scores for condition 2, and then find the sum of all these squared scores.

The sum of the squared scores for the control condition is 65.92. Thus

$$\sum X_2{}^2 = 65.92$$

Step 13. Sum all the scores for condition 2, and then square this sum.

The squared sum of scores for the control condition is 657.41. Thus

$$\left(\sum X_2\right)^2 = 657.41$$

Step 14. Divide the result of step 13 by the number of scores in condition 2 (N_2).

For our data

$$\frac{\left(\sum X_2\right)^2}{N_2} = \frac{657.41}{10} = 65.74$$

Step 15. Subtract the result of step 14 from the result of step 12.

In the present case

$$\sum X_2{}^2 - \frac{\left(\sum X_2\right)^2}{N_2} = 65.92 - 65.74 = 0.18$$

Step 16. Add the result of step 15 to the result of step 11.
We find that

$$\left[\sum X_1{}^2 - \frac{(\sum X_1)^2}{N_1}\right] + \left[X_2{}^2 - \frac{(\sum X_2)^2}{N_2}\right] = 0.16 + 0.18 = 0.34$$

Step 17. Add the number of scores in condition 1 to the number of scores in condition 2 and then subtract 2.
For our data

$$N_1 + N_2 - 2 = 10 + 10 - 2 = 18$$

Step 18. Divide the result of step 16 by the result of step 17.
We find that

$$\frac{\{\sum X_1{}^2 - [(\sum X_1)^2/N_1]\} + \{X_2{}^2 - [(\sum X_2)^2/N_2]\}}{N_2 + N_2 - 2} = \frac{0.34}{18} = 0.019$$

Step 19. Divide 1 by the number of scores in condition 1.
In the present case

$$\frac{1}{N_1} = \frac{1}{10} = 0.1$$

Step 20. Divide 1 by the number of scores in condition 2.
In the present case

$$\frac{1}{N_2} = \frac{1}{10} = 0.1$$

Step 21. Add the results of step 19 to the results of step 20.
For our data

$$\frac{1}{N_1} + \frac{1}{N_2} = 0.1 + 0.1 = 0.2$$

Step 22. Multiply the result of step 21 by the result of step 18.
We find that

$$\left(\frac{\{\sum X_1{}^2 - [(\sum X_1)^2/N_1]\} + \{\sum X_2{}^2 - [(\sum X_2)^2/N_2]\}}{N_1 + N_2 - 2}\right)\left(\frac{1}{N_1} + \frac{1}{N_2}\right) = 0.2 \times 0.019$$

$$= 0.0038$$

Step 23. Find the square root of the result obtained in step 22.

$$\sqrt{\left(\frac{\{\sum X_1{}^2 - [(\sum X_1)^2/N_1]\} + \{\sum X_2{}^2 - [(\sum X_2)^2/N_2]\}}{N_1 + N_2 - 2}\right)\left(\frac{1}{N_1} + \frac{1}{N_2}\right)} = \sqrt{0.0038}$$

$$= 0.0616$$

We round this result to .06. This is the denominator of Eq. (C.25.1).

Step 24. Divide the result of step 7 by the result of step 24, to obtain the calculated t value.
Our final result is

$$t_{calc} = \frac{-0.24}{0.06} = -4$$

Step 25. State your alpha level.
   As usual, we assume an alpha level of .05

$$\alpha = .05$$

Step 26. Determine whether you are doing a one-tailed or two-tailed test of the null hypothesis.
   The alternative hypothesis for the *t*-test analysis in the present case predicts that the mean reaction time for the classical music condition will be less than the mean reaction time for the control condition. Because the alternative hypothesis specifies the direction of the difference, we adopt a one-tailed test.

Step 27. Determine the degrees of freedom, from the formula

$$df = N_1 + N_2 - 2$$

   In the present case

$$df = 10 + 10 - 2 = 20 - 2 = 18$$

Step 28. Look in a standard *t* table (Table B.12) to determine the critical *t* value for a one-tailed test with $\alpha = .05$ and 18 degrees of freedom.
   According to Table B.12, the critical *t* value is -1.734.
   Although Table B.12 includes the appropriate sign of the critical *t* value, some tables do not. You must then refer back to your alternative hypothesis. If you are predicting that the first mean will be less than the second mean, as in the present example, the critical *t* value is located in the left tail of the sampling distribution and will have a negative value. If you were predicting that the first mean will be greater than the second mean, the critical *t* value would be in the right tail of the sampling distribution and have a positive value.
   We state our result formally as follows

$$(t_{crit} = -1.734;\ df = 18;\ \alpha = .05;\ \text{one-tailed})$$

Step 29. Compare the calculated *t* value to the critical *t* value. If the absolute value of the calculated value is equal to or geater than the absolute value of the critical *t* value, you must reject the null hypothesis. If not, you must not reject the null hypothesis.
   The calculated *t* value for our data (-4) is greater in absolute value than the critical *t* (-1.734); therefore, we reject the null hypothesis.

Step 30. State your conclusion in a standard statistical format using appropriate statistical symbols.
   An appropriate statement is as follows

$$(t_{calc} = -4;\ df = 18;\ p < .05;\ \text{one-tailed})$$

Step 31. State your statistical conclusion in words.
   If the null hypothesis were true, the probability of arriving at a calculated *t* value of -4 with 18 degrees of freedom and a one-tailed test would be less than .05. Therefore, the null hypothesis is *probably* not true, and the alternative hypothesis is a better bet.

Step 32. State your final conclusion in plain English.
   Given the data and the statistical conclusion, it is reasonable to argue that the reaction time was reduced by listening to classical music.

Calculation C.26 *t*-Test for Dependent Groups (Within Groups or Matched Groups)

Type of research: Experiment
Number of dependent variables: 1
Level of measurement: Interval/ratio
Assumptions met: Yes
Number of independent variables: 1
Conditions of independent variable: 2
Type of design: Matched groups
Choice of analysis: *t*-test for dependent groups

Motivation for Research: A researcher believes that listening to classical music will improve a person's reaction time.

Description of Research: The researcher randomly selects 20 people from the general population. Their reaction times are first measured on a standard task. After this initial reaction time measurement, these 20 people are ranked from fastest to slowest and placed into matched pairs. (The first and second ranked people are identified as one pair, the third and fourth ranked people as another pair, and so on.) Then one member of each matched pair is randomly assigned to the control condition, and the other member is assigned to the experimental condition. After all matched assignments are made, there are 10 subjects in the control condition and 10 subjects in the experimental condition. Each of the 10 subjects in the control condition is asked to sit in a room for 15 minutes and to try to relax. After this 15-minutes relaxation period, the reaction times of the 10 people are measured again on the same standard task. Each of the 10 subjects in the experimental condition is asked to sit in a room for 15 minutes and to try to relax while listening to classical music. After this 15-minute relaxation period, the reaction times of the 10 people are measured again on the same standard task.

Type of Conclusion Possible: The *t*-test for dependent groups analysis will allow the researcher to determine whether the mean reaction time for the experimental group is significantly lower than the mean reaction time for the control group.

Comments: If the results of the *t*-test indicate that the mean reaction time is significantly lower for the experimental group, the researcher may conclude that listening to classical music had the significant effect of improving the reaction times of the subjects.

Assumptions: Suppose that the parametric assumptions are met.

Test Data:

Classical music group		Control group	
Person	Reaction time	Person	Reaction time
1	2.58	11	2.69
2	2.49	12	2.58
3	2.34	13	2.41
4	2.46	14	2.49
5	2.32	15	2.47
6	2.31	16	2.34
7	2.59	17	2.68
8	2.66	18	2.70
9	2.48	19	2.56
10	2.58	20	2.62

Specifics Regarding the Analysis: The t-test for dependent groups helps the researcher to determine whether or not two sample means differ significantly from what would be expected by chance.

Research Hypothesis: The researcher believes that listening to classical music will decrease reaction time. Symbolically, the research hypothesis—the alternative hypothesis—appears as follows

H_{alt}: $\mu_{music} < \mu_{control}$

In plain English, the researcher is predicting that the average reaction time after listening to classical music will be significantly lower than the average reaction of the control group.

Null Hypothesis: As we noted in Chapter 9, we state the null hypothesis for the sake of argument, on the assumption that our research hypothesis is incorrect. In the present case, the null hypothesis is that there is *no difference between the average reaction time without the classical music and the average reaction time after the classical music.* Symbolically

H_{null}: $\mu_{music} = \mu_{control}$

Organizing the Raw Data: When you prepare the data for entry into the t-test formula—whether you do the calculations by hand or by computer—you need to identify the following:

- the independent variable: music, in the present case.

- the two conditions of the experiment: classical music and control group.

- the number of subjects in each condition: 10 and 10.

- the dependent variable: reaction time.

Note that the subjects are matched in the present case.

t-Test Calculation

Once these values have been identified, you may enter them into the computer or use the calculation formula as follows.

Step 1. List your obtained data.
        The test data have already been tabulated.
Step 2. Identify the conditions of the experiment.
        In the present case, we have the classical music condition (condition 1) and the control condition, with no music (condition 2).
Step 3. Calculate the mean for condition 1.
        The mean of the scores for the classical music group is 2.481. Thus

$\bar{X}_1 = 2.481$

Step 4. Calculate the mean for condition 2.
        The mean of the scores for the control group is 2.554. Thus

$\bar{X}_2 = 2.554$

Step 5. Calculate the difference between the means for conditions 1 and 2.
        In the present case

$\bar{X}_1 - \bar{X}_2 = 2.481 - 2.554 = -0.073$

Step 6. Determine the null-hypothesis difference between the population mean for condition 1 and the population mean for condition 2.
        If the null hypothesis were true, the difference between the population mean for the classical music group and the population mean for the control group would be zero. Thus

$\mu_1 - \mu_2 = 0$

Step 7. Subtract the result of step 6 from the result of step 5.
We find that

$$(\bar{X}_1 - \bar{X}_2) - (\mu_1 - \mu_2) = -0.073 - 0 = -0.073$$

Step 8. Find the difference between the scores for each matched pair. Then square each of these differences, and sum both the differences and the squared differences.
The results for the present case are shown in Table C.26.1.

Step 9. Determine the calculated t value, by substituting the results obtained into the formula

$$t_{dep} = \frac{(\bar{X}_1 - \bar{X}_2) - (\mu_1 - \mu_2)}{\sqrt{\dfrac{\sum D^2 - [(\sum D)^2/N]}{N(N-1)}}} \tag{C.26.1}$$

where N is the total number of data pairs.
For our data, $N = 10$, and thus

$$t_{calc} = \frac{-0.073}{\sqrt{\dfrac{0.0671 - [(-0.73)^2/10]}{10(9)}}}$$

$$= \frac{-0.073}{\sqrt{\dfrac{0.0671 - (0.5329/10)}{90}}}$$

$$= \frac{-0.073}{\sqrt{\dfrac{0.0671 - (0.05329)}{90}}}$$

$$= \frac{-0.073}{\sqrt{\dfrac{0.0138}{90}}}$$

$$= \frac{-0.073}{\sqrt{0.0001533}}$$

TABLE C.26.1 **Differences and Squared Differences**

	X_1	X_2	Difference (D)	D^2
	2.58	2.69	−0.11	0.0121
	2.49	2.58	−0.09	0.0081
	2.34	2.41	−0.07	0.0049
	2.46	2.49	−0.03	0.0009
	2.32	2.47	−0.15	0.0225
	2.31	2.34	−0.03	0.0009
	2.59	2.68	−0.09	0.0081
	2.66	2.70	−0.04	0.0016
	2.48	2.56	−0.08	0.0064
	2.58	2.62	−0.04	0.0016
Sum			−0.73	0.0671

$$= \frac{-0.073}{0.01238}$$

$$= -5.8966$$

Step 10. State your alpha level.

> As usual, we adopt an alpha level of .05

$$\alpha = .05$$

Step 11. Determine whether you are doing a one-tailed or two-tailed test of the null hypothesis.

> The alternative hypothesis predicts a specific direction for the difference between the two groups; therefore, this is a one-tailed hypothesis.

Step 12. Determine the degrees of freedom, from the formula

$$df = N - 1 \quad \text{where } N = \text{number of matched pairs}$$

For our data

$$df = 10 - 1 = 9$$

Step 13. Look in a standard t table (Table B.12) to determine the critical t value for a one-tailed test with $\alpha = .05$ and nine degrees of freedom.

> According to Table B.12, the critical t value is -1.833.
>
> Although Table B.12 includes the appropriate sign of the critical t value, some tables do not. You must then refer back to your alternative hypothesis. If you are predicting that the first mean will be less than the second mean, as in the present example, the critical t is located in the left tail of the sampling distribution and will have a negative value. If you were predicting that the first mean will be greater than the second mean, the critical t would be located in the right tail of the sampling distribution and would have a positive value.
>
> We state our result formally as follows

$$(t_{crit} = -1.833; df = 9; \alpha = .05; \text{one-tailed})$$

Step 14. Compare the calculated t value to the critical t value. If the absolute value of the calculated t is equal to or greater than the absolute value of the critical t, you must reject the null hypothesis. If not, you must not reject the null hypothesis.

> The calculated t value for our data (-5.8966) is greater in absolute magnitude than the critical t (-1.833); therefore, we reject the null hypothesis.

Step 15. State your conclusion in a standard statistical format using appropriate statistical symbols.

> An appropriate statement is as follows

$$(t_{calc} = -5.8966; df = 9; p < .05; \text{one-tailed})$$

Step 16. State your statistical conclusion in words.

> If the null hypothesis were true, the probability of arriving at a calculated t value of -5.8966 with nine degrees of freedom and a one-tailed test would be less than .05. Therefore, the null hypothesis is *probably* not true, and the alternative hypothesis probably is true.

Step 17. State your final conclusion in plain English.

> Given the data and the statistical conclusion, it is reasonable to argue that the reaction time was reduced by listening to classical music.

Calculation C.27 *t*-Test (Single Mean)

Type of research: Observation
Number of variables: 1
Levels of measurement: Interval/ratio
Choice of analysis: *t*-test for single mean

Motivation for Research: A researcher believes that listening to classical music will improve a person's reaction time.

Description of Research: The researcher randomly selects 20 people from a population of people who have already been measured for their reaction times. Each of these people is then asked to listen to classical music for 15 minutes; then the reaction time of each person is measured by the technique used for the original population.

Type of Conclusion Possible: The *t*-test analysis will allow the researcher to determine if the mean reaction time for the 20 people is significantly lower than the mean reaction time for the original population.

Comments: This scenario falls into the gray area between uncontrolled observation and controlled experiment. Notice that there is no true independent variable.

Assumptions: Suppose that the parametric assumptions have been met.

Test Data:

Person	Reaction time
1	2.36
2	2.20
3	2.10
4	2.57
5	2.19
6	2.06
7	1.98
8	2.03
9	2.09
10	1.95
11	2.10
12	2.24
13	2.09
14	1.97
15	2.09
16	1.99
17	2.12
18	2.09
19	2.06
20	2.13

Specifics Regarding the Analysis: The *t*-test for a single mean helps the researcher to determine whether or not a particular sample mean is close enough to the original population mean that the sample can be said to be from the same population.

The *t*-test analysis results in a single *t* value, which is compared to a critical *t* value. If the calculated *t* is greater than the critical *t*, the null hypothesis is rejected.

Research Hypothesis: The researcher believes that listening to classical music will decrease reaction time. Symbolically, the research hypothesis—the alternative hypothesis—appears as follows average reaction time after listening to classical music is faster than the original reaction time. This supports the researcher's argument that listening to classical music will improve a person's reaction time.

Calculation C.28 Theta (Correlation Coefficient)

Type of research: Observation
Number of variables: 2
Levels of measurement: One ordinal variable, one nominal variable
Choice of analysis: Theta

Motivation for Research:. A researcher believes that a person's academic rank upon graduation from college can be used to predict his or her political perspective five years after graduation. More specifically, those of higher academic rank (where the first in the class is understood to have the highest rank) will be more likely to label themselves as liberal five years after graduation.

Description of Research: The researcher randomly selects 20 students from the population of seniors in college. Each of these 20 students is asked to state his or her class rank at the time of graduation from college, as determined by the Registrar's Office (the student with the highest grade point average is ranked first, and so on). Five years later, these same students are contacted and asked to choose which of two labels — liberal or conservative — is most appropriate to describe their political perspective.

Type of Conclusion Possible: The theta analysis will allow the researcher to determine if a person's academic class rank in the senior year of college is correlated with his or her political perspective five years after graduation. If there is a sufficiently high degree of correlation, then the researcher may conclude that academic class rank in senior year, as operationally defined in this study, may be used to predict political perspective five years after graduation, as here defined.

Comments: One of the variables being measured — academic class rank — is at the ordinal level. The other variable — political perspective — is at the nominal level.

Test Data:

Person	Academic rank	Political perspective
1	120	Conservative
2	10	Liberal
3	15	Liberal
4	80	Conservative
5	25	Conservative
6	160	Conservative
7	1	Liberal
8	33	Liberal
9	88	Conservative
10	101	Conservative
11	18	Liberal
12	4	Liberal
13	156	Conservative
14	67	Liberal
15	12	Conservative
16	6	Liberal
17	35	Liberal
18	110	Liberal
19	3	Liberal
20	87	Conservative

$$H_{alt}: \mu_{music} < \mu_{original}$$

In plain English, the researcher is predicting that the average reaction time after listening to classical music will be less than the average reaction time in the original population.

Null Hypothesis: As we noted in Chapter 9, we state the null hypothesis, for the sake of argument, on the assumption that our research hypothesis is incorrect. In the present case, the null hypothesis is that there is *no difference between the mean after listening to classical music and the mean of the original population*. Symbolically

$$H_{null}: \mu_{music} = \mu_{original}$$

Organizing the Raw Data: When you prepare the data for entry into the *t*-test formula — whether you do the calculations by hand or by computer — you need only identify the dependent variable. (Note, however, that strictly speaking this is not a true experiment with an independent variable and a dependent variable.) In the present case, the dependent variable (the X variable) is the reaction time (in seconds).

t-Test Calculation

Once the X values have been identified, you may enter the data into the computer or use the calculation formula as follows.

Step 1. List your data.
         The test data have already been tabulated.

Step 2. Square each data value. Sum the original data values. Sum the squared data values. Summarize the results.
         The results for the present case are summarized in Table C.27.1.

Step 3. Calculate the mean for the data.

TABLE C.27.1 Results of Summing and Squaring

Person	X	X^2
1	2.36	5.5696
2	2.20	4.8400
3	2.10	4.4100
4	2.57	6.6049
5	2.19	4.7961
6	2.06	4.2436
7	1.98	3.9204
8	2.03	4.1209
9	2.09	4.3681
10	1.95	3.8025
11	2.10	4.4100
12	2.24	5.0176
13	2.09	4.3681
14	1.97	3.8809
15	2.09	4.3681
16	1.99	3.9601
17	2.12	4.4944
18	2.09	4.3681
19	2.06	4.2436
20	2.13	4.5369
Sum	42.41	90.3239

The mean is

$$\bar{X} = \frac{\sum X}{N}$$

where N is the total number of data values. In the present case, $N = 20$, and thus

$$\bar{X} = \frac{42.41}{20}$$

$$= 2.12$$

Step 4. Calculate the unbiased estimate of the standard deviation of the population by means of the formula

$$\tilde{\sigma} = \sqrt{\frac{\sum (X^2) - \frac{(\sum X)^2}{N}}{N - 1}}$$

For our data

$$\tilde{\sigma} = \sqrt{\frac{90.3239 - \frac{(42.41)^2}{20}}{20 - 1}}$$

$$= \sqrt{\frac{90.3239 - \frac{1798.608}{20}}{19}}$$

$$= \sqrt{\frac{90.3239 - 89.9304}{19}}$$

$$= \sqrt{\frac{0.3935}{19}}$$

$$= \sqrt{0.02071}$$

$$= 0.1439$$

Step 5. Calculate the standard error of the mean.
The corresponding formula is

$$s_{\bar{X}} = \frac{\tilde{\sigma}}{\sqrt{N}}$$

We find that

$$s_{\bar{X}} = \frac{0.1439}{\sqrt{20}}$$

$$= \frac{0.1439}{4.472}$$

$$= 0.03217$$

Step 6. Determine the population mean corresponding to the null hypothesis.
According to our null hypothesis

$$\mu_{null} = 2.56$$

Step 7. Calculate the t value by means of the formula

$$t_{calc} = \frac{\bar{X}_{observed} - \mu_{null}}{s_{\bar{X}}} \qquad \text{(C.27.1)}$$

Substituting our results into this formula, we find that

$$t_{calc} = \frac{2.12 - 2.56}{0.03217}$$

$$= \frac{-0.44}{0.03217}$$

$$= -13.677$$

Step 8. State your alpha level. [We assume .05 unless otherwise specified]

$$\alpha = .05$$

Step 9. Determine whether you are doing a one-tailed or a two-tailed test of your null hypothe
The alternative hypothesis specifies that the observed mean will be less than null-hypothesis mean; therefore, we are doing a one-tailed test in the lower tail of distribution.

Step 10. Determine the degrees of freedom by means of the following formula

$$df = N - 1$$

For our data

$$df = 20 - 1 = 19$$

Step 11. Look in a table of critical t values (Table B.12) to determine the critical t for a o with $\alpha = .05$ and 19 degrees of freedom.
Although Table B.12 indicates the sign of the critical t value, most sta do not. In such cases you will have to determine the sign of the critical t on th alternative hypothesis.
The critical t value for an alpha of .05, 19 degrees of freedom, an hypothesis predicting a negative difference is -1.729.
We state this result formally as follows

$$(t_{crit} = -1.729; df = 19; \alpha = .05; \text{one-tailed})$$

Step 12. Compare the calculated t value to the critical t value.
In the case of positive critical values, you must reject the n calculated t is greater than or equal to the critical t.
In the case of negative critical values, you must reject the calculated t is less than or equal to the critical t.
The calculated t value for our data (-13.677) is less than therefore, we reject the null.

Step 13. State your statistical conclusion in a standard format using appro
An appropriate statement is as follows

$$(t_{calc} = -13.677; df = 19; p < .05; \text{one-tailed})$$

Step 14. State your statistical conclusion in words.
If the null hypothesis were true, the probability of -13.678 with 19 degrees of freedom and a one-tailed test wo the null hypothesis *probably* isn't true, and the alternative h

Step 15. State your final conclusion in plain English.
Given the data and the statistical conclusion, it see

Specifics Regarding the Analysis: The theta analysis helps the researcher to determine whether or not there is a significant correlation between two variables when the predictor variable is at the ordinal level and the predicted variable is at the nominal level. These two variables must represent a pair of observed measurements for each pair of subjects or items in the observation. In the present study, the two observed measurements for each of the 20 subjects are class rank and political perspective. For person 13, for example, the measurements are: 156 and conservative.

The calculations result in a single theta value ranging from 0 to +1.00. Higher theta corresponds to a greater correlation between the two variables. In the present example, the research hypothesis predicts a correlation such that those with relatively high class ranks (where the first in the class is understood to be the highest rank) would tend to have a liberal political philosophy, while those with relatively low class ranks would tend to have a conservative political philosophy.

Research Hypothesis: The researcher believes that class rank is a factor in predicting a person's political philosophy. Note, however, that this is *not* an experiment in which class rank is manipulated as an independent variable and political philosophy is measured as a dependent variable. Instead, class rank and political philosophy are simply measured for each of the 20 subjects in the study. Therefore, the research hypothesis being tested here is that the class rank (ordinal level variable) will be correlated with the measured political philosophy (nominal level variable). Symbolically, the research hypothesis — the alternative hypothesis — appears as follows:

$$H_{alt}: \theta_{R,P} > 0$$

In plain English, this means that the researcher is predicting that the correlation between class rank (R) and measured political philosophy (P) will be greater than zero in the population from which the sample was drawn.

Null Hypothesis: As we noted in Chapter 9, we state the null hypothesis, for the sake of argument, on the assumption that our research hypothesis is incorrect. In the present case, the null hypothesis is that there is *no correlation between class rank and political philosophy.* Symbolically

$$H_{null}: \theta_{R,P} = 0$$

Organizing the Raw Data: When you prepare the data for entry into the theta calculation formula — whether you do the calculations by hand or by computer — you must first label one of the variables as the X variable and the other as the Y variable. The X variable should be the variable that could logically be used to predict the Y variable. In the present case, the intention is to predict the political philosophy of a person on the basis of that person's class rank. Therefore, in the present example, class rank is identified as the X variable, and political philosophy — operationally defined as either conservative or liberal — is identified as the Y variable.

After determining which is the X variable and which is the Y variable, you need to identify the X value and Y value for each observation in the sample. There is one pair of X, Y values for each of the 20 people in this observation. Each X value and each Y value can be subscripted for identification. For example, X_5, Y_5 correspond to the fifth person in our sample and, thus, according to our test data

$$X_5 = 25$$

$$Y_5 = conservative$$

Having identified the X and Y values, you must make sure that the X variable is at the ordinal level of measurement. In the present case, even though the class rankings are already at the ordinal level, these rankings should be reranked (from 1 to 20) for the 20 persons who were sampled. After this ranking, the data appear as follows.

Person	Revised academic rank	Political perspective
1	18	Conservative
2	5	Liberal
3	7	Liberal
4	13	Conservative
5	9	Conservative
6	20	Conservative
7	1	Liberal
8	10	Liberal
9	15	Conservative
10	16	Conservative
11	8	Liberal
12	3	Liberal
13	19	Conservative
14	12	Liberal
15	6	Conservative
16	4	Liberal
17	11	Liberal
18	17	Liberal
19	2	Liberal
20	14	Conservative

Theta Calculation

You may now enter the data into the computer or use the following calculation formula

$$\theta = \frac{\sum (f_{i>j} - f_{j>i})}{\sum (N_i N_j)}$$

(C.28.1)

The procedure is as follows.

Step 1. Sort the ranks and indicate the corresponding nominal category for each rank.
The sorted ranks for our data are shown in Table C.28.1.

Step 2. Make a table that includes each possible comparison of nominal categories.
In the present case, the table is very simple.

Comparisons
Conservative versus liberal

Step 3. Count the number of times a rank that falls in the first category is greater than a rank that falls in the second category, and the number of times a rank that falls in the second category is greater than a rank that falls in the first category.

Looking at Table C.28.1, we calculate that a conservative (category 1) has a higher rank number than a liberal (category 2) on 85 occasions. The conservative with a rank of 20 has a higher rank number than the 11 liberals below; the conservative with a rank of 19 also has a higher rank number than the 11 liberals below; and so on.

Table C.28.1 also shows that a conservative has a lower rank number than a liberal on 14 occasions.

TABLE C.28.1	Sorted Ranks and Corresponding Categories

Sorted Ranks	Category
20	C
19	C
18	C
17	L
16	C
15	C
14	C
13	C
12	L
11	L
10	L
9	C
8	L
7	L
6	C
5	L
4	L
3	L
2	L
1	L

We summarize these data in Table C.28.2.

Step 4. Calculate the difference between the frequencies.
From Table C.28.2

$$f_{1>2} - f_{2>1} = 85 - 14 = 71$$

Step 5. Determine the total number of cases in each category.
In the present case

$$N_1 = 9, N_2 = 11$$

Step 6. For each comparison, multiply the number of cases for the two categories being compared.
We find that

$$N_1 N_2 = 9 \times 11$$
$$= 99$$

TABLE C.28.2	Frequency Values for Comparisons

Comparison	$f_{1>2}$	$f_{2>1}$
C versus L	85	14

Step 7. Summarize the results of steps 4 and 6 in a table.
Our results are summarized in Table C.28.3.

TABLE C.28.3 **Summary of Results**

Comparison	$f_{1>2}$	$f_{2>1}$	$f_{1>2} - f_{2>1}$	N_1N_2
C versus L	85	14	71	99

Step 8. Calculate the sum of the differences obtained in step 4 and the sum of the products obtained in step 6.

In the present example there are only two nominal categories being compared. This will not always be the case. Thus, for our data

$$\sum (f_{i>j} - f_{j>i}) = f_{1>2} - f_{2>1} = 71$$
$$\sum (N_iN_j) = N_1N_2 = 99$$

Step 9. Calculate theta by substituting the results into Eq. (C.28.1).
In the present case

$$\theta = \frac{71}{99}$$

$$= .7172$$

Step 10. Calculate the Kruskal-Wallis H value or the chi square value.
The theta calculation results in a numerical value ranging from 0 to 1. Higher theta corresponds to greater correlation between the two variables. To test the significance of theta, imagine that the data represent the results of an experiment in which the nominal variable was the independent variable, and conduct a Kruskal-Wallis analysis, to obtain a calculated H value (Calculation C.11).

If there are fewer than five subjects in each nominal category, compare the calculated H with the critical H from a standard table (Table B.10). If the calculated H is beyond the critical H, the null hypothesis can be rejected, and the correlation may be regarded as significant.

If, as in the present case, there are more than five subjects in each nominal category, the calculated H is compared to the critical chi square (Table B.3); the corresponding degrees of freedom are calculated by subtracting 1 from the number of nominal categories. Once again, if the calculated H is beyond the critical chi square, the null hypothesis is rejected, and the correlation is regarded as significant.

Applying the Kruskal-Wallis procedure (Calculation C.11) in the present case, we find a calculated H of 7.2742.

Step 11. Determine the degrees of freedom by means of the following formula

$$df = N_{nom} - 1$$

where N_{nom} is the number of nominal categories.
In the present case

$$df = 2 - 1$$

$$= 1$$

Step 12. Determine the alpha level. [We assume .05, unless otherwise specified]

$$\alpha = .05$$

Step 13. Determine the critical Kruskal-Wallis (or chi square) value from standard tables.
According to Table B.3, the critical chi square value with one degree of freedom and an alpha level of .05 is 3.841.

Step 14. Compare the calculated H value with the critical value. If the calculated H is greater than or equal to the critical value, you must reject the null hypothesis; otherwise, you cannot reject the null.
The calculated H value for our data (7.2742) is greater than the corresponding critical chi square value (3.841); therefore, we reject the null.

Step 15. State your statistical conclusion in a standard format using appropriate statistical symbols.
An appropriate statement is as follows

$$(\theta = .7172;\ H = 7.2742;\ df = 1;\ p < .05)$$

Step 16. State your statistical conclusion in words.
If the null hypothesis were true, the probability of obtaining a calculated H of 7.2742 with one degree of freedom would be less than .05. Therefore, the null hypothesis is *probably not true*, and the alternative hypothesis probably is true.

Step 17. State your final conclusion in plain English.
Given the data and the statistical conclusion, it is reasonable to argue that academic rank and political perspective are significantly correlated. This supports the researcher's argument than a person's academic rank upon graduation from college can be used to predict his or her political perspective five years after graduation.

Calculation C.29 Unbiased Estimate of Population Standard Deviation

The calculation formula for an unbiased estimate of the population standard deviation is as follows

$$\hat{\sigma} = \sqrt{\frac{\sum (X^2) - \frac{(\sum X)^2}{N}}{N - 1}} \qquad \text{(C.29.1)}$$

The sample data for the present calculation, originally stated in Table 4.23, are the measured arm lengths (in inches) for five people (randomly selected from Database A.7)

34, 27, 31, 28, 24

Here are the steps you should follow when calculating the standard deviation for a set of data.

Step 1. Square each of the data values in the data set.
The results for our data are shown in Table C.29.1.

Step 2. Sum all of the squared data values obtained in step 1.
In the present case

$$\sum (X^2) = 1156 + 729 + 961 + 784 + 576 = 4206$$

Step 3. Sum all of the data values.
We find that

$$\sum X = 34 + 27 + 31 + 28 + 24 = 144$$

TABLE C.29.1 Results of Squaring the Data

X	X^2
34	1156
27	729
31	961
28	784
24	576

Step 4. Square the sum of the X values.
For our data

$$(\sum X)^2 = 144^2 = 20{,}736$$

Step 5. Divide the result of step 4 by the total number of data values in the data set (N).
In the present case, $N = 5$, and so

$$\frac{(\sum X)^2}{N} = \frac{20{,}736}{5} = 4147.2$$

Step 6. Subtract the result of step 5 from the result of step 2.
For our data

$$\sum(X^2) - \frac{(\sum X)^2}{N} = 4206 - 4147.2 = 58.8$$

We have now calculated the numerator of Eq. (C.29.1).

Step 7. Divide the result of step 6 by $(N - 1)$.
In the present case

$$\frac{\sum(X^2) - \frac{(\sum X)^2}{N}}{N - 1} = \frac{58.8}{4} = 14.7$$

We have now calculated the part of Eq. (C.29.1) within the square root sign. This is actually the variance for the data set.

Step 8. Take the square root of the result of step 7. This gives the unbiased estimate of the population standard deviation.
For our data

$$\tilde{\sigma} = \sqrt{11.76}$$
$$= 3.43$$

Calculation C.30 Using a Table of Random Numbers

The following steps represent one way to use a table of random numbers.

Step 1. Establish an ordinal sequence of numbers for a given sample. For example, if you wish to select a sample of 20 people, then establish the ordinal sequence: 1, 2, 3, 4, 5, 6, ..., 20.

Step 2. Enter the random numbers table at a randomly chosen point. For example, close your eyes and stab your finger at the table to find the starting point.

Step 3. Randomly choose a direction to move. For example, toss a die: If it lands on 1, move horizontally to the left; if 2, horizontally to the right; if 3, vertically upward; if 4, vertically downward.

Step 4. Move in the randomly chosen direction until the first available sequence number is reached. For example, if the ordinal sequence is 1–20, move until you find one of the following two-digit sequences: 01, 02, 03, 04, 05, 06, 07, 08, 09, 10, 11, 12, 13, 14, 15, 16, 17, 18, 19, 20. In order to be truly random, the number of digits in the sequence must always be equal to the number of digits in the largest number of the ordinal sequence. Therefore, if 20, a two-digit number, is the largest number, you should consider two digits at a time as you move through the table.

Step 5. If you are randomly selecting without replacement, then any particular number that you find in the sequence cannot be used again. If you are randomly selecting with replacement, each number in the sequence can be used repeatedly.

Calculation C.31 Variance

The calculation formula for the variance is as follows

$$\text{Variance} = \frac{\sum (X^2) - \dfrac{(\sum X)^2}{N}}{N} \tag{C.31.1}$$

The sample data for the present calculation, originally stated in Table 4.23, are the measured arm lengths (in inches) for five people (randomly selected from Database A.7)

34, 27, 31, 28, 24

Here are the steps you should follow when calculating the standard deviation for a set of data.

Step 1. Square each of the data values in the data set.
The results for our data are shown in Table C.31.1.

Step 2. Sum all of the squared data values obtained in step 1.
In the present case

$$\sum (X^2) = 1156 + 729 + 961 + 784 + 576 = 4206$$

TABLE C.31.1 **Results of Squaring the Data**

X	X^2
34	1156
27	729
31	961
28	784
24	576

Step 3. Sum all of the data values.
   For our data

$$\sum X = 34 + 27 + 31 + 28 + 24 = 144$$

Step 4. Square the sum of the X values.
   We find that

$$\left(\sum X\right)^2 = 144^2 = 20{,}736$$

Step 5. Divide the result of step 4 by the total number of data values in the data set (N).
   In the present case, $N = 5$, and thus

$$\frac{\left(\sum X\right)^2}{N} = \frac{20{,}736}{5} = 4147.2$$

Step 6. Subtract the result of step 5 from the result of step 2.
   For our data

$$\sum (X^2) - \frac{\left(\sum X\right)^2}{N} = 4206 - 4147.2 = 58.8$$

   We have now calculated the numerator of Eq. (C.31.1).

Step 7. Divide the result of step 6 by the total number of data values in the data set.
   We find that

$$\frac{58.5}{5} = 11.76$$

   This is the final result.

Step 8. Refer to the final result in the following ways.
   If all the data values in a sample were used in Eq. (C.31.1), as in the present case, the result is the variance of a sample and may be stated symbolically as follows

$$s^2 = 11.76$$

   This is a statistic.
   If all the data values in a population were used in Eq. (C.31.1), the result is the variance of the population and may be stated symbolically as follows

$$\sigma^2 = 11.76$$

   This is a parameter.
   If you do not know whether the data are a sample or a population, then the results can be stated generically as follows

Variance = 11.76

or

Var. = 11.76

Calculation C.32 Wilcoxon (Nonparametric, Within Groups)

Type of research: Experiment
Number of dependent variables: 1
Level of measurement: Interval/ratio
Assumptions met: No
Number of independent variables: 1
Conditions of independent variable: 2
Type of design: Within-groups (w-g)
Choice of analysis: Wilcoxon

Motivation for Research: A researcher believes that listening to classical music will improve a person's reaction time.

Description of Research: The researcher randomly selects 10 people from the general population. The reaction time of each person is first measured on a standard task. Then, each person is asked to sit in a room for 15 minutes and to try to relax by listening to classical music. At the end of the 15-minute relaxation period, the reaction time of each person is measured again on the same standard task.

Type of Conclusion Possible: The Wilcoxon analysis will allow the researcher to determine if the overall change in the reaction times after the relaxation session represents a significant decrease from the initial reaction times.

Comments: If the results of the Wilcoxon analysis indicate that the ranked reaction times are significantly lower after the relaxation session, then the researcher may conclude that listening to classical music had the significant effect of improving the ranked reaction times.

Test Data:

Before relaxation		After relaxation	
Person	Reaction time	Person	Reaction time
1	2.79	1	2.36
2	2.58	2	2.10
3	2.41	3	2.60
4	2.49	4	2.32
5	2.47	5	2.14
6	2.34	6	2.30
7	2.68	7	2.45
8	2.70	8	2.47
9	2.56	9	2.58
10	2.62	10	2.46

Specifics Regarding the Analysis: The Wilcoxon analysis is appropriate if, as in the present case, the researcher is beginning with data at the interval or ratio level but cannot meet the parametric assumptions. In that case, the data must be ranked before proceeding with the analysis.
     The Wilcoxon analysis is also appropriate if the initial data are at the ordinal level.
     This analysis helps the researcher to determine whether or not two samples differ significantly, with respect to the ordinal ranks, from what would be expected by chance.

Research Hypothesis: The researcher believes that listening to classical music will decrease reaction time. Symbolically, the research hypothesis—the alternative hypothesis—appears as follows

$H_{alt}: \mu_{ranks_{after}} < \mu_{ranks_{before}}$

In plain English, the researcher is predicting that the average rank of the reaction times after listening to classical music will be significantly lower than the average rank of the reaction times before listening to classical music.

Null Hypothesis: As was noted in Chapter 9, we state the null hypothesis, for the sake of argument, on the assumption that our research hypothesis is incorrect. In the present case, the null hypothesis is that there is *no difference between the average rank of the reaction times before listening to classical music and the average rank of the reaction times after listening to classical music.* Symbolically

$$H_{null}: \mu_{ranks_{before}} = \mu_{ranks_{after}}$$

Organizing the Raw Data: When you prepare the data for entry into the Wilcoxon test formula—whether you do the calculations by hand or by computer—you need to identify the following:

- the independent variable: music, in the present case.

- the two conditions of the experiment: before and after.

- the number of subjects in each condition: 10 and 10.

- the dependent variable: reaction time.

Wilcoxon Test Calculation

Once these values have been identified, you may enter them into the computer or use the calculation formula as follows.

Step 1. List your data.
  The test data have already been tabulated.

Step 2. Find the difference between the before and after scores for each subject. Rank the differences, disregarding the positive or negative signs, from 1 (lowest) to N (highest). Place the results of these operations into a summary table.
  The results for our data are summarized in Table C.32.1. When ranks are tied, we average the corresponding ranks. For example, in Table C.32.1, the tied differences of 0.23 share the rank 6.5, which is the average of the ranks of 6 and 7.

Step 3. Sum the positive ranks and label this sum as $T+$.
  In the present case

$$T+ = 9 + 10 + 4 + 8 + 2 + 6.5 + 6.5 + 3$$
$$= 49$$

TABLE C.32.1 Summary of Ranked Differences

Before	After	Difference	Ranked difference
2.79	2.36	0.43	+9
2.58	2.10	0.48	+10
2.41	2.60	-0.19	-5
2.49	2.32	0.17	+4
2.47	2.14	0.33	+8
2.34	2.30	0.04	+2
2.68	2.45	0.23	+6.5
2.70	2.47	0.23	+6.5
2.56	2.58	-0.02	-1
2.62	2.46	0.16	+3

Answers to Selected Exercises

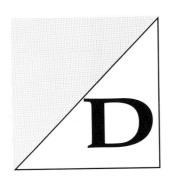

CHAPTER 1

1.6 It is more correct to say "The data are..." because *data* is the plural and *datum* is the singular form.

1.7 5 ft 8 in. is a parameter because it is based on the population. 5 ft 9 in. is a statistic because it is based on a sample.

1.8 The sample of 500 would not represent people who are not listed in the telephone book.

1.9 The primary purpose of inferential statistics is to make decisions about populations of data on the basis of samples of data that represent the populations.

1.10 The primary purpose of descriptive statistics is to accurately describe the population or the sample that the data represent.

CHAPTER 2

2.2 A. The behavior of the body temperature is being observed.
B. The I.Q. variable has not changed.
C. John's heart rate behavior is being monitored.
D. Wisconsin's snowfall behavior is being reported.

2.3 The independent variable is the amount of time since his dog has eaten. The dependent variable is the dog's running speed.

2.4 Hair color could be measured at the nominal level by matching it with color charts or hair samples that have already been labeled dark brown, auburn, blond, and so on.

2.6 A. Grade point average can be considered a ratio level measurement if you are willing to assume, for example, that a 4.00 is twice as high as a 2.00. If not, you might settle for the interval level of measurement.
B. Class rank at graduation is an ordinal measurement.
C. Yearly income is a ratio level measurement.
D. Rating scales are at least ordinal; beyond this it is debatable.
E. Same as D.
F. Inches of rainfall is a ratio level measurement.
G. Percentage correct is a ratio level measurement.

2.7 We often make assessments based upon subjective impressions that are not highly operational.

2.8 It is not possible to average letters, and so the letters would first have to be converted to numbers. In a grading scheme where A = 4 and F = 0, the average would be 20/6 = 3.33. This value could then be converted into a letter grade (B or B−) according to the grading scheme.

2.9 It is not possible to average categories, and so the categories would first have to be converted to numbers: gold = 1; silver = 2; bronze = 3. Using this scheme, the average would be the sum of the numbers (1 + 1 + 2 + 3 + 3 = 10) divided by 5; that is, 2. However, it would be awkward to say that "silver" was the average for his olympic performances because the medal categories have qualitative meaning and are difficult to quantify. Consider a case where the average would be 2.5! What would you say then?

2.10 Mark's system appears to be more precise because the units of change in the symbols are smaller.

CHAPTER 3

3.5 As the number of class intervals increases, the size of the class intervals decreases; and vice versa.

3.6 Real limits: 3.15–3.45, and 3.45 − 3.75.

3.7 Real limits: 3.015–3.045, and 3.045 − 3.075.

3.8 Upper real limit = upper apparent limit + (half the highest degree of precision).

Lower real limit = lower apparent limit − (half the highest degree of precision).

3.9 A frequency count for a particular class interval states the number of cases in each class interval. A cumulative frequency count for a particular class interval states the total number of cases below the upper real limit of that class interval.

3.10 A possible score value is a value on some scale where a case could conceivably fall. An actually measured score is a score on a scale where a particular case does fall.

CHAPTER 4

4.1 Mean = 51.5.
Median = 51.5.
Mode = 41.

4.2 R (method 1) = 31.
R (method 2) = 32.
s^2 = 94.05.
s = 9.70.

4.4 For Tom:
R (method 1) = 40.
R (method 2) = 41.
ADD = 13.33.
s^2 = 266.67.
s = 16.33.
For Mary:
R (method 1) = 20.
R (method 2) = 21.
ADD = 6.67.
s^2 = 66.67.
s = 8.165.

4.5 This is a matter of opinion. Some might choose Mary because she is more predictable. Others might choose Tom because he has shown the potential for high scores.

4.6 Mary's scores are more homogeneous. Tom's scores are more heterogeneous.

4.7 σ is the population standard deviation; s is the sample standard deviation.

4.8 σ is the population standard deviation; σ^2 is the population variance.

4.9 $\sigma = 4.6$; $s = 4.3$.

4.10 Conceptual formulas are based upon the logical purpose of the formula, without concern for ease of calculation. Calculation formulas are modifications of the conceptual formulas for the purpose of making the calculations easier.

CHAPTER 5

5.4

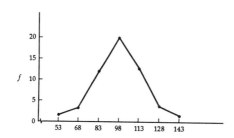

5.5

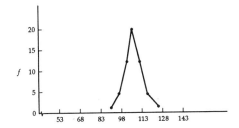

CHAPTER 6

6.1 $\bar{X} = 58.9$.

6.2 $s = 8.65$.

6.3 $Z = +1.05$.

6.4 Assuming a normal distribution, the 50th percentile is the same as the mean: 58.9. Or, finding the median of the sample, the 50th percentile is 58.5.

6.5 Based on a Z value of $+1.645$, the 95th percentile is 73.13.

6.6 85.31; or approximately the 85th percentile.

6.7 Only 5% of the scores fall below 44.67.

6.8 Only 5% of the scores fall above 73.13.

6.9 2.5% of the scores fall below 41.95, and 2.5% of the scores fall above 75.85.

6.10 $\bar{X} = 52.56$.

6.11 $s = 9.08$.

6.12 $Z = +1.70$.

6.13 Assuming a normal distribution, the 50th percentile is the same as the mean: 52.56. Or, finding the median of the sample, the 50th percentile is 52.

6.14 Based on a Z value of $+1.645$, the 95th percentile is 67.50.

6.15 95.54; or approximately the 96th percentile.

6.16 Only 5% of the scores fall below 37.61.

6.17 Only 5% of the scores fall above 67.50.

6.18 2.5% of the scores fall below 34.76, and 2.5% of the scores fall above 70.36.

6.19 The sample from the population (58.9 > 52.56).

6.20 The sample that rode the exercise bike (9.08 > 8.65).

6.21 Stronger than 93.7% of the population. Given the population mean of 49.72 and the population standard deviation of 11.98, we find that the score of 68 has a Z score of 1.53. This point in the distribution is such that 93.7% of the distribution falls at or below it.

6.22 We can infer that the original population has a higher average hand strength than the new hypothetical population represented by the sample of nine people. We can also infer that the original population is more heterogeneous since the standard deviation of the original population is 11.98 and the unbiased estimate of the new hypothetical population, based on the sample data, is 9.63. The answers to Exercises 6.9 and 6.18 also suggest that the middle 95% of the original population falls between a narrower range of scores than does the middle 95% of the new hypothetical population.

CHAPTER 7

7.1   Dynamic, circular, no final answers.

7.2   A tentative explanation stated with the expectation of being challenged.

7.3   A prediction that is made before gathering the relevant information.

7.4   A law is generally a theory that is so widely accepted that it is not challenged.

7.5   A theory is an explanation regarding some event that has already-been observed; but a hypothesis is a prediction regarding some event that has not yet been observed.

7.6   Theories are generally more tentative and open to challenge.

CHAPTER 8

8.4   A.   Internal validity is poor. There are many possible variables that could affect mood.
         B.   Internal validity is good. It is a reasonably well-controlled experiment.

8.5   A.   External validity is not possible when there is no internal validity. In other words, results that are known not to be internally valid cannot be generalized.
         B.   External validity is relatively poor. Nursing home patients are not representative of the general population.

8.6   A.   Hypothesis.
         B.   Theory.
         C.   Hypothesis.
         D.   Theory.

8.7   No. Random selection does not guarantee that all variables relevant to the hypothesis and theory will be appropriately represented in the sample.

8.8   The purpose of random assignment is to obtain internal validity. The purpose of random selection is to obtain external validity.

8.9   *Uncontrolled observations* have no true independent variable, no true dependent variable, and, therefore, questionable internal validity. Variables that are naturally present can be measured and evaluated for the degree of relationship among them. The external validity of any relationships that are found is reasonably good. *Controlled experiments* have a genuine independent variable, a genuine dependent variable, and, therefore, good internal validity. The more artificial the conditions, however, the less external validity there will be.

8.10   Compare your answer to the criteria at the beginning of this chapter.

CHAPTER 9

9.10   If replacement is assumed, 0.000,035. If no replacement is assumed, 0.000,003,69.

9.11   0.0456.

9.12   0.05.

9.13   0.05.

9.14   0.05.

9.15 $+1.645$.

9.16 -1.645.

9.17 -1.96 and $+1.96$.

CHAPTER 10

10.3   Four ounces of alcohol will have no effect on reaction time.

10.4   The average reaction time (accurate to one-hundredth of a second) for the ten people who drink four ounces of alcohol will be the same as the average reaction time of the control group.

10.5 $H_0: \mu_{4oz} = \mu_{control}$.

10.6   Four ounces of alcohol will increase reaction time.

10.7   The average reaction time (accurate to one-hundredth of a second) for the ten people who drink four ounces of alcohol will be greater than the average reaction time of the control group.

10.8 $H_0: \mu_{4oz} > \mu_{control}$.

10.9   This is a one-tailed alternative hypothesis, assuming that you predicted that alcohol would increase reaction time.

10.10   A sampling distribution of differences between sample means.

10.11   When alpha is set at .05. In that case, you are more likely to reject the null hypothesis.

10.12   Situation B. The smaller the sample size, the less the statistical power.

CHAPTER 11

11.1   A. t-test for independent groups.
  B.   Pearson r correlation coefficient.
  C.   ANOVA, then Scheffe.
  D.   Kruskal-Wallis.
  E.   Two-way ANOVA, then Scheffe.

11.5   Mann-Whitney U.

11.6   Wilcoxon.

11.7   1.   Normal distribution of the dependent variable.
  2.   Random selection of subjects or items from the population.
  3.   Homogeneity of variance.

11.8   In a between-groups design, there is a separate group of subjects for each condition of the experiment. In a within-groups design, each subject experiences each condition of the experiment.

11.9   In a before-after design, each subject is measured before the introduction of the experimental condition, and measured again after its introduction. In a matched-groups design, subjects are assigned to pairs on the basis of some measurement related to the dependent variable; then, the two members of each pair are randomly assigned to the experimental conditions.

11.10   Kruskal-Wallis.

CHAPTER 12

12.3   For the Pearson r, compare your answer to Eq. (12.1). For Z, compare your answer to Eq. (12.5). For t, compare your answer to Eqs. (10.4) and (12.6). For F, compare your answer to Eq. (12.7).

12.4 A. Three possible comparisons.
       B. Six possible comparisons.
       C. Fifteen possible comparisons.

12.5 Because of inflated alpha; in other words, there would be an increased probability of making a type-I error.

12.6 1. Within-groups versus between-groups designs.
       2. More than two conditions of each independent variable.
       3. More than one independent variable.

12.7 There would be two indepedendent variables, each with three conditions, resulting in nine separate experimental conditions.

12.8 Inflated alpha occurs if multiple t-tests are performed on a given set of data. The Scheffe analysis is specifically designed to maintain a constant alpha level.

12.9 Two independent variables are said to interact when one of the independent variables has a different effect under the different conditions of the other.

12.10 Systematic variation can be attributed to a specific source that is varying systematically. For example, in a perfectly controlled experiment, systematic variation in the dependent variable can be attributed to systematic changes in the independent variable. Unsystematic variation is any variation that cannot be attributed to systematic changes in a specific source.

CHAPTER 13

13.1 A. $t = +1.68$; $df = 18$; n.s.; one-tailed.
       B. $t = -1.76$; $df = 18$; $p < .05$; one-tailed.
       C. $t = -1.72$; $df = 18$; $p < .05$; one-tailed.
       D. $t = +2.36$; $df = 22$; $p < .05$; two-tailed.
       E. $t = +1.82$; $df = 18$; $p < .05$; one-tailed.
       F. $F = 3.36$; $df_s = 2$; $df_u = 27$; n.s.
       G. If four categories are on one dimension, then we have a simple chi square

          $\chi^2 = 8.1$; $df = 3$; $p < .05$

       If the four categories represent two categories in each of two dimensions, then we have a chi square test of independence

          $\chi^2 = 8.1$; $df = 1$; $p < .05$

       H. $r = -.46$; $df = 14$; $p < .05$; one-tailed.
       I. $r = +.46$; $df = 14$; n.s.; one-tailed.
       J. $r = +.38$; $df = 16$; n.s.; one-tailed.
       K. $r = .40$; $df = 16$; n.s.; one-tailed.
       L. $r_s = -.46$; $N_{pair} = 16$; $p < .05$; one-tailed.
       M. $r_s = +.46$; $N_{pair} = 16$; $p < .05$; one-tailed.
       N. $r_s = +.38$; $N_{pair} = 18$; n.s.; one-tailed.
       O. $r_s = +40$; $N_{pair} = 19$; n.s.; two-tailed.

13.3 Compare your answer to the guidelines stated at the beginning of this chapter.

13.4 One-tailed tests are conducted when the alternative hypothesis specifies a particular direction for the results. Two-tailed tests are conducted when no particular direction is specified.

13.5 Generally the calculated statistics must have an absolute value that is equal to or greater than the critical value. The important exceptions to this general rule are the Mann-Whitney U and the Wilcoxon analyses.

13.6 Generally speaking, the null hypothesis is rejected when the results obtained would be very unlikely if the null hypothesis were true. This is usually determined by comparing a calculated statistic, such as a calculated t value, to a critical value for that statistic. This comparison establishes whether or not the calculated statistic would have a probability of .05 or less if the null hypothesis were true.

13.7 Generally speaking, the results of the statistical analysis are significant if they would occur 5% of the time or less on the assumption that the null hypothesis is true. In other words, if the null hypothesis is unlikely, the alternative hypothesis is preferred and the results are said to be statistically significant.

13.8 We make a type-I error when we reject a null hypothesis that is actually true. It is important to remember that we cannot make a type-I error unless we actually reject the null hypothesis.

13.9 The researcher determines the probability of making a type-I error when she or he sets the alpha level. Usually the alpha level is set at .05. In the absence of specific statements to the contrary, $\alpha = 0.5$ should be assumed.

13.10 1% of the time.

13.11 Compare your answer to the guidelines stated in this chapter.

REFERENCES

Blair, R. C., & Higgins, J. J. (1985). Comparison of the power of the paired samples *t*-test to that of Wilcoxon's signed-ranks test under various population shapes. *Psychological Bulletin, 97*, 119–128.

Harshbarger, T. R. (1977). *Introductory statistics: A decision map.* (2nd ed.) New York: Macmillan.

Perry, W. G. (1970). *Forms of intellectual and ethical development in the college years: A scheme.* New York: Holt, Rinehart & Winston.

Petrinovich, L. F., & Hardyck, C. D. (1969). Error rates for multiple comparison methods: Some evidence concerning the frequency of erroneous conclusions. *Psychological Bulletin, 71*, 43–54.

Stevens, S. S. (1946). On the theory of scales of measurement. *Science, 103*, 667–680.

CREDITS

The author wishes to express his appreciation to the authors and publishers whose material was used to generate the values for the following tables:

Table B.1 Z Values and Corresponding Normal Curve Areas

SOURCE: The values in this table have been generated by a computer program authored by R. Maleske. The program makes use of standard formulas pertaining to the normal curve.

Table B.2 Critical Z Values

SOURCE: Values selected from Table B.1.

Table B.3 Critical Chi Square Values

SOURCE: Values taken from Table D.4 of Kirk, R. E. (1990) *Statistics: An Introduction* (3rd ed.). Chicago: Holt, Rinehart & Winston.

Table B.4 Critical Pearson *r* Values

SOURCE: Values for $df = 1$ through 16 taken from Table G of Couch, J. V. (1987) *Fundamentals of Statistics for the Behavioral Sciences* (2nd ed.). St. Paul: West Publishing Co. Values for $df = 17$ through 120 were generated by a computer program authored by R. Maleske. The program makes use of a derivation of the formula

$$t = \frac{r_{xy}\sqrt{df}}{\sqrt{1 - r^2_{xy}}}$$

in which *r* is isolated on the left side of the equal sign. Then critical r values are calculated after placing *df* values and corresponding critical *t* values in the equation.

Table B.5 Critical Spearman r_s Values

SOURCE: Values for $df = 1$ through 10 taken from Table H of Couch, J. V. (1987) *Fundamentals of Statistics for the Behavioral Sciences* (2nd ed.). St. Paul: West Publishing Co. Values for $df = 11$ through 120 were generated by a computer program authored by R. Maleske. The program makes use of a derivation of the formula

$$t = \frac{r_s \sqrt{df}}{\sqrt{1 - r_s^2}}$$

in which r_s is isolated on the left side of the equal sign. (For more information regarding this formula see Harshbarger, T. R. (1977). *Introductory Statistics: A Decision Map* (pp. 433–434). New York, NY: Macmillan. Then critical r_s values are calculated after placing df values and corresponding critical t values in the equation.

Table B.6   Critical Eta Values

SOURCE: All values generated by a computer program authored by R. Maleske. The program makes use of a derivation of the formula

$$F = \frac{\widetilde{\eta}^2(N - J) + (J - 1)}{(1 - \widetilde{\eta}^2)(J - 1)}$$

in which η is isolated on the left side of the equal sign. (Note: J = number of nominal predictor categories; N = number of data pairs). (For more information regarding this formula see Harshbarger, T. R. (1977). *Introductory Statistics: A Decision Map* (pp. 465–466). New York, NY: Macmillan.) Then critical η values are calculated after placing J, N, and corresponding critical F values in the equation.

Table B.7   Critical Lambda Values

SOURCE: This table is based upon Harshbarger's (1977) discussion of lambda. (See Harshbarger, T. R. (1977). *Introductory Statistics: A Decision Map* (pp. 481–482). New York, NY: Macmillan.)

Table B.8   Critical Mann-Whitney U Values

SOURCE: Values taken from Table H of Spatz, C. (1993) *Basic Statistics: Tales of Distributions* (5th ed.). Pacific Grove, California: Brooks/Cole Publishing Company.

Table B.9   Critical Wilcoxon T Values

SOURCE: Values taken from Table J of Spatz, C. (1993) *Basic Statistics: Tales of Distributions* (5th ed.). Pacific Grove, California: Brooks/Cole Publishing Company.

Table B.10   Critical Kruskal-Wallis H Values

SOURCE: These are actually Chi Square values taken from Table D.4 of Kirk, R. E. (1990) *Statistics: An Introduction* (3rd ed.). Chicago: Holt, Rinehart & Winston.

Table B.11   Critical Friedman Values

SOURCE: These are actually Chi Square values taken from Table D.4 of Kirk, R.E. (1990) *Statistics: An Introduction* (3rd ed.). Chicago: Holt, Rinehart & Winston.

Table B.12   Critical t Values

SOURCE: The table is the author's own format. The values in this table have been generated by a computer program authored by R. Maleske. The program makes use of standard formulas pertaining to the t variations of the z distribution.

Table B.13   Critical F Values

SOURCE: The table is the author's own format. The values are taken from Snedecor, G. W. and Cochran, W. G. (1967) *Statistical Methods* (6th ed.). Ames: Iowa State University Press.

Table B.14   Random Numbers

SOURCE: The values in this table have been generated by a computer program authored by R. Maleske.

INDEX

probabilistic, comparing test results to, 165–166
μ (population mean), 67
Multiplicative rule, of probability, 166–167

n, and size of sample, 76
ns (not significant), 246
N:
    and binomial formula, 180
    and size of data set, 60
    and Pearson r formula, 221
Natural conditions, 150
$_N C_r$:
    example, 182
    formula, 182
    related to binomial formula, 181
Nondirectional hypothesis, vs. directional, 151
Nonparametric analyses, 232–233, 245
Nonreplacement, and probability, 169
    vs. parametric analyses, 209
Normal distribution (*See also* Normal curve):
    as a model, 184–186
Normal curve, 104–105, 108–122
    to estimate percentiles, 118–119
    formula, 179–180
    grading on, 112–114
    as a model, 108–114
Normally occurring variance, estimate of, 220
Null hypothesis, 160–162, 218–219
    for analysis of variance:
        between groups, one independent variable, 316
        between groups, two independent variables, 331
        mixed factorial, 343–344
        within groups, 324
    for binomial test, 357
    and causality, 205
    for chi square test of independence, 364
    for controlled experiments vs. uncontrolled observations, 218
    and correlation, 204
    for eta correlation analysis, 369
    for Friedman analysis, 374
    for Kruskal-Wallis analysis, 390
    for lambda correlation analysis, 394
    for Mann-Whitney U analysis, 401
    for Pearson r analysis, 404
    rejecting, 245–246
    for Scheffe analysis, 320, 339, 354
    for sign test, 412
    for simple chi square analysis, 361
    for Spearman r analysis, 415
    stating, 185, 191–192
    symbol for, 185
    for t-test analysis:
        between groups, 422
        dependent groups, 427
        matched groups, 427

        for single mean, 431
        within groups, 427
    for theta correlation analysis, 435
    for Wilcoxon analysis, 444

Observation:
    and choice of analysis, 204–205
    and experience, 20–21
    uncontrolled versus experiment, 204–205, 212
One-tailed:
    alternative hypothesis, 191–192
    vs. two-tailed alternative hypothesis, 242
Operational definition:
    definition, 24–25
    of hypotheses, 164–165
Ordinal level measurement, 30

p:
    and binomial formula, 180
    $< .05$, 241 (*See also* Statistical, significance)
    $> .05$, 241 (*See also* Statistical, significance)
P, and binomial formula, 181
Parameters:
    definition, 12
    estimating, 124
Parametric:
    analysis, 208–209
    assumptions, 208–209
    vs. nonparametric analysis, 209
Pearson r analysis, 204, 212, 221–222, 239–242
    conceptual formula, 221
    critical values, 276–281, Table B.4
    example, Appendix C.17
Percentile, 118
Percentile rank, 118
Perfect experiment, 149
Perry, W. G., 140
Pie charts, 91–92
Plain English conclusion, examples for:
    analysis of variance:
        between groups, one independent variable, 320
        between groups, two independent variables, 338
        mixed factorial, 353
        within groups, 329
    binomial test, 359
    chi square test of independence, 367
    eta correlation analysis, 373
    Friedman analysis, 377
    Kruskal-Wallis analysis, 392
    lambda correlation analysis, 397
    Mann-Whitney U, 403
    Pearson r analysis, 409
    Scheffe analysis, 323, 341, 356
    simple chi square analysis, 363
    sign test, 413
    Spearman r analysis, 417

DECISION TREE
For Selecting Statistical Analyses

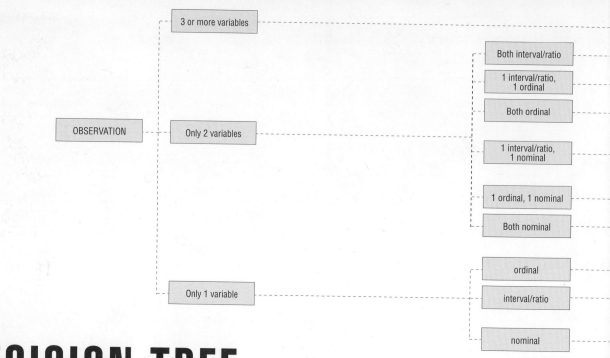

OBSERVATION
- 3 or more variables
- Only 2 variables
  - Both interval/ratio
  - 1 interval/ratio, 1 ordinal
  - Both ordinal
  - 1 interval/ratio, 1 nominal
  - 1 ordinal, 1 nominal
  - Both nominal
- Only 1 variable
  - ordinal
  - interval/ratio
  - nominal

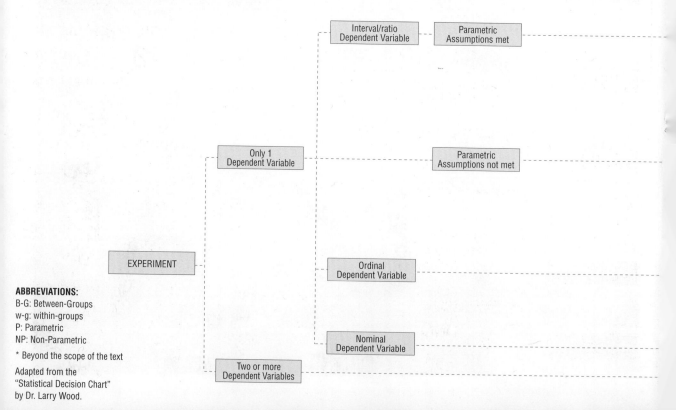

EXPERIMENT
- Only 1 Dependent Variable
  - Interval/ratio Dependent Variable
    - Parametric Assumptions met
    - Parametric Assumptions not met
  - Ordinal Dependent Variable
  - Nominal Dependent Variable
- Two or more Dependent Variables

ABBREVIATIONS:
B-G: Between-Groups
w-g: within-groups
P: Parametric
NP: Non-Parametric

* Beyond the scope of the text

Adapted from the
"Statistical Decision Chart"
by Dr. Larry Wood.